Jonah
Through the Centuries

Wiley Blackwell Bible Commentaries

Series Editors: Ian Boxall, Andrew Mein, Lena-Sofia Tiemeyer
Founding Editors: John Sawyer, Christopher Rowland, David M. Gunn

John Through the Centuries
Mark Edwards

Revelation Through the Centuries
Judith Kovacs and Christopher Rowlands

Judges Through the Centuries
David M. Gunn

Exodus Through the Centuries
Scott M. Langston

Ecclesiastes Through the Centuries
Eric S. Christianson

Esther Through the Centuries
Jo Carruthers

Psalms Through the Centuries: Volume I
Susan Gillingham

Galatians Through the Centuries
John Riches

Pastoral Epistles Through the Centuries
Jay Twomey

1 & 2 Thessalonians Through the Centuries
Anthony C. Thiselton

Six Minor Prophets Through the Centuries
Richard Coggins and Jin H. Han

Lamentations Through the Centuries
Paul M. Joyce and Diana Lipton

James Through the Centuries
David Gowler

The Acts of the Apostles Through the Centuries
Heidi J. Hornik and Mikael C. Parsons

Chronicles Through the Centuries
Blaire French

Isaiah Through the Centuries
John F.A Sawyer

Psalms Through the Centuries: Volume II
Susan Gillingham

Matthew Through the Centuries
Ian Boxall

Jonah Through the Centuries
Lena-Sofia Tiemeyer

Jonah
Through the Centuries

Lena-Sofia Tiemeyer

WILEY Blackwell

This edition first published 2022
© 2022 John Wiley & Sons Ltd

Registered Office
John Wiley & Sons, Inc., 111 River Street, Hoboken, NJ 07030, USA
John Wiley & Sons Ltd, The Atrium, Southern Gate, Chichester, West Sussex, PO19 8SQ, UK

Editorial Office
9600 Garsington Road, Oxford, OX4 2DQ, UK

For details of our global editorial offices, customer services, and more information about Wiley products visit us at www.wiley.com.

Wiley also publishes its books in a variety of electronic formats and by print-on-demand. Some content that appears in standard print versions of this book may not be available in other formats.

Limit of Liability/Disclaimer of Warranty
The contents of this work are intended to further general scientific research, understanding, and discussion only and are not intended and should not be relied upon as recommending or promoting scientific method, diagnosis, or treatment by physicians for any particular patient. In view of ongoing research, equipment modifications, changes in governmental regulations, and the constant flow of information relating to the use of medicines, equipment, and devices, the reader is urged to review and evaluate the information provided in the package insert or instructions for each medicine, equipment, or device for, among other things, any changes in the instructions or indication of usage and for added warnings and precautions. While the publisher and authors have used their best efforts in preparing this work, they make no representations or warranties with respect to the accuracy or completeness of the contents of this work and specifically disclaim all warranties, including without limitation any implied warranties of merchantability or fitness for a particular purpose. No warranty may be created or extended by sales representatives, written sales materials or promotional statements for this work. The fact that an organization, website, or product is referred to in this work as a citation and/or potential source of further information does not mean that the publisher and authors endorse the information or services the organization, website, or product may provide or recommendations it may make. This work is sold with the understanding that the publisher is not engaged in rendering professional services. The advice and strategies contained herein may not be suitable for your situation. You should consult with a specialist where appropriate. Further, readers should be aware that websites listed in this work may have changed or disappeared between when this work was written and when it is read. Neither the publisher nor authors shall be liable for any loss of profit or any other commercial damages, including but not limited to special, incidental, consequential, or other damages.

Library of Congress Cataloging-in-Publication Data
Names: Tiemeyer, Lena-Sofia, 1969- author.
Title: Jonah through the centuries / Lena-Sofia Tiemeyer.
Description: Hoboken, NJ : John Wiley & Sons, Inc., 2022. | Includes
  bibliographical references and indexes. | Summary: "The reception
  history of the book of Jonah offers a rich web of interpretations. This
  brief introduction outlines some of the key interpretative trends in
  Jewish, Christian, Muslim, and secular readings"-- Provided by
  publisher.
Identifiers: LCCN 2021021853 (print) | LCCN 2021021854 (ebook) | ISBN
  9781118973349 (hardback) | ISBN 9781118973318 (pdf) | ISBN 9781118973325
  (epub) | ISBN 9781118973332 (ebook)
Subjects: LCSH: Bible. Jonah--Criticism, interpretation, etc.
Classification: LCC BS1605.52 .T54 2022 (print) | LCC BS1605.52 (ebook) |
  DDC 224/.9206--dc23
LC record available at https://lccn.loc.gov/2021021853
LC ebook record available at https://lccn.loc.gov/2021021854

Cover image: © Life of William Blake (1880), Volume 2, Job illustrations by Cygnis insignis is licensed under CC BY-SA
Cover design by Wiley

C098227_190821

Table of Contents

Author's Preface	vii
Introduction	1
Jonah 1	12
Jonah 2	88
Jonah 3	163
Jonah 4	203

Conclusion 244

Biography 249
Bibliography 252
Index of Biblical Texts 279
General Index 286
Index of Authors 290

Author's Preface

It is a gargantuan task to cover the uses and misuses of the Book of Jonah throughout the last two millennia. The present commentary does not set out to do so; rather, it aims to showcase some of the more influential re-readings of the book in Jewish, Christian, Muslim, and secular traditions. My starting point will always be the biblical text itself. I shall show how all the retellings ultimately originate within the text itself: sometimes in its theological or literary ambiguities, sometimes in its choice of words, and sometimes in a syntactical construction. In parallel, retellings are fuelled by the interpreter's preconceived ideas of what the text ought to say, ideas that are often influenced by the interpreter's religious background and cultural assumptions. As a result, we shall frequently observe how several retellings form clusters according to the interpreters' religious affiliations: one set of retellings may be labelled typically mediaeval Jewish, whereas another set may be found nearly exclusively in Patristic circles.

Interpretative clusters, Jewish and Christian alike, should never be understood to exist in a vacuum. Rather, they are influenced by one another. A Christian interpretation often triggered a Jewish counter-interpretation, and vice versa. I shall endeavour to explain the dynamic behind this interchange and highlight what societal and religious factors gave rise to a given interpretation.

Many of the Christian interpretations are strongly anti-Jewish, and some of the Jewish interpretations are, although to a significantly lesser extent, anti-Christian. I neither excuse nor condone these interpretations. It is my hope that the readers of this volume will recognize them for what they are and neither encourage nor propagate their use.

The notion of interpretative clusters also influences the structure of my commentary. I have arranged the interpretations thematically rather than strictly chronologically. In practical terms, I shall begin with the earliest interpretation and follow that line of thought through to modern times before turning to the next-oldest interpretation, and so forth.

My commentary progresses slowly through the Book of Jonah, verse by verse and sometimes even word by word. Some verses have given rise to a plethora of interpretations, whereas others have seldom been cited. The commentary reflects this unevenness, with the result that the discussions of key verses, such as Jonah 1:1, 3, and 2:1, will stretch over many pages. Other verses are treated much more succinctly due to the relative lack of interest shown by exegetes.

The reception of the Book of Jonah interacts not only with the Masoretic text (MT), i.e. the received Hebrew text, but also with a wide range of translations, predominantly the Septuagint (LXX), the Aramaic Targum (TJ), and the Syriac Peshitta (S), among others. Yet, most interpretations, predominantly but not exclusively Jewish ones, have their origin in aspects associated with the Hebrew text. I have therefore opted to open the discussion of each verse with my own very literal translation of the MT into English. I have made limited effort to arrive at an idiomatically pleasing translation; rather, the translation serves to give readers insight into the exact rendering of the Hebrew text. When citing from other passages in the Bible, the translations are from the NIV (unless otherwise stated).

Throughout the commentary, I have avoided, by and large, using Hebrew characters and instead have opted for a simplified form of transliterations. At times, however, I have chosen to include the germane Hebrew words and expressions so that readers familiar with the language can grasp the logic behind a given interpretation. Likewise, when an interpretation stems from the Greek translation of Jonah, I have similarly included the Greek text to enable readers to comprehend the rationale behind the retelling. The same is true for interpretations depending on the Latin text of the Vulgate, etc. In all cases, I provide the original language, accompanied by an English translation.

In addition, I have endeavoured to find English translations of the original sources. This means that the Jewish Sages, the Church Fathers, the Reformers, and so forth, are not cited in the original Hebrew, Aramaic, Greek, Latin, or German but in the extant English translations. For more details concerning the translations, please see the bibliography. When no translations exist, I have translated the source myself (or asked kind friends for help).

Reception history is truly synchronic insofar as few interpreters prior to the twentieth century interpreted the Book of Jonah on its own. Jonah was considered a book within a larger canon, and interpreters allowed the rest of that canon to inform the events and concepts within the book. As a result, we should not be surprised to find interpreters drawing from a wide range of biblical passages to support or refute a given interpretation of a passage in Jonah.

On a related note, I am fully aware that many of the perceived contradictions in the final form(s) of the Book of Jonah can be and have been explained by modern scholarship from source-critical and redaction-critical perspectives. A case in point is the tension between the narrative in Jonah 1, 3–4 and the psalm in Jonah 2. I have wilfully excluded such diachronic interpretations. This approach should be construed as neither endorsement nor rejection of diachronic explanations but as an attempt to preserve the focus of the present commentary on the received text in its final form(s).

Finally, some technical details.

- I refer to God as a masculine singular entity called either God or Yhwh. This is a linguistic rather than ontological decision that seeks to reflect how God has been perceived for most of the last 2500 years.

- Many people have written commentaries to the Book of Jonah. In each case, unless otherwise specified, the references to their writings go to the germane verse in their commentary. In the case of the *Glossa Ordinaria* and the Geneva Bible Notes, unless stated otherwise, the reference belongs to the verse under discussion. With reference to the Church Fathers, this is true also for Jerome (transl. MacGregor), Cyril of Alexandria (transl. Hill), and Theodore of Mopsuestia (transl. Hill); with reference to the reformers, the same principle applies to Calvin (transl. Owen) and Luther (transl. Oswald). In the case of Luther, I shall further indicate whether his comment appears in his Latin or his (longer) German commentary. The interpretations of the mediaeval Jewish commentators (Rashi, Ibn Ezra, Radak, Abarbanel) are all taken from the Rabbinic Bible, as found in the Bar Ilan Judaic Digital Library (the Responsa Project). As above, their views are expressed in their commentary to the particular verse under discussion (transl. Bob) unless otherwise specified.

- English translations of the following primary sources are taken from the following texts unless otherwise indicated: the Jewish-Hellenistic sermon *On Jonah*, see Muradyan and Topchyan; Rabbinical sources (Mishnah, the talmudim, Mekhilta, Genesis Rabbah, etc.), see Neusner; Targum Jonathan, see Cathcart and Gordon; *Pirqei de-Rabbi Eliezer*, see Friedlander; *Glossa Ordinaria*, see Litteral; 'Patience', see Koertge; the Qur'an, see Pickthall; the Zohar, see Wineman.

It has been a rare scholarly privilege to spend the last five years in the company of the Book of Jonah. I wish to thank the series editors John F.A. Sawyer and David Gunn for their invitation to write this commentary and for their continuous and ever-gracious and constructive support along the way. I am also very grateful to the series editor Andrew Mein, who read through the penultimate version of this book and gave constructive and encouraging feedback. I am further indebted to the students in my seminar 'Jonah and His Fish' that I gave in the autumn of 2019 at the University of Aberdeen. Their questions and insights constantly prompted me to think deeper about the issues raised in this commentary. I especially wish to thank Dr Hei Yin Yip, Amy Bender, Dorothy Plummer, and Caitlin Yool for pointing out a plethora of typos and less felicitous English constructions, thus helping me to write a better book. I am also, as always, grateful to my husband Andreas Tiemeyer for his constant willingness to discuss yet another theological issue, yet another interpreter, and yet another textual problem. It is not an exaggeration to say that Jonah and his fish have become members of our family!

Lena-Sofia Tiemeyer
Örebro, Sweden, November 2020

Introduction

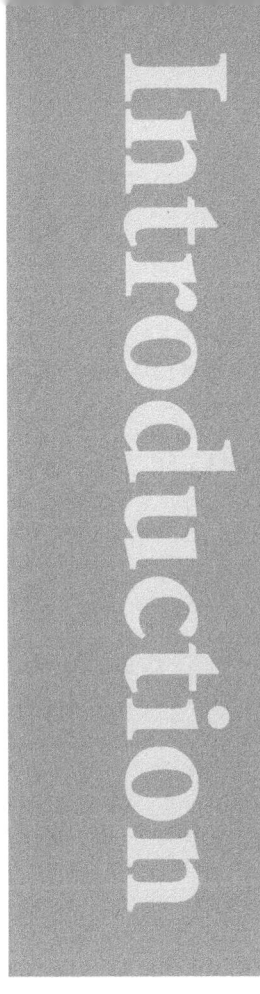

The reception history of the Book of Jonah offers a rich web of interpretations. This brief introduction outlines some of the key interpretative trends in Jewish, Christian, Muslim, and secular readings.

Jewish Interpretations

Jewish interaction with the Book of Jonah is varied, having begun in the intertestamental period and continuing to modern times.

Jonah Through the Centuries, First Edition. Lena-Sofia Tiemeyer.
© 2022 John Wiley & Sons, Ltd. Published 2022 by John Wiley & Sons, Ltd.

Early Jewish Interpretations

There is some evidence of interpretation as early as the Septuagint (LXX). The Greek translation offers four readings that attest either to a Hebrew text that differs from the Masoretic text (MT) or, more likely, interpretations of the MT. First, LXX Jonah 1:6 finds Jonah 'snoring', whereas Jonah in the MT 'sleeps deeply'. Many later interpreters adopt this reading and explore its theological consequences. Second, whereas the MT Jonah 1:9 has Jonah present himself as a 'Hebrew', the LXX defines Jonah as 'as servant of the Lord'. Third, the LXX understands the MT's fish as some kind of sea monster. This interpretation may be inspired by Greek mythology, where the same term denotes the sea monsters which were slain by the heroes Perseus and Heracles. Fourth, whereas Jonah in the MT gives the people of Nineveh forty days to repent, the LXX gives them a mere three days. Several later Christian interpreters preferred the latter reading as it lent additional support to their typological interpretation of Jonah as a type for Christ (see further below).

There are multiple other examples of Second-Temple-period Jewish interaction with the Book of Jonah. Jonah is mentioned in, for example, the Book of Tobit, *Joseph and Aseneth*, *Testament of the Twelve Patriarchs*, *3 Maccabees*, and *Hellenistic Synagogal Prayers*.

A more substantial treatment is found in the Hellenistic sermon *On Jonah*, probably originating in the synagogue in Alexandria between 25 BCE and 50 CE. One significant difference appears in its retelling of Jonah 1:15 where Jonah, according to the sermon, decides to commit suicide rather than allow the sailors to toss him overboard. Another variation concerns Jonah's time inside the fish. According to the sermon, the fish cares for Jonah as a mother cares for the baby in her womb and takes Jonah on a sightseeing tour of the wonders of the ocean. This 'detour' becomes very influential and is later adopted and enhanced by other retellings of the Jonah narrative, exemplified by the Jewish midrash *Pirke de-Rabbi Eliezer* (*PRE*).

The Jewish historian Josephus offers an abbreviated version of Jonah in his *Ant.* 9.206–214, featuring only chs 1–2. He treats the biblical text as a historical record and downplays God's active role in the narrative, together with all its miraculous aspects. In his hands, the Book of Jonah is turned into a narrative about Jonah's disobedience and his later prayer to God. Nineveh and its (possible) repentance lose all significance, presumably because Josephus and his intended audience knew about its destruction in 612 BCE by, among others, Neo-Babylonian and Median forces.

Among the Qumran scrolls, parts of the Book of Jonah are attested in five manuscripts (4Q76, 4Q81, 4Q82, Mur88, and 8Hev1). These manuscripts preserve three very minor variations, none of which alter the content of the book in any salient way.

1. 4Q82 reads Jonah 2:7 [Eng. 2:6] 'You brought up from the pit my life, **My soul**, o YHWH my God', in contrast to the MT of the same verse, which reads 'You brought up from the pit my life, o YHWH my God'.
2. 4Q76 reads Jonah 3:2 'the proclamation **like the one that I spoke**', whereas the MT reads 'the proclamation **that I am speaking**'.
3. 4Q82 and the MT of Jonah 4:6 use different appellations for God. Yet, although they use different names, both traditions would have been read and pronounced the same way.

Rabbinical and Mediaeval Jewish Interpretations

There are ample references to the Book of Jonah in various midrashic compendiums (e.g. *Genesis Rabbah*, *Pesikta de-Rab Kahana*). One dominant trend in rabbinical interpretation is to flesh out the Jonah narrative with details of the prophet's background. Traditional Jewish exegesis equates the prophet Jonah with the eponymous prophet in 2 Kgs 14:23–25, as well as with the anonymous prophet who was active during Jeroboam II's reign in 2 Kgs 9:1. In parallel, Jonah is commonly identified as the son of the widow of Zarephath, who died and was resurrected by Elijah (1 Kgs 17).

These backstories are then read into the fabric of the Book of Jonah. The identification of Jonah with the prophet in 1 Kgs 14 provides Jonah with a reason for his flight. Jonah had previously had bad experiences with non-fulfilment of his prophecy, and he feared that the same would happen if he went to Nineveh, thus causing people to consider him to be a false prophet (e.g. *Seder Olam Rabbah*, *PRE*). Another interpretation, also found among Christian interpreters, is that Jonah did not want to go to Nineveh because he was afraid that Nineveh's repentance would reflect badly on Israel's failure to repent (e.g. *Mekhilta Attributed to R. Ishmael*). In contrast, the identification of Jonah with the resurrected son in Zarephath often serves to develop Jonah's life after his journey to Nineveh. *The Lives of the Prophets*, for example, describes how Jonah and his mother chose to settle in Tyre following his return from Nineveh, the reason being that Jonah was now regarded as a false prophet in his homeland.

The mediaeval Jewish exegetes continue to debate many of the same questions (e.g. Rashi, Ibn Ezra, Radak) although they often advocate different solutions. Investigating the particular issue of Jonah's flight from his mission, Abarbanel portrays Jonah as a martyr, who decided to disobey God to ensure

Israel's survival: if Nineveh was not given the chance to repent, then God would have to destroy the city, which in turn would mean that Assyria would not be able to annihilate the Northern Kingdom of Israel. Further, in contrast to *The Lives of the Prophets*, Abarbanel maintains that Jonah's resurrection occurred in childhood and thus sheds light upon Jonah's reference to God having (already) saved him from Sheol in Jonah 2:3 [Eng. 2:2].

Christian Interpretations

Turning to Christian readings of the Book of Jonah, they generally emphasized how Jonah, along with other characters in the book, foreshadows aspects of Jesus's life and death. This type of exegesis often fostered strong anti-Jewish sentiments, which in turn led to Jewish polemical responses.

Typology

To appreciate fully the Christian uses of the Book of Jonah, we must begin in the New Testament (NT). The NT mentions Jonah in Matt 12:38–41; 16:1–4 and in Luke 11:29–32, two of which refer to the so-called 'sign of Jonah' (Matt 12:39; Luke 11:29). The NT authors aim (among other things) to show how Jesus is the fulfilment and culmination of the Hebrew Bible/Old Testament (OT). Read from this perspective, the texts in the OT have been either fulfilled or superseded. Fulfilment is understood to take place broadly in the person of Jesus in a collective, corporate, and individual way.

This approach was further developed in patristic exegesis. Much of the writings of the Church Fathers focussed on the relationship between the OT and the NT, emphasizing either the dichotomy between the two testaments (e.g. Marcion), their identity and essential sameness (e.g. the Alexandrian Fathers), or the continuity and development between the OT and the NT, where a sound reading of the OT begins in the NT and works backwards (e.g. the Antiochene Fathers). Both the Alexandrian and the Antiochene Fathers use typology: the correspondence between people and events of the past, present, and future. Typology is based on the conviction that God acts consistently and that earlier acts of God 'prefigure' his later acts (e.g. Matt 24:37; in John 3:14). To the Church Fathers, an OT character can be a 'type', i.e. a prophetic image that points forward to and is fulfilled by Jesus Christ, or an 'anti-type', i.e. a figure or situation that is opposite to that found in the NT.

Christian exegetes took an active interest in the Book of Jonah, partly due to its typological potential. Among the Church Fathers, the interpretations of St Cyril of Jerusalem, Gregory of Nazianzus, Jerome, John Chrysostom, and Augustine stand out. The reformers followed suit. Luther, Bugenhagen, and Calvin each wrote a full-length treatise on the book. Their exegesis was informed by its typological aspects, but they also interpreted the book in a relatively literal manner with an eye to its relevance to the theological debates of their time.

The widespread Christian typological understanding of Jonah has its origin in the reference to the 'sign of the prophet Jonah' in Matt 12:39/Luke 11:30. There are three main typological events in Jonah's life:

1. Jonah being tossed into the sea by the sailors is a precursor for Jesus's crucifixion (Jonah 1:15).
2. Jonah's three days inside the belly of the fish is a precursor for Jesus's death (Jonah 2:1b).
3. Jonah being vomited out of by the fish is a precursor for Jesus's resurrection (Jonah 2:10).

Beginning with the second and third points, the Church Fathers agree almost unanimously that the three days and the three nights in Jonah 2:1b point to Jesus's death and resurrection (e.g. Augustine, Cyril of Jerusalem). In parallel, many patristic interpreters stress the distinction between Jonah and Jesus. Cyril of Alexandria highlights that not everything which befell Jonah should be understood as relevant and applicable to the process of seeing Jonah as a type for Christ. Jonah tried to flee from God's command, unlike Jesus, who did not display any reluctance or lack of enthusiasm for his ministry, nor did he flee from the face of God. Furthermore, while Jonah was disappointed in God's compassion, Jesus was not disappointed to see the nations saved. Thus, inherent in many of the typological interpretations is a sense that Jonah is an imperfect type or even an 'anti-type' of Christ, ultimately to be replaced by the perfect 'true Jonah', namely Jesus. This view became prevalent in much Christian writing and often conveyed anti-Jewish replacement theology.

Turning to the first point, many Christian exegetes (e.g. Jerome) treat the sailors as 'anti-types' and compare them to the Jews at the time of Jesus, to the detriment of the latter. Whereas the sailors hesitated to throw Jonah into the sea, the Jews at the time of Jesus shouted for Jesus's crucifixion. Turning to the 'types', a significantly smaller group of Christian retellings, yet equally anti-Jewish in their outlook, depicts the sailors as brutal Jewish men ready and willing to kill Jonah.

In addition to these three main typological readings, many interpreters maintain the virtue of the people of Nineveh. Despite the brevity of Jonah's message, they turned to the God of Israel in penitence. Many Christian exegetes use the Ninevites' repentance to highlight the perceived failure of the Jews to accept Jesus as their Messiah (e.g. Jerome, Justin Martyr, Cyril of Alexandria, Ephrem the Syrian). This type of anti-Jewish comparison remains prevalent among the reformers. In his German commentary to Jonah, Luther lauds Nineveh's behaviour, comparing it with that of the centurion in Matt 8:10, while lamenting Jerusalem's rejection of Jesus. It also persists in later protestant sermons on Jonah. The eighteenth-century English congregational minister Thomas Bradbury, for example, contrasts the people of Nineveh with the people of Israel. The former believed Jonah – a mere messenger – and repented of their sins, whereas the latter neither believed nor repented despite hearing God's own son in the flesh.

Finally, the worm in Jonah 4:7 has been read typologically to foreshadow Jesus's victory on the cross and the triumph of the Gospel. According to Augustine, followed by Luther, the worm is a type for either Christ or the Gospel, who devours the plant (*kikayyon*), which represents the Old Covenant. Again, this image is strongly anti-Jewish in its insistence that God's covenant with Israel has been superseded by that with the Christian Church.

Jonah in Christian Art

Jonah is used in a similar typological way in much of Christian art. Such a 'Jonah cycle' consists of three main scenes:

1. Jonah is tossed overboard by the sailors and swallowed by the fish.
2. Jonah is vomited out of the fish (Jonah 2:11).
3. Jonah reclines under the *kikayyon* (Jonah 4:6–7).

The iconography thus concentrates on those elements that convey the central Christian message; these three motifs are selected because they represent key Christian tenets of faith. The tossing of Jonah overboard and his subsequent re-emergence carry the dual function of symbolizing Jesus's own death and resurrection and, by extension, also Christian baptism whereby a Christian is understood to die and rise with Christ. In contrast, the repentance of the people of Nineveh, such a prominent theme in Christian texts (see above), seldom appears in graphic form. Michelangelo's depiction of Jonah, in the Sistine chapel, offers a formidable example of Christian Jonah symbolism. The fish represents Jesus's triumphant resurrection, whereas the plant in the background stands for the cessation of the Old Covenant.

Jewish Responses to Christian Polemic

Due to the prevalent and often very anti-Jewish quality of much Christian interaction with the Book of Jonah, many Jewish interpreters reacted to this polemic. For instance, many Jewish interpreters problematized the typological interpretations of the sailors by turning them into either Jewish converts or persecuting Christians. Likewise, Jewish interpreters responded to the Christian praise of the Ninevites by casting doubts upon the sincerity and longevity of their repentance. This line of exegesis receives support from a comparative reading of Jonah and Nahum, where the latter book describes Nineveh's historical destruction in 612 BCE. It gains further momentum by the references to the fasting animals in Jonah 3:7: according to many rabbis, the Ninevites' decision to withhold water from innocent animals demonstrated their inherent cruelty (e.g. *y.Tan.* 2:1).

Islamic Interpretations

Jonah, or Yunus as he is called in Arabic, is remembered in Islamic traditions as a prophet who was faithful to God and delivered his message. He is often also named Dhul-Nun (Arabic: ذو النون, meaning 'The One of the Whale') and Sahib al-hut (Arabic: صاحب الحوت, meaning 'The Man of the Whale'). Most of the material about Jonah in the Qur'an serves to support Muhammad: it provides insight into and a precedent for the initial opposition that Muhammad faced from the people of Mecca.

Jonah appears six times in the Qur'an (Sura 4:163; 6:86; 10:98 [Yunus]; 21:87-88; 37:139-48; 68:48-50). These references are opaque and difficult to forge together into a coherent and cohesive narrative. It is likely that the original readers were familiar with the Book of Jonah, along with the references in the NT, and thus able to interpret the extant elusive Qur'anic references in their light.

As time went by, however, the biblical narrative faded from memory, and the Qur'anic fragments became the building blocks for creating new and alternative Jonah narratives with a sequence of events that differs drastically from the biblical original. A common outline runs as follows: God sends Jonah to Nineveh to preach a message. The people of Nineveh refuse to listen to Jonah. As a result, Jonah leaves Nineveh and boards a ship. Because of the storm, the sailors cast lots and realize that Jonah is the cause of the storm, whereupon they throw him into the sea. A gigantic fish swallows Jonah. Inside the fish, Jonah repents and glorifies God, and the fish spits him out. As Jonah is very sore from having been inside a fish, God provides a gourd plant to offer shade, and the archangel Gabriel gives him clothes (a scene often portrayed in Islamic art). In this manner, Islamic traditions transformed the biblical Book of Jonah into a new narrative with a new theme: God sends messengers, the people reject their message, and God sends punishment. They also give it a new climax: Jonah's prayer and glorification of God inside the fish.

This modified narrative was subsequently interpreted by Islamic traditions (*hadīth*) and Qur'anic exegesis (*tafsīr*). These interpretations caused the Islamic Jonah traditions to evolve even further as they germinated new narrative details and prompted new theological questions. Two key intertwined issues came to dominate the exegetical discussions: (1) the specific character of Jonah's sin and (2) the specific occasion when he sinned. The prevalent understanding among Islamic interpreters (e.g. Al-Qummī, Zamakhsharī, Ibn Kathīr) was that Jonah's sin was *anger* and that he committed it when he ran away in wrath *after* his mission to Nineveh. Many Islamic scholars accordingly sought to elucidate with whom Jonah was angry (e.g. God, the Israelites, the Ninevites) or flatly maintained that, in fact, he was *not* angry (as prophets were infallible and thus *could not* be angry). Ultimately, Muhammad was compared with Jonah (Sura 68). Both prophets felt rejected by the people to whom they were sent to preach. Jonah's enraged departure should not, however, be emulated by Muhammad; rather, Muhammad should be patient and see that God would sort things out. In parallel, other later traditions, such as the ones found in Al-Kisā'ī's *Tales of the Prophets*, elaborated further, and included folkloristic motifs known from other, non-Islamic traditions.

Modern Literary Interpretations

The biblical Book of Jonah has been the subject of multiple literary retellings, ranging from individual poems to whole novels and theatrical dramas. In addition, a huge number of literary works contain allusions to the Jonah narrative. In these retellings, Jonah often becomes a representative of humanity: haunted by God, persecuted, and exiled. Jonah is turned into our alter ego as he embodies our own struggles with God. There are three prevalent tropes in these modern retellings: Jonah who runs away from his calling, Jonah the refugee, and Jonah who questions God's justice.

Jonah Running Away from His Calling

Many scholars have pondered the issue of Jonah's flight from God's command in Jonah 1:3. In literature, Jonah's flight is often used to explore the futility of fleeing from God and his calling. A good example is the Swedish novel *Guldspiken* (*The Golden Nail*) by Peter Nilson. Using the motif of a lay preacher seeking to escape his calling, the novel dialogues with the Book of Jonah in order to explore a person's feeling of despondency when faced with the inability of avoiding their God-ordained fate.

Jonah's flight and his ensuing time inside the fish is sometimes more widely understood to represent the human struggle with God and our sense of alienation from God and the world. Paul Auster, for example, employs the motifs of 'being inside the whale' as a leitmotif throughout his book *The Invention of Solitude* to designate the estrangement that characterizes much of post-holocaust Jewry. Jonah's struggle with God is also the topic of several poems. Gabriel Preil compares himself to Jonah, as he describes an existence torn between faith and a desire to flee from it. Enrique Lihn likewise expresses his own sense of unease with the fickleness of his existence through the lens of the Book of Jonah.

A subset of these retellings deals with the Jewish experience of never being able to run away from being chosen by God. The notion of the Jewish people carrying a burden and having a responsibility towards God and towards the Gentile world is expressed poignantly by Kadia Molodowsky in her poem 'Jonah'. It expresses in a heart-breaking manner the Jewish experience through the lens of Jonah's calling. Jonah the Jew can never escape from being part of God's chosen people.

Jonah the Refugee

Other, related retellings turn the trope of 'the fleeing Jonah' into 'Jonah the refugee': Jonah is a man whom God abandoned. These retellings stem from Jonah 2:5 [Eng. 2:4], where Jonah expresses how he is cast out from God's presence. They gain further inspiration from the affinity between the dialogue of God and Jonah in Jonah 4 and that of God and Cain in Gen 4. The comparison is triggered by the shared use of the Hebrew verb *ḥarah* = 'to be angry', as well as by the shared rare expression *milifne Adonai* = 'from before the Lord' (Jonah 1 and Gen 4). This intertextuality fashions Jonah as a type for the 'wandering Jew'. This notion comes to the forefront in the novel *The Strange Nation of Rafael Mendes* by Moacyr Scliar, where the Jonah narrative lends structure to the novel.

Jonah and God's Justice

In the biblical narrative, Jonah's flight from God is explained in Jonah 4:2 – Jonah knew that God is prone to showing compassion. The question then becomes: why did Jonah not wish God to show compassion on Nineveh? Many modern retellings of the Book of Jonah maintain that the key problem is God's failure to uphold justice and the concomitant failure to withhold mercy. The pivotal issue is the balance between mercy and justice: can true mercy exist in the absence of true justice? Put aptly by the literary theorist Terry Eagleton,

Jonah refused to obey God because there did not seem to be any point in obeying him. This issue forms the central question in a range of modern literary interactions with the Book of Jonah, among them Robert Frost's play *A Masque of Mercy*, where the central figure Jonah Dove argues that God is obliged to punish the wicked; he must do so in his role as supreme and just deity. God, however, has failed to carry out this task. Taking a more explicit stand, Harald Tandrup envisages Jonah as ultimately rejecting God's perspective. What is the point when God does not punish the guilty? Other retellings lament Jonah's failure to be compassionate. The musical rendering by Samuel Adler, *Der Mann ohne Toleranz*, for instance, mourns Jonah's inability to accept God's decision to pardon Nineveh.

The Fish

No introduction to the Book of Jonah is complete without discussion of the fish. Notwithstanding its relatively minor role in the biblical narrative, it has fascinated most interpreters and as a result has generated what might seem to be a disproportionally large number of interpretations. Frankly, most people are familiar with the story of how the fish swallowed Jonah; significantly fewer people can say something insightful about the message of the Book of Jonah.

The fish is particularly interesting because of its varied reception. It metamorphoses throughout the centuries: from being God's obedient servant, it turns into a monster which ultimately becomes a symbol of death and hell. This 'monstrification' of the fish has already begun in the intertestamental literature, where Jonah's ordeal in the fish is compared with Daniel's ordeal in the lions' den (e.g. *Joseph and Aseneth*, *Hellenistic Synagogal Prayers*). By contrast, later rabbinical Jewish interpretation takes pains to uphold its benevolent character, to the point that the fish becomes Jonah's guide through the netherworld (e.g. the Jewish-Hellenistic sermon *On Jonah*, PRE).

A unique aspect of Jewish interpretation of the fish is surely the concern about its biological gender. This issue stems from the changes to the Hebrew word for 'fish', from being referred to as *dag* to *daga* and then back to *dag* again. The longer form has traditionally been understood as a feminine form, giving rise to a set of wondrous interpretations that Jonah was being swallowed by two consecutive fish: first a male fish and then a female fish. At first, Jonah was swallowed by the male fish, but he was not sufficiently uncomfortable in its belly to turn to God. To rectify this apparent problem, God appointed a female fish, pregnant with multiple little fish. Once inside her, Jonah was so cramped that he began to pray to God for his deliverance. This interpretation continued to have its adherents in the mediaeval ages (e.g. Rashi), whereas others sought alternative explanations of the changing vocabulary (e.g. Ibn Ezra).

Turning to Christian interactions with the fish, very early on it becomes a symbol of death (Matt 12:40). This tradition culminates in mediaeval art, as exemplified in the various depictions of hell as the mouth of a massive sea monster (e.g. the old English poem 'The Whale'). The same tradition is also found, albeit in a very different form, in Jewish mysticism (*The Zohar*). In patristic interpretation, two intertwined motifs appear: the womb and the tomb. For Cassiodorus, for example, the fish is a type for hell where Jesus spent the time between Good Friday and Easter morning, yet it was also a safe haven for the prophet Jonah where he was kept alive and safe from a watery death. In later Protestant interpretations, Luther and Calvin return to the more biblical imagery: they agree that the fish was a horrific monster, yet nonetheless it kept Jonah alive.

Finally, the obsession with the fish persists into modern days, where Jonah's time inside the fish often serves as a symbol of life in exile or the diaspora, both in art (e.g. Zalmanovich Abeshaus) and in literature (e.g. Rodoreda).

Jonah 1

The first chapter of the Book of Jonah features God's calling to Jonah to go to Nineveh to preach repentance. It also speaks of Jonah's attempted flight to Tarshish to avoid that same calling. We shall explore how interpreters through the ages have embellished the character of Jonah, with focus on his origin, his character, the reasons behind his disobedience, and his interaction with the sailors on board the ship.

Jonah Through the Centuries, First Edition. Lena-Sofia Tiemeyer.
© 2022 John Wiley & Sons, Ltd. Published 2022 by John Wiley & Sons, Ltd.

Jonah 1:1

And the word of YHWH came to Jonah, the son of Amittai, saying

The first verse of the Book of Jonah raises several questions. The ensuing discussion will focus on two key issues. First, what information can we glean from the description of Jonah as the 'son of Amittai'? Who were his parents and where did he live prior to his flight from Yafo? Second, was this the first time that 'God's word came to Jonah' or had God already commissioned Jonah to serve as a prophet earlier in his career?

Jonah's Identity and Ancestry

2 Kgs 14:25 gives interpreters their chief starting point for establishing Jonah's identity. This verse refers to a person named Jonah, son of Amittai, who was a contemporary of Jeroboam II. We further learn that this Jonah was from Gath-Hepher. This reference compels most pre-critical scholars to identify the prophet in the Book of Jonah with this man, with the result that the events in the Book of Jonah are assumed to have taken place in the Northern Kingdom of Israel during the eighth century BCE.

The Jewish sages sought to find out even more about Jonah's background story and family connections. Whereas 2 Kgs 14:25 states clearly that Jonah's father was Amittai, his mother's identity is more difficult to establish. Rabbinic traditions commonly identify Jonah's mother with the woman of Zarephath, who hosted Elijah (1 Kgs 17) and whose son Elijah resurrected. The basis of this identification can be found in the use of the word 'truth' (*emet*) in 1 Kgs 17:24. This word is then connected with Jonah's patrilineage Amittai (*amitai*), a name that contains the same three Hebrew letters *aleph*, *mem*, and *tav*. By extension, the whole narrative in 1 Kgs 17 is understood to provide information that is useful for uncovering Jonah's identity. God commands Elijah to go to Zarephath of Sidon, where God has commanded a widow to supply him with a place to stay (v. 9). In the ensuing narrative, Elijah performs a miracle whereby the woman has enough flour and oil to last until God would again bless the country with rain (vv. 13–16). Later, the woman's son becomes ill and finally stops breathing (v. 17). Elijah carries the boy upstairs, stretches himself out on top of the boy, and pleads with God to let the boy live (vv. 18–21), with the result that the boy's life is restored (vv. 22–24).

In many rabbinic stories, the resurrected boy is identified with Jonah, yet there is no consensus whether his resurrection took place before or after his mission to Nineveh. In the mediaeval midrash *Pirqei de-Rabbi Eliezer* 33 (henceforth *PRE*), for example, Rabbi Simeon says:

Owing to the power of charity, the dead will be quickened in the future. Whence do we learn this? From Elijah the Tishbite 'For he betook to Zarephath, and a woman (who was) a widow received him with great honour'. She was the mother of Jonah and they were eating and drinking his bread and oil; he, she, and her son, as it is said, 'And she did eat', and he also (1 Kgs 17:15) was entreated of him, as it is said, 'And the Lord hearkened unto the voice of Elijah' (1 Kgs 17:22).

The Lives of the Prophets (*Vitae prophetarum*), a document of Jewish origin written in Greek, elaborates on the same tradition (see Schwemer 2020). Taking the end of the Book of Jonah as its starting point, it narrates how Jonah, *after* having been to Nineveh, settles in Tyre together with his mother, the reason being that he was now considered a false prophet in his homeland Israel. At this time, Elijah had fled from Israel after having called a famine upon the land as part of his rebuke of the house of Ahab. Elijah stayed with Jonah and his mother in the region of Tyre. Jonah died at this point but was brought back to life again by Elijah. After the famine ended, Jonah and his mother moved to Judah. On the way, however, his mother died, and Jonah buried her.

Elijah was at that time rebuking the house of Ahab and having called a famine upon the land he fled. Coming to the region of Tyre he found the widow and her son, for he himself could not lodge with the uncircumcised. He brought her a blessing; and when her child died, God raised him from the dead through Elijah, for he wished to show him that it is not possible to flee from God.

This intertextual dialogue between the Jonah narrative and the Elijah narrative serves two purposes. It not only provides the reader with more information about the prophet Jonah, it also offers an explanation as to how and why Elijah was able to stay in Tyre: the widow in whose house he stayed was in fact an Israelite (and not a Gentile).

By contrast, the Portuguese Jewish statesman and philosopher Abarbanel (1437–1508 CE) argues that this event took place in Jonah's childhood and thus prior to his mission to Nineveh. In his commentary to Jonah 2:3 [Eng. 2:2], he explains Jonah's reference to God having saved him from Sheol as a reference to Elijah's miracle in 1 Kings when he brought Jonah back to life. Along similar lines, a few modern scholars position Jonah's death experience in his childhood and understand it as a key to his later behaviour in the Book of Jonah. Zornberg, for instance, explains Jonah's fear of facing God as a result of his earlier trauma of survival (cf. below, Jonah 1:3) (Zornberg 2008: 291–293). Fishman likewise explores what it would have meant for Jonah to know that his early resurrection and subsequent fate depended on the acts of 'a desperate impulsive mother and a feckless purveyor of false promises who occasionally gets lucky' (Fishman 2008: 312).

Several Christian sources also attest to this identification. In the prologue to his commentary on Jonah, Jerome (347–420 CE) appears to accept the Jewish tradition that Jonah was the son of the woman of Zarephath, and it is also found in the prologue to the Book of Jonah in the *Glossa Ordinaria*. Ephrem the Syrian (303–373 CE) likewise adheres to the same tradition, as he writes that Jonah, after completing his mission to Nineveh, retired to Tyre with his mother (Ephraem, *Repentance of Nineveh*, Introduction). Other Christian interpreters reject this line of thinking, instead maintaining that the woman of Zarephath was a non-Jew. This line of interpretation is supported by Luke 4:25–26:

> [25]I assure you that there were many widows in Israel in Elijah's time, when the sky was shut for three and a half years and there was a severe famine throughout the land. [26]Yet Elijah was not sent to any of them, but to a widow in Zarephath in the region of Sidon.

Luther (German commentary), for instance, uses this passage to prove that the woman of Zarephath was a Gentile. The fact that Jonah identifies himself as a Hebrew in Jonah 1:9 means, according to Luther, that Jonah could not have been the son of the (Gentile) woman of the Elijah narrative. Instead, Jonah was 'an excellent and estimable man in the kingdom of Israel'.

Islamic traditions also provide Jonah with a mother. The tradition preserved in *Tales of the Prophet* and attributed to Kaab al-Ahbar names Jonah's mother Sadaqa ('righteousness'). Furthermore, according to the same tradition, Jonah's birth was miraculous as Sadaqa gave birth to him when she was no longer of childbearing age (Burge 2017: 588. Eng. transl. W. M. Thackston, al-Kisai, *Tales of the Prophets*, 321).

Some traditions do not stop with Jonah's parents but also, somewhat surprisingly given the complete lack of textual support, provide Jonah with a wife. Several classical Jewish texts associate her with pilgrimage to Jerusalem. Among them, *Mekhilta Attributed to R. Ishmael* 17:1, speaking of people who fulfil ritual requirements, mentions Jonah's wife:

> The wife of Jonah used to go up for festivals to Jerusalem.

Thus, a woman never mentioned in a biblical book is reported as having set out on a pilgrimage to Jerusalem (Ginzberg 1913: 4:253). This widespread tradition is also attested in the Jerusalem Talmud (*y.Ber* 2:2–3, cf. *y.Ber* 9:1, and *b.Erub.* 10:1–2), stating that Jonah's wife used to go on pilgrimage but at one point was sent home. From this we can learn that women (as well as slaves and children) are exempt from the obligations of reciting the *Shema* and from wearing *tefillin*.

They asked: Lo, Michal daughter of Kushi used to wear Tefillin. And Jonah's wife used to go up to Jerusalem on the pilgrimages, and the sages did not object.

R. Hezekiah in the name of R. Abbahu, 'they sent the wife of Jonah home and the sages objected to Michal the daughter of Kushi's actions'.

Some traditions even name Jonah's wife. Several Islamic traditions describe how Jonah, together with his wife Anak and their two sons, went to Nineveh together (Burge 2017: 587–588. Eng. transl. W. M. Thackston, al-Kisai, *Tales of the Prophets*, 321–322). Much more recently, the libretto by Paul Goodman, accompanying the opera *Jonah* by Jack Beeson (1921–2010 CE), names Jonah's wife Hephzibah (to be sung by a contralto or mezzo soprano). This name, meaning 'my delight is in her', appears twice in the Bible: in 2 Kgs 21:1 referring to Hezekiah's wife and the mother of Manasseh and in Isa 62:4 referring to Jerusalem. It is unclear whether either of these two passages influenced Goodman in his choice of name.

Having established Jonah's family connections, many interpreters proceed to determine his tribal affiliation. The biblical account in 2 Kgs 14:25 informs us that Jonah came from Gath-Hepher, a place known from Josh 19:10–13, Judg 1:3, and 1 Kgs 17:9, yet its exact location is unknown. Readers of the Jonah narrative thus sought to establish more firmly the whereabouts of Jonah's hometown, as well as his tribal affiliation. The section on Jonah in *The Lives of the Prophets*, for instance, claims that Jonah came from the district of Kiriath-maon near the Gentile city of Ashdod (Azotus) on the sea. Based on this location, Jonah belonged to either the tribe of Asher or the tribe of Zebulun. To narrow down the possibilities, the rabbis appealed to the above-mentioned biblical passages:

> [10]The third lot came up for Zebulon according to its clans: The boundary of their inheritance went as far as Sarid. [11]Going west it ran to Maralah, touched Dabbesheth, and extended to the ravine near Jokneam. [12]It turned east from Sarid toward the sunrise to the territory of Kisloth Tabor and went on to Daberath and up to Japhia. [13]Then it continued eastward to Gath Hepher and Eth Kazin; it came out at Rimmon and turned toward Neah. (Josh 19:10–13)

> [31]Nor did Asher drive out those living in Akko or Sidon or Ahlab or Akzib or Helbah or Aphek or Rehob. [32]The Asherites lived among the Canaanite inhabitants of the land because they did not drive them out. (Judg 1:31–32)

> [8]Then the word of the LORD came to [Elijah]: [9] 'Go at once to Zarephath in the region of Sidon and stay there. I have directed a widow there to supply you with food'. [10]So he went to Zarephath. When he came to the town gate, a widow was there gathering sticks. He called to her and asked, 'Would you bring me a little water in a jar so I may have a drink?' (1 Kgs 17:8–10)

Gen.Rab. 98:11, for example, reports a discussion between Rabbi Levi and Rabbi Yohanan. According to Rabbi Levi, citing Josh 19:10–13, Jonah, as indicated by his origin in Gath-Hepher (2 Kgs 14:25), came from the tribe of Zebulon. By contrast, according to Rabbi Yohanan, citing Judg 1:31–32 and 1 Kgs 17:9, Jonah came from Asher, as indicated by the above-mentioned identification of Jonah with the son of the woman of Zarephath near Sidon. Offering a compromise, Rabbi Levi concludes that whereas Jonah's mother came from Asher, his father came from Zebulon (cf. *y.Sukk.* 5:1). The mediaeval Jewish exegetes also debated this issue. The mediaeval Jewish commentator David Kimhi (henceforth Radak, 1160–1235 CE), for example, used Josh 19:10, 13 to argue that Jonah was from the tribe of Zebulun.

At this point, it should be noted that the Book of Jonah never specifies Jonah's starting point. In Jonah 4:2, Jonah's reference to his home can literarily be translated to read 'on [his] own ground'. This vague reference has caused especially Muslim retellings to detach Jonah from the Land of Israel and instead to see him as a Ninevite. As implied in the writings of both Ibn Isḥāq and Al-Thaʿlabī, Jonah was commanded to speak to his fellow citizens of Nineveh. Quoting Ibn ʿAbbas, Ibn Isḥāq states that 'God, the Most High, sent Jonah to the people of his town, and they opposed what he brought to them and resisted them' (Gregg 2015: 416. Eng. transl. Newby 1989: 224). Along similar lines, Al-Thaʿlabī, citing other scholars, situates Jonah on a mountain in Nineveh, in the region near Mosul (Gregg 2015: 421. Eng. transl. Brinner 2002: 681).

Jonah's Prophetic Career

In parallel, interpreters have asked questions about Jonah's prophetic career, both prior to and after his mission to Nineveh.

Jonah, Elisha's Disciple

A rabbinic tradition argues that Jonah, following his resurrection by Elijah, became Elijah's disciple. This tradition probably comes from *b.San.* 113a, which speaks about Elijah's student Joshua (!) and the curse that he would utter. Several other rabbinic traditions identify Jonah with the anonymous prophet in 2 Kgs 9:1–4 (e.g. Ginzberg 1913: 4, Chapter 8; opening statement in *PRE* 11; Rashi, *Rabbinic Bible*, 2 Kgs 9:1). After Elijah's death, Jonah joined Elisha's many disciples and was sent to anoint King Jehu (prior to his mission to Nineveh in Jonah).

> The prophet Elisha summoned a man from the company of the prophets and said to him, 'Tuck your cloak into your belt, take this flask of oil with you and go to Ramoth Gilead. ²When you get there, look for Jehu son of Jehoshaphat, the son of Nimshi.

> Go to him, get him away from his companions and take him into an inner room. ³Then take the flask and pour the oil on his head and declare, "This is what the LORD says: I anoint you king over Israel". Then open the door and run; don't delay!' ⁴So the young man, the prophet, went to Ramoth Gilead. (2 Kgs 9:1–4).

Seder Olam Rabbah 19 (Part 2 [the prophets], sections 25–26 [Joash]) also preserves this tradition. This retelling conflates the material in 1–2 Kings with that in the prophetic books in an attempt to identify which prophet was active during which king's reign:

> Elisha went to Damascus and anointed Hazael as king over Aram and sent Jonah son of Amittay to anoint Jehu at Ramoth Gilead.

Seder Olam Rabbah (Part 2 [the prophets], sections 23–24 [Asa to Ahaziah]) makes the additional claim that all the prophecies to the House of Jehu were given through Jonah (cf. Scherman 1978: xxv).

> Jehu ruled over Israel for 28 years. (2 Kgs 10:30) 'And the Eternal said to Jehu: Since you were good and did the right things in my eyes, all my intentions you executed on the dynasty of Ahab, your Children of the fourth generation will sit on the throne of Israel'. Who said that to him? Jonah son of Amittai. (2 Kgs 10:31–32)

Gen.Rab. 21:5–6 also identifies Jonah with one of Elisha's disciples, more exactly with the one who was cutting down a tree and whose iron axe-head fell into the water (2 Kgs 6:5):

> Resh Lakish said: [He has become] like Jonah, [of whom is written], But as one was felling a beam, etc.

Jonah, the Prophet during Jeroboam II's Reign

The identification of Jonah with the eponymous prophet in 2 Kgs 14:24–25 tells us that Jonah delivered prophecies during the reign of Jeroboam II. This identification provides Jonah with both prophetic experience and prophetic credentials.

> He did evil in the eyes of the LORD and did not turn away from any of the sins of Jeroboam son of Nebat, which he had caused Israel to commit. He was the one who restored the boundaries of Israel from Lebo Hamath to the Sea of the Arabah, in accordance with the word of the LORD, the God of Israel, spoken through his servant Jonah son of Amittai, the prophet from Gath Hepher.

The Roman-Jewish scholar and historian Josephus (37–100 CE), for example, includes Jonah in his retelling of the events during the reign of Jeroboam II (*Ant.* 9:10) and emphasizes his previous prophetic assignments.

> Now one Jonah, a prophet, foretold to him that he should make war with the Syrians, and conquer their army, and enlarge the bounds of his kingdom on the northern parts to the city Hamath, and on the southern to the lake Ashaltitis; for the bounds of the Canaanites originally were these, as Joshua their general had determined them. So Jeroboam made an expedition against the Syrians, and overran all their country, as Jonah had foretold.

Several Church Fathers follow suit. Cyril of Alexandria (376–444 CE), identifying Jonah in the Book of Jonah with the prophet in 2 Kgs 14:24–25, states that 'you could find him uttering a great number of oracles to the Jewish populace, transmitting the word of God on high and clearly foretelling the future'. Cyril further attributes the prophecies in 1 Kgs 25:25–27 to Jonah. The Protestant reformer Martin Luther (1483–1546 CE) likewise argues in his German commentary that this identification is certain and that it 'contributes to a proper understanding of a man's book if one knows his time, his place of residence, his person, and his background'. Luther accordingly concludes that Jonah first served and aided Jeroboam in his own country Israel before being sent further afield to Nineveh.

The notes to the Geneva Bible also appeal to these earlier missions, even though their assessment of Jonah's success is different. These notes were compiled by a group of reformers in Geneva between 1560 CE and 1599 CE, among them John Calvin, John Knox, Miles Coverdale, William Whittingham, Theodore Beza, and Anthony Gilby. According to their comments to Jonah 1:1, 2, Jonah had prophesied in Israel but had been unsuccessful insofar as Israel's conversion was concerned. Therefore, God charged him to go and pronounce his judgement against Nineveh, with the aim of making Israel realize how their disbelief had kindled God's wrath.

In addition to these prophetic assignments during Jeroboam II's reign, *PRE* 10 mentions yet another mission, namely to Jerusalem (Eng. transl. Adelman 2009: 219):

> The second time, the Holy One blessed be he sent him to Jerusalem to destroy it, but because they repented God took pity on them, and changed His mind about the decree of doom and did not destroy it. And the Israelites called Jonah a false prophet.

In sum, the identification of Jonah in the Book of Jonah with the eponymous prophet in 2 Kgs 14:25 not only gives Jonah a family background and tribal affiliation, but it also provides him with a history of prior prophetic commissions. As we shall see further below, these prior commissions afford an explanation of Jonah's reluctance to obey God.

A few modern retellings pick up the notion of Jonah having had a prophetic career prior to his mission to Nineveh. The children's film *Jonah: A VeggieTale Movie* (2002), for instance, begins with Jonah being an effective and God-fearing prophet in Israel. Less seriously, James Bridie's play *Jonah and the Whale* (Act 1) (1932) portrays Jonah as a very successful prophet in his small provincial town of Gath-Hepher in Zebulon. Before Jonah set to work, his town was in a pretty bad shape:

> Jonah: This parish, Bilshan, was only a few short years ago a pretty obvious target for thunderbolts. Every man, woman and child in it, every domestic fowl moved in continual jeopardy; and their state was none the less shocking that they were unaware of the fact. They were given up to every unseemly hobby, from adultery to idolatry. I can only assume that Jahveh held His hand because He was stunned by their impudence.

In response to this situation, Jonah girded up his loins and got to work, with the result that 'in three weeks the place was unrecognisable'. The modern choral work *Jonah: A Musical Morality* (1989) by the Welsh composer William Mathias, and with text by Charles Causley, likewise opens with the speaker declaring:

> […] There lived a prophet,
> A preacher,
> An all-electric speaker,
> A hard-time teacher
> Of the old, old School
> His speech was thunder
> And it wasn't a wonder…
> And he told it well
> He told all the people
> Of Israèl

Jonah's Longevity

According to several rabbinic sources, Jonah lived to a great age. As noted above, *Seder Olam Rabbah* 18 maintains that Jonah was alive to anoint Jehu. If Jonah was a boy during the lifetime of Elijah, old enough to anoint Jehu in 841 BCE, i.e. when he is estimated to have begun his reign (r. 841–814 BCE), and still alive during the reign of Jeroboam II (r. 786–746 BCE), he must indeed have lived to be very old (see Scherman 1978: xxxvi). Abarbanel, in his commentary to Jonah 3:1, does the maths more explicitly: if Jonah anointed Jehu in the year 3062 from the creation of the world and lived until Zechariah who ruled Israel in the year 3164, Jonah must have lived another 102 years after his first occasion of prophecy. Slightly differently, *Eccl.Rab.* 8:10, discussing the identity of the 'wicked buried' referred to in Eccl 8:10, claims that Jonah was never buried (my translation):

> Rabbi Judah son of Simon said: The, by Ezekiel, newly resurrected dead cannot be meant here, as they were not sinners but righteous. The son of the woman from Zarephath is also not referred to here, as he was never buried.

Going one step further, *Midrash Tehilim* 26:7 postulates an ever-living Jonah. He is described as completely righteous and therefore able to enter the Garden of Eden while still alive. In this context, Jonah is compared with the son of the Shunammite: whereas this boy died (2 Kgs 4:18), came to life, but ultimately died again because of his wickedness, the son of the woman from Zarephath (i.e. Jonah) never died (my translation):

> But the son of the widow from Zarephath, i.e. Jonah ben Amittai, was a perfectly righteous man, purified by being devoured by the fish and in the depths of the sea, and he did not die, but 'the Eternal One spoke to the fish and it vomited Jonah onto dry land' (Jonah 2:11), and he entered into Paradise in his life in his glory.

The Church Fathers, in contrast, highlight that Jonah's longevity meant that his prophetic career coincided with many of Israel's other prophets. Jerome, for example, in the Prologue to his commentary, notes that Jonah must have been a contemporary of Hosea, Amos, and Isaiah.

Jonah's Name and Character

The basic meaning of the name 'Jonah' is 'dove'. The rabbis connected the name Jonah with the 'perfect dove' in Song 6:9a. Understanding God as the speaker in the verse and the addressee as Israel, the rabbis argued that Jonah's greatest characteristic was his perfection and his utter loyalty to God. It would thus be impossible that his flight to Tarshish was in any way a flight away from God; instead, his motivation was to ensure that Israel would not be slighted (cf. below).

More recent Jewish scholarly discussions have highlighted how the image of the dove connects the Jonah narrative to the flood narrative, where the dove plays a pivotal role. According to Keiter, the prophet Jonah is very much like the dove in the flood narrative: they both lack empathy, and neither gives enough thought to the severity of the destruction that God has foretold. The outcomes of the two narratives are also interconnected: in the flood story, God goes ahead with the punishment, whereas in the Jonah narrative, God's mercy prohibits any act of punishment (Keiter 2012; cf. Amar 2006/7; Greenstein 2016).

The name Jonah has also been understood as referring to 'suffering'. This dual sense comes to the forefront in many Christian typological interpretations. Jerome (*Commentary to Jonah*, 1:1–2), for instance, explores both meanings in his discussion of Jonah's role as a precursor of Christ. He connects Jonah's name 'dove' with the Holy Spirit that descended in the form of a dove upon Jesus at his baptism (Mark 1:10; Luke 3:22; John 1:32–33). In parallel, Jonah's name 'suffering' predicts Jesus's passion (cf. Isa 53:5) and his weeping for Jerusalem (Luke 19:41). In the concluding remarks in his German commentary, Luther likewise identifies Jonah as a symbol of the Holy Spirit. The reformer Johannes Bugenhagen (1485–1558 CE) challenges Jerome's allegorical interpretation and instead favours a spiritual meaning whereby Jonah 'is a dove, that is, a Christian [...] He is the son of Amittai, that is, a true preacher and confessor of the word of God'. Thus, Jonah is not a type for Christ in Bugenhagen's reading; Jonah is a representative of all Christians and embodies their calling to preach God's word (Lohrmann 2012: 91).

Yet other retellings offer either puns or interpretations of the name 'Jonah'. The long poem 'A Feast for Worms' from 1620 by Francis Quarles (1592–1644 CE), for example, has God tell Jonah to go forth to Nineveh 'Not like a Dove, but like a Dragon go; Pronounce my Judgment and denounce my Woe' (section 1).

A few modern scholars have connected the name Jonah ('dove') with the legend of Semiramis. Although the best-known version of this legend is preserved in the second book (1–20) of the *Bibliotheca historica* by the first-century BCE Roman historian Diodorus of Sicily (or Diodorus Siculus), it has much earlier roots. The legendary Queen Semiramis is probably based on the historical Assyrian queen Sammu-ramat, who served as regent for her son Adad-narari III (r. 810–783 BCE) during the early years of his reign. Weinfeld, and in greater detail also Frahm, have pointed to four shared aspects between the Semiramis legend and the Book of Jonah: the name Semiramis may stem from the Akkadian word for 'dove' (*summu/summatu*), her mother is the fish goddess Derceto, she is associated with Ashkelon (cf. Yafo), and she is the queen of Nineveh. Based on these similarities, Frahm argues that the Book of Jonah forms a midrash on the Semiramis legend (Weinfeld 1991; Frahm 2016).

The contemporary biblical scholar Jione Havea, looking at the Book of Jonah from the perspective of the Pasifika (the region, peoples, and cultures of Pacific Islands, South Sea Islands, Oceania), highlights that the name 'Jonah' has both positive and negative connotations. On the one hand, parents who name their son 'Jonah' wish their son to be at one with the sea. On the other hand, when trouble visits a family or community, they ask 'who is the Jonah', i.e. who is to blame (Havea 2020: ch. 1).

Jonah 1:2

> Rise, go to Nineveh, the great city, and call out against it, because its/their evil has risen before me.

Verse 2 speaks of God's call to Jonah to go to the Gentile city of Nineveh and proclaim that God has become aware of its wickedness. This command raises the question of whether God's salvation is only for the Jews or also for the Gentiles. Luther, for example, appeals to this verse (alongside Rom 3:29) as part of his argument that circumcision and the Law of Moses are not prerequisites for piety and pleasing God. It follows, according to Luther, that the Jews are mistaken in their claim that all must become Jews and accept and observe the Laws of Moses (German commentary to Jonah 1:2).

'Nineveh, the great city'

Nineveh, the capital city of the Neo-Assyrian Empire, was one of the largest cities in the ancient Near East. In the Bible, it is known from 2 Kgs 19:36 as the capital city of Sennacherib. Within the narrative of Jonah, set ostensibly in the eighth century BCE (cf. above, Jonah 1:1), it constituted Israel's mightiest and most feared enemy. It was sacked in 612 BCE by, among others, Neo-Babylonian and Median forces. The Hebrew Bible is aware of Nineveh's destruction, as indicated by the Book of Nahum. It can thus be readily assumed that all subsequent interpreters of Jonah, and probably also its original author, were aware of Nineveh's demise (Tiemeyer 2017b). The Spanish biblical commentator Abraham ben Meir Ibn Ezra (henceforth Ibn Ezra, 1089–1167 CE), for example, notes pertinently that Nineveh was the capital of Assyria and that it is nowadays destroyed.

Alongside its political significance, the city of Nineveh conjures up images from Genesis. It is mentioned in Gen 10:10–11 as one of the mighty cities of Mesopotamia. The association with Shinar in Gen 10:10 creates a textual link between the city of Nineveh and the narrative of the tower of Babylon, set on the plain of Shinar (Gen 11:2). As a result, the name Nineveh very early on came to serve as the epitome of godlessness. Jerome, for example, connects Nineveh with the builders of the tower of Babel, stating that the city was sinful even back then as its inhabitants constructed a 'tower of pride'.

Although a symbol of wickedness, Nineveh also projects the notion of a pious and successful imperial city (cf. also Jonah 3). The German Protestant reformer and theologian Johannes Brenz (Latinized as John Brentius) (1499–1570 CE) transforms the image of Nineveh into a model for imperial

England that is worthy of emulation. Through Jonah's preaching, Nineveh became a beacon of light to the (less fortunate) nations around it, thus justifying and legitimizing the actions of the imperial centre (Staffell 2008: 493–496). In his commentary to Jonah 3:4 (*News from Niniue*, p. 46), Brentius writes:

> For as Ionas could not go from house to house generally throughout ye Citie of Niniue, but stoode in a convenient place of ye City, that the fame of his preaching might come to all men, even so the word of the Lord is not wont to be carried to every corner of every region, but it is revealed & published in the speciall and principall kingdomes, that by them the fame thereof might be spred abrode throughout the whole world, that no man might have excuse.

George Abbot (1562–1633 CE), the Archbishop of Canterbury, expresses similar sentiments in his series of sermons on Jonah (*Exposition*, p. 17). For him, Nineveh was the celebrated and powerful imperial centre of the Orient, yet in his own time was replaced by London. In his first lecture, devoted to Jonah 1:1–2, he both praises Nineveh for its piety and warns London that unless it shows the same willingness to repent, it may also ultimately be replaced by a more God-fearing city (see Staffell 2008: 497–498).

> Our Prophet in his preaching need find no such fault: his charge hath a name: it is Niniue that great Citie, which ruled over the earth, the seat of the Empire, the Ladie of the East, the Queene of nations, the riches of the world, where more people did inhabit, then are now in some one kingdome.

The notion of Nineveh as 'a great city' in Jonah 1:2 anticipates the references to its large land area and huge population later in Jonah 3:2–3 and 4:11. The Geneva Bible Notes to Jonah 1:2 claim rather specifically that it was about 48 miles in circumference, had 1,500 towers and 120,000 children (cf. below, Jonah 4:11). Its great size is also stressed in Judith 1:1: 'Nebuchadnezzar, who reigned over the Assyrians in Nineveh the great city' (Ueberschaer 2020).

Modern scholars have noted the prevalent use of the term 'great' (Heb. root *gdl*) throughout the Book of Jonah. Not only is Nineveh 'great' (1:2; 3:2, 3; 4:11), but there is also a 'great storm' (1:4) causing a 'great fear' (1:10, 16), as well as a 'great fish' (2:1 [Eng. 1:17]), Jonah's 'great joy' over the *qiqayyon* (4:6), and the verbal form 'to grow' (4:10) (Halpern and Friedman 1980: 81–82).

Not all commentators take the reference to Nineveh literally. The *Glossa Ordinaria*, for example, argues that the term 'city' here refers to the world. As such, it is a prophecy of how the world will accept Jesus, whom the Jews have disdained.

'and call out against her'

The statement 'and call out against her' raises the question: what is Jonah to cry out? The biblical text does not spell out the content of Jonah's message. The simple answer, according to the French rabbi and biblical commentator Shlomo ben Itzchak (henceforth Rashi, 1040–1105 CE), is God's proclamation. A few scholars, however, have assigned exegetical significance to the absence of a concrete message. Radak discusses the possibility that Jonah fled from his mission simply because he objected to go to Nineveh without knowing what exactly God wanted him to say. Radak ultimately rejects this interpretation, favouring instead the alternative that Jonah was aware of God's message to the people of Nineveh and fled *because* he knew exactly what God wanted him to say. In Radak's view, Jonah knew precisely that his message was going to be 'and Nineveh will be overturned/destroyed' (Jonah 3:4). Coming from a different angle, the Vilna Gaon (1720–1797 CE), commenting on Jonah 1:2, connects this statement with Isa 40:6–8 and suggests that the deeper intention of Jonah's message was to convey humanity's temporal frailty in contrast to God's eternity (Shapiro 1997: 12).

Exploring the purpose of Jonah's proclamation, two lines of thinking dominate: (1) its purpose was to foretell Nineveh's imminent destruction or (2) its purpose was to cause the Ninevites to repent, with the aim of averting the foretold destruction. A few scholars maintain that Jonah here, as in 3:4, is simply commanded to convey God's decision to destroy Nineveh. The Russian biblical commentator and Kabbalist Rav David Luria (henceforth Radal, 1798–1855 CE), for example, in his commentary to *PRE* 10.5, states that the proclamation here is the same as in Jonah 3:4, i.e. Nineveh's destruction. As this interpretation is potentially problematic, given that it removes part of the impetus for Jonah to flee, most exegetes instead think that Jonah is commanded to convey God's desire that they repent. For example, the Russian rabbi, grammarian, and biblical commentator Meir Leibush ben Yehiel Michel Wisser (henceforth Malbim, 1809–1879 CE) argues in his commentary to Jonah 1:3 that God commanded Jonah to encourage the Ninevites to repent, as the decree of their punishment had not yet been sealed. In a very outspoken fashion, the modern choral work *Jonah: A Musical Morality*, by the Welsh composer William Mathias, declares upfront that Jonah is supposed to preach repentance and to offer God's forgiveness. The choir sing:

> Go now to Nineveh, the good Lord said. […] Preach them repentance and God's good grace. […] Preach repentance. Offer the gift of God's forgiveness. Redemption, forgiveness to all the people. Throw away your narrow pride, Jonah. Open your mind. Open your heart to all peoples. The love of God, the forgiveness of God is for all the people.

Seeking a middle path, Ibn Ezra maintains that Jonah was merely given the task of stating that God's message at this time was that Nineveh's wickedness had become known to God, i.e. the content of verse 2b, yet he was (more indirectly) entrusted with calling the people of Nineveh to repent (commentary to Jonah 1:1).

At this point, a few scholars try to exonerate Jonah's anticipated disobedience in Jonah 1:3. The Egyptian Jewish rabbi, philosopher, and biblical commentator Sa'adia HaGaon (882–942 CE), as quoted by Ibn Ezra in his commentary to Jonah 1:1, attempted to explain the verb 'call against it' (וקרא עליה) as an invitation rather than as a command to prophesy by appealing to Exod 2:20, where Moses's future father-in-law asks his daughters to 'call' Moses so that he could eat bread. Ibn Ezra rejects this interpretation, however, stating that the two passages are hardly parallels. Rather, Ibn Ezra chooses to compare Jonah's behaviour here with that of Moses's series of objections in Exod 3:11, 13; 4:1, 10, 13. Moses' hesitation was, in fact, worse than Jonah's, insofar as Moses was merely tasked with bringing his chosen people out of Egypt, whereas Jonah was saddled with the much more onerous commission of bringing repentance to Nineveh.

'its wickedness has ascended before Me'

The final letter *mem* of the word *ra'atam* can be understood in two ways. It can either be a possessive m.pl. suffix 'their' and thus refer to the inhabitants of Nineveh, rendering the phrase 'their evil'. Alternatively, it can be understood as an enclitic mem that is attached to a f.sg. suffix, rendering the phrase 'its evil' (referring to the city). The Vulgate (*malitia eius*) and the LXX (τῆς κακίας αὐτῆς) support the second reading (see further Sasson 1990: 75–76).

The phrase 'its wickedness has ascended [to God]' echoes two passages in Genesis. First, as pointed out by the prologue to the Book of Jonah in the *Glossa Ordinaria*, it recalls the similar statement in Gen 18:20–21 pertaining to Sodom and Gomorrah. The glossator argues that because Jonah was ignorant of the dispensation of God who desires the salvation of all men (cf. 2 Pet 3:9) and therefore did not want the pronounced divine judgement to be revoked, Jonah decided to flee from before God's face. Second, it recalls Gen 4:10, where Abel's blood cries out to God from the earth. These two allusions to Genesis serve to establish Nineveh as a symbol of extreme evil, an impression that is reinforced in 1:3 by Jonah's flight: Nineveh is the very last place that Jonah wishes to visit (Lindsay 2016).

The phrase by itself raises the question of whether God refers to a specific (act of) wickedness. The Hellenistic-Jewish sermon *On Jonah* (chs 4–5) comments on this issue at length. The young people of Nineveh searched for (illicit) sexual pleasures, whereas the old people tricked each other. More generally, the sermon stresses the Ninevites' lack of gratitude to God for his abundant blessings upon their city (e.g. fecundity, fair weather) and their lack of justice towards one another. Other commentators focus more on Nineveh's acts of evil against Israel. The French Jewish biblical commentator Yosef Kara (1065–1135 CE), for example, argues that this statement refers to Nineveh's destruction of the Northern Kingdom and the exile of the ten northern tribes (Zlotowitz 1978: 80).

Focusing more on the sins that the Ninevites did *not* commit, Ibn Ezra, on the basis of the phrase 'a great city to God' in Jonah 3:3, maintains that Nineveh only recently had become a wicked city. Further, the people of Nineveh cannot have been guilty of idolatry, given that biblical text fails to mention that they destroyed their idols as part of their repentance. In other words, quoting Ibn Ezra, had they been guilty of idolatry, they would have destroyed the idols (otherwise their repentance would have been insufficient) (cf. below Jonah 3:10).

Why Did God Send a Prophet to Forewarn Non-Jews about the Consequences of Their Wickedness?
The notion that God is concerned with the sins of the foreign, Gentile city of Nineveh prompts the wider question as to why God called Jonah in the first place. The Hellenistic-Jewish sermon *On Jonah* 2:1–3, originally written in Greek but preserved to us in an old Armenian translation, likens God to a healer who wishes to cure the world:

> [A]s a good doctor He sought after the right medicine for the city's illness, in order to stop the spread of the illness and to outstrip the menace by His help. And this medicine had a reputation contradicting salvation, for wishing to keep alive and protect the city, He dispatched a prophet, threatening it with ruin – correctly, I think, and [in this way] teaching [it] the genuine craft of the doctors (as the most skilful of them [do]); they promise to keep the sick alive and set them upright by curing with fire and water.

On Jonah thus refers to the predicted disaster as the necessary cure, i.e. the essential impetus to bring about Nineveh's repentance. It derives the notion of God as a healer from, among other texts, Exod 15:26; Ps 103:2–3; and Deut 32:39 (Muradyan and Topchyan 2013: 776–777).

Looking at the related issue as to why God bothered with the *Gentile* city, Radak, informed by Amos 3:2, notes that God acts on the evil of the nations of the world in those specific cases when their evil is related to 'violence' (*ḥamas*). This was the case at the time of Noah (Gen 6) and this was the case of Sodom (Gen 19). God is less concerned with their other sins; in this respect, God treats

Israel distinctively in that he notes *all* its sins (and thus holds his chosen people to a higher standard). Radak claims that the Ninevites' particular sins were robbery and oppression. Further, inspired by the statement 'the violence of their hands' in Jonah 3:8 and the occurrence of the same word 'violence' in the flood narrative (Gen 6:11, 13), Radak argues that God had to intervene because his creation was at stake.

Several commentators, Christians and Jewish alike, argue that the true focus of God's command to Jonah is Israel rather than Nineveh. Among Christian interpreters, Theodore, Bishop of Mopsuestia (350–428 CE), claims in the Introduction to his commentary on Jonah that God sent Jonah to the nations because the Jews were unbelieving and reluctant to heed his prophecies. Among Jewish interpreters, Abarbanel (in the Introduction to his Jonah commentary) and later also Malbim highlight that God wished the people of Nineveh to repent, as their repentance would enable God to use Assyria as a rod to punish Israel (cf. Isa 10:5). If they had remained as sinful as they were in Jonah's days, so the logic goes, God could not justifiably have used them as his tools. Knowing that Israel's future survival was at stake, Jonah decided to disobey God for the sake of saving Israel (see further below).

Turning to the even wider issue of why God is in the habit of sending prophets as harbingers of his imminent judgement, Luther, in his German commentary to Jonah 1:1, declares that 'whenever God's wrath is about to be kindled, He usually first sends His Word to save a few'. In support of this claim, Luther mentions that God sent, among others, Noah before obliterating the earth (Gen 6), Lot before annihilating Sodom (Gen 19), and Moses before afflicting Egypt. He further sent Hosea before doing away with Israel; now Jonah is sent before destroying Nineveh. Ultimately, God sent Jesus before the appearance of the final wrath at the Last Judgement. In this manner, Luther stresses that the possibility of repentance and thus our salvation is imbedded in God's very sending of a prophet. The details of Luther's opinion are, however, unsupported by the biblical text insofar as nothing in the narratives about Noah and Lot implies the possibility of repentance; this aspect is being read into the narratives by later readers.

In fact, when we read Jonah intertextually with Gen 18–19, Jonah's *lack* of intercession stands out. In contrast to Abraham, who fulfilled his prophetic role of intercessor, Jonah made no attempt to change God's mind (McLaughlin 2013: 76–77; Schellenberg 2015: 356). On a different level, however, Jonah and Abraham are carrying out the same function, namely to make sure that God upholds justice. For Abraham, that justice means that God should not punish the innocent with the guilty; he does not argue that God should spare the guilty (Schmidt 1976: 160–164). The link between Jonah and Gen 18–19 is accentuated, and further problematized when we add Jer 20:16 into the mix. This verse reports how God did not 'change his mind' (*niphal* of root *nḥm*, cf. Jonah 3:9, 10) but instead went ahead and 'overthrew' (root *hpk*, cf. Gen 19:21; Jonah 3:4) 'the cities' (i.e. Sodom and Gomorrah). Nineveh in Jonah thus serves as the opposite of Sodom and Gomorrah in Genesis as it was *not* overthrown, because God *did* change his mind. The real historical Nineveh (and also the literary Nineveh in Nahum), however, becomes Sodom and Gomorrah's successor, which in the end is also overthrown.

Jonah 1:3

> And Jonah rose to flee to Tarshish from before Yhwh, and he went down to Yafo and he found a ship coming [to/from] Tarshish and paid its fare and went down into it to come with them to Tarshish from before Yhwh.

The imagery of this verse is beautifully captured by Melville in Father Mapple's sermon on Jonah in Chapter 9 of *Moby-Dick*:

> He skulks about the wharves of Joppa [...] with slouched hat and guilty eye, skulking from his God; prowling among the shipping like a vile burglar hastening to cross the sea. So disordered, self-condemning is his look, that had there been policemen in those days, Jonah, on the mere suspicion of something wrong, had been arrested ere he touched a deck. How plainly he's a fugitive! No baggage, not a hat-box, valise, or carpet-bag – no friends accompany him to the wharf with their adieux. (Herman 1851 / Richard Bentley / Public domain)

Melville, through this portrayal of Jonah, suggests that the potentially comical prophet of the biblical narrative is really a troubled and isolated man, whose rebellion against God reflects his anguished spirit. The hat seeks to hide him from God's eyes, yet the prophet himself knows fully well the futility of this endeavour (Rathbun 1991: 4).

'And Jonah rose to flee'

The opening statement of Jonah 1:3 raises one of the central theological questions of the Book of Jonah, namely, why Jonah decided to defy God's command. We shall explore five widely held and influential interpretative lines. Many of these interpretations share the notion that Jonah, due to his prophetic office, knew that Nineveh would repent, a notion that is emphasized later in Jonah 4:2. Expressed differently, the statement in Jonah 4:2 is often, but not always, read back into the fabric of Jonah 1:3 and understood to provide the key to Jonah's disobedience.

1. God's Habitual Compassion

A dominant explanation for Jonah's flight is Jonah's knowledge of what we may call 'God's habitual compassion'. To a certain extent, this explanation walks hand in hand with the related explanation that Jonah fled because he feared being called a false prophet, as well as the idea that Israel would be compared unfavourably to the nations. The biblical narrative itself supports this line of exegesis: in Jonah 4:2, Jonah admits that God is a 'gracious and compassionate God, slow to anger and abounding in love, a God who changes his mind with regard to planned evil'. Thus, a significant number of (predominantly rabbinic) scholars claim that Jonah did not want to go to Nineveh lest he be vilified. Past experiences had taught him about God's mercy in the face of repentance, and so he did not want to be considered a false prophet.

1.1 Fear of Being a False Prophet

Many interpreters suggest that Jonah fled for fear of being called a false prophet. The origin of this interpretation is the belief that a prophet whose prophecy does not come true is a false prophet (Deut 18:22):

> If what a prophet proclaims in the name of the LORD does not take place or come true, that is a message the LORD has not spoken. That prophet has spoken presumptuously, so do not be alarmed.

Schellenberg has argued that Jonah's anger at God sparing Nineveh and Jonah's subsequent wish to die is a conscious allusion to Deut 18:20, 22, serving to portray Jonah as an 'anti-prophet' (Schellenberg 2015: 359).

This notion of prophethood is, however, not in line with the general Israelite (and ancient Near Eastern) notion of prophecy. In contrast to, say, a meteorologist, a prophet's reputation does not depend on the correctness of his/her forecast but on his/her ability to effect spiritual transformation. Ezekiel's watchman, for example, warns the people of the oncoming danger with the aim of making them change their behaviour and thus to forestall the danger (Ezek 3:17; 33:1–11) (cf. Tiemeyer 2005; see also Bickerman 1967: 33, 40; Adelman 2011: 83). As put very aptly by Eagleton, 'the only successful prophet is an ineffectual one, one whose warnings fail to materialize [...] What they get done is to produce a state of affairs in which the state of affairs they describe won't be the case. Effective declarations of imminent catastrophe cancel themselves out, containing as they do a contradiction between what they say and what they do' (Eagleton 1990: 233).

Nevertheless, many rabbinical texts explain Jonah's flight as a matter of saving his own prophetic reputation. This interpretation is often influenced by the identification of Jonah with not only his namesake in 2 Kgs 14:25 but also with the anonymous prophet in 2 Kgs 9:1 (see above Jonah 1:1). This identification informs readers that Jonah had already carried out at least two prior missions, namely, to anoint Jehu (2 Kgs 9:1) and to prophesy regarding Jeroboam's restoration of the borders of Israel (2 Kgs 14:24–25). The second prophecy in 2 Kgs 14:24–25, however, caused Jonah grief. Since Jeroboam was a bad king, the very fact that this prophecy came true was unfortunate. As a result, Jonah's reputation as a prophet took a dent, later leading to Jonah not wanting to go to Nineveh where, so the logic goes, his reputation as a prophet would be given its death warrant (see further Adelman 2009: 220). Expressed in the words of the opening section of *PRE* 10 (Eng. transl. Adelman 2009: 219):

> The fifth day of the week was also the day on which Jonah fled from God's presence. And why did he flee? Because the first time, He (God) sent him to restore the borders of Israel and his words were fulfilled, as it says [2 Kgs 14:25].

Later, *PRE* 10 speaks of yet another mission, this time to Jerusalem:

> The second time, the Holy One blessed be He sent him to Jerusalem to destroy it, [but because they repented] God took pity on them, and changed His mind about the decree of doom and did not destroy it. And the Israelites called Jonah a false prophet.

In *PRE* 10, this reputation, in turn, becomes one of two reasons why Jonah did not want to go to Nineveh:

> The third time, he was sent to Nineveh to destroy it. Jonah deliberated to himself, 'I know that these Gentiles are close to repenting. Now when they repent, the Holy One, Blessed be He, will be filled with mercy towards them [onto the enemies of Israel] and transfer His fury [onto Israel]. Is it not enough that the Israelites call me a false prophet, must the nations of the earth call me a false prophet as well?'

Jonah's past experiences had taught him that God shows mercy when (His) people repent. Therefore, as he suspected that the Ninevites might repent, Jonah decided to refuse God's mission to save his prophetic reputation. Mixed in with this fear is another danger, hinted at in the last quote from *PRE* (above), namely, that if the Gentiles repented, God would compare Israel unfavourably with them and use the nations to punish Israel.

A few Jewish commentators offer a more nuanced interpretation, as they distinguish between Jonah's own perception of prophecy (cf. above) and the less sophisticated beliefs of the people around him. As expressed by Radal in his commentary to *PRE* 10.5, whereas the wise would have realized that repentance changes God's decree and thus understood Jonah to be a true prophet, the ignorant masses, as well as the whole Assyrian nation, would have considered Jonah to be false one. Jonah, having tasted the bitterness of vilification earlier, was not inclined to risk his reputation again and thus fled (Scherman 1978: xxxvii).

From a modern Jewish American perspective, Oren and Gerson compare Jonah's dilemma with that of a president faced with the option of going to war in order to prevent an anticipated massacre, yet as the massacre is prevented, they are often blamed for starting a war. The moral of the story is that it is almost impossible to receive credit 'for averting cataclysms that never occur' (Oren and Gerson 2007).

Several Church Fathers are aware of this interpretation (cf. also Jonah 4:2). Tertullian, for example, claims that Jonah foresaw that God's mercy would be poured out on the heathens, thus causing Jonah to fear that that would prove him to be a false prophet (*On Purity*, 10). Likewise, John Chrysostom (349–407 CE), the Archbishop of Constantinople, states explicitly in his Homily 2:18–20, 'On Repentance and Almsgiving', that Jonah did not want to go to Nineveh due to God's customary philanthropy:

> He hastily fled far away into exile, for he said, 'I am going away to preach; you repent as a lover of mankind, and then I am executed as a false prophet' [...] He spoke about them, and, in this manner, Jonah was considered a false prophet.

Later, Francis Quarles's poem 'A Feast for Worms' (section II) voices the same opinion that Jonah was afraid of being called a false prophet:

> I know my god is gentle, and inclin'd
> To tender mercy, apt to change his mind.
> Upon the least repentance: Then shall I
> Be deem'd as false, and shame my Prophecy.

Gregory of Nazianzus (329–390 CE), Archbishop of Constantinople, likewise states in his *Oration* 2.106 that

> [Jonah] fled from having to announce the dread and awful message to the Ninevites, and from being subsequently, if the city was saved by repentance, convicted of falsehood: not that he was displeased at the salvation of the wicked, but he was ashamed of being made an instrument of falsehood, and exceedingly zealous for the credit of prophecy, which was in danger of being destroyed in his person, since most men are unable to penetrate the depth of the Divine dispensation in such cases.

Yet, Gregory ultimately rejects this interpretation as unworthy of a prophet of God who undoubtedly would not be so 'ignorant of the design of God'. He would surely also not have imagined that he could ever flee from God's presence, knowing – both as a prophet and as a sensible man – that God's power is everywhere (*Oration* 2.107–108). Instead, Jonah fled to save Israel (*Oration* 2.196):

> When he saw the falling away of Israel, and perceived the passing over of the grace of prophecy to the Gentiles – this was the cause of his retirement from preaching and of his delay in fulfilling the command.

Luther also rejects the notion that Jonah would have been afraid of being considered a false prophet: according to the narrative logic of the book, Jonah obviously did not know what would happen. If he had known, why would he have been sitting outside the city in Jonah 4:5 to see what would happen? (German commentary, Jonah 1:3).

1.2 Fear of Israel Being Compared Unfavourably with the Nations

Other interpreters propose an interrelated reason as to why Jonah fled, namely, that he feared that Israel would be compared unfavourably with Nineveh and thus found wanting. In other words, if the nations repented, then their repentance would point an accusing finger at sinful Israel, with the result that Jonah would have been instrumental in bringing about Israel's terrible condemnation.

Several Church Fathers favour this explanation. Jerome, for instance, states that Jonah, through the inspiration of the Holy Spirit, was aware that the repentance of the people (of Nineveh) would be the destruction of the Jews. Once the Gentiles had come to believe, then Israel would surely perish. When realizing the danger that Nineveh's repentance would constitute for Israel, Jonah decided to save his people by fleeing. Jonah's disobedience to God can thus be compared with Moses's expressed willingness to die on behalf of Israel (Exod 32:31–32, cf. below). Thus, according to Jerome, Jonah's behaviour was, if not fully laudable, at least honourable. Furthermore, in Jerome's view, Jonah felt that God was unduly punishing him by sending him to a place like Nineveh that was characterized by idolatry and ignorance of God.

Theodore of Mopsuestia, in the introduction to his commentary to Jonah (cf. also Jonah 1:1–2), also speaks of Jonah not wanting to go to Nineveh because he feared an unfavourable comparison between the Gentiles and the Jews. For Theodore, the events at Nineveh pointed forward to Jesus: the move '*en masse* to godliness' of the Gentiles would inevitably put the Jews to shame as they remained unresponsive and resistant to Christ the Lord despite having had him in their midst. Like Jerome, Theodore further explains Jonah's decision to flee as an act of compassion. Like Paul in Rom 9:1–5, who preferred being cut off from Christ for the sake of his brothers, Jonah's flight stemmed from his desire to save his people: Jonah opted to flee thinking that he would thus avoid prophesying to the Ninevites and so preserve Israel's honour.

On this issue, Cyril of Alexandria's comment to Jonah 1:3 is another case in point. Cyril states quite frankly that Nineveh's repentance was Israel's condemnation, as hinted at in Matt 12:41 (cf. also the Prologue of the *Glossa Ordinaria*):

> They were convicted of being forward, unresponsive, paying little heed to the laws of God. After all, at a single prophet's preaching, the Ninevites were instantly brought around to a sense of obligation to repent, despite suffering from extreme deception, whereas those others set at naught Moses and prophets, and spurned Christ himself, the Saviour of us all, despite his supporting his teachings with miracles, through which they should have been convinced quite easily that he was God by nature and became man to save the whole earth under heaven, and them before all others.

Cyril further argues that Jonah feared that the fate proclaimed by him would not take effect and that the people of Nineveh

> [...] though unaware of the kindness of the compassionate God, might take advantage of it and do away with him as a charlatan, deceiver, and liar who had persuaded them to make needless efforts. Barbarians, you see, are ever disposed to anger and quite ready to act like a bull, even without any real basis for their frenzy.

The Jewish sages and the mediaeval Jewish commentators give this line of interpretation a different slant. In their hands, Jonah becomes a martyr for Israel who had to choose between obeying God and defending Israel's honour. To shield Israel from God's anger, Jonah, therefore, chose not to go to Nineveh. Using the rabbinic terminology of 'father' (i.e. God) and 'son' (i.e. Israel), Rabbi Scherman aptly states that Jonah had to choose between obeying God and defending the honour of Israel. 'In order to shield the child from the wrath of its Father, he chose not to go to Nineveh'.

This notion is connected to a wider discussion of prophetic responsibility. The *Mekhilta Attributed to R. Ishmael* 1:3 outlines three types of prophets:

1. Those who are aware of honouring the father and also aware of honouring the son: e.g. Jeremiah
2. Those who are aware of honouring the father but not aware of honouring the son: e.g. Elijah
3. Those who are aware of honouring the son but not aware of honouring the father: e.g. Jonah

The *Mekhilta* thus highlights two opposite sides of the prophetic office, namely, whether prophets should accentuate their role as God's spokespersons before Israel or their role as Israel's intercessors before God. Jonah, in the view of the *Mekhilta*, is doing the latter and should accordingly be compared with Moses, who was willing to die for the sake of Israel (Exod 32:32, cf. Jerome above). In this way, Jonah, like other prophets before him, was willing to give his life for Israel's survival:

> R. Nathan says, 'Jonah went only to commit suicide in the sea, as it is said, "And he said to them: 'Take me up and cast me forth into the sea.'" As so you find that the patriarchs and prophets gave their lives for Israel'.

The Jerusalem Talmud (*y.San* 11:5) makes the point poignantly, quoting Jonah as saying that he had no choice but to flee:

> Jonah said: 'I know that these Gentiles are nigh unto repentance, and lo, I shall go and prophecy against them, and they shall repent, and the Holy One, blessed be he, consequently will come and inflict punishment on [those who hate] Israel [meaning, on Israel itself]'. 'So what should I do? [I have no choice but to] flee'.

Jonah was prepared to endanger his prophetic calling and to forfeit God's grace for the sake of Israel. In other words, he was willing to commit a transgression for a noble cause.

Many mediaeval Jewish exegetes pick up this line of exegesis (e.g. Rashi [Jonah 1:3], Radak [Jonah 1:1]). Ibn Ezra, in his commentary to Jonah 1:1, rejects the idea that Jonah resented being called a false prophet for three reasons. First, Jonah did at this point not know God's message to Nineveh (which was only given in Jonah 3:4); second, the notion that Jonah would be inflamed because the people of Nineveh would call him a false prophet is absurd, given that he did not live among them; third, the people of Nineveh were no fools – they would have figured out that Jonah's prophecy would be conditional; why else would God bother sending this message in the first place? In parallel, Ibn Ezra accepts the idea that Jonah prioritized the well-being of Israel over against following God's command, citing the rabbinic idiom that Jonah 'prioritized the honour of the son and did not prioritize the honour of the father'.

Lam.Rab. 31:2, inspired in part by the association of the name Jonah with the verb 'to oppress', compares the fate of Jerusalem with that of Nineveh. In words akin to Jesus's lament over Jerusalem in Matt 23:37–39, the midrash bemoans that Jerusalem did not learn a lesson from Nineveh but persisted in its evil ways and accepted no correction:

> The oppressing city: should she not have learned from the city of Jonah, which is Nineveh. One prophet did I send to Nineveh, and the city repented, but to the

Israelites in Jerusalem how many prophets did I send: 'Yet the Lord forewarned Israel and Judah by the hand of every prophet and seer, saying "Turn from your evil ways and keep my commandments and my statutes"' (2 Kgs 17:13). 'And though I sent to you all my servants the prophets, sending them daily and early' (Jer 7:25), 'daily and early' means rising up early to send them in the morning and likewise at night. 'She listens to no voice, she accepts no correction' (Zeph 3:2).

2. Foreknowledge that Nineveh would Later destroy Israel

Another less prevalent line of interpretation may be labelled 'historical' insofar as it takes the destruction of Israel in 721 BCE by the Neo-Assyrian Empire as a given. It is also biblical in the sense that it places the Book of Jonah in dialogue with the Book of Nahum, which (depending on its date of composition) either predicts or laments the Neo-Assyrian obliteration of Israel. One of its chief advocates is the Portuguese Jewish statesman and philosopher Abarbanel. In the introduction to his commentary to Jonah, he rejects the above-mentioned reasons, namely, that the nations were close to repentance and that their repentance would somehow shame Israel:

> This is a very weak explanation. For perhaps in the repentance of the people of Nineveh the Israelites would be shamed. And they would repent from their sins turning to The Eternal who would have mercy on them for their personal acts [of repentance].

Abarbanel then also dismisses the explanation that Jonah feared being called a false prophet in case the people of Nineveh repented, and God pardoned them:

> This also does not make sense to me. For the people of Nineveh believed in [the words of] Jonah and therefore performed repentance growing out of [the words of] his mouth. And he knew that if they returned in repentance as a result of his words they had already believed in [the validity of] his prophecy. If they had not believed in it they would not have returned in repentance.

Having eliminated these two widespread explanations, Abarbanel offers his own take on the matter:

> Jonah did not want to go to Nineveh for he knew of the future difficulties which would befall the [ten] tribes of [the Northern Kingdom of] Israel. Therefore, he closed his soul to God's call for the purpose that the nations of Assyria and Nineveh its capital would be destroyed.

In other words, Jonah chose to be a martyr on behalf of Israel (cf. above). He knew that Assyria would soon threaten the Northern Kingdom. Therefore, by refusing to prophesy (lest he encourage the Ninevites to repent), Jonah sought to ensure Nineveh's destruction and concurrently safeguard Israel's survival. In fact, Jonah fully expected his disobedience to cost him his life, as he would under normal circumstances have drowned in the sea when the sailors tossed him overboard. In this regard, Abarbanel, as Jerome and others before him, compares Jonah with Moses, whose statement in Exod 32:33 reveals his desire to save Israel at the potential cost of his own life (Abarbanel, Commentary to Jonah, Answer to the second question, cf. Tiemeyer 2017b).

A few, predominantly modern, interpreters add an extra dimension to this interpretation, namely, that Jonah actively *hated* the Neo-Assyrians, due to the immense suffering that they caused Israel and many other people groups in the ancient world. Jonah's flight from God's commission stemmed from his hatred of, or at least deep feelings of hurt associated with, the Assyrians. Given what they had done and were going to do to Israel and others, they did not deserve God's mercy. Stefan Andres's novel *Der Mann im Fisch*, written in 1963, reflects on the parallels between Assyria at the time of Jonah and his own generation in Germany. Jonah, when hearing the call to go to Nineveh, refuses to go as he thinks that the people of Assyria deserve to perish due to their crimes. They are not worthy of being given the opportunity to repent and live. Jonah thus flees from God and sinks into oblivion as he is hurled overboard, only suddenly to find himself in the twentieth century and to realize that wars are still going on and that whole cities are bombed and turned to dust and ashes. Jonah's faith in God collapses and, once back in his own time again, he refuses to be God's puppet in his dealings with Nineveh. Although he rages against God, Jonah ultimately ends up bowing in submission to a God who is inconsistent and incomprehensible, yet also almighty and merciful (see further Liptzin 1985a: 246–247).

Auster, in his *The Invention of Solitude* (p. 169), makes a similar comparison. After highlighting the Assyrians' animosity and violence against Israel as expressed through the words of the prophet Nahum, he states pertinently:

> Not only does [Jonah] run away, he goes to the limit of the known world. This flight is not difficult to understand. Imagine an analogous case: a Jew being told to enter Germany during the Second World War and preach against the National Socialists. It is a thought that begs the impossible.

This aspect is also found in modern scholarly literature, where Nineveh's cruelty and acts of destruction towards Israel are compared with those of Nazi

Germany. André and Pierre-Emmanuel Lacocque ask poignantly (LaCocque and LaCocque 1990: 121–122):

> Where is the Auschwitz survivor who would go to Berchtesgaden or Berlin carrying God's salvation?

Yvonne Sherwood postulates that the author of Jonah may, in fact, be creating fantastic stories to try out the principle of universal mercy in the most extreme circumstances, asking a fantastic 'What if' (Sherwood 1998: 67):

> What if Nineveh, the 'bloody city' as Nahum puts it, the equivalent of Berlin of the Third Reich, repents?

3. Jonah was Afraid

Several (predominantly but not exclusively Christian) interpreters suggest that the true reason behind Jonah's flight was fear. The idea that Jonah ran away because he was afraid to go to Nineveh is, to my knowledge, first attested in Josephus's retelling of the Jonah narrative (*Ant.* 9:10): 'But he went not, out of fear'. This interpretation gains momentum at the time of the persecution of the early Christians. In his encouragement to his fellow Christians not to fear death and torture as a martyr ('On Flight in Time of Persecution'), the North-African Christian apologist Tertullian (160–220 CE) refers to Jonah. Rather than fleeing as Jonah did, and having God confine him in a beast, unable either to find death or escape, Tertullian advocates staying firm and doing God's will, no matter what:

> A certain bold prophet also had fled from the Lord, he had crossed over from Joppa in the direction of Tarsus, as if he could as easily transport himself away from God; but I find him, I do not say in the sea and on the land, but, in fact, in the belly even of a beast, in which he was confined for the space of three days, unable either to find death or even thus escape from God. How much better the conduct of the man who, though he fears the enemy of God, does not flee from, but rather despises him, relying on the protection of the Lord.

This idea of Jonah's fear of the people of Nineveh reappears in the fourteenth-century English homiletic poem 'Patience' (lines 74–80):

> Greatly was he wroth in his wit, and wildly he thought:
> 'If I bow to His bidding and bring them this tale,
> And I am taken in Nineveh, my trouble begins:
> He tells me those traitors are drunken shrews;
> I come with those tidings, they take me quickly.
> Pen me in a prison, put me in stocks,
> Wind me in a warlock, wrest out my eyes.'

Jonah is often seen as a type for Christ, yet the poet responsible for 'Patience' presents Jonah more as an anti-type by emphasizing the difference between the two. Although Jonah and Jesus shared the same vocation (to preach to the Gentiles) and the same plight (to spend three days and three nights in the land of the dead), Jonah is depicted as the very opposite of Christ (lines 74–80). The ensuing lines 95–96, which speak about stripping and crucifixion, allude unequivocally to Jesus's passion. The reader of the whole poem thus cannot help but realize that Jonah angrily refused to undertake a task to which Jesus later submitted willingly (Andrew 1973: lines 130–231).

> Though I am taken to Nineveh and robbed naked,
> Ruthlessly rent on a cross, by many ruffians.

'Patience' further uses the Book of Jonah to teach patience, courage, and facing hardship without complaint. In the poet's hand, although Jonah first sought to avoid his fate by fleeing from God's command, his subsequent voyage to Nineveh constitutes his acceptance of death, in this case brought about by vicious madmen in Nineveh. God's call to Jonah was thus intended not only to save the people of Nineveh but also for the benefit of the prophet's own soul (Davis 1991: 277–278). 'Patience' was set to music by the American composer Dominick Argento (1927–2019 CE) in his choral work *Jonah and the Whale* (1973). He translated the entire poem into modern English himself and used parts of it as the backbone of the libretto. Argento follows the lead of the poem and attributes fear as the chief reason for Jonah's flight.

This interpretation resurfaces at the time of the Reformation. Luther (German commentary, 1:2–3) remarks on the courage that it would have taken for Jonah to go to Nineveh. He draws a comparison between Jonah's task and a hypothetical situation in his own life: what courage would he need if God were to call him to rebuke the Turkish Emperor? Any man would have been afraid of going with such a message to a mighty king in a foreign land. Yet, even though such a calling might be almost absurd, the foolishness of God is wiser than men (1 Cor 1:25). Along similar lines, Calvin offers a three-part explanation to the question of Jonah's reluctance to go to Nineveh (Lecture 72). First, it was a novel thing for (the Israelite) prophets to preach abroad. Second, given Nineveh's reputation as a licentious city, Jonah doubted that they would heed his call and be converted. Third, Jonah feared what the people of Nineveh would do to him on hearing his message of doom. Not only would they not believe him; they would harm him for taking the liberty of preaching such a message.

Fear also appears in the oratorio *Jonas* by the Italian composer Giacomo Carissimi (1605–1674 CE). This piece features 21 sections and is scored for soloists, choir, 2 violins, violoncello, obligato, and basso continuo. In the third section, sung by 'the Historian', Jonah 'feared greatly' when he heard God's voice and decided to flee (*et timuit timore magno*).

Thomas Bradbury, an English congregational preacher (1677–1759 CE), hints at the notion of fear in his sermon 'The Repentance of Nineveh: Consider'd and Apply'd, in two Sermons', from 1720. He emphasizes how Jonah went 'to a People, thus swell'd up with Plunder' (Nah 3:1) (p. 7), how Jonah had to 'throw himself into such a Crown, and tell them that in the publick Streets, which would make every one that heard it abhor him' (p. 8), how Jonah did not have 'Angels to protect him from a ravenous Multitude' (p. 9), and how his message was 'the most dangerous to him' (p. 12). Drawing a parallel to Paul's preaching to a 'roaring Mob' in Ephesus (inferred from 1 Cor 16:8), Bradbury declares that just as God protected Jonah in Nineveh, so he will always protect those who faithfully deliver his Word (p. 10).

In more recent times, the character of Father Mapple in *Moby-Dick* offers a similar interpretation in his sermon on Jonah (ch. 9). Father Mapple's Jonah, however, does not resemble the biblical character very much, lacking the latter's desire to see Nineveh destroyed. Rather, Father Mapple's Jonah flees because he fears the hostility that the people of Nineveh will show to him as they hear his message. In *Moby-Dick*, it is instead Captain Ahab who personifies the biblical Jonah, as he pursues a path of hatred and destruction to fulfil what he believes to be his destiny. In this pursuit, Captain Ahab, like Jonah, endangers the lives of his crew (Wright 1940: 191–192; eadem 1975: 54. Cf. Rathbun 1991: 4–8; Sprang 2011: 453–457). In Melville's hand, the Jonah of his sermon accepts God's correction, whereas Ahab (not unlike the Jonah of the Bible) rejects it and instead displays his anger against God (Herbert Jr 1969: 1614).

Laurence Housman's play, *The Burden of Nineveh*, likewise considers fear to have been the main reason why Jonah chose to run away (scene 1). This fear, however, is concerned less with what the people of Nineveh might do to him and more with the possibility that the prophecy would all be a mistake: Jonah has not heard God correctly:

Jonah: How do I know that His Word has come to me?

Shemmel: You may not know how – but you know it has come, Jonah … Don't you?

[…]

Shemmel: When the Word of the Lord comes to you, it's no question of wanting, then. It takes hold of you – won't let you go. You become a different man … You are not your own any more. Five years ago, when you told Israel (so proud as they were then of having beaten Syria three times) that three times wasn't enough, and that Syria would beat them yet – they were so angry that some were wishing to kill you. But you were not afraid of them: you were the true prophet then. And you didn't get that from yourself.

Jonah: No; I got that from our Lord and Father Elisha just before he died. 'Twas his prophecy, not mine. That's how I came by it – just took it from him. And being his, I was sure of it.

This opening scene alludes to the aforementioned Rabbinic tradition of Jonah being one of Elisha's disciples (see Jonah 1:1). Jonah expresses the fear that although he has heard God's voice correctly in the past (i.e. in 2 Kgs 14:24–25), that was together with Elisha; now he is on his own for the first time.

The chapter 'Three Simple Stories' by Julian Barnes, part of his book *A History of the World in 10½ Chapters*, hints at this understanding as well, yet twists it into a poignant criticism of God who moves his characters to his own liking with no regard for their suffering:

> Jonah, disliking the task for unexplained reasons which might have had something to do with a fear of being stoned to death by the partying Ninevites, ran away. (p. 175)

In Barnes's hand, Jonah's position is vindicated. He juxtaposes the Jonah story with a story of a boatload of Jewish refugees who ultimately, being denied the right to disembark the ship at every port, are sent back to continental Europe to die in concentration camps. Jonah's distrust of God thus turns out to be justified (Sherwood 2000: 166–168).

4. Jonah was Angry

Predominantly Islamic sources explain Jonah's disobedience as a result of his anger. The Qur'anic retelling of the Jonah narrative in Q37 states that Jonah ran away 'like a slave from captivity'. This statement is often conflated in Islamic retellings with the material in Q21:87–88, the end result being that Jonah ran away in anger.

> And Yunus, when he went away in **wrath**, so he thought that We would not straiten him, so he called out among afflictions: There is no god but Thou, glory be to Thee; surely I am of those who make themselves to suffer loss. So We responded to him and delivered him from the grief and thus do We deliver the believers.

The statement in Q21.87 'And Yunus, when he went away in wrath' came to be problematic to later Islamic traditions, due to the principle of prophetic infallibility ('*iṣma*). Qur'anic exegetes therefore often tried to explain (away) this matter in a number of different ways: Was Jonah's anger directed against God or against someone else? Was he angry before or after his mission to Nineveh?

As recorded in Al-Tha'labī's 'Jonah, son of Amittai' and Al-Ṭabarī's *History of al-Ṭabarī*, early interpreters/*Ḥadīth* transmitters suggested five possible reasons (cf. Burge 2017: 587):

1. Ibn ʿAbbās: Jonah was angry at Hezekiah, King of Israel, and the prophet Isaiah (Al-Tha'labī).
2. Al-Ḥasan al-Baṣrī: Jonah was angry with God because God did not allow Jonah to prepare properly before going to Nineveh (Al-Tha'labī).
3. Ibn ʿAbbās: Jonah wanted to procure a riding animal before going to Nineveh, but the angel Gabriel prevented him (Al-Tha'labī, Al-Ṭabarī).
4. Ibn ʿAbbās: God removed the punishment from Nineveh (Al-Ṭabarī).
5. Ibn ʿAbbās: Jonah was angry at the Israelites for their unbelief (Al-Tha'labī).

Other interpreters when faced with the same issue, among them Ibn Kathīr, opted for active denial: Jonah was not angry at all, the rationale being that Jonah, as a prophet of God and thus infallible, *could not* have been angry (with God).

Additionally, this sura raises a problem regarding the sequence of events: at what point in the narrative did Jonah 'call out among afflictions'? In short, did Jonah's stay in the fish precede or follow his mission to Nineveh (cf. below Jonah 2:2)? Beginning with those interpreters who maintain that Jonah ran away *prior* to his mission to Nineveh (i.e. following the storyline of the Hebrew Bible), the Persian scholar, historian, and exegete of the Qur'an, Al-Ṭabarī (839–923 CE), fleshes out the aforementioned third possible reason for Jonah's anger. He claims that Gabriel commanded Jonah to go to Nineveh in haste. Jonah wished for a camel and then shoes, but Gabriel denied him both, claiming that the matter was too urgent. As a result, Jonah fled in anger at Gabriel.

A greater number of Muslim interpreters, however, argue that Jonah ran away *after* his mission to Nineveh. This interpretative move can partly be explained by a desire to align Jonah's mission with that of Muhammad. Just as Muhammad and his followers encountered hostility from the people in Mecca, so Jonah's first mission to Nineveh failed due to the hostility of the city. Further, just as Muhammad, after his interlude in Medina, returned to and seized control of Mecca, so Jonah returned and converted Nineveh. The Persian Shi'ite scholar Al-Qummī (923–991 CE) claims in his *tafsir* (a commentary on the Qur'an[1]) that Jonah announced God's punishment and fled the city before that dreadful hour. When God later withdrew his punishment, Jonah ran away in anger at God (*Tafsir Qumi* 1:318–319, on Q10.98, as cited by Reynolds 2010: 122–123). Likewise, the Persian theologian al-Zamakhsharī (1075–1144 CE) claims in his *tafsir* that Jonah went to Nineveh twice. He fled after his first, unsuccessful visit. Al-Zamakhsharī admonishes Jonah, stating that he should have been patient and waited for permission from God to leave the people of

Nineveh (*Al-Kashshaaf* 3:131, on Q21.87, as cited by Reynolds 2010: 121, 124). Along similar lines, the Syrian Sunni scholar Ibn Kathīr (1300–1373 CE) maintains that Jonah was swallowed by a fish only after his initial visit to Nineveh, to where he later returned (*Tafsir Ibn Kathīr*, Vol. 6 [Surat Al'Isra', verse 39 to the end of Surat Al'Mu'minûn, surat Yūnus]).

5. Jonah was Mad
Last but not least, in John Kitto's *Cyclopedia of Biblical Literature* (p. 142), the entry 'Jonah' offers madness as the reason for Jonah's flight from before God's presence:

> His attempt to flee from the presence of the Lord must have sprung from a partial insanity, produced by the excitement of distracting motives in an irascible and melancholy heart. The temerity and folly of the fugitive could scarcely be credited, if they had not been equalled by future outbreaks of a similar peevish and morbid infatuation. The mind of Jonah was dark and moody, not unlike a lake which mirrors in the waters the gloomy thunder-clouds which overshadow it, and flash over its sullen waves a momentary gleam.

Was Jonah Guilty of Suppressing Prophecy?
In addition to the question of motive, Jonah's flight raises questions of sin. First, is it a sin to suppress prophecy and, if so, did Jonah commit that sin? Second, was Jonah's disobedience a sin in itself? In broad terms, Jewish scholars have concerned themselves with the first issue while Christian scholars have explored the second.

The Babylonian Talmud (*b.San.* 10:5 [89a]) reports how a Tannaitic authority is quoted before Rabbi Hisda that a person who suppresses his prophecy is to be flogged. Rabbi Hisda objects, asking how anyone would know about this fact (since the prophecy was, in fact, suppressed). Rabbi Abbayye responds that the prophet's fellow prophets would know, as God does nothing without telling his servants the prophets (Amos 3:7). Rabbi Hisda voices the theoretical possibility that God might choose not to carry out his decision, as in the case of Jonah (how, so the logic goes, would anyone then know that Jonah resisted the prophecy). Rabbi Abbayye retorts that Jonah was told that Nineveh would be 'turned' (3:4); he was not told whether it was for good or bad.

A similar discussion, yet with a different verdict, is found in the Tosefta (*Sanhedrin* 14:15, cf. Sifré to Deuteronomy 177:1), in the context of identifying a false prophet. There Jonah is listed alongside Zedekiah, the son of Kenaanah, who prophesied what he had not heard (1 Kgs 22:11); Hananiah, the son of Azzur, who disagreed with Jeremiah (Jer 28:1–17); the companions of Micaiah (1 Kgs 20:35); and those like Iddo, who transgressed his own words (2 Chron 9:29);

as well as any person who changed his prophecy, or a stranger who ministered in the temple, or someone who ministered before being fully cleansed, etc. All these people are subject to the death penalty.

Later Jewish commentators attempted to exonerate Jonah from this misdemeanour. Malbim, in his commentary to Jonah 1:2, solves the conundrum by postulating a difference between 'prophesying' and 'calling to repentance'. In this way, according to Malbim, God's initial calling, which Jonah refused, was not to prophesy (i.e. it did not predict Nineveh's destruction), but to call them to repentance. The aforementioned Talmudic decree, therefore, does not apply to Jonah. In fact, Jonah fled towards Tarshish lest he be given a more specific message in the form of a prophecy (which he would not have been able to refuse as its suppression would have led to his death warrant).

Looking more at the aspect of disobedience itself, Luther, in his German commentary to Jonah 1:3, argues succinctly that rather than trying to defend Jonah's defiance and to describe it as something else, due to a misguided notion that prophets cannot sin, 'we shall stick rigidly and inflexibly to the Word of God and agree that Jonah here committed a grave and serious sin'. He sinned as gravely as Adam did in Paradise, and for that, he was duly punished by having to spend three days in the fish. These three days stood in direct proportion to the enormity of Jonah's sin (cf. below, Jonah 2:1). In line with Luther's overarching theological understanding, Jonah's ultimate salvation was not due to any act that Jonah himself committed inside the fish but was solely owing to God's mercy. In parallel, Luther emphasizes that Jonah did not despair in his sin but clung firmly to God's mercy: 'If he had despaired, he would never have come forth from the whale's belly. His strong faith in the midst of his sin makes it impossible for God to forget him; He must again deliver him'.

In modern scholarship, the notion that a prophet would refuse to prophesy after having received a word from God has been compared with Amos 3:7–8:

> Surely the Sovereign LORD does nothing without revealing his plan to his servants the prophets. The lion has roared – who will not fear? The Sovereign LORD has spoken – who can but prophesy?

According to Schellenberg, these two verses emphasize God's task of sharing his future plans with his prophets, and the prophets' task of responding to it. In her view, Jonah's refusal to fulfil this role contributes to the portrayal of Jonah as an 'anti-prophet' (Schellenberg 2015: 361–362).

Fleeing from God – Mythical, Fictional, and Scholarly Retellings
The notion of a person trying to flee from God is common in myths. It is indeed so common that it is often impossible to determine whether (1) a given myth

is a source of influence for the Book of Jonah, (2) Jonah is a source of influence for the myth, or (3) both texts are part of the same phenomenon. Here, I shall discuss a few texts which are likely inspired by the biblical texts, without ruling out other sources of influence.

There are several intriguing parallels between the Book of Jonah and material inspired by the life of the Irish missionary monk St Columba (521–597 CE), called *Colm Cille* (meaning 'dove of the church') in Irish. As the very name 'dove' conveys a possible allusion to Jonah, hearers are encouraged to connect the two characters (see further Layzer 2001: 75). In the *Life of St. Columba* by Adomnán of Iona (624–704 CE), for example, St Columba is likened to Jonah. Adomnán continues to tell a story which occurred when St Columba was living on Iona. As brother Berach planned to sail for Tiree, St Columba told him not to take the normal route lest he be terrified by a monster of the deep. Yet Berach did not follow the advice and duly soon encountered an enormous whale. At that point he remembered St Columba's words and was filled with awe. This tale is then repeated but with a distinct difference: another brother, Baithéne, is told by St Columba that he would encounter a great whale. In response, Baithéne expressed his confidence in God who holds both him and the whale in his hand. Upon hearing this, St Columba told Baithéne to go in peace as his faith in Christ would shield him from danger (*Adomnán, Vita Sancti Columbae* §1.19, cf. Sharpe 1995: 125–126). As Layzer has shown, both brothers, Berach and Baithéne, are analogous to Jonah. While Berach may be likened to Jonah pre-fish, i.e. the Jonah who disobeys God, Baithéne may be likened to Jonah post-fish, i.e. the Jonah who carries out God's command (Layzer 2001: 85–87).

The notion of a person trying to flee from God is a common trope in fiction. The Swedish novel *Guldspiken* (*The Golden Nail*, 1985) by Peter Nilson (1937–1998 CE) forms a sustained allusion to the Book of Jonah, made explicit already in its opening statement through a reference to Jonah and the fish. In his novel, Nilson explores a lay preacher's attempt to flee from his calling to preach. This motif comes to the forefront when the chief protagonist, the poor boy Elias, hears a voice from heaven telling him to go to hell and preach there. He flees, only to experience hell on earth aboard a ship to Africa (pp. 98–100, 109–131).

Jonah's flight is sometimes more widely understood to represent his struggle with God and his sense of alienation from God and the world, as well as the latter's lack of belief in him. As Sherwood aptly states, Jonah becomes 'a patron saint of all those who feel the need to curse' due to the unsettledness and fickleness of their existence. (Sherwood 2000: 171). Paul Auster (b. 1947), for example, employs the motifs of being 'inside the whale' and of 'shipwreck' as leitmotifs throughout his book *The Invention of Solitude* (part II 'The Book of Memory', 1982, p. 83) to designate the estrangement that characterizes much of post-holocaust Jewry. In his commentary on modern-day urban existence, the character George Oppen uses the term 'shipwreck of the singular' to refer to his own sense of being separated and even banished from the rest of humanity (p. 83, cf. p. 96). The 'Book of Memory, book 7', contains the strongest reference to the Jonah narrative. Auster/Oppen likens his own existence to Jonah running away from the presence of the Lord to meet his doom by shipwreck. In Auster's hand, the story of Jonah is one of solitude. Jonah is not, like Jeremiah, merely reluctant to speak; he refuses to speak (pp. 132–135). As to the reason for Jonah's fleeing, Auster puts it movingly (pp. 134–135):

> If the Ninevites were spared, would this not make Jonah's prophecy false? Would he not, then, be a false prophet? Hence the paradox at the heart of the book: the prophecy would remain true only if he did not speak it. But then, of course, there would be no prophecy, and Jonah would no longer be a prophet. But better to be no prophet at all than to be a false prophet 'Therefore now, O lord, take, I beseech thee, my life from me; for it is better for me to die than to live'.

> Therefore, Jonah held his tongue. Therefore, Jonah ran away from the presence of the Lord and met the doom of shipwreck. That is to say, the shipwreck of the singular.

Auster further alludes to the character of Jonah by repeated references to Pinocchio (pp. 83, 139–143, 174–176), who is yet another incarnation of the recalcitrant prophet (cf. below) (Hau 2010: 236, note 121). Auster returns to the image of Jonah in the belly of the whale towards the end of the book. Oppen sits in his small room in the same way as Jonah sits in the belly of the fish, abandoned not only by God but also by his creative muse and desperately trying to reconnect with his creativity (p. 169).

Jonah's struggle with God is also the topic of several poetic retellings. The American poet Gabriel Priel (1911–1993 CE) compares himself to Jonah, and describes an existence torn between faith and a desire to flee from it:

> The prophet Jonah ran from his angry Master
> And I to my ship empty of God and man
> [...]
> I, God willing, while escaping my Master, hope to find
> A minute of refuge in a season of faith and ripeness.

The Chilean poet Enrique Lihn (1929–1988 CE) likewise expresses his own sense of unease with the fickleness of his existence through those of Jonah:

> I could damn everything equally, just don't ask me in the name of what.

> In the name of Isaiah, the prophet, yet with the grotesque and unfinished gesture of his colleague Jonah,

who never managed to get through with his simple task, given to the ups and downs

of good and evil, to the fickle circumstances of history that plunged him into the whale's belly.

[...]

And Jehova's doubts about him, wavering between mercy and anger, grabbing him and tossing him that old instrument whose use is doubtful

no longer used at all any more.

[...]

Another group of modern scholars have sought to bridge psychoanalysis and Jewish and biblical scholarship. They all agree that 'fleeing' is the dominant motif in the Book of Jonah, with focus on Jonah's flight from dialogue with God and his inability or refusal to face his own traumas. In the central essay, Zornberg understands Jonah to address the eternal human dilemma of fleeing from God's presence. Jonah refuses to stand vulnerable between life and death before God in prayer; he refuses to face his conscience, and struggles to receive forgiveness (Zornberg 2008). Shulman's response to Zornberg stresses Jonah's attempt to escape not only from God but also from himself (Shulman 2008). Salberg elaborates further as she emphasizes Jonah's despair due to his lack of capacity for self-reflection and his inability to deal with his own feelings. In her view, Jonah's death wish presents an easy way out of his despair (Salberg 2008).

From a very different perspective, the Israeli poet Maya Bejerano (1993) uses Jonah's flight to explore the modern Israeli search for God in her poem 'Midrash Jonah'. In her hands, Jonah is not fleeing God as much as seeking a new understanding of him:

> Jonah
> Jonah how much courage
> courage to know was in you
> [...]
> for it was just that which you wanted,
> carried and cast into the story sea of possibilities
> [...]
> your daring flight to Tarshish transformed into determined diving towards Him
> [...]

Jacobson, responsible for this translation from Hebrew into English, understands the poem to express how our modern search for God may result in our acceptance of the divine will, as well as our uncertainty about what such an acceptance might entail (Jacobson 1997: 234–240).

Fleeing from Oneself

In the commentary to the Book of Jonah in the *Queer Bible*, Michael Carden argues that Jonah's flight from and subsequent acceptance of his God-given mission can be read as a story of coming out. According to Carden, Jonah's flight and subsequent hiding in the ship may be likened to the experience of the closet, in the sense that he is fleeing from who he really is. Realizing that his flight and his time in the fish provides but an illusory security, he is ultimately forced to face reality (Carden 2006: 466–467; Havea 2020: ch. 7).

'to Tarshish'

Jonah 1:3 continues to state that Jonah rose to flee 'to Tarshish'. The exact location of Tarshish has been much debated through the ages. There are three main lines of interpretation (all reaching across the Jewish-Christian divide):

A first group of scholars, among them Josephus (*Ant.* 9:10), Cyril of Alexandria, Saadia Gaon (as quoted by Ezra, *Rabbinic Bible*, Commentary to Jonah 1:3), and Calvin (Lecture 72), identifies Tarshish with Tarsus in Cilicia (the south-eastern coastal region of Asia Minor, corresponding to the modern Turkish region of Çukurova). The main problem with this identification is that Tarsus is inland and thus unlikely to have a port.

A second group of interpreters maintains that Tarshish is a city in the western part of the Mediterranean, i.e. as far away from Nineveh as it is possible to reach by ship. The Antiochene theologian and bishop Theodoret of Cyrus (393–466 CE) identifies it with Carthage (cf. Lipiński 2004: 260, fn. 179), while Ibn Ezra suggests Tunis, as does Abarbanel. In the much later novel *Moby-Dick*, ch. 9, Father Mapple declares that Tarshish must be Cadiz in Spain, as is 'the opinion of learned men':

> Because Joppa, the modern Jaffa, shipmates, is on the most easterly coast of the Mediterranean, the Syrian; and Tarshis or Cadiz more than two thousand miles to the westward from that, just outside the Straits of Gibraltar. See ye not then, shipmates, that Jonah sought to flee world-wide from God? (Herman 1851 / Richard Bentley / Public domain)

A third group suggests that Tarshish is not the name of an actual city but instead another word for 'the sea'. Targum Jonathan translates the term Tarshish consistently as 'sea' ('and Jonah rose to flee to the sea', cf. Targum Onkelos, Exod 28:20). Jerome is aware of this interpretation and cites Ps 43:8 and Isa 23:1 in support. In his view, Jonah had no desire to go to a specific place; he merely wished to flee *anywhere*. During the Reformation, Luther (German commentary to 1:3) adopts this interpretation. He points out that Hebrew has two words for 'sea'. Whereas the Hebrew term *yam* may be used for either a lake (e.g. Gen 1:10) or the sea, the Hebrew term *tarshish* denotes only the sea, as can be gleaned from 1 Kgs 9:26–28; Isa 23:1; and Ps 72:10. Furthermore, like Jerome, Luther argued that the indefinite translation 'sea' is more in tune with the narrative, as Jonah had no reason to flee *to* a specific city; his only concern was rather to flee *from* Israel.

In parallel, the reference to Tarshish can be understood symbolically. The *Glossa Ordinaria* sees Tarshish as a reference to 'joy': the prophet hurries to Tarshish in order to experience the joy of rest and contemplation of beauty and the variety of knowledge. This interpretation is anchored to the biblical narrative through the reference to Yafo, which means 'beauty', in the same verse.

'and he went down to Yafo'

Having decided to flee to Tarshish, Jonah 'went down to Yafo'. Yafo/Jaffa/Joppa is an ancient port city that was settled already in the Bronze Age. Today it forms the oldest part of Tel-Aviv-Yafo. It is mentioned both in the Hebrew Bible (Jonah 1:3; Ezra 3:7; 2 Chron 2:16) and the New Testament (Acts 10:10–23; 11:4–17), and it is also known from the mythological story of Andromeda. As noted by Jerome, the city of Yafo is the place where Andromeda was chained to the rock and later saved by Perseus from being devoured by the sea monster (see below, commentary to Jonah 2:1).

The choice of Yafo as the port is bewildering, given that Jonah lived in Gath-Hepher (according to 2 Kgs 14:25). The Jerusalem Talmud (*y.Suk.* 5:1) asks pertinently why Jonah, if he came from the Northern Kingdom, went to Yafo in the south. Would it not have been better for him to flee to Akko instead? Rabbi Jonah solves the problem by claiming that Jonah had earlier gone down (to Jerusalem) to celebrate the festivals. This interpretation implies that Jonah, being a prophet of Yhwh, was one of the few Northerners who rejected the temple in Israel and instead continued to worship in the temple in Jerusalem.

'from the presence of Yhwh'

Jonah fled 'from before the presence of Yhwh'. This statement raises several questions. On a literal level, some exegetes ask whether, in fact, there are places where God's presence is not manifest. By an elaborated use of proof texts, it is conceivable to reach the conclusion that the sea is the one place on earth where God is relatively less present. As expressed by *PRE* 10 (Eng. transl. Adelman 2009: 224):

> Rather, I will get up and flee from His Presence to the Sea, to the place where His glory is not said to be. But not to the Heavens! [About the Heavens it is said: 'His glory

is above the Heavens' (Ps 113:4)]. And about the Earth it is said, 'His presence fills all the Earth' (Isa 6:3). No, I shall flee to the Sea, where His Presence is not said to be.

Jonah's decision to escape to the sea is thus a logical choice, the only remaining option after having eliminated all other possibilities. Refuting this line of interpretation, *Mekhilta to Rabbi Ishmael* (Bo, Tractate Passha 1) points out that Jonah's decision to flee in Jonah 1:3 may cause a person to infer (wrongly) that God's presence would not be found outside the Land of Israel. The *Mekhilta* accordingly proceeds to contest this interpretation step by step: God is found in heaven, in the netherworld, and at the end of the world (Ps 139:7; cf. Amos 9:2–4); God's eyes roam the entire earth (Zech 4:10), they are in every place (Prov 15:3), and there is no darkness where sinners can hide from him (Job 34:22). Reaching the same conclusion, albeit via a different route, the Hellenistic-Jewish sermon *On Jonah* 6:2 stresses Jonah's delusion, as he 'was frivolous enough, hoping to escape from the Creator of all'. God, however, initially allowed him to flee in order to demonstrate His power and thus to reproach the prophet and to make his proclamation to Nineveh more powerful.

Adhering to the same logic, God's less palpable presence at sea may, in turn, cause prophecy there to diminish. As expressed by Targum Jonathan, Jonah hoped that by fleeing he would be rendered *unable* to prophesy, an interpretation that is based on the belief that prophecy could only take place on the soil of Israel (Gordon 1982: 124–126). The mediaeval Jewish commentators later fine-tuned this interpretation. Rashi states that the word *tarshisha* indicates the sea (see above), namely a place outside the Land of Israel. As far as Jonah is aware, the Shechinah does not dwell abroad, yet God refutes him by highlighting that he has agents whom he can send after Jonah to retrieve him from anywhere. In Ibn Ezra's view, Jonah, of course, knew that God's presence is everywhere. The case here is rather Jonah's attempt to flee from *serving* God. To reach this interpretation, Ibn Ezra (commentary to Jonah 1:1) compares the statement in Jonah 1:3 with the similar one in Gen 4:16 where Cain departs 'from before the presence of Yhwh' (Heb. *milifnei* Yhwh). As this statement is negated by Cain himself in Gen 4:14 ('can I be hidden from your presence?'), Jonah is accordingly not trying to flee from God's presence but from standing *before* him in service. Following suit, Abarbanel postulates a difference between *mipnei* Yhwh which denotes 'from Yhwh's presence', i.e. his knowledge and his omniscience, and *milifnei* Yhwh, which denotes 'from being before the presence of Yhwh', i.e. in a position to receive prophecy. Jonah thus flees in order to avoid the burden of prophecy. Building on this line of exegesis, Malbim argues that prophecy requires an elevated degree of holiness that is only possible to obtain within the Land of Israel. Or, more exactly, given that a few cases of prophecy outside of Israel exist (Elijah prophesied on Mt Horeb [1 Kgs 19:9]; Ezekiel prophesied in a foreign land), the sea route was by far the 'safer' place for not receiving prophetic inspiration. From a slightly different angle, Radak emphasizes that Jonah desired not to flee from God's presence but instead, motivated by his love for Israel and not wishing to see it destroyed, decided to flee from 'that which was before Him', i.e. prophetic inspiration, which, according to Jonah's belief, was only possible within the Land of Israel.

A few Christian exegetes also adhere to this way of thinking. Theodore of Mopsuestia argues that Jonah's fleeing from the face of the Lord should be understood to mean that he fled not from God himself – who is everywhere – but from the place where God made his appearance, i.e. the temple in Jerusalem. Focusing more on Jonah's failure to flee from before the Lord, the Roman poet and senator Paulinus of Nola (354–431 CE) suggests in his 'Poem 22' that it teaches us that 'sea and star are moved under God's control'.

A very different interpretation is found in the *Glossa Ordinaria*, where Jonah's flight is read mystically as a precursor of Christ taking on flesh, thus fleeing his home (heaven) to the 'sea of this world' (cf. above, where Tarshish is understood as a reference to the sea).

'and he found a ship coming Tarshish'

The statement 'and he found a ship coming Tarshish' is problematic because the Hebrew text lacks a preposition between the verb 'to come' and the name 'Tarshish'. As a result, it is unclear whether the ship came *from* Tarshish or was going *to* Tarshish. The problem is aggravated by the fact that the Hebrew verb for 'to come' is accented on the ultimate syllable as a participle and thus best rendered as 'coming'. Nevertheless, from the perspective of the Jonah narrative, it makes the most sense to translate the phrase as 'going *to* Tarshish'. To solve this preposition issue, diverse suggestions abound. Targum Jonathan translates the phrase 'coming Tarshish' as 'sea-bound ship', implying a direction away from Yafo towards the sea (see Cathcart and Gordon 1989: 105, fn. 4), whereas Radak argues that the ship is 'coming [to] Tarshish' i.e. it was going back and forth between Tarshish and Yafo.

PRE 10 resolves the matter by combining both options. When Jonah arrived in Jaffa, the ship to Tarshish had departed two days ago. In order to test Jonah, God sent a storm which forced the ship to return to port in Jaffa. Jonah understood the divine intervention as a sign of divine approval of his plan (Eng. transl. Adelman 2009: 228):

> Jonah went down to Joppa, but he could not find a ship to board. The ship that he eventually boarded was already at sea, a two-day distance away, in order to test Jonah. What did the Holy One, blessed be He, do? He brought upon it a stormy

wind, and forced it to return to Joppa. When Jonah saw the ship, he rejoiced, saying to himself, 'Now I know that my path is justified before me'.

Other scholars argue that the boat was just returning *from* Tarshish. Malbim, for example, interprets the fact that Jonah had to pay 'its entire fare' (see below) as a sign that the boat had just returned (and thus was not ready to set out just yet, unless bought by Jonah). Malbim continues by postulating that Jonah wished to depart quickly: he wished for few passengers on board because (1) Jonah feared that the ship would be in danger due to his disobedience to God and (2) he did not wish to endanger more people than necessary. The same idea of innocent suffering because of Jonah's flight, although seen from the opposite angle, is taken up by Luther (German commentary, Jonah 1:4), as he comments that many people are obliged to suffer for the sin of an individual. Yet, according to Luther, we should not assume that the sailors were without sin, as nobody is sinless before God.

'and paid its fare'

Having found a ship, Jonah paid 'its fare' (*shecharah*). Once more, an intriguing textual issue has given rise to a wide range of interpretation. The object suffix ('its') on the noun 'fare', being f.sg., cannot refer to (the male) Jonah but must instead refer to the ship, i.e. the nearest preceding f.sg. noun. Thus, rather than paying his own fare, it appears that Jonah paid the fare of the entire boat. Among the mediaeval Jewish commentators, Rashi states that contrary to the usual custom of seafarers paying when disembarking, Jonah paid in advance as he was in a hurry to go. Not only that, he paid the fare of the whole boat rather than for his single seat. Ibn Ezra rejects this interpretation, however, and claims that Jonah only paid what was required for his own place.

Based on the phrase 'paid its fare', the Jewish sages further concluded that personal wealth was a necessary quality for prophetic calling, alongside strength, wisdom, and humility. The Babylonian Talmud (*b.Ned.* 38a), for example, states:

> Said Rabbi Yohanan, 'All of the prophets were wealthy'. How do we know it? From the cases of Moses, Samuel, Amos, and Jonah. Jonah: 'And he found a ship going to Tarshish, so he paid the fare thereof and went down into it' (Jonah 1:3). And in this connection noted Rabbi Yohanan, 'He paid for the rent of the whole ship'. Rabbi Romanus said, 'The fee to rent the whole ship was four thousand gold denarii'.

This interpretation was later endorsed by, among others, Radak, who states that prophecy only falls on rich men.

The idea of Jonah paying for more than his own place on board the ship resurfaces in *Moby-Dick* (ch. 9). In his sermon, Father Mapple depicts the captain as a relatively corrupt man in whose ship 'sin that pays its way can travel freely, and without a passport'. He charges Jonah triple the price for the journey, and when Jonah willingly obliges, the captain knows that his gut feeling, namely, that Jonah is up to no good, is correct, yet he still allows Jonah on board because of the money that he has paid.

'and went down into It'

After going down to Yafo, Jonah goes further down into the ship. Modern scholarship has noted the significance of the downward and upward movements present throughout the Book of Jonah. Jonah 'goes down' to Yafo and 'down into' the ship (1:3). Later, Jonah goes down into the hold (1:6) and then ultimately down to the base of the mountains (2:7 [Eng. 2:6]). As pointed out by Halpern and Friedman, this downward spiral represents Jonah's flight further and further away from God. In parallel, there is an upward movement: God brings Jonah up (2:7 [Eng. 2:6]), the *qiqayyon* goes up (4:6), and the sun goes up (4:7) at dawn. The interplay between the Hebrew roots *yarad* ('go down') and *'ala* ('go up') is thus part of the narrative fabric of the text and has theological import (Halpern and Friedman 1980: 80–81; Sutskover 2014).

Jonah 1:4

> And Yhwh hurled a great wind towards the sea, and there was a great storm on the sea, and the ship threatened to be broken up.

'And Yhwh hurled a great wind towards the sea'

The fourth-century poem *De Jona et Nineveh*, traditionally attributed to Tertullian but nowadays mostly assigned to Cyprianus Gallus or Pseudo-Cyprian, conveys the storm in magnificent words (lines 50–56):

> With black encirclement; the upper air
> Down rushes into darkness, and the sea
> Uprises; nought of middle space is left;
> While the clouds touch the waves, and the waves all
> Are mingled by the bluster of the winds
> In whirling eddy. 'Gainst the renegade,
> 'Gainst Jonah, diverse frenzy joined to rave.

Carissimi's oratorio *Jonas* from 1650, using the choir to emphasize the force of the wind, specifies that the winds that faced the ship were the south wind, the east wind, and even the African wind, accompanied by rain clouds, flooding, whirlwind, hail, thunderstorm, thunder, and lightning:

Much traditional Jewish scholarship envisages a local, albeit not less fierce, storm. The reasons are twofold: first, because God sent the storm, the storm was abnormal. Second, because God was responsible, the storm only endangered those who were guilty. According to *Gen.Rab.* 24:3, the storm in Jonah was one of the three most terrible storms that the world has ever seen. The other two were the storm in the days of Job (Job 1:19) and the storm in the days of Elijah (1 Kgs 19:11) (cf. also *y.Ber.* 9:2 and *Lev.Rab.* 15:1). This final storm in Jonah 1:4, however, was the most curious one. Noting the definite article on the Hebrew term $w^e haoniyah$ ('and *the* ship'), *Gen.Rab.* 24:3, citing R. Yudah, argues that the storm that came at the time of Jonah came against that ship alone. Only Jonah's ship was in danger of being shipwrecked; all the other ships were fine. The storm that killed Job's children was likewise a 'localized' storm as it destroyed only Job's oldest son's house. In contrast, the storm that Elijah experienced in the wilderness affected the whole world.

In Paulinus of Nola's poetic retelling of the Jonah narrative ('Poem 22'), Nature is a sentient being and God's faithful servant:

> By vainly seeking to flee from God the controller of all things whom none can escape, he aroused the anger of both sky and sea. Nature, which belongs to the almighty Lord, realised that he was revolting and she was afraid to play conspirator by transporting the guilty man safely through her demesne; she chained the runaway with winds and waves.

The sea is also a sentient being in the modern ecological reading suggested by Jione Havea. Here, however, God commits an act of violence against the sea. First, as the creator, God is expected to protect and nurture the creation, rather than using its forces for his own personal vendetta. Second, storms disturb the seafloor and destroy the lifelines and homes of sea creatures, and it takes many years for marine life to recover from the devastation of a one-day storm (Havea 2020: chs. 2 and 8).

'and the ship threatened to be broken up'

The expression 'and the ship threatened' can be rendered literally as 'the ship thought'. It is noteworthy because of its use of the verb 'to think' with an inanimate object (i.e. the ship). Rashi explains this statement as figurative speech to express that it seemed as if the boat were going to break. Somewhat differently,

Ibn Ezra compares it with the notion in Ezek 14:13, where 'the land' is sinning (the land thus being used to represent its inhabitants). Radak agrees, stating that the verb 'to think' in Jonah 1:4 implies that the men on board the ship thought that the ship was going to break.

Jonah 1:5

> And the sailors were afraid and cried out, each to his own god, and they hurled the utensils, which were in the ship, into the sea to lighten [it] of them. And Jonah had gone down into the innermost parts of the boat, laid down, and fallen asleep.

Jonah 1:5 introduces readers to the sailors. The text sets up a deliberate contrast between the frantic behaviour of the sailors who, due to their fear of death, begin to toss the cargo overboard, and Jonah who is sound asleep in the 'innermost parts of the ship'.

'The sailors were afraid and cried out, each to his own god'

The claim that the sailors called out to their individual gods has given rise to two interrelated exegetical queries. First, given that they had different gods, readers are led to assume that they must have come from different places. This assumption is entirely reasonable, given that naval crews in all times have formed an ethnic 'United Nations'. Second, given the sailors' diverse ethnicity, who were these deities to whom they cried out?

Seeking to respond to both queries, an influential rabbinic interpretation suggests that the sailors here represent the 70 nations, i.e. all the nations of the world. *PRE* 10, for instance, offers an extended version of Jonah's time aboard the ship. The sailors are presented as worshippers of idols. Among them were representatives of all 70 languages/nations on earth, and each sailor worshipped his own idol that he had brought on board. This notion of (70) nations, which is not attested in the text of Jonah, stems from a conflation of Jonah 1:5 and Micah 4:5, the latter stating that 'all the nations will walk, each man in the name of his god'. In a sense, *PRE* 10 presents here the ship as the world in miniature (cf. Rashi).

Later readers of Jonah have also wondered when, in the Jonah narrative, these sailors ceased to worship these gods and instead began turning to the God of Israel. The biblical text indicates that the changes took place in Jonah 1:14, which states that they beseeched Yhwh. According to Targum Jonathan, however, their turning to the God of Israel happened earlier, as evidenced by the addition in TJ at the end of verse 5. Having prayed, each man to his idol, TJ adds that 'they saw that they were useless'. The sailors thus abandoned their beliefs in their own deities *prior* to both the calming of the storm and Yhwh's miraculous saving of Jonah through the fish.

Other readers have sought to establish the precise identity of these foreign deities, among them the fourteenth-century English homiletic poem 'Patience' (lines 164–167):

> But each one cried to his god that availed him best;
> Some to Vernagu there vouched solemn vows.
> Some devout ones to Diana, and bold Neptune,
> To Mahomet and to Margot, the Moon and the Sun.

The apparent idolatry of the sailors especially caused the Protestant reformers to frown at them. In his Latin commentary to Jonah 1:5, Luther betrays his low opinion of the sailors. Although the sailors' behaviour is natural, according to Luther, it is nevertheless idolatrous. Further, even though the sailors were not total atheists, their gods were of their own making. In his longer commentary to the same verse in German, Luther appears more charitable towards the sailors. Granting that the sailors did not have true faith in God, they nonetheless acknowledged God's ability to respond in a situation of need.

'And they hurled the utensils, which were in the ship, into the sea to lighten [it] of them'

The sense of the Hebrew text is clear, namely, that the sailors threw their cargo into the sea in order to make the boat lighter. The exact syntax is, however, less lucid. It is especially difficult to determine whether the m.pl. suffix of the preposition 'from upon them' (Heb. *me'alehem*) refers to the sailors (i.e. that the boat was lighter for [the sailors]), or to the utensils (i.e. that the boat was lighter without [the utensils]). Given the prevalent use of the preposition *me* with the meaning 'from' throughout the Book of Jonah, the latter sense is slightly more convincing.

Commenting on the sailors' endeavour, Chrysostom, in his Homily 5:8, 'On Repentance and Almsgiving', notes that despite their effort to lighten their ship, the heaviest burden remained on board, namely Jonah's sin, 'for nothing is so heavy and onerous to bear as sin and disobedience'. In support of his interpretation, Chrysostom cites Zech 5:7, where sin is likened to a piece of lead.

Reading the Book of Jonah from an ecological perspective, Jione Havea faults the sailors for throwing their baggage, i.e. rubbish, into the sea (Havea 2020: ch. 8).

'And Jonah had gone down into the innermost parts of the boat, laid down, and fallen asleep'

While the sailors were calling out, each to their own god, Jonah was otherwise busy. Rather than being among the sailors, he had instead withdrawn, presumably curled up in the bowels of the ship, where he was sound asleep.

The Hebrew text uses two verbs, 'lying down' (*wayishkav*) and 'sleeping' (*wayerdam*) to denote Jonah's actions. In contrast, the LXX attests to a different reading (καὶ ἐκάθευδεν καὶ ἔρρεγχεν), namely, that Jonah was not only asleep but that he also *snored*. This reading has influenced several later traditions. In the Hellenistic-Jewish sermon *On Jonah* 9:3, for example, we read that the captain hears the snoring, and realizes that someone is asleep and thus not calling out to his deity (as he ought to be doing). *On Jonah* further declares that Jonah was not snoring 'so much for a natural reason as due to the punishment imposed [on him] for the reproof of sinners'. Several of the Church Fathers also mention Jonah's snoring (Jerome, Theodore of Mopsuestia, and Cyril of Alexandra), as does the *Glossa Ordinaria* ('his deep sleep resounds through raucous nostrils'). The fourth-century poem *De Jona et Nineveh* attributed to Tertullian portrays a calmly sleeping (and snoring) Jonah in lines 81–84:

> Unconscious of all this, the guilty one
> 'Neath the poop's hollow arch was making sleep
> Re-echo stertorous with nostril wide
> Inflated

Jonah's rather surprising behaviour – sleeping rather than praying – has been noted by many commentators. Why did Jonah not pray alongside the sailors? Jerome offers several possible interpretations. Could it be that Jonah was so peaceful and that his spirit was so at rest that he had gone down to enjoy a peaceful sleep? Alternatively, could it be that Jonah's sleep was unnatural and rather a sign of his worry? In other words, knowing himself to be a fugitive and a sinner, maybe Jonah had retired to his bed in order to hide from the world and the roaring waves. For Jerome, Jonah is like a man who has 'fallen asleep from the drug of wickedness' as he ignores the wrath of God. Along similar lines, the Hellenistic-Jewish sermon *On Jonah* 7:5 explains how Jonah, seeking complete oblivion, left the deck of the ship and descended into its belly. There he surrounded himself with oblivion and the sadness in his heart. Along similar lines, the *Glossa Ordinaria* suggests that Jonah sleeps out of melancholy, like the apostles in the Lord's passion (Luke 22:45).

From a different perspective, Abarbanel focuses on Jonah's feelings of shame. Given that Jonah knew fully well not only the source of the storm but also its reason, to pray for its ceasing would have been both futile and insincere. Instead,

Jonah went down expecting to die. Along somewhat similar lines, Ibn Ezra's comment (to Jonah 1:6) seems to suggest that Jonah had entered the ship when the storm was already raging. Jonah is thus consciously hiding from the storm rather than being oblivious to it (cf. Bob 2013: 25). Some of the Church Fathers voice similar sentiments. John Chrysostom, in his Homily 5:8, 'On Repentance and Almsgiving', states that Jonah's sleep was the result of his sorrow and his faintheartedness due to his sin of disobedience. Luther likewise states in his German commentary that Jonah's sleep may be termed a 'sleep of death' that had come upon him shortly before he was doomed to die. Jonah had sinned but, as God's punishment tarried, 'Jonah felt secure and loses his fear, lies down, goes to sleep, and fails to see the disaster and the great storm gathered over him which will arouse him horribly' [...] 'There he lies and snores in his sin'. In contrast, the Geneva Bible follows the MT ('fast asleep').

Cyril of Alexandria finds Jonah's sleeping incompatible with what one might expect from a prophet. He, therefore, shifts the chronology of the narrative, a change made possible by the *qatal* form of the Hebrew verb *yarad* ('had gone down'), and positions Jonah's sleep earlier in the narrative before the storm began. In Cyril's view, Jonah's going down to the hold of the ship was a mark of one accustomed to being on his own; 'after all, it is always a preference and a concern for the saints to avoid hubbub, absent themselves from crowds, and be on their own'. In support of this reading, Cyril cites Lam 3:27 which he presumes to be written by Jeremiah. Jonah was thus dozing – not ignoring his duty –*prior to* the storm.

Looking at Jonah asleep on the boat from the perspective of Christian typology, Jonah 1:5 foreshadows Matt 8:24. To cite the Syrian Church Father Jacob of Serug (451–521 CE) (Eng. transl. Kitchen 2011: 34):

> Our Lord slept and the sea was disturbed against the disciples
> And this type was demonstrated in the sleep of Jonah.
> That is, he was asleep and they woke him up as in the typology
> which was performed by the disciples to our Saviour. (13.387:13–18)

In some literary retellings, Jonah's sleep has turned into an expression of his fear of death or even a symbol of his death wish. In Melville's hands, Jonah's time in his room on board the ship is a premonition of his time inside the fish:

> Jonah feels the heralding presentiment of that stifling hour, when the whale shall hold him in the smallest of his bowel's wards.

Even though Jonah is tired, he is afraid where he is lying in his berth. When he has no strength to be terrified anymore, he falls into a deep stupor, 'as over the man who bleeds to death, for conscience is the wound, and there's naught to staunch it' (*Moby-Dick*, ch. 9).

The notion that Jonah is asleep and wished to continue to sleep is picked up in the evocative poem 'Tal vez me llame Jonás' ('Perhaps I am called Jonah') by the Spanish poet León Felipe (1884–1968 CE). Felipe fought in the Spanish Civil War for the Spanish Republican Army and later left Spain in 1938 for a voluntary exile in Mexico, where he later died. The poet begins by identifying himself with 'nobody' (*Yo no soy nadie*) and ends by saying that he 'is Jonah' (*Yo soy Jonás*).[2] The poem is filled with echoes of the imagery of Jonah, such as a storm calling out to him, telling him to go to Nineveh, but also how the poet ignores the voice and flees, only to hear the voice yelling at him again, telling him to wake up. In response to the attempts to wake him, the poet claims that he is nobody and pleads to be allowed to sleep. One day, the poet is thrown into the abyss, where he proceeds to describe his experience in the water in words very similar to Jonah 2. The poet exclaims that he has been in hell (*Quiero decir que he estado en el infierno*) (cf. Jonah 2:2 [Eng. 2:3]). Even so, he refuses to preach destruction (*y no canto la destrucción*).

Jonah 1:6

> And the captain drew near to him and said to him: 'How can you sleep! Get up, call to your God! Maybe God will consider us so that we will not perish'.

Jonah 1:6 contains the captain's speech to Jonah. In the biblical narrative, the captain plays the role of Jonah's better self, who seeks to convince Jonah to do his duty towards his fellow travellers on board the ship. In doing so, the captain attributes power to Jonah's God and conveys the impression that Jonah holds the fate of the ship in his hands.

This impression is strengthened in the Hellenistic-Jewish sermon *On Jonah* 9:5, where the shipmaster not only tells Jonah to get up and call to his own God but also indicates that he is aware that Jonah is at fault and the cause of the storm:

> Do you not see those who were sailing safely before you got on board the ship, and that they have been at peril since you have boarded?

The *Zohar* goes one step further in its depiction of the captain as the voice of Jonah's conscience. In its metaphorical retelling of the Book of Jonah, the *Zohar* depicts Jonah as a symbol of the human soul. Just as Jonah goes down into the ship and later into the fish, so the human soul descends first into a human being and later into the grave. While in the human world, the soul is exposed to trials and tribulations. A human being sins and flees from his Master, but God sends a storm to persecute him and demands his punishment, yet the soul lies sick. In this retelling, the captain is identified with the 'good inclination' (*yetser hatov*) that calls upon the soul to repent:

> Zohar 83: Who is the shipmaster? The Good Inclination that guides everyone.

The Gentile shipmaster has thus come a long way from his pagan origin insofar as he now represents the God of Israel. At the same time, despite its Jewish flavour, there is something both timeless and universal about the depiction in the Zohar. True to its genre of Jewish mysticism, the shipmaster in the Zohar is neither Jew nor Gentile; he is the good intention in every human being. As such, the Jonah story in its entirety is turned into a treatise about the universal conditions of humanity.

Significantly less complimentary, Luther compares the captain with his contemporary Catholics (Latin commentary). In times of crisis, it is human nature to turn not to God directly but to another human who, they believe, can save them through their intercessions. Thus, when pressed in their conscience by sin and thus seeking consolation, the sailors turned to Jonah in the same way that people around Luther would turn to a monk.

Jonah 1:7

> And one man said to his fellow man: 'Let us cast lots so that we will know on whose behalf this evil is' and they threw lots and the lot fell on Jonah.

This verse tells how the sailors decided to cast lots in order to determine on whose behalf the storm raged.

A Matter of Narrative

The story line demands that Jonah leaves 'the innermost of the ship' after being commanded to pray by the shipmaster (v. 6) and before the throwing of lots (vv. 7–8), yet the biblical text omits any reference to Jonah joining the sailors on deck. Seeking to fill this narrative gap, the Hellenistic-Jewish sermon *On Jonah* 10:1 describes how Jonah woke up and ascended to deck, where he saw the waves and heard the wailing of men and the crying of children. (So far in the sermon, the audience has not encountered these children: where did they come from and what were they doing on board the ship? The sermon does not answer these questions.) Later, in 10:2–3, the sermon makes the salient point that Jonah was consoled when he saw the misfortune of the others, 'for human beings are accustomed to enduring pain more easily when many people are involved; this creates equality, and each one derives a consoling remedy for his pain from the misfortune of others'.

According to the biblical narrative, the sailors then cast lots (Jonah 1:7). As the lots fall on Jonah, the sailors proceed to ask him a series of questions, although none of them touch upon the reason for the storm (Jonah 1:8). Instead, the discussion in verses 8–9 is concerned only with Jonah's origin, occupation, and ethnicity. The reader learns only later (v. 10b, 'because Jonah had told them') that Jonah at one point must have informed the sailors about his flight from God. It would, however, make narrative sense for Jonah to have mentioned this matter already in verse 7, i.e. immediately after the lots had revealed his culpability.

To resolve this chronological issue, the sermon *On Jonah* 11 changes the sequence of events here. Presumably for reasons of narrative cohesion, the sermon seeks to establish when exactly the sailors realized that Jonah was responsible for the storm. Thus, as soon as Jonah appears on deck, the sailors ask him from whence he came etc. (cf. Jonah 1:8). Already at this point, the sailors seem to be aware of Jonah's situation, as they tell Jonah that 'You are small in stature but a burden for the boat, and we are afraid that with the load of your deeds you are going to sink the ship' (*On Jonah* 11:3). Jonah, however, only mentions to the sailors such things as are for his own benefit, such as being a servant of YHWH, while keeping silent about his flight. It is at this point that the sailors decide to cast lots, through which God reveals to them beyond a shadow of a doubt that Jonah is indeed guilty (Jonah 1:7).

'let us cast lots'

Many commentators have explored and evaluated the sailors' action of 'casting lots'. Viewing the action positively, *On Jonah* portrays the sailors as pious people. As to the reasons behind this portrayal, Siegert suggests that the author of the sermon lived in a multicultural setting, and his audience probably included Gentiles, as well as Jews with liberal leanings (Siegert 1994: 52–58). The lot throwing is thus portrayed as a very pious endeavour, in the sense that the sailors allowed God to be the judge rather than a human being, who might have been swayed by ulterior motives.

By contrast, several Christian commentators focus on the vice of lot casting. The *Glossa Ordinaria* argues that in the case of Jonah and Matthias (Acts 1:26), the outcome was due to the power of God. When this is not the case, however, we should not trust in or use lots. Luther, in his Latin commentary, does not take kindly to the casting of lots in Jonah 1:7. It is evil to cast lots in order to tempt God; it is not evil, but still not ideal, to do so in a case of real distress (such as that of Jonah and the sailors). Luther tempers his views somewhat in his German commentary, where he distinguishes between casting lots and tempting God. The former may, in fact, be 'a real act of faith', unless it is misused to arbitrarily satisfy one's own inquisitiveness. Ultimately, 'it is fitting that Christians abstain from casting lots in a spirit of levity'.

Luther (Latin commentary) also holds Jonah's participation in the lot casting against him. He scathingly states that Jonah knew that he was guilty, yet nevertheless took part in the enterprise in the hope that he would somehow escape. Thus, he cannot be excused from sin. Luther (German commentary) further compares Jonah with Adam: if God had not come upon Adam and Eve, they would never have paid any attention to their sin. But, as God approached, they hid from him. Luther thus castigates Jonah for his cowardly hiding:

> He is not pious enough to come out into the open and confess his sin, but he lets these poor people endure such terror and danger and distress for his sake until he is betrayed by the casting of lots and God wrests a confession of his sin from him. That is also one of the tender virtues of sin: it renders people mute. It conceals itself; it is ashamed.

Calvin, following suit, states that the sailors' lot casting was a sign of weakness and doubt. Calvin is initially more positive than Luther, deeming it to be a lawful undertaking in certain (but not all) circumstances, such as the one in which the sailors found themselves. In this case, God ruled over the outcome. Even so, the sailors do not completely escape Calvin's criticism. In his view, all men are guilty of offence, yet the sailors did not own up to their fault, and none of them confessed any sin (Lecture 73).

Some retellings of the Jonah narrative detect in Jonah 1:7 an allusion to the soldiers casting lots for Jesus's clothes (John 19:23–24), thus emphasizing how aspects of Jonah's life make him a type for Christ. The drama-oratorio 'Jona ging doch nach Ninive' by the Russian/Swiss composer Wladimir Vogel (1896–1984 CE) provides an interesting example. Although Vogel based his text on Martin Buber's translation (rather than on a Christian translation) and made hardly any alterations to the overarching storyline, he nevertheless included several Christian allusions through his music. Among them, the depiction of the sailors casting lots in Part One is, to cite Geiger, 'an obvious allusion to the chorus of soldiers casting lots for Christ's raiment in Bach's St. John Passion' (Geiger 2001: 12).

A few Muslim exegetes also comment on the sailors' lot casting in their commentaries to the Quran. In his *Tafsīr al-Qurʾān al-ʿAẓīm* to Q21:87–88, drawing from Q37:141 ('Then he [agreed to] cast lots, and he was among the losers'), Ibn Kathīr states that the sailors cast lots not only once but three times, in an attempt to avoid having to toss Jonah overboard:

> Yunus, meanwhile, went and travelled with some people on a ship, which was tossed about on the sea. The people were afraid that they would drown, so they cast lots to choose a man whom they would throw overboard. The lot fell to Yunus, but they refused to throw him overboard. This happened a second and a third time.

As we shall see shortly, this interpretation is reminiscent of the tradition in *PRE* 10 where the sailors 'dip' Jonah into the water several times (see below, Jonah 1:13).

'so that we will know on whose behalf this evil is'

This rather curious statement, explaining the reason for the casting of lots, suggests that the sailors suspected that the storm was due to someone on their ship. As asked poignantly by Radak, why did the sailors think that someone on *their particular ship* was responsible for the storm? Were there no other ships in the sea? This train of thought caused early Jewish and Christian exegetes, among them Theodore of Mopsuestia, to argue that *only* the ship on which Jonah was aboard was afflicted by the storm (cf. above, Jonah 1:4). In the words of *PRE* 10:

> They had travelled one day's journey, and a mighty tempest on the sea arose against them on their right hand and on their left hand; but the movement of all the ships passing 'to and fro' was peaceful in a quiet sea, but the ship into which Jonah had embarked was in great peril of shipwreck, as it is said, 'But the Lord sent out a great wind into the sea, and there was a mighty tempest in the sea, so that the ship was like to be broken' (Jonah 1:4).

Many of the mediaeval Jewish commentators follow suit. Rashi, for instance, states that the other boats were travelling peacefully while the ship that held Jonah was breaking apart.

The fourteenth-century English homiletic poem 'Patience' goes beyond the biblical text, having the sailors declare that whoever is found guilty will be tossed overboard (lines 168–174):

> Then spoke the readiest, almost in despair:
> 'I believe some traitor is here, some lawless wretch,
> Who has grieved his god and goes here among us! Do!
>   All sink in his sin, and for his guilt perish.
> I propose that we lay out lots on each man.
> And whosoever the loss falls on, fling him overboard'.

In contrast to the biblical narrative, the retelling by the Swedish poet and posthumous Nobel prize laureate in literature (1931) Erik Axel Karlfeldt (1864–1931 CE), in his poem 'Jone havsfärd' (Eng. 'Jonah's sea travel') portrays the drunk captain as eager to throw the pale, fat, and sickly looking prophet overboard to calm the storm. Jonah pleads with them to take another man, yet the sailors claim that he is a good choice as he is so fat that he will float (my translation).

> And they place their hand upon Jonah,
>   but he pleads: 'Please, spare,
> Because I am a spiritual man and a venerable prophet'.
>   But they responded: 'If you have the throne,
>   then you can tread water, Jonah,
> Though you probably float on the speck, o prophet, fat like a parson'.

Jonah 1:8

> And they said to him: 'Tell us, please, on whose behalf this evil is. What is your occupation and where are you from? What is your country and from what people are you?'

The sailors ask a series of questions. From a narrative perspective, however, it is unclear why they need to know so many details about Jonah – profession, place of origin, ethnicity – at this point in the story. Both Jewish and Christian exegetes have therefore explored possible reasons behind their inquisitiveness. According to Cyril of Alexandria, for example, the sailors, being pagans, wished to figure out *what exact* deity Jonah had offended. John Chrysostom, in his Homily 5:8, 'On Repentance and Almsgiving', focusing more on the sailors' manner of questioning, argues that the sailors established a court of justice on board the ship. They charged Jonah but also allowed him to defend himself. Chrysostom is in fact very impressed by the sailors and points out that they were far from eager to charge and convict Jonah, even though they knew that he had committed a sin (in contrast to Chrysostom's implied readers who unfortunately act in the opposite manner).

Looking more specifically at the questions that the sailors asked Jonah, Rashi suggests that the sailors suspected Jonah to have sinned in his profession, that there was a decree against the people in his place of origin, or that his people had sinned. Radak, in his commentary to Jonah 1:7, expands on this issue by suggesting that the sailors asked Jonah whether he had swindled someone or been violent and thus was going to be charged. Objecting to this line of interpretation, Ibn Ezra points out its logical flaws: if God had indeed decreed death to a certain people, God would surely have been able to single out an individual from that guilty people and not included innocent bystanders in his punishment. The sailors would accordingly have had no reason to fear. Given that they did fear, however, another interpretation must be sought. In Ibn Ezra's view, it was simply the custom that most people had a trade. To ask about that trade would inevitably provide vital clues to the reason behind their actions and could thus explain why they happened to be in a certain place. Ibn Ezra's interpretation was to some extent already anticipated by Jerome, who argued that these types of questions would shed light upon the reason for 'the wickedness'.

In sharp contrast to the biblical portrayal, the sailors are depicted as being exceedingly rude in Dominick Argento's choral work *Jonah and the Whale*:

> Chorus:
> What the devil have you done, doltish wretch?
> What do you seek on the sea, sinful shrew?
> Would you destroy us all with your wicked works?
> What country do you come from, do you call your own?

This impression persists throughout the work, emphasized by the later description of how the sailors accused Jonah of being sinful and how they threw Jonah *roughly* into the sea (unsupported by the biblical text of Jonah 1:15):

> Chorus:
> Have you no governor, guardian, or god to call upon?
> Where in the world were you wanting to go?
> See, how your sins have sealed your fate!
> Give glory to your god before you go further!
>
> Narrator:
> Roughly they took him by top and by toe,
> And into the tumultuous sea he was thrown.

It is possible that this negative portrayal stems from Argento's other key source of inspiration, namely, the depiction of Jonah and the sailors in Härkeberga Church, Sweden, where the sailors are treated as a type for the Jews who crucified Jesus (see Jonah 1:13)

Jonah 1:9

> And he said to them: 'I am a Hebrew and I fear YHWH, the God of the heaven, who has made the sea and the dry land'.

'And he said to them "I am a Hebrew"'

Jonah states that he is 'a Hebrew' in Jonah 1:9. This is an unusual statement insofar as the word 'Hebrew' is seldom attested in the Hebrew Bible; it is far more common for the expression 'people of Israel' to denote Israelite ethnicity. Its rare use explains Ibn Ezra's need to explore the origin of the term 'Hebrew' (*i'vri*). He derives it from Gen 10:21, which states that Shem was the father of all the children of Eber. It may also explain the 'modernizing' attempt in Targum Jonathan, where Jonah states that he is 'a Jew'.

The LXX preserves a different reading, namely, that Jonah is a 'servant of the Lord' (δοῦλος κυρίου). It is possible that this reading preserves a misreading of the Hebrew text where the orthographically similar letters *resh* and *daleth* have been mixed up.[3] The Greek translator may have read the Hebrew expression עברי as עבד י ('servant of Yhwh'), where the final *yod* was understood as an abbreviated reference to Yhwh.

In later interpretations, Jonah's Hebrew/Jewish identity conjures up notions of exile and estrangement. Already Jerome connected Jonah's words in Jonah 1:9 with Ps 39:13 [Eng. 39:12], where the psalmist states that he is 'a stranger with you, a dweller like all my fathers'. The notion of Jonah being a foreigner is later picked up in literature. The novel *Die Antwort des Jona*, written by the German-Israeli author Schalom Ben-Chorin (1913–1999 CE), uses Jonah's declaration in Jonah 1:9 as its starting point. For Ben-Chorin, Jonah is a symbol of the Jews and his flight from God representing the Jews' eternal struggle to deal with their position as God's chosen people and their calling to be God's witness in the world. Jonah is the stranger and the eternal outsider who remains a Jew. He can never fully assimilate and become German or French etc. This is true even though he believes in the God who is the God of the entire universe (Ben-Chorin 1966: 13–22; see further Liptzin 1985a: 247–248).

The notion of the Jewish people carrying a burden and having a responsibility towards God and towards the Gentile world is expressed poignantly by the Russian-Jewish author Kadia Molodowsky (1894–1975 CE) in the Yiddish poem 'Jonah' (1965). It expresses in a heart-breaking manner the Jewish experience through the lens of Jonah's calling (see further Liptzin 1985a: 248–249):

> […]
> You will lie in the ditch, pelted with stones,
> There, with flesh wounds, burns, plagues, you will stay.
> Still, God will mark you with fire in your bones:
> Go to Nineveh,
> And what I command you, – say.

[...]
You are chosen for mercy and for pain,
Go to Nineveh,
And purify its sin.

In a very different manner, James Bridie's play *Jonah and the Whale* has Jonah denying who he is. On board the ship bound for Tarshish, Jonah is recognized by the commercial traveller Bilshan. In a scene not unlike the one where Peter denies Jesus (Matt 26:33–35/Mark 14:29–31/Luke 22:33–34/John 13:36–38), Jonah denies being Jonah and he denies his mission to Nineveh (Act I).

> Bilshan: [...] You're the local Prophet, aren't you?
>
> Jonah: I'm not Jonah. I – I think I know the man you mean. We are often mistaken for one another. But I assure you, you are wrong.
>
> Bilshan: I should think you're a true prophet all right. You could never have made much of a reputation at lying. Let me see ... let me see...Oh, you ... Aren't you in the wrong boat?
>
> Jonah: No ... no. I hope not.
>
> Bilshan: The usual route to Nineveh is to go up to Damascus and to cross the desert by caravan. This is precisely in the opposite direction.
>
> Jonah: I know that. I have no intention of going to Nineveh. I – I never had.

Modern interfaith dialogue has appealed to Jonah's encounter and interaction with the sailors. For example, the Anglican minister Rev. Geraldine V. Wiliame, in her interfaith work in Fiji, has used Jonah's declaration as an example of maintaining one's own identity yet respecting that of the 'Other' when seeking to bridge the gap between different religious groups (Wiliame 2005; cf. Tiemeyer 2017a).

'Who has made the sea and the dry land'

The *Glossa Ordinaria* connects this expression with the details about Jonah's flight in Jonah 1:3. Building on the common interpretation that Tarshish symbolizes 'the sea' (cf. above, v. 3), Jonah is here referring to the origin of his flight ('the dry land') and the destination of his flight ('the sea'). A few modern scholars have also connected the notion of 'the dry land' with the creation narrative in Gen 1:1–2:4 (see, e.g. Kamp 2003: 205–209).

Jonah 1:10

> And the men feared greatly and they said to him: 'What is this that you have done?' because the men knew that he was fleeing before Y<small>HWH</small> for he had told them.

'And the men feared greatly'

The Hebrew verb *yareh* = 'fear' can mean either to worship, as in 'fearing Y<small>HWH</small>', or to be afraid. In verse 9, it is reasonable to assume that the sailors would have understood Jonah's statement 'I fear Y<small>HWH</small>, the God of heaven' to mean that he 'worships' him. In contrast, when the same verb is repeated in verse 10, now with the sailors as its subject, the sense is that the sailors 'feared greatly'. Due to this repetition of the verb *yareh*, although with a change of subject (Jonah versus the sailors), commentators have wondered not only in what way the sailors 'feared', but also, in retrospect, in what way the sailors understood Jonah's statement that he 'feared' Y<small>HWH</small>. A few commentators suggest that the sailors in fact misunderstood Jonah to have said that he was *afraid* (of God's retribution). As a result, the sailors also 'feared' in the sense that they became frightened. Abarbanel, for example, interprets Jonah's confession in Jonah 1:9bα that he fears Y<small>HWH</small> as an acknowledgement that he had sinned against him.

'And they said to him: "What is this that you have done?"'

Cyril of Alexandria asks how, upon hearing that Jonah was a Hebrew, the sailors knew that he was fleeing from God. He concludes that Jews were not permitted to leave the country that was allotted to them, to visit foreigners, or to enter cities given over to idolatry. As the sailors saw Jonah outside the borders of Israel, they accordingly deduced that he must have repudiated life within the Law and thus would be fleeing from God.

Speaking more generally about the sailors' assumption of Jonah's guilt, Ben-Chorin ponders the reasons and the responsibility for the storm and the resulting plight of the ship. Is Jonah guilty, as the seamen would argue ('what have *you* done [to cause this storm]')? The answer must be 'yes' if we take God's role in the story into account. Jonah is trying to flee, and God is trying to stop him. Ben-Chorin further applies the interplay between Jonah and the seamen as a lens through which to view the interaction between Jews and Gentiles over the past 2000 years. Gentiles make the Jews (the eternal foreigners) into scapegoats for the problems in the world. The Gentiles cast lots to find the guilty one, and the lot falls on the Jew (Jonah 1:7). In this way, according to Ben-Chorin (*Die*

Antwort des Jona, pp. 14–15), the Gentiles demand to know the reason for the Jews' existence (Jonah 1:8) as they assume that there is a correlation between that and their own misfortune (my translation):

> They ask him as the foreigner, the primal foreigner, and they ask him immediately about their own misfortune. He, the persecuted one, should tell them why they are experiencing evil. He, the foreigner, must have the key to the misfortune of the nations. They themselves also flee from their fate and from God. They do not ask themselves, they do not look inside themselves, but they approach the sleeping Jew, the foreigner, and ask him.

From a different angle, Hesse and Kikawada detect here an allusion to Gen 3:13, where God asks Eve 'what is this that you have done?' (Hesse and Kikawada 1984: 12) This allusion emphasizes anew the assumption of guilt.

'for he had told them'

The idea that Jonah had already told the sailors that he was fleeing from God is seldom commented upon (but cf. *On Jonah*, above). One rare example of giving words to Jonah is found in the fourth-century poem *De Jona et Nineveh* attributed to Tertullian (lines 99–104):

> He avows himself
> A servant, and an over-timid one,
> Of God, who raised aloft the sky, who based
> The earth, who corporally fused the whole:
> A renegade from Him he owns himself,
> And tells the reason.

In the modern choral work *Jonah: A Musical Morality* by William Mathias, Jonah explicitly admits his sin at this moment (rather than at an earlier moment): 'I have defied my God. I have defied my God'.

Jonah 1:11

> And they said to him: 'What should we do to you so that the sea will quieten for us?' because the sea was becoming increasingly stormy.

In this verse, the sailors ask Jonah what they should do with him, given that the storm was getting rougher and rougher. In short, should they save Jonah, or should they save themselves? In the Hellenistic-Jewish sermon *On Jonah* 12, the sailors elaborate on this question, declaring that their single overarching aim is to survive. To do so, they need to get rid of the storm. If there is a way for them to accomplish this without harming Jonah, then let him, by all means, suggest it. If, however, by seeking to save Jonah's life they will all die, 'then for us the salvation of many is preferable to one man's death' (*On Jonah* 12:3, cf. Jonah 1:14).

According to the *Glossa Ordinaria*, the sailors put the responsibility for any decision-making upon Jonah: Jonah, as the author of the sin that caused the storm, ought to come up with the solution. The sailors knew that if they killed him (by tossing him overboard), they would ease God's anger, yet it is up to Jonah to command them to do so.

For Calvin (Lecture 74), who has so far been rather critical of the sailors, they grow in his opinion as the narrative proceeds. Calvin lauds their behaviour in Jonah 2:11. Rather than throwing Jonah overboard and thus saving themselves – now that they know that Jonah brought about the storm – they are restrained by their fear of God.

The final part of verse 11 speaks of the sea. For Chrysostom, the sea is a sentient (female) subject who has found Jonah, recognized him, and wants him. She thus threatens to sink the entire ship if the sailors will not surrender Jonah to her (Homily 5.3.8, 'On Repentance and Almsgiving').

Jonah 1:12

> And he said to them: 'Pick me up and throw me into the sea and the sea will quieten for you, because I know that it is because of me that this great storm is upon you.'

Jonah 1:12 forms the epigraph of Albert Camus's short story *Jonas, ou l'artiste au travail*. This epigraph, together with the name of the main character (Gilbert Jonas), invites the reader to make a connection between the short story and the biblical narrative. One of the more poignant allusions to the biblical Jonah can be found in one of its final images, when Jonas is sitting alone and motionless in his loft, trying to paint, after a prolonged time of what might be called 'painter's-block' caused by his own success. The darkness in the loft is restful and he listens to the silence within himself. He describes himself as being at work although his canvas remains blank, apart from a word in the centre of the canvas, written in very small letters, which could read either *solitary* or *solidary*. The story ends with Jonas collapsing, although the doctor assures his wife that Jonas will soon recover.

'Pick me up and throw me into the sea'

Several traditions see Jonah's willingness to be thrown into the sea as the ultimate sign of Jonah's love for Israel. Not only was Jonah prepared to sin (by running away), he is now ready to sacrifice his life in order to save Israel. The Hellenistic-Jewish sermon *On Jonah* is a case in point. The sailors approach Jonah and ask him to leave the ship and go to another ship so that the storm would leave their own ship in peace. In response, Jonah offers a long soliloquy wherein he declares that the sailors' confidence in his ability to do the right thing should not be put to shame: 'I will justify your confidence to my last breath' (*On Jonah* 13:4). He realizes that he should not seek his own salvation but instead show himself to be a God-fearing prophet; to save the human beings on the ship, Jonah thus 'threw himself into the wavy sea' (14:3). Siegert, in his commentary to the sermon, argues that although the notion of sacrificing your life to save humanity could be understood as an alternative (and competing) reference to Jesus's teaching, it is more likely to be part of a shared Hellenistic ethical-religious ideal of self-sacrifice so that others might live (Siegert 1992: 134).

The idea that Jonah committed suicide on behalf of others is alluded to also in *Mekhilta Attributed to R. Ishmael* I.III (7–8):

> 7.A. R. Nathan says, 'Jonah went only to commit suicide in the sea
> 7.B. as it is said "And he said to them,
>   'Take me up and cast me forth into the sea'" (Jonah 1:12)'.
> 8.A. And so you find that the patriarchs and prophets gave their lives for Israel.
> [...]
> 8.D. Lo, in every passage you find that the patriarchs and prophets
>   gave their lives for Israel.

Jerome is likewise impressed by Jonah's resolve and willingness to confess his sins here. Jonah is neither evasive nor tries to hide his guilt; rather he graciously accepts his punishment. Moreover, he would rather die than let the innocent sailors die. Along similar lines, Cyril, Bishop of Jerusalem (313–386 CE) holds up Jonah's readiness to die as an example for people to confess their sins and take their due punishment ('Catechetical Lecture' 6:26):

> Ought then he, who shared the guilt of murder, to be worshipped? Ought he not to have followed the example of Jesus, and said, If ye seek Me, let these go their way? Ought he not to have said, like Jonas, Take me, and cast me into the sea: for this storm is because of me? (Jonah 1:12)

More neutrally, Josephus (*Ant.* 9:10) states that '[Jonah] persuaded them to cast him into the sea'. Although they did not want to do so at first, they were in the end 'animated to do it by the prophet himself'.

From a different perspective, Ibn Ezra argues that Jonah's desire not to be the instrument of Nineveh's repentance was so strong that he desired and requested to die, yet he did not state this openly in case the sailors took him to Nineveh. Abarbanel, following suit, maintains that Jonah's gesture was his saving grace. Jonah chose to stifle his soul and die in the depths of the sea to avoid going to Nineveh and thus to save Israel from being destroyed by the Neo-Assyrians (cf. above, Jonah 1:3). In contrast, other classical Jewish texts interpret Jonah's behaviour in Jonah 1:12 more negatively. *PRE* 10, for example, depicts Jonah as a sacrifice, but he is not the one who offers himself up. Rather, in line with the biblical account, he pushes the burden and responsibility of the sacrifice upon the sailors (Adelman 2009: 231).

The Babylonian Talmud connects Jonah's death by drowning with his refusal to prophesy. According to *b.Suk.* 53b, the form of death for withholding prophecy is asphyxiation (but it does not mention Jonah – rather, the example given is David). On this basis, so the argument goes, by drowning, Jonah was made to suffer the appropriate death sentence.

Other, predominantly Christian, commentators maintain that Jonah's willingness to die in Jonah 1:12 was a great sin. The fourth-century poem *De Jona et Nineveh*, attributed to Tertullian, describes the event with a focus on Jonah's despair and lack of hope in God (lines 109–117):

> Words prompted by the Spirit of the Lord:
> 'Lo! I your tempest am; I am the sum
> Of the world's madness: 'tis in me', he says,
> 'That the sea rises, and the upper air
> Down rushes; land in me is far, death near,
> And hope in God is none! Come, headlong hurl
> Your cause of bane: lighten your ship, and cast
> This single mighty burden to the main,
> A willing prey!'

Even more sharply, Luther, in his Latin commentary, asks how Jonah could want to die, knowing that God was angry with him and knowing that he would be responsible for the death of the men around him. This is an instance, all too common, of one ungodly person causing an entire state and whole nation to perish and be in great misery. Luther's views are somewhat more nuanced in his German commentary where he, in fact, states that Jonah's willingness to die demonstrates the power and effect of a pure heart's faith. Jonah realizes that he alone is culpable, while the others are blameless. This insight, in turn, prompts him to accept and bear the burden of sin, reconcile himself with his fate, even pronounce his own verdict, and submit in agony to the punishment. All these things combined fall upon Jonah, drive him to utter despair of God's grace, and ultimately urge him to depart from faith.

In Calvin's view, although Jonah's offer to be thrown overboard was definitely a sign of his despair, his willingness to die nonetheless shows his awareness of his guilt and his patient submission to God's punishment. In fact, he 'willingly bears his charged guilt and his punishment' (Lecture 74).

Jonah 1:13

> But the men rowed to return [him] to the dry land, but they did not manage because the sea was becoming increasingly stormy.

Verse 13 depicts how the sailors pay no heed to Jonah's offer to be thrown into the sea but instead attempt to row back to dry land. Several commentators have commented positively on their endeavour to save both themselves and Jonah. Abarbanel, for example, argues that the sailors decided to row back in order to remove Jonah from their boat and to send him on his mission to Nineveh. God, however, wanted Jonah to repent by choosing this path freely; he therefore did not grant the sailors success. Chaim Dov Rabinowitz (1909–2001 CE), in his commentary to Jonah in *Daat Soferim*, provides a different explanation. The sailors realized that if Jonah drowned, any remaining possibility for him to carry out God's command would be utterly lost. Thus, fearing God's fury and ensuing punishment if they let Jonah drown, the sailors sought to save him with all their might.

PRE 10, exaggerating the positive impression that the biblical account gives, paints these sailors as men of compassion and love. Although they by now had identified Jonah as the source of the storm, the sailors nonetheless initially refused to throw him overboard and instead tried alternative solutions in order to save his life. They lowered him to the knees in the water whereupon the sea calmed. When they took him out of the water, the storm commenced again. After repeating this effort twice more, each time putting more of Jonah in the water, with the same result, they saw no other way out than to throw Jonah into the water, whereupon the storm abated. This whole exercise emphasizes the sailors' righteousness, but it also, as Adelman points out, depicts them as 'foils to Jonah in his anti-mission. They pity the prophet [...] while Jonah, wishing to abort the salvation of the Ninevites [...] risks all his shipmates' lives in the storm' (Adelman 2009: 232–233).

Many of the Church Fathers are very appreciative of the sailors. In his Homily 3.8, 'On Repentance and Almsgiving', John Chrysostom encourages his audience to be like the sailors, who, in Jonah 1:12–13, 'neither despise a single soul nor neglect a single body'. He further stresses that the sailors were not eager to condemn Jonah. Rather than throwing the prophet into the water after discovering that he had sinned and thus being responsible for the calamities facing them, they tried to save him. 'They demonstrated tolerance and constraint'. Theodore of Mopsuestia is somewhat less enthusiastic about the sailors, simply stating that they thought it would be dangerous to cast out into the sea a man who was close to God.

At times, the Christian appreciation of the sailors has been combined with anti-Jewish sentiments. Several Christian exegetes have compared the sailors with the Jews at the time of Jesus, to the detriment of the latter. As Jerome writes:

> They refused to shed blood, preferring rather to die than kill. O how changed are they now! The people that had served God (Deut 10:12) saying, 'crucify him, crucify him' (Luke 23:21).

This type of anti-Jewish polemic is systemic to much of Jerome's Jonah commentary (cf. below, Jonah 1:14).

Another, significantly smaller, group of Christian retellings, equally anti-Jewish in their outlook, cast the sailors in the Book of Jonah in a bad light. Behind this interpretative move is the desire to reinforce the typology of Jonah and Jesus. The sailors are depicted as brutal men, in direct opposition to their presentation in the biblical narrative. Moreover, they are painted as Jews rather than Gentiles.

For example, in the illustrations (see Figure 1) of the Jonah narrative in Härkeberga Church (Sweden) by the mediaeval German-Swedish

FIGURE 1   Illustrations of the Jonah narrative in Härkeberga Church (Sweden) by the mediaeval German-Swedish painter Albrekt Målare (Latinized as Albertus Pictor) (1440/45–1509 CE). Medieval paintings of Jonah and the whale by Albertus Pictor. Source: Xauxa Håkan Svensson. Licensed under CC BY-SA 3.0.

painter Albrekt Målare (Latinized as Albertus Pictor) (1440/45–1509 CE), the sailors are portrayed as cruel men with grotesque noses and conical hats, both associated with European mediaeval Jewry (cf. Jonah 2:11) (see further Malmberg; Melin 2009).[4] The sailors are thus here depicted as Jews, or rather what a person in the mediaeval ages would have associated with Jewry (Friedman 1988: 128). The onlookers would, as a result, have interpreted Jonah 1:13 as a precursor to the passion narrative: the sailors/Jews killed Jonah/Jesus.

Jonah 1:14

> And they called to YHWH and said: 'Please, YHWH, may we not perish for the sake of this man, and do not bring upon us innocent blood. For you are YHWH. As you have wanted, you have done'.

In verse 14, the sailors' prayer to YHWH emphasizes his power, authority, and omnipotence. Again, we note the Christian proclivity for appreciating the sailors. Jerome, for example, in his *Against the Pelagians*, 2.23, highlights the sailors' faith in God. Despite not knowing the reasons as to why Jonah, a prophet of God, needed to be punished, the sailors nevertheless justified God and trusted in his character as a just judge. In his Jonah commentary, Jerome goes one step further and contrasts the sailors' strong faith and their willingness to die on behalf of Jonah with the Jews who in response to Pontius Pilate stated that Jesus's blood might be upon them and their children.

> This seems to be the confession of Pilate, as he washes his hands and says, 'I am clean of the blood of this man' (Matt 27:24). The Gentiles do not want Christ to die, and affirm that it is innocent blood. And the Jews say, 'let his blood fall upon us again and on our son' (Matt 27:25).

The idea of saving the many while sacrificing a single man is also found, although in a non-judgemental manner, in the Hellenistic-Jewish sermon *On Jonah* 12:3 (cf. Jonah 1:11). It later reappears in the fourteenth-century poem 'Patience', where the sailors state (line 172) that 'Do! All sink in his sin, and for his guilt perish'. As Andrew points out, this is in all likelihood a conscious echo of the High Priest Caiaphas's words in John 11:50 ('You do not realise that it is better for you that one man die for the people than that the whole nation perish'). Later in the same poem (lines 225–228), the sailors cry out:

> First they pray to the Prince that prophets serve,
> That He give them the grace to grieve Him never,

> Because they mingle their hands in blameless blood,
> Though that man were His that they here killed.

Andrew argues that we again hear an echo from the Gospel, this time from Pilate's words in Matt 27:24 (cf. above). This echo does not equate Jonah with Jesus, however, but serves instead to emphasize the *difference* between Jesus's innocence and Jonah's deserved treatment (Andrew 1973: 231–232).

Jonah 1:15

> And they lifted Jonah and threw him into the sea, and the sea ceased from its raging.

'And they lifted Jonah and threw him into the sea'

To jump or not to jump – that is one question that is debated in the reception history of Jonah 1:15. Did Jonah jump or was he thrown into the water? Further, if he was indeed thrown, did Jonah comply without a fight or did he resist the sailors? The biblical text states unequivocally that the sailors lifted Jonah and threw him overboard. This, however, has not restrained interpreters from envisaging other scenarios. The Hellenistic-Jewish sermon *On Jonah* 14:3 offers the unusual viewpoint that Jonah threw himself into the sea, yet there is also an alternative textual variant of the sermon where Jonah was thrown. It is possible that this variant was written because some people objected to Jonah's apparent suicide (Siegert 1992: 134). The same idea – that Jonah not only volunteered to be tossed into the sea but actually jumped willingly – is also attested in a few Muslim traditions. In his *Tafsīr al-Qur'ān al-'Aẓīm*, commentary to Q21:87 (but commenting on Q37:141), Ibn Kathīr states that 'Yunus stood up, removed his garment, and cast himself into the sea'. In his subsequent commentary to Q37:139–148, Ibn Kathīr writes that Jonah 'took off his garment so that he could throw himself into the sea, and they tried to stop him'. Jerome, staying closer to the Hebrew text, maintains that the sailors were responsible for Jonah ending up in the water. This act, however, was carried out in a most gentle manner. According to Jerome, the choice of words in Jonah 1:15 shows that the sailors 'took' him rather than 'seized' him or 'threw' him, which in turn indicates that the sailors did not discharge Jonah into the sea with repugnance. It further indicates that Jonah went of his own accord. Jerome's commentary here is not in line with the Hebrew text; instead, as the next Hebrew word makes clear, the sailors did indeed 'throw' Jonah into the sea (*wayetiluhu*).

Jonah 1:15 forms the pinnacle of the sixteenth-century set of sermons on the Book of Jonah by the English Protestant reformer (and later martyr) John Hooper (1495–1555 CE). In these sermons, Jonah represents a wide array of dissenting (Catholic) elements ('Jonases') in society that seek to disrupt the ship of state that is England. Although this group contains representatives of all classes, the unruly masses form the greatest threat. Hooper's advice to the young (and ill) King Edward VI, to whom the sermons are preached, is to get rid of these dissenting Jonases, either by death or enslavement (1831: 115, 125, 127):

> Among the common people ye shall also find many Jonases […] and so displeases the majesty of God, that he will never cease from sending tempests, till those Jonases are amended, or cast into the sea
>
> […]
>
> Is it possible to sail or live quietly with so many obstinate Jonases? Nay, doubtless. What remedy then? Let them be cast all into the sea […] whom the king's majesty must cast into the sea, or send to the gallies.
>
> […]
>
> The sloth and idleness, the impatience and rebellion of the people, must be punished and amended, or else they will cast the ship, the shipmaster (that is the king and his council), yea, and themselves also, into the sea, and bring this realm to desolation and utter destruction.

Jonah 1:15 thus illustrates how the worthy men of England's 'ship of the commonwealth' toss the Jonases that are 'rocking the boat' overboard. Hooper's reading of the Book of Jonah thus encourages a social system of 'docile bodies' accepting the authority of the King, Word-Magistrate, and (Protestant) Preacher (Sherwood 1997: 379–388, eadem 2000: 39–42. See also Gane 1981: 100; Staffell 2008: 489–492).

A few retellings omit any reference to the sailors' act. The dramatic cantata *The Whale: A Biblical Fantasy*, composed by John Tavener (1944–2013 CE) between 1965 and 1966 and first performed by the London Sinfonietta and the London Sinfonietta Chorus on 24 January 1968, skips over Jonah 1:13–16. Likewise, the sung part of the modern choral work *Jonah: A Musical Morality* by William Mathias, jumps from Jonah 1:14 to 1:16, thus omitting the sailors throwing Jonah overboard. In the music, there is a long silence (a bar's rest) between the two verses, causing the listeners to 'fill in the blank'. When the singing recommences, the choir states: 'And the blood of Jonah was not upon their hands'.

The Sailors' Violation of the Code of Hospitality
The sailors ultimately decided to save themselves by throwing Jonah into the sea. In many ways, their behaviour violates the code of hospitality. In the words of the Romanian-born writer, Nobel Peace Prize laureate (1986), and Holocaust survivor Elie Wiesel (1928–2016 CE), the sailors (Wiesel 1981: 141):

> dispose of a helpless passenger in order to save their own skins […] Although Jonah is not one of their own, he is their guest, their passenger. Don't they know that a ship's crew is duty-bound to save the lives of the passengers before their own? And remember: Jonah is not a stowaway; he has, after all, paid his fare.

The sailors' violation of the code of hospitality has been a topic in several fictional interactions with the Book of Jonah. The novel *The Strange Nation of Rafael Mendes* (*A estranha nação de Rafael Mendes*) by the Jewish Brazilian author Moacyr Scliar (1935–2011 CE) is inspired by the biblical Jonah narrative (see also Jonah 4). The main character Rafael appears again and again throughout history in different incarnations. The Rafael Mendes who lived during the Inquisition is a 'New Christian'. After imprisonment and prolonged torture, Rafael and his companion Afonso manage to escape, only to end up on a ship run by Jew-hating sailors. Near the coast of Brazil, the weather suddenly changes. The sailors blame the two 'descendants of Christ's killers' on board:

> 'Divine punishment has befallen us', muttered the sailors, 'for we are harbouring two heretics, two descendants of Christ's killers'. Tension kept mounting, and one night Rafael and Afonso woke up with shouts and the clangor of swords. […] 'Save yourselves', the captain shouted at them, 'jump into the sea'. (p. 126)

In the penultimate incarnation, Rafael Mendes seeks to return to Spain to fight with the Republicans. He does not reach Spain but instead dies aboard the ship and, like Jonah, his body is thrown into the sea (Barr 1996: 43). The characters in the Book of Jonah are thus read and interpreted through the lens of the last 2000 years of Jewish persecution. Rafael Mendes has a much clearer understanding of the Jewish relationship with the Gentile world than the biblical Jonah ever had. As a result, Scliar does not have the strength, or possibly the patience, to treat the sailors as upright, decent men; instead he reads the past Jewish encounters with the Gentile world into his depictions of the sailors (Tiemeyer 2017a: 259–279). Norma Rosen expresses the same sentiments in her modern midrash on Jonah, where the fish has told the prophet what is to come: inquisitions, expulsions, ghettos, pogroms, death camps, and crematoria (Rosen 1992: 93).

Melville's *Moby-Dick* likewise employs the character of Jonah as a type for the downtrodden and enslaved. In Chapter 93 ('The Castaway'), Pip, a cheerful, young, black ship's boy, is washed overboard when they chase the whale.

> Now upon the second lowering, the boat paddled upon the whale; and as the fish received the darted iron, it gave its customary rap, which happened, in this instance, to be right under poor Pip's seat. The involuntary consternation of the moment caused him to leap, paddle in hand, out of the boat; and in such a way, that part of the slack whale line coming against his chest, he breasted it overboard with him, so as to become entangled in it, when at last plumping into the water. That instant the stricken whale started on a fierce run, the line swiftly straightened; and presto! poor Pip came all foaming up to the chocks of the boat, remorselessly dragged there by the line, which had taken several turns around his chest and neck. [...] 'Damn him, cut!' roared Stubb; and so the whale was lost and Pip was saved. [...] Stubb suddenly dropped all advice, and concluded with a peremptory command, 'Stick to the boat, Pip, or by the Lord, I won't pick you up if you jump; mind that. We can't afford to lose whales by the likes of you; a whale would sell for thirty times what you would, Pip, in Alabama'. (Herman 1851 / Richard Bentley / Public domain)

This passage emphasizes how Pip is saved, yet the other sailors stress his meagre value and his dispensability. Later, in the same Chapter 93, Melville highlights further the parallels between Jonah and Pip. In his hands, Pip becomes an inverted Jonah who, through his ordeal in the abyss, is saved; yet his sanity is lost (see further Pardes 2008: 71; Sprang 2011: 455–357):

> By the merest chance the ship itself at last rescued him; but from that hour the little negro went about the deck an idiot; such, at least, they said he was. The sea had jeeringly kept his finite body up, but drowned the infinite of his soul. Not drowned entirely, though. Rather carried down alive to wondrous depths, where strange shapes of the unwarped primal world glided to and fro before his passive eyes; and the miser-merman, Wisdom, revealed his hoarded heaps; and among the joyous, heartless, ever-juvenile eternities, Pip saw the multitudinous, God-omnipresent, coral insects, that out of the firmament of waters heaved the colossal orbs. He saw God's foot upon the treadle of the loom, and spoke it; and therefore his shipmates called him mad. So man's insanity is heaven's sense; and wandering from all mortal reason, man comes at last to that celestial thought, which, to reason, is absurd and frantic; and weal or woe, feels then uncompromised, indifferent as his God.

The Polish-British novelist and mariner Joseph Conrad (1857–1924 CE) wrote several novels that feature life at sea. In his works *Lord Jim* (1899–1890) and *Typhoon* (1902), Conrad uses a scenario that echoes that of Jonah 1:6–15 in order to explore a seaman's responsibility towards not only his crew but also his passengers. In both novels, a moment of stress provides a moment of insight that their human cargo is different from the bales of hay and the bolts of cloth that they also have on board. The Arab pilgrims and the Chinese coolies respectively are human beings for whom the captain and his crew have an obligation (Masback 1961: 329).

In *Lord Jim*, the captain fears that the boat *Patna* is about to sink. He and his crewmen, including the seaman Jim, get into the lifeboats while leaving the 800 Muslim passengers to their fate. A few days later, they learn that their ship was brought safely to shore after all. An investigation begins into the circumstances that led the crew to leave the passengers in the lurch, with the result that the crew is vilified for abandoning the ship and its passengers for the sake of saving their own lives. Jim spends the rest of his life wracked by guilt. Speaking with hindsight about his thoughts when he believed that the ship was going to sink (ch. 7), Jim muses:

> 'You must remember he believed, as any other man would have done in his place, that the ship would go down at any moment; the bulging, rust-eaten plates that kept back the ocean, fatally must give way, all at once like an undermined dam, and let in a sudden and overwhelming flood. He stood still looking at these recumbent bodies, a doomed man aware of his fate, surveying the silent company of the dead. They were dead! Nothing could save them! There were boats enough for half of them perhaps, but there was no time. No time! No time! It did not seem worthwhile to open his lips, to stir hand or foot'.
>
> [...]
>
> 'He protested he did not think of saving himself. The only distinct thought formed, vanishing, and re-forming in his brain, was: eight hundred people and seven boats; eight hundred people and seven boats'.

Turning to the novella *Typhoon*, the opposite situation occurs. Captain Mac-Whirr steers the ship *SS Nan-Shan* into a typhoon when sailing on the Chinese Sea. As they fear that the ship is going to sink, questions arise concerning what to do with the Chinese passengers on board:

> A minute passed. Some of the stars winked
>   rapidly and vanished.
> 'You left them pretty safe?' began the Captain
> abruptly, as though the silence were unbearable.
> 'Are you thinking of the coolies, sir? I rigged
>   lifelines all ways across that 'tween-deck'.
> 'Did you? Good idea, Mr. Jukes'.
> 'I didn't ... think you cared to ... know', said
>   Jukes – the lurching of the ship cut his speech

> as though somebody had been jerking him
> around while he talked – 'how I got on
> with … that infernal job. We did it. And it
> may not matter in the end'.
> 'Had to do what's fair, for all – they are only
> Chinamen. Give them the same chance
> with ourselves – hang it all. She isn't lost
> yet. Bad enough to be shut up below
> in a gale –'
> 'That's what I thought when you gave me the
> job, sir', interjected Jukes, moodily.
> '– without being battered to pieces', pursued Cap
> tain MacWhirr with rising vehemence.
> 'Couldn't let that go on in my ship, if I knew
> she hadn't five minutes to live. Couldn't bear
> it, Mr. Jukes'.

Conrad's *The Shadow Line* and *The Nigger of the Narcissus* stand even closer to the Book of Jonah. In both cases, the ship is in great danger due to circumstances that appear almost supernatural and to have been caused by just one man. Just like Jonah, that man (Mr Burns/Jimmy Wait) is not part of the crew. He, again like Jonah, is isolated and does not respond well to the crew's kindness. As Masback highlights, each of these two novels feature six motifs that are each reminiscent of the Book of Jonah: (1) both 'Jonah types' appear suddenly and disconcertingly and disrupt the normal order on board the ship, (2) both 'Jonahs' are fleeing from something in their past, (3) both 'Jonahs' are set apart from the rest of the people on board the ship, (4) both 'Jonahs' seem to anticipate that they will be sacrificed, yet the crew show them only compassion, (5) there are reasons to believe that both 'Jonahs' are actually, at least to some extent, responsible for the calamity that is facing the ship, and (6) both 'Jonahs' are involved in putting an end to the calamity: Mr Burns appears on deck, returned to health, and the heat that has faced the ship is eased by a strong breeze; Jimmy Wait dies, and his body is consigned to the sea with the result that the wind begins to blow and the ship can journey further. Despite these parallels to the Book of Jonah, however, these two narratives form a marked contrast to the biblical narrative. First, neither crew forsakes the afflicted man. Second, it is implied that the ship survives *thanks to* the crew's charitable behaviour towards the man. For Conrad, according to Masback, 'the only hope for man is to act out of courage, out of a conviction of the solidarity of the human race'. In this manner, Conrad shames the sailors in the Jonah narrative, who acted out of cowardice and who were willing to assign Jonah to his death in order to save themselves (Masback 1961: 331–333).

In yet another novella by Conrad, *The Secret Sharer*, the Jonah narrative meets the Cain and Abel narrative. The character Leggatt is a man on the run. Like Cain, he has murdered a fellow crew member on board his ship. He is spotted by the captain, who is on board another ship, while swimming away from his ship and thus fleeing from justice. The captain takes him on board, hides him, and eventually drops him back into the sea so that he can swim to freedom. Leggatt is both a type for Cain and a type for Jonah, fused together by their shared wandering and their flight from justice/God (cf. Jonah 1:3; 4:4) (Leiter 1960: 159–175).

'and the sea ceased from its raging'

The sailors' action caused the sea to calm, with the result that the remaining crew on board the ship was safe. Christian literature commonly expands upon the notion that Jonah is cast into the sea to *save* the sailors: Jonah, the single man who dies for the sake of redeeming the many, is understood as a type of Jesus's death upon the cross. This interpretation conflates Jonah's willingness to be thrown overboard to save the sailors' lives (Jonah 1:12) and Jesus's willing sacrifice on the cross. Jacob of Serug, for example, observes that the sailors bound Jonah, wished him peace, and expressed their belief that they would be saved by his atoning blood (26.411–12). Later in the same poem, the typology is made between the sailors and Pontius Pilate (Eng. transl. Kitchen 2011: 34–35):

> Jonah stood before the sailors while being questioned
> Just as also our Lord was tried by Pilate.
> The sailors implored God on account of Jonah
> Lest they be destroyed by the blood of a man who was righteous.
> The judge too washed his hands on account of our Lord
> Lest he be defiled by the holy blood which was innocent. *(28. 413.4–9)*

Another similar approach, lines 111–112 of the fifth-century poem 'Hymnus Ieiunantium' ('Hymn for those who fast') by the Christian poet Prudentius, read:

> The man whose guilt the urn declares
> Alone must die, the rest to save.

Augustine expresses this typology explicitly in his *Letter* 102, section 34 (question 6), where he reads Jonah through the lens of Matt 12:39–40:

As, therefore, Jonah passed from the ship to the belly of the whale, so Christ passed from the cross to the sepulchre, or into the abyss of death. And as Jonah suffered this for the sake of those who were endangered by the storm, so Christ suffered for the sake of those who are tossed on the waves of this world.

Early Christian art often presents the scene when Jonah is being thrown into the sea to still the storm as a prototype for the crucifixion. In some cases, the symbolism is spelled out; in others it is not. For example, a third-century mosaic 'Jonah and the Fish' and a fourth-century sarcophagus, both found under St Peter's Basilica in Rome, depict how the sailors toss Jonah overboard. Likewise, the Catacomb of Saint Peter and Saint Marcellino in Rome preserves a (probably fourth-century) depiction (see Figure 2) of the sailors throwing Jonah overboard, notable not least because of the rather charming and very non-fishlike fish:

Looking at depictions of Jonah in early Christian art more broadly, a 'Jonah cycle', consisting of three key episodes, can be observed: (1) Jonah being tossed overboard by the sailors and swallowed by the fish (Jonah 1:15–2:1 [Eng. 1:17]), (2) Jonah being vomited out of the fish (Jonah 2:11 [Eng. 2:10]), and (3) Jonah reclining under the *qiqayyon* (Jonah 4:6–7). A good example can be found on

Figure 2 The Catacomb of Saint Peter and Saint Marcellino, Rome, Italy. Picture of the prophet Jonah being thrown into the Sea. Public Domain.

the wall paining from the catacomb of Callixtus, Rome (see further Davis 2000: 78 [Codex Palatinus Latinus 871, fol. 15 r.]). The iconography concentrates on those elements that convey the central Christian message, and these three motifs are selected because they represent key Christian tenets of faith. The tossing of Jonah overboard and his subsequent re-emergence carry the dual function of symbolizing Jesus's own death and resurrection and, by extension, also Christian baptism, whereby a Christian is understood to die and rise with Christ (Jensen 2000: 51, 78, 85). The Jonah story thus reminded viewers that baptism is a type of death and rebirth (Jensen 2000: 87–88). Other elements in the biblical narrative, such as the sins of Nineveh, are seldom depicted (Davis 2000: 72–83; Jensen 2000: 69, 75, 93).

The three scenes, right to left, are clearly seen on the sarcophagus in the Lateran Museum in Rome (fourth-century CE; see Figure 3).

There are also other sets of scenes that capture the typology between Jonah and Jesus. In the *Biblia Pauperum* ('Paupers' Bible'), a type of illustrated Bible that aimed to visualize the typological correspondences between the Old and New Testaments, Jonah is often depicted alongside Jesus being placed in the tomb. Along similar lines, Codex Palatinus Latinus 871, fol. 15 r., a manuscript from 1425 to 1450 and preserved in the Vatican Library, offers a threefold comparison. On the right, Jonah is put into the mouth of a whale that waits for him in the sea; in the centre, Jesus is placed in his coffin; and on the left, Joseph is cast into the pit.

The German pastor, theologian, and anti-Nazi dissident Dietrich Bonhoeffer (1906–1945 CE) alludes to the last line of Jonah 1:15 in his poem 'Jonah', written from his prison cell on 5 October 1944. The poem ends with the words 'Da stand das Meer', a literal translation of the Hebrew expression *waya'amod hayam*. It is likely that Bonhoeffer penned this poem, which conjures up a vivid image of fear and trembling, at the very moment when he gave up hope of escape and instead accepted the likelihood of death (Plant 2013: 66).

FIGURE 3   Sarcophagus, The Lateran Museum, Rome.

> They screamed in the face of death, their
> frightened bodies clawing
> at sodden rigging, tattered by the storm,
> [...]
> And Jonah spoke: "Tis I!'
> In God's eyes I have sinned. Forfeited is my life.
> 'Away with me! The guilt is mine. God's
> wrath's for me.
> The pious shall not perish with the sinner!'
> They trembled much. But then, with their
> strong hands,
> they cast the guilty one away. The sea stood still.

Bonhoeffer uses the Jonah story as a hidden criticism of the Third Reich and its narrow nationalism. Through its interaction with the Jonah narrative, the poem targets those who are indifferent to the fate of a people other than their own. Jonah himself, however, realizes the plight of others and refuses to let them die (cf. Liptzin 1985a: 242-244). Jonah committed a sin when he refused to go to Nineveh and call the Ninevites to repentance. This sin cannot be changed, yet in the present, when Jonah confesses his sin and places his life humbly before the judgement of God, then God alone can still the storm and calm the sea (Plant 2013: 60). Jonah's acknowledgement of his guilt and his instruction to the sailors to cast him overboard indicates that he has given up any attempt to justify himself; instead he has chosen to take responsibility for his guilt and in parallel also take responsibility for the lives of others (Plant 2013: 69-70). As to the sailors, Liptzin argues that they symbolize the German people in their hour of distress on board a German ship of state (Liptzin 1985a: 244).

Jonah 1:16

> And the men feared Yhwh greatly and they sacrificed sacrifices and vowed vows.

Verse 16 tells how the sailors, having thrown Jonah into the sea, feared Yhwh greatly and offered sacrifices to him. The second part of this claim has caused predominantly Jewish interpreters some concerns. Sacrifices to Yhwh should only be offered in the temple in Jerusalem (e.g. 2 Chron 7:12); what the sailors were doing in the middle of the sea was therefore wrong. As a result, many interpreters rewrite the text or at least seek to explain the sailors' unorthodox (and also impractical) behaviour.

Josephus is responsible for what is probably the most extreme modification. In sharp contrast to the biblical account, Josephus nowhere depicts the sailors praying to the God of Israel. They also never make any vows and they most certainly never offer any sacrifices. In fact, God is largely missing from Josephus's account of Jonah's adventures (*Ant.* 9:10) (Feldman 1992: 10). The 'missing' fear of Yhwh and the 'missing' sacrifices, evident in the biblical text of Jonah 1:16, is, according to Feldman, likely to be the result of a conscious strategy employed by Josephus to assure his Roman target readers that the Jewish community did not seek to proselytize. The proselyting movement in Rome was at its peak when Josephus was writing his *Antiquities*, yet it was frowned upon by certain circles in Rome. Josephus thus had to tread carefully lest he offend his Roman hosts. He accordingly downplayed all references which could be (mis)-understood as propagandizing for proselytes (Feldman 1992: 22–24). Some modern retellings follow this trend of omitting verse 16. Notably, the paraphrase 'Der Prophet Jona' from 1896 by the German poet and dramatist Otto Erich Hartleben (1864–1905 CE) adheres to the plot of the Book of Jonah carefully with this one exception: it excludes any mention of the sailors' vows and sacrifices.

To solve the theological issue raised by the ban against performing sacrifices outside the Jerusalem temple, many rabbinic texts relocate the sailors' sacrifices into the future. Targum Jonathan, followed by many of the mediaeval Jewish commentators, translates Jonah 1:16 as 'and [the sailors] *promised* to offer a sacrifice before the Lord'. This reading is inspired by the extended meaning of the Hebrew verb *nadar* = 'to vow', i.e. 'to promise'. Radak, following suit, claims that the sailors *promised* to make (future) sacrifices before God (in the temple in Jerusalem), whereas Ibn Ezra simply states that the sailors sacrificed 'after they had left the ship'. By pushing the sacrifices into the future and by changing their location, this line of interpretation solves the problem of having Gentiles offering sacrifices to Yhwh outside the temple in Jerusalem (Cathcart and Gordon 1989: 106, fn. 29; see further Sasson 1990: 139). The sacrifices are no longer random sacrifices taking place in the middle of the Mediterranean; they are proper, cultic sacrifices carried out in the central sanctuary in Jerusalem.

PRE, at the end of Chapter 10, attests to a variant of this interpretation of Jonah 1:16 (see further Smolar and Aberbach 1983: 123, who suggest that TJ forms the basis for the midrash preserved in *PRE*). As the sailors saw all the miracles that God performed for Jonah (i.e. his salvation by and adventure together with the fish; see below), they abandoned their idolatry, returned to Yafo, went up to Jerusalem, and circumcised the flesh of their foreskins. As Friedlander comments, the term 'sacrifice' here is reinterpreted to refer to the sacrifice of the blood of the covenant that is shed during circumcision (cf. Adelman 2009: 233, fn. 57). Accordingly, when the sailors sacrificed and made vows, they were really converting (to Judaism). *PRE* 10 ends with a reference to the thirteenth blessing of the *Amidah* (the central prayer in Jewish liturgy, consisting of nineteen blessings), i.e. to pray for the welfare of the righteous converts (Adelman 2009: 234, fn. 60). Along similar lines, Rashi maintains that the sailors vowed to *convert* (to the worship of the God of Israel). As demonstrated by Adelman, the conversion of the sailors in PRE 10 likely formed part of an overarching anti-Christian polemic in PRE. The sailors serve as a counterpoint to those Jews mentioned in Matt 12:39 who do not become followers of Jesus: the sailors of Jonah 1 do not become Christians; they become Jews. Furthermore, the satirical depiction of Jonah targets the Christian use of Jonah as a type for Christ. Indirectly, PRE 10 thus offers a veiled critique of Jesus as a messianic figure (Adelman 2009: 236).

Although the Church Fathers do not share the same theological concern as the rabbinic interpreters, many nevertheless comment on the sheer impracticality of performing sacrifices on board a ship. Jerome argues that, given that the sailors were in a boat at sea, any physical sacrifice would have been out of the question. Instead, the sailors offered a sacrifice of praise and vows to the Most High (cf. Ps 50:14; Isa 19:21 where sacrifices are offered by Gentiles) (cf. Timmer 2013). Theodore of Mopsuestia likewise considers it unlikely that the sailors performed actual sacrifices at sea; rather they completely abandoned their idols and instead devoted themselves wholeheartedly to the worship of God, promising to join his service and to make due sacrifices to him in the future.

A few commentators take the text at face value. Luther, especially, is full of admiration for the sailors. In his view, the sailors must have thought that Jonah had drowned and was dead. Furthermore, they must have felt that they had been instrumental in killing him, although reluctantly and only in compliance with God's will. They now become pious and true servants of God; all their previous gods have been forgotten (German commentary, Jonah 1:17). By contrast, the Geneva Bible Notes to Jonah 1:16 express doubts regarding the sailors' sincerity. Rather, the sailors' worship of the one true God 'was done for fear, and not from a pure heart and affection'.

Notes

1 In a *tafsīr*, the complete qur'anic text for comment is cited (lemma) and accompanied with comment (Calder 1993: 101).
2 I am grateful to my friend Laura Giancarlo, Pontificia Universidad Católica Argentina, Buenos Aires, who kindly translated this poem for me.
3 This possibility was pointed out to me by my insightful Hebrew student, Dorothy Plummer.
4 For the demand that Jews wear tall, conical hats as a distinguishing mark, in accordance with the decrees of the fourth Lateran Council (1215), see Gottheil and Deutsch 1906.

Jonah 2

The second chapter of the Book of Jonah introduces the reader to the fish. God commands it to swallow Jonah in verse 1 and to spit him out again in verse 11. The rest of the chapter features Jonah's prayer to God while ensconced inside the fish. We shall investigate how interpreters through the centuries have conceptualized the fish and how they have envisaged Jonah's survival inside it. We shall also explore the theological issues raised by Jonah's prayer.

Jonah Through the Centuries, First Edition. Lena-Sofia Tiemeyer.
© 2022 John Wiley & Sons, Ltd. Published 2022 by John Wiley & Sons, Ltd.

Jonah 2:1 [Eng. 1:17]

> And Yhwh appointed a big fish to swallow Jonah and Jonah was in the belly of the fish three days and three nights.

Jonah 2:1 is probably one of the most commented-upon verses in the entire Hebrew Bible. The first part of our discussion will explore the statement in verse 1a that Yhwh appointed a 'big fish' to swallow Jonah. The second part will investigate the claim in verse 1b that Jonah spent three days and three nights inside the fish. The matter of the (grammatical/biological) gender of the fish will be discussed in conjunction with Jonah 2:2.

'And God appointed a big fish to swallow Jonah'

What creature swallowed Jonah? Was it a fish, a sea monster, or a whale? Furthermore, was it a benevolent creature or a vicious monster?[1] We shall begin by looking at four common interpretations: (1) the fish as Jonah's helpful saviour, (2) the fish as a monster, (3) the fish as death, and (4) the fish as a matter of embarrassment. In addition, we shall explore depictions of the fish in (5) poetic descriptions, (6) retellings that give the fish a voice, and (7) *Pinocchio*. We shall conclude by investigating (8) what the fish may have looked like and (9) 'what really happened'.

1. The Helpful Saviour of Jonah

The Masoretic Text (MT) of Jonah portrays the fish as a vehicle of deliverance. This portrayal is firmly anchored in the text. In the narrative part of Jonah, Yhwh 'appoints' the fish (2:1 [Eng. 1:17]) to swallow Jonah when he has been thrown overboard, thus saving him from drowning. It further keeps Jonah alive during the three-day journey to safety on dry land, and it finally, again following Yhwh's command, spits out the prophet so that he can fulfil his God-given task (2:11 [Eng. 2:10]). Turning to the poetic part of the book, Jonah praises God for saving him 'from the belly of Sheol' (2:3 [Eng. 2:2]) (Ackerman 1981: 215). A contextual reading suggests that the fish is the saviour, while 'the belly of Sheol' is the netherworld where Jonah would have ended up had he drowned. Jonah cried out to God before the fish came around. When the fish appeared, he was saved. Put succinctly, Jonah is *not* in the 'belly' of the netherworld precisely because he *is* in the belly of the fish. Although a few passages in the psalm in Jonah 2, such as 2:7 [Eng. 2:6], can be (and have been; see below) understood as references to Jonah's time inside the fish, the overall impression in the MT is that the fish is God's obedient servant who follows the divine commands and thus saves Jonah.

The notion of a sea creature saving the protagonist of a story from drowning and bringing him to safety on dry land may have been a common trope in ancient storytelling. The Greek tale of the musician Arion, for example, depicts how Arion's ship is captured by pirates. Arion is given the choice between suicide and being thrown overboard. To win time, Arion asks if he could sing one last song. As he finishes, he leaps into the water, yet is saved by dolphins that had been attracted by his music. He is thus saved and brought safely to shore in Corinth on the back of a dolphin (see further Liptzin 1985b: 237–238; cf. Bickerman 1967: 11–12; Ziolkowski 2007: 83).

The Hellenistic-Jewish sermon *On Jonah* 16:1 follows the cue of the MT and portrays the fish as a benevolent creature that does God's bidding, saves Jonah from certain death, and offers him a safe (and comfortable) haven:

> Now, having healed both illnesses and having taught the man that no one should regard God as unaware or be an obstacle to His love for human beings, He supplied him with a vessel: a huge fish swimming there, which he considered to be a killing beast, but it was the salvation and the guard of salvation; and while the prophet was swimming, the huge fish drew him inside like breath and conceived him alive in its belly.

The word denoting Jonah's fish in the Armenian text is the Greek loanword κῆτος (*ketos*), used also in the Septuagint (LXX) to denote the fish in Jonah (cf. below). Jonah's fish thus belongs to the larger categories of big sea-living creatures (Siegert 1992: 135–136).

A few of the Church Fathers also see the fish as God's benevolent servant, even though they often emphasize in parallel the more punitive aspects of Jonah's time inside the fish (cf. below). Although John Chrysostom, in his Homily 5.9, 'On Repentance and Almsgiving', first likens the fish to a prison from which Jonah cannot escape and where he is placed due to his sin of trying to run away from God's command, he later states explicitly that the creature saved Jonah and returned him to the city. The prayer by Paulinus of Nola (Poem 24.205) similarly states that Jonah was imprisoned in a 'living gaol', yet although he was 'physically incarcerated, the prophet emerged in spirit to return to God'.

The Reformers likewise stress the salvific aspects of the fish, even though they also emphasize the torment that Jonah suffered while in its belly. Luther, in the Preface to his Latin commentary, teaches that the 'fish' (*piscis*) was God's tool in the sense that God had appointed him for the very purpose of keeping Jonah alive. Turning to his much longer German commentary (1:12), the character of the fish is more nuanced and also more monstrous. The 'fish' has become a 'whale' (*Walfissch*), and Jonah's time inside this whale is referred to as a second death:

> One death does not suffice, and he must pass through the jaws of the whale. God takes on a glowering mien. It seems that His anger is not appeased by the death and the penalty, to which Jonah is willing to submit, and that He cannot avenge Himself fiercely enough on him. It must have been a horrifying sight to poor, lost, and dying Jonah when the whale opened its mouth wide and he beheld sharp teeth that stood upright all around like pointed pillars or beams and he peered down the wide cellar entrance to the belly. Is that being comforted in the hour of death? Is this the friendly glance in dying, that dying and death are not even sufficient? [...] For the tumultuous sea wants to drown him, and as the whale devours him and wants to consume him, so a conscience feels nothing but the tempest of God's wrath and of death, and hell and damnation threaten to make short shrift of the soul and consume it [...].

In Luther's subsequent commentary to Jonah 2:10, the creature is a fish again. Luther argues that after being a vehicle of death, it now must serve to further life! Calvin also sees the fish as a most benevolent being, to be likened to a hospital!

> [F]or [Jonah] was received inside of the fish as though it were into a hospital; and though he had no rest there, yet he was as safe as to his body, as though he were walking on land.

Even so, Calvin underscores time and again the torment that Jonah must have endured while inside the fish (Lecture 76, commentary to Jonah 1:17). Jonah suffered a 'continual execution', and he languished in 'continual torments'.

The modern pop cantata *Jonah-Man Jazz* (1967) by the composer Michael John Hurd (1928–2006 CE) finally also sees the fish as Jonah's saviour. When Jonah falls into the ocean, he confesses his sins of disobedience. In response, God sends to fish to save him (Song 5):

> [...]
> Oh Lord I'm very sorry that your word I've disobeyed,
> if you will only come and help me I will do as you command;
> [...]
> When Jonah has repented him the Lord he didn't fail,
> although the sea was tropical he sent along a whale!
> It promptly swam right up to Jonah and its mouth was open wide.
> Before he'd even noticed it poor Jonah was inside!

1.1 A Helper Appointed by God on the Fifth Day of Creation

Jonah 2:1 [Eng. 1:17] states that 'YHWH appointed a fish'. This statement has caused several interpreters to ask *when exactly* this appointment took place, whether right then and there or a long time before.

The retelling of the Jonah narrative in *PRE* opts for the latter interpretation. In fact, the account of Jonah in *PRE* 10 appears as part of the wider discussion that began in *PRE* 9 about the events of the fifth day of creation (Gen 1:21). As the biblical account makes clear, the fifth day saw the creation of the great 'serpents'/'sea monsters'. Jonah's fish, as it turns out, is to be counted as one of these creatures. As stated by Rabbi Tarphon:

> That fish was specially appointed from the six days of Creation to swallow up Jonah, as it is said, 'And the Lord had prepared a great fish to swallow up Jonah' (Jonah 2:1 [1:17]).

The identification furthermore implies that this type of fish is not contrary to nature; rather it is built into the world as part of the creation and thus subject to God's authority. Jonah's fish is on a par with other happenings such as when the Re(e)d Sea was divided (Exod 14:21) and when the sun stood still in Ayalon (Josh 10:12–14): although they appear to be abnormal at first glance, they actually form part of God's plan. According to Rabbi Jeremiah ben Eleazar (*Gen.Rab.* 5:5), God declared already at the time of creation:

> That is in line with this verse in Scripture: 'I, even my hands, have stretched out the heavens and all their host have I commanded' (Isa 45:12). 'I commanded the sea to divide. I commanded the heaven to be silent before Moses: "Give ear, heaven" (Deut 32:1), I commanded the sun and the moon to stand still before Joshua, I commanded the ravens to bring food to Elijah, I commanded the fire not to harm Hananiah, Mishael, and Azariah, I commanded the lions not to harm Daniel, the heaven to open before Ezekiel, the fish to vomit up Jonah'.

A few mediaeval Jewish commentators follow suit. Radak argues that God assigned the fish for the specific task of swallowing Jonah when he fell into the water. This occurrence, moreover, is not natural but constitutes a miracle. Among the Church Fathers, Jerome likewise maintains that God created the fish already at creation, using Ps 104:26, which mentions how God created the Leviathan to play in the sea, as proof text.

2. The Fish as a Monster

Other traditions have focused on the monstrous qualities of Jonah's fish. Whereas the Hebrew MT uses the neutral term *dag/dagah* = 'fish' throughout Jonah 2, the Greek LXX employs the term *ketos* (κῆτος) (Jonah 1:17; 2:1, 10) rather than *ichthys* (ἰχθύς), i.e. the general Greek term for 'fish' (cf. LXX Gen 1:26). In ancient Greece, the term *ketos* (Latinized as *cetus*) denoted any large sea-dwelling animal, among them a large fish, a whale, a shark, or indeed a sea monster (Sasson 1990: 149). The Latin word for 'whale' is derived from this term, yet the Greek term has much wider connotations.

2.1 Greek Connotations of ketos

For those readers familiar with Greek mythology, the choice of *ketos* for the creature in Jonah 2:1 would have conjured up a wide range of tales featuring less-than-benevolent monsters of the deep sea. Notably, this term designates the sea monsters that the heroes Perseus and Heracles killed. Neither of these myths are retellings of the Jonah narrative. Rather, they provide sources that later interpreters combined with the Jonah narrative as they shaped their own readings.

The tale of Perseus and the sea monster begins with Cassiopeia boasting that her daughter Andromeda is more beautiful than the Nereids. This claim invokes Poseidon's anger and causes him to send a *ketos*. Cassiopeia and her husband Cepheus decide to sacrifice their daughter Andromeda to Cetus. They chain her to a rock near the ocean, traditionally associated with the city of Yafo (cf. Pliny the Elder). Perseus finds Andromeda and, when Cetus subsequently appears, he kills it (see further Flusser 1976: 1080–1083). Given the shared location of Yafo, it is possible that the Greek translators of the Book of Jonah were familiar with the legend about Perseus and chose the translation *ketos* to forge a connection between the Greek legend about Andromeda, Perseus, and the sea monster in Yafo and the story about the prophet Jonah who was swallowed by a big fish after boarding a ship in Yafo (Jonah 1:3).

The LXX reading of Jonah may also be indebted to the legend of Heracles and the Trojan princess Hesione, found in the *Bibliotheca*, Book II (Heracles, and the Heraclids – The Belt of Hippolyte). The *Bibliotheca* (also called Pseudo-Apollodorus) is a compendium of myths and heroic legends, arranged in three books, generally dated to the first or second centuries CE (Apollodorus 2008: 79). King Laomedon refuses to pay for the building of the walls of Troy. In his anger at this refusal, Poseidon sends a sea monster (*ketos*) to destroy Troy, with the caveat that if King Laomedon allows the sea monster to devour his daughter Hesione, then Troy will be delivered. King Laomedon accordingly has his daughter chained to a rock near the seashore, whereupon Heracles comes along and kills the monster.

It is finally also possible that the mythological figure Keto (derived from *ketos*), denoting the primordial sea goddess in Greek mythology who is known as the mother of a host of monstrous children called the Phorcydes, played a part in the development of Jonah's fish into a sea monster (see further Hard 2004: 58–64).

2.2 The Intertestamental Period

The interpretative trend to view Jonah's fish as a dangerous monster continues and is strengthened in the intertestamental period. Four Jewish texts, *Joseph and Aseneth*, *The Testament of the Twelve Patriarchs*, *3 Maccabees* 6:7–8, and *The Hellenistic Synagogal Prayers* testify to the notion of a sea monster that swallows people. As above, these texts are not retellings of the Jonah narrative in the strictest sense; instead, they provide background material that testifies to the transformation of Jonah's fish from being God's helpful servant into a monster that opposes God.

In *Joseph and Aseneth* 12:10, a tale which probably was composed in the Jewish community in Egypt sometimes after 100 BCE, the speaker (Aseneth) fears being thrown into the sea and swallowed by the *ketos*. In view of the parallelism within the passage, the reader is encouraged to equate the Devil's act of devouring (v. 9) with the fate of being swallowed by *ketos* (v. 10) and thus to understand the *ketos* as God's opponent who seeks to kill Aseneth (Angel 2006: 87–89; Eng. transl. Cook 1984: 485).

> [9]For lo, the wild primaeval Lion pursues me;
> And his children are the gods of the Egyptians that I
> have abandoned and destroyed;
> And their father the Devil is trying to devour me.
>
> [10]But do thou, O Lord deliver me from his hands,
> And rescue me from his mouth,
> Lest he snatch me like a wolf and tear me,
> And cast me into the abyss of fire, and into the tempest of the sea;
> And let not the great Sea-monster swallow me.

A similar tradition is attested in the section about Judah in the *Testament of the Twelve Patriarchs* 21:6–9 (Hollander and de Jonge 1985: 220–224). The text is of uncertain date and origin, stemming from either a Jewish or a Christian context (or both) and composed sometime between 200 BCE and 190 CE (Angel 2006: 110–111). The reference to sea monsters that swallow men like fishes, in a context that also mentions false prophets, brings Jonah and his fish to mind. The fish in Jonah swallowed a man to save him; here, kings are likened to sea monsters that swallow men like fish (Eng. transl. Hollander and de Jonge 1985: 221):

> [6]But you will be king in Jacob and you will be for them as the sea: for as on the sea just and unjust men are tossed about [...]. [7]For those who reign as kings will

be like sea-monsters, swallowing men like fishes [...] ⁹And false prophets will be like tempests, and they will persecute all righteous men.

3 Maccabees 6:7–8 is part of the same strand of reception. This passage, making an explicit reference to Jonah, tells the story of the persecution of the Jews during the reign of Ptolemy IV Philopator (r. 221–204 BCE), i.e. some decades before the Maccabean uprising in 166 BCE (Johnson 2004: 129–141). In his prayer in 3 Macc 6:8, the priest Eleazar mentions Jonah and how he was 'wasting away' 'in the belly of a sea monster' and how God restored him unharmed to all his family. It is not clear from verse 8 whether the fish is harmful or benevolent, yet the context suggests the former. In the preceding verse 7, Eleazar refers to God's act of saving Daniel in the lion's den. The parallelism between these two verses suggests that the 'sea monster' and the 'lions' are vicious beasts from which God saves men. This tradition in 3 Maccabees is strongly reminiscent of the above-mentioned interpretation in *Gen.Rab.* 5:5, yet with a crucial difference. There, the comparison between the fish in Jonah with the lions in Daniel emphasizes the subordination of the animals, alongside the sun, the sea, fire, and Elijah's raven, to God's will. In contrast, the comparison in 3 Maccabees shows how God saves his prophets from animals that would normally kill them.

The same connection is made in *The Hellenistic Synagogal Prayers*, again referring explicitly to Jonah. Chapter 6 contains a prayer of invocation that enumerates people whose prayers God has heard, pleading with God to hear also the present supplicants' prayers. Verse 11 states (Eng. transl. Darnell 1983: 2:685; cf. Limburg 1993: 103):

'Daniel in the hole of the lions; Jonah in the belly of the whale; the three children in a furnace of fire'.

Although the verse does not state explicitly that the fish is a monster on a par with the lions or a danger on a par with the furnace, such comparisons are implied.

This tradition is later picked up in the rabbinic literature. In the Jerusalem Talmud (*y.Ber.* 9:1), Rabbi Judah, in the name of Rabbi Isaac, refers to Jonah in order to show the reliability of God's salvation:

But the Holy One, blessed be He, [saves his subjects, just as he] saved Jonah from the belly of the fish. Lo, it says, 'And the Lord spoke to the fish, and it vomited out Jonah upon dry land' [Jonah 2:10].

This statement reveals that the fish is no longer thought of as God's vehicle of salvation; rather, it is something from which Jonah needs saving. The following chapter (*y.Ber.* 10:1) conveys the same thought with even stronger terms, as it compares Jonah's fish with Pharaoh, the fiery furnace in Dan 3, and the lions in Dan 6:

> He saved Moses from the sword of Pharaoh. He saved Jonah from the belly of the whale, Shadrach, Meshach and Abednego from the fiery furnace, and Daniel from the lion's den.

We encounter a slightly different situation in the Book of Tobit. Tob 6:2–4 narrates how another big fish tried to swallow Tobit's son Tobias (Eng. transl. Jacobs 2018: 109):

> And the lad went out and the angel with him and the dog went out with him and the first night came upon them and they camped by the Tigris river. And the lad went down into the Tigris to wash off his feet and a great fish, leaping up from the water, wished to gulp down the foot of the lad and he cried out. And the angel said to the lad, 'seize and hold fast to the fish' and the lad seized the fish and carried it up upon the land.

The connection between Tobias's fish and Jonah's fish is at best tangential: whereas Jonah's fish is large enough to swallow a man, Tobias's fish is small enough for a man to catch. It should be noted, however, that the size of the fish was a matter of dispute, as reflected in the various manuscript traditions. While G[I] states that the fish tried to devour Tobias whole, G[II] indicates that the fish nipped at Tobit's foot/genitals (it is possible that the term 'foot' is a euphemism for 'genital'; cf. Ruth 3:7b) (Moore 1996: 199). At the same time, a certain affinity exists. Two factors support a general connection between the Book of Tobit and the Book of Jonah. First, the shared narrative setting in Nineveh suggests a strong literary connection. Second, Jonah is mentioned twice in the conclusion in Chapter 14 (verses 4 and 8), where Tobias, at the extreme age of 127 years, rejoices at the news of Nineveh's destruction by Nebuchadnezzar and Ahasuerus in apparent fulfilment of Jonah's prophecy against the Assyrian capital. There are two textual versions of Tob 14:4; the one mentioning Jonah is probably the earlier one, whereas the one mentioning Nahum is likely the later one (Sherwood 2000: 124–125 fn. 185).

Vis-à-vis the fish motif, Levine suggests that the account in Tobit is an intentional parody of Jonah's fish. While Jonah, who sought to flee from God, was swallowed by the fish, Tobias, who acted responsibly, was given the power to overcome the fish (Levine 1992: 46). The use of the verb καταπιεῖν ('to swallow') invites comparisons with the Hebrew verb 'to swallow' (root *bala'*) in Jonah

2:1. This connection is strengthened by the Tobit texts from Qumran, where 4Q197, offering a Hebrew text of Tobit 6:3-4, uses the root *bala'* to denote the action of Tobias's fish. As Jacobs has shown, the use of this verb connects the fish in Tobit not only with the Ugaritic deity of Death, Mot (cf. below), but also with Jonah's fish (Jacobs 2018: 109–112).

The fish in the Book of Tobit is clearly a fish (*ichthys*) rather than a monster (*ketos*), as implied not only by the vocabulary used but also by the fact that Tobias later eats it (Moore 1996: 199). At the same time, Tobias's fish is violent and threatening. Notably, Tobias's struggle with the fish occurs at night, a time when evil is the dominant power. Nowell goes so far as to say that the fish here serves as a symbol of death, and that Tobias's victory over it stands for life and a new beginning. In support of her reading, Nowell connects the fish with the primeval watery chaos, as well as with the chaos monster Tiamat over whom Marduk was victorious (*Enuma Elish*). What we have here in the Book of Tobit is thus Tobias's struggle and victory over evil (Nowell 1983: 219, as cited by Moore 1996: 199).

3. The Fish as Death

The Book of Tobit bridges the traditions of Jonah's fish as a monster and as a symbol of death. If the connotations of 'death' are merely implicit in the Book of Tobit, they are explicit in a motley assortment of other texts: in the New Testament and subsequently also in the writings of the Church Fathers, in select *Midrashim* such as *Midrash Jonah* and *Yalkut Shimoni*, and in the *Zohar*. The Christian strand of this tradition culminates in mediaeval art, exemplified in the various depictions of Hell as the mouth of a massive sea monster and in the identification of Jonah's fish with the Leviathan and ultimately also with the Devil.

3.1 Jonah's Fish in Research on Myth

The conception of Jonah's fish as a symbol of death ultimately has its root in myths and folktales. The account of Jonah and the fish has gathered interest among scholars of myth and religious rituals and experiences. The imagery in the Book of Jonah may be indebted, consciously or subconsciously, to the Sumerian myth of 'Inanna's Descent to the Netherworld'. In this myth, the goddess Inanna descends to the netherworld, the domain of her sister Ereshkigal, where she dies because of her hubris. She is resurrected three days later and re-ascends to the world of the living (Landes 1967: 11–12).

More than a century ago, Simpson read the Jonah narrative from what he called 'a comparative mythologist' perspective and suggested that Jonah's three-day-stay in the fish was a ceremony connected with the initiation into the priesthood (Simpson 1899: 98). More recently, the Jonah narrative has been compared with initiatory ordeals that consist of being swallowed by a monster. As discussed by Mircea Eliade, Jonah's experience – being swallowed by the fish, spending time in its belly, and being vomited out – depicts symbolic death and rebirth. It is furthermore comparable with myths that speak about heroes being swallowed by marine monsters which they later kill and from which they emerge victorious. To cite Eliade, '[t]here can be no doubt that the fish that swallows Jonah and the other mythical heroes symbolizes death; its belly represents Hell' (Eliade 1960: 218–223). At the same time, this death experience also symbolizes the acquisition of wisdom. The hero enters the monster and stays there in seclusion (in the belly/Hell). During this time, he obtains wisdom and learns secret traditions. Ultimately, death leads to spiritual regeneration (Eliade 1960: 225–227). From a slightly different perspective, Maud Bodkin connects Jonah's descent into the sea and into the body of the fish with the experience of liberation and rebirth. Jonah descends amid slime and corruption before he can experience a renewal of life (Bodkin 1934: 52–53).

3.2 Jonah's Fish, the Ancient Near East, and Modern Scholarship

More specifically, the conceptualization of Jonah's fish as a symbol of death has roots in ancient Near Eastern mythology. Using the verb 'swallow' in Jonah 2:1 as the starting point, modern scholarship has, like *PRE* 10 (above), connected the fish in Jonah 2:1 with the great 'serpents'/'sea monsters' in Gen 1:21, yet has taken this affinity in a very different direction. Jonah's fish is placed alongside the Leviathan in Ps 104:26, as well as the Ugaritic deity of death Mot, who 'swallows' his prey. In the Ugaritic Baal cycle (KTU 1.5–6), for example, Mot describes his ferocious appetite and how his victims enter his mouth and descend (down his throat), using the same Semitic root for 'to swallow' as that in Jonah 2:1 (KTU 1.5 I 18) (Döhling 2013: 21–23; Noegel 2015: 242, Eng. transl. of the relevant part of the Baal Epic, see Cho and Fu 2013: 120–125).

3.3 The Fish in the New Testament

The notion that Jonah's time in the fish symbolizes his death features strongly in Matt 12:40. This statement, in turn, is the key impetus for the later Christian tradition of Jonah as a type for Jesus, where his three days in the belly of the fish prefigure Jesus's death and resurrection (cf. also below).

Beginning with matters of language, the text of Matt 12:39–41 clearly depends on the LXX and accordingly uses the same term *ketos* in reference to Jonah. Following suit, Jerome translates the Greek term *ketos* used in Matt 12:40 as *cetus*, i.e. the Latinized form of the Greek term (*sicut enim fuit Ionas in ventre ceti tribus diebus et tribus noctibus*). In contrast, in his Vulgate translation of the Book of Jonah, he employs the term *piscis*, which denotes 'fish' (*piscis grandis*). This distinction is reflected in later English Bible translations. Tyndale differentiates, as Jerome does, between the Hebrew Bible and the New Testament. While he renders the animal in Jonah 2:1 as a 'greate fyshe' in line with the Hebrew text, he translates the reference to the same animal in Matt 12:40 as 'whale' in line with the Greek text. Tyndale's translation was later incorporated into the Authorized Version of 1611. Markedly, Tyndale's translation of the NT is the first occurrence of the translation 'whale' in English Bibles. Since then, not only Matt 12:40 but also Jonah 2 have often been understood to speak about a 'whale'.

Turning to matters of interpretation, Matt 12:39–41 transforms Jonah and his fish into a typology for Jesus's death and resurrection.

> He answered, A wicked and adulterous generation asks for a miraculous sign! But none will be given it except the sign of the prophet Jonah. For as Jonah was three days and three nights in the belly of a huge fish, so the Son of Man will be three days and three nights in the heart of the earth. The men of Nineveh will stand up at the judgment with this generation and condemn it; for they repented at the preaching of Jonah, and now one greater than Jonah is here.

Matt 12:40 makes clear that Jonah is a type for Jesus, and the fish is a type for death. By contrast, the parallel passage in Luke 11:30 does not refer to the fish.

> As the crowds increased, Jesus said, 'This is a wicked generation. It asks for a miraculous sign, but none will be given it except the sign of Jonah. For as Jonah was a sign to the Ninevites, so also will the Son of Man be to this generation [...] The men of Nineveh will stand up at the judgment with this generation and condemn it; for they repented at the preaching of Jonah, and now one greater than Jonah is here'.

The chronological relationship between the two passages is unclear. Whereas Edwards maintains that Luke 11:29–32 contains the most original form, with Matthew attesting to an extended version that includes the three-day typology (Edwards 1971: 71–109), Bolin argues that Matthew preserves the original version (Bolin 1997: 20).

3.4 The Fish in the Zohar

The connotations of 'death' and 'resurrection' found in the New Testament are shared by and, if possible, made even more overt in the retelling of the Jonah narrative in the *Zohar*. The *Zohar* (*Wayakhel* 198b/7:81–97) draws a parallel between Jonah's downward journey into the sea and the descent of the human soul into this world to dwell in a physical body. The *Zohar* thus reconceptualizes the Jonah story as a universal story about the fate of humanity (Wineman 1998: 103–105). In this retelling, the fish is identified with the grave and Sheol (the term used throughout the Hebrew Bible for the still, dark place to where people, righteous and wicked alike, go after death). Jonah lies in this grave for three days and three nights. After a subsequent period of 30 days of pain, a voice sounds among the graves, calling the people to life again. At this moment, the graves cast forth their corpses to be resurrected. God thus commanded the fish and it spewed Jonah out.

> When they brought him into the graveyard following the judgement, the decree of judgment that had been raging now calmed from its fury. The fish that swallowed him is really the grave: What is written? 'And Jonah remained in the fish's belly' (Jonah 2:1). The belly of this fish is actually the belly of She'ol. On what basis is this identity established? It is written, 'From the belly of She'ol I cried out' (Jonah 2:3). And should it otherwise be understood simply as the belly of the fish and nothing more, it is here clearly written, 'the belly of the Netherworld'. (Wayakhel 7:88–89)

Using Exod 7:21 as proof text, where it is written that the fish of the Nile died, the *Zohar* further explicates that the fish does not only represent a tomb; the fish itself really dies after swallowing Jonah. At the same time, death also means healing, as death paradoxically serves as the gateway to life. The fish is restored to life three days later, in time to spit Jonah out. The fish is thus understood as a sign of both death and the resurrection of the dead (Wineman 1998: 105–109).

> In the account of the fish one finds words of healing for all the world, for upon swallowing Jonah the fish died, but after Jonah was inside the fish for three days, the fish was restored to life and cast out Jonah.

The notion that Jonah is a symbol of the soul is attested also in *Midrash Yonah*, a late Aggadic work in two parts traditionally read in the synagogue on the Day of Atonement. While the first part contains the midrash proper, the second part, featuring an allegorical rendering of the Jonah narrative, contains roughly the same material as the *Zohar*. A version of this text is preserved in the anthology *Yalkut Shimoni*. Commenting on Jonah 2:1 (part ii. §§ 550–551), it states that the belly of the fish should be understood as the belly of Sheol, as indicated by Jonah 2:3 (Eng. 2:2).

3.5 The Fish in the Writings of the Church Fathers

The Church Fathers show virtually no interest in the fish itself; only its symbolic value is important. There are two prevalent trends of interpretation: the womb and the tomb. Cyril of Jerusalem, for example, states in his 'Catechetical Lecture 14.7':

> Jonah was cast into the belly of a great fish, but Christ of his own will descended to the abode of the invisible fish of death. He went down of his own will to make death disgorge those it had swallowed up, according to the Scripture.

Implied in this comparison is the idea that the fish corresponds to both the tomb and the netherworld.

The Roman statesman Cassiodorus (485–585 CE) goes one step further in his 'Exposition on the Psalms 129.1'. In one and the same sentence, he manages not only to liken the fish to hell but also to acknowledge, in line with the biblical account, that the fish is Jonah's saviour:

> Finally from these depths Jonah, who was set in the whale's belly and had entered hell alive, spoke to the Lord with silent vehemence. The whale was a house of prayer for the prophet, a harbour for him when shipwrecked, a home amid the waves, a happy resource at a desperate time. He was not swallowed for sustenance but to gain rest; and by a wondrous and novel precedent the beast's belly yielded up its food unharmed, rather than consumed by the normally damaging process of digestion.

Referring explicitly to the dual connotations of the womb and the tomb, Jacob of Serug maintains that Jonah's sojourn in the fish prefigures Jesus's conception in the Virgin Mary (Eng. transl. Kitchen 2011: 35–36):

> A wronged dead one who is alive in destruction and is not destroyed
> The Living One who was not dead, they carried off and buried, casting him away.
> [...]
> A new foetus which entered through the mouth to the belly of his mother
> And he became a conception without intercourse by a great miracle. (31. 418:3–8)
> [...]
> Three days in the heart of the earth Jonah was buried
> So that the road of our Lord which was to the tomb should be explained.
> The prophet in the fish and the Lord of the prophets in the death which he desired
>   (35. 422:17–19)

In contrast, the Christian martyr Zeno of Verona (300–371 CE) focuses exclusively on the connotations of hell (*Tractatus* 2.17) (Eng. transl. Ziolkowski 2007: 389):

> We have no doubt that the whale is hell; just as Jonah was in the belly of the whale three days and three nights and upon being vomited out betook himself to the city of Nineveh, so too the Lord, the day after being resurrected from hell, betook himself to the city of Jerusalem before going to heaven.

The *Glossa Ordinaria* offers the somewhat incongruous comment that as much as the fish/hell rejoiced in consuming Jonah, it lamented just as much in vomiting him up.

The understanding of the fish as hell is also attested, although to a significantly lesser extent, in the writings of the Reformers. It features prominently in the Geneva Bible notes to Jonah 2:1, 2, and 6, where the fish is being likened to death and its belly to a grave and a place of darkness.

3.6 The Fish in Mediaeval Depictions

Building on the conceptualization of Jonah's fish as a symbol of hell, the fifth-century poem *Hymnus Ieiunantium* ('Hymn for those who fast') by the Roman Christian poet Prudentius (348–405/413 CE) envisages the fish that swallowed Jonah as 'a vast and living grave' (lines 113–115):

> Hurled headlong from the deck, he falls
> And sinks beneath the engulfing wave,
> Then, seized by monstrous jaws, is plunged
> Into a vast and living grave.

The fourteenth-century English poem 'Patience' likewise employs references to Hell in its long and detailed description of the horrors of the fish (lines 274–275, 306):

> And stood up in Warlow's stomach, that stank as the devil.
> There in fat and filth that savoured of hell,
> [...]
> Out of the hole you heard me, from hell's womb

The same link between Jonah's fish and Hell is made in art. In many mediaeval paintings, the entrance to Hell resembles the gaping mouth of a huge (marine) monster. It is commonly held that this imagery first appeared in Anglo-Saxon art and then spread across Europe, and continued to be prevalent in depictions of the 'Last Judgement' and 'Harrowing of Hell' until the Renaissance (Schmidt 1995: 13–16). At one point in this process, the demonization of Jonah's fish led to its conflation with the Leviathan as a symbol of the Devil, i.e. someone whom

Jesus – the 'true Jonah' – killed when he defeated death through his resurrection (Friedman 1981: 106–109, 122). The Leviathan/Jonah's fish thus came to be conceptualized as a monstrous animal whose mouth swallows the damned during the Last Judgement (Schmidt 1995: 52–60). The Anglo-Saxon collection called *Vercelli Homilies* (4:46–48), for example, likens Satan to a dragon which is swallowing the damned (Eng. transl. Hofmann 2008: 85):

> [they] never come out of the pit of snakes and of the throat of the dragon which is called Satan.

It is not self-evident how mediaeval readers arrived at the identification of Jonah's fish with the Leviathan and the Devil. What follows here is a possible scenario. A likely starting point is Job 40:25 [Eng. 41:1], a passage that conjures up the image of the Leviathan being captured by a hook as if it were a fish. Other passages in the Hebrew Bible also describe the Leviathan as some form of dragon or sea monster.[2] These passages were then put into dialogue with Rev 12:9, which identifies 'the great dragon' (Greek *drakon*) with the Devil, as well as with Rev 20:2, where 'the dragon, that old serpent' likewise is equated with the Devil. As Jonah's fish began to be depicted in early Christian art as a sea monster, inspired by the term *ketos* in the LXX (cf. Davis 2000: 77), the steps to associate the fish with the Devil and to identify it with the Leviathan were not so far. According to Noegel, who has traced the development from Jonah's fish to Leviathan, via the Greek translation in the LXX, the LXX chose the translation *ketos* in order to encourage readers to identify Jonah's fish with the great *tannin* ('sea monster', e.g. Gen 1:21), a term which in turn is connected with the Leviathan. Moreover, the Book of Jonah itself contains a web of textual allusions which serve to link not only the fish but also Jonah himself to the sea monster of Chaos (Noegel 2015: 237, 240–258).

Be that as it may, later readers certainly made this connection, whether intended by the LXX translator or not. In *The Whale*, for instance, an Old English poem preserved in the tenth-century *Exeter Book* (Exeter Cathedral Library MS 3501, folio 96b–97b), the mouth of Hell is compared to a whale's mouth, and the whale is understood as the servant of the Devil or even as the Devil himself. In this poem, the monster/whale is given the name *Fastitocalon* and is described as a cunning monster that sinks seafarers and lures fish into its mouth to be devoured. The fish thus serves simultaneously as a symbol of Hell itself and as the Devil personified who entices the unaware sinners towards destruction. This description of the creature probably owes its imagination partly to the Leviathan and partly to Jonah's fish (Schmidt 1995: 62–63; Eng. transl. Thorpe 1842: 360–364).

The depiction of the entrance to Hell as a giant set of jaws is a prevalent image in Christian art. Ödeshög Church, Sweden, for example, features

FIGURE 4   Illustrations of Hell mouth from Ödeshög church, Sweden.

a painting from 1736 by Daniel Blavér and Annika Jönsdotter Daggren (see Figure 4). Christ features as the judge of the world, whereas the archangel Michael separates between the 'sheep' and the 'goats'. The latter group (on the right) are entering hell through the mouth of a sea creature.[3]

The Christian conflation of Jonah's fish with a monster of Hell is also well illustrated in the Church of Saints Peter and Paul, situated in the town of Duszniki-Zdroj in the Lower Silesia Province of Poland (see Figure 5). In a clear reference to the Jonah narrative, its Baroque pulpit is shaped as a whale. The preacher stands inside the mouth of the fish while preaching (presumably) on the dangers of sin and the need for repentance.

The same conflation of Jonah's fish with the Leviathan is found in the Elizabethan stage play *A Looking Glass for London and England* (lines 1460–1479),

FIGURE 5   Photo of the Baroque pulpit in the Church of Saints Peter and Paul, situated in the town of Duszniki-Zdroj in the Lower Silesia Province of Poland. Source: Jacek Halicki. Licensed under CC BY-SA 3.0.

written by Shakespeare's contemporaries Thomas Lodge (1558–1625 CE) and Robert Green (1558–1592 CE). In the play, Jonah laments that he has been swallowed by the Leviathan ('the proud Leviathan that scours the seas', line 1467) and compares the whale's belly to 'deepest hell' (line 1478). To visualize this on stage, a hell mouth theatrical 'prop' was used to represent the whale. It probably consisted of a wooden frame in the shape of a mouth, which belched smoke, fire, and fireworks (Sager 2013: 53, 64).

> Lord of the light, thou maker of the world
> Behold thy hands of mercy reares me up,
> Loe from the hideous bowels of this fish,
> Thou hast returnd me to the wished aire,
> Loe here apparant witnesse of thy power,
> The proud Leviathan that scoures the seas,
> […]
> Out of the belly of the deepest hell,
> I cride, and thou didst heare my voice O God.

We can observe some related imagery in Francis Quarles' poem 'A Feast for Worms', section VI, from 1620:

> Even so the Leviathan set open
> His beam-like jaws, (prepar'd for such a boon)
> And at a morsel swallowed Jonah down,
> [...]
> Jonah was Tenant to his living Grave
> Embowell'd deep in this stupendious Cave.

3.7. The Fish as a Prison (as Hospitable as Hell)

A few modern poetic retellings use Jonah's time inside the fish to express conflict and alienation between God/the fish on the one hand and Jonah on the other. In words of the American poet Hart Crane (1899–1932 CE), Jonah asks God to keep him in the fish, unforgiven, to keep the distance between them. His poem 'After Jonah', a title that suggests both the sense of 'departing from' and 'in the footsteps of', depicts God as a hellish deity who tortures Jonah (cf. Sherwood 2000: 172–173):

> [...]
> There is no settling tank in God. It must be borne
> that even His bowels are too delicate to board
> a sniping thief that has a pious beard.
> We must hail back the lamb that went unsheared.
> O sweet deep whale as ever reamed the sky
> with high white gulfs of vapor, castigate
> our sins, but be hospitable as Hell.
> And keep me to the death like ambergris,
> sealed up, and unforgiven in my cell.

From a different perspective, the biblical scholar Jione Havea likens the fish both to a 'maximum prison' and a 'sanctuary'. He further highlights the significance of the verb 'to swallow' in this context: those biblical characters (such as the deep [Ps 69:15], Sheol [Prov 1:12], the earth [Exod 15:12], and the ground [Num 16:30]) that swallow objects do so in order to punish or destroy them (Havea 2020: ch. 7).

4. The Fish as a Matter of Embarrassment

A few ancient authors, when tasked with the retelling of the Jonah narrative, were clearly embarrassed by the whole 'fish incident', given its fantastic dimensions. Josephus (*Ant.* 9, 213) glosses over the fish as quickly as possible. Apparently following the LXX, he claims that the fish that swallowed Jonah was a *ketos* and reports the whole incident rather matter-of-factly (Eng. transl. Whiston 1987: 260):

> It is also related that Jonah was swallowed down by a whale, and that when he had been there three days, and as many nights, he was vomited out upon the Euxine Sea, and this alive, and without any hurt upon his body.

Josephus's retelling betrays no indication that the creature that swallows Jonah was monstrous in any manner of speaking. In fact, Josephus consistently aims at downplaying the miraculous aspects of the Book of Jonah. God never speaks to the fish, and Jonah prays only after leaving its belly. Rather, in a detached manner, Josephus reports that according to the 'story' of Jonah, Jonah was swallowed by a fish. Likewise, using passive voice, Jonah was *cast up* on the shore of the Black Sea (Feldman 1992: 14–16).

5. The Fish as Symbol of Human Life

The image of the fish swallowing Jonah has captured the imagination of poets aplenty. Many of these poetic descriptions share the sense of dread, power, and monstrosity. The fourth-century poem *De Jona et Nineveh* attributed to Tertullian illustrates these aspects well, as it describes the appearance of the fish (lines 124–129):

> And from the eddy's depth a whale
> Outrising on the spot, scaly with shells,
> Unravelling his body's train, 'gan urge
> More near the waves, shocking the gleaming brine,
> Seizing-at God's command-the prey; which, rolled
> From the poop's summit prone, with slimy jaws.

In more recent retellings (cf. also Jonah 1:12), the fish commonly becomes a symbol of a person's life. In the poem 'Jonas' by the French poet and journalist Jean-Paul de Dadelsen (1913–1957 CE), for instance, people are referred to as those who 'lived with us in the mouth of the whale' (*Ils ont habité avec nous dans la gueule de la baleine*), and life is conceived as a 'journey in the whale' (*notre voyage à nous, c'est/le voyage dans la baleine*) (part one: 'Invocation liminaire'). The poem continues by declaring that everything – war, the city, the country, society, its taboos, its vanity, its ignorance, marriage, love of self, life incarnate, the creation – is attributed to the fish. In this way, life in 'the whale' is life itself, and to be swallowed up by the whale is to be swallowed up by all that threatens to consume us (Showalter Jr 1982: 42, 44–45, cf. Frieling 1999: 71–87).

The fish in the poem 'Jonah's prayer' (*Jónás imája*) by the Hungarian poet Mihály Babits (1883–1941 CE), written in 1938 after the *Anschluss*, conveys similar sentiments, where the fish is a symbol for both the struggles in life and the final death (Eng. transl. Zollman).

> [...]
> as lazy Jonah shirked to no avail,
> and then for three days rotted in the Whale,
> I too went down and shared those deadly bays
> of hot throbbing pain, but for thirty days,
> for thirty years or three hundred, who knows,
> to find, before my book will firmly close
> an even blinder and eternal
> Whale shall swallow my last departing journal,
> [...].

In Albert Camus's short story *Jonas, ou l'artiste au travail* (cf. above, Jonah 1:12), the fish likewise serves as a symbol of the forces that engulf Jonas – the city, society, vanity, marriage, self-love, and sexuality – and from which he flees when he retreats up to the loft. In parallel, Jonas's loft, like Jonah's fish, becomes the place where the protagonist takes refuge. The loft itself is a kind of fish where Jonas is trapped but which also gives him security, albeit potentially insubstantial. Jonas's time in the loft is symbolic of his feelings of 'betweenness'. Jonas declares that he is content inside the loft, never having to work again; he can listen in on humankind yet is spared from actual interaction with it. Ultimately, however, Jonas falls down (from the loft and into his house) (Showalter Jr 1982: 41). While in the loft, Jonas is alone (*solitaire*) because nobody has crawled in there to share his space, yet he is not fully alone as he is able to talk with his family. Jonah is also not abandoned but rather part of a community (*solidaire*) because, being in his own home, he depends on his family to bring him food, oil for his lamp, and general maintenance (McGregor 1995: 55–56). Jonas learns finally that the common condition of life – the very essence of existence – is solitude, yet solitude together with others: 'he now no longer participates in the fantasized and rationalized existence of evasive existentialism, but in the raw, unadorned absurd reality of universal exile [...] with all humanity' (McGregor 1995: 64).

The parallels between Jonas and the biblical Jonah are clear: they share the same name, they spend time inside a dark space, and they come out alive. In the words of Dücker, Camus's short story speaks of Jonas's symbolic death and cultural rebirth (Dücker 2011: 348). Further, as argued by McGregor, their similar points of departure are significant: they both personify their respective societies and the individual's struggle with that same society. Jonah, the prophet, must leave his close-knit Israelite society and venture out alone to rescue others, and Jonas, the artist, is an individual who must reject the status quo. Yet they also differ from one another: whereas Jonah remains confident in God's ability to save and exits the fish not that much different from when he entered it, Jonas leaves the loft a changed man who is ready for an open-ended future. Finally, according to McGregor, while Jonah in Jonah 1:12 is being punished for wilful disobedience against God, Jonas's failures belong more in the realm of personal shortcomings against family, friends, and social amenities (McGregor 1995: 65–67). At this point, McGregor's reading is not supported by the biblical narrative. Jonah is not tossed overboard as a punishment; he is tossed to still the storm which God has set in motion in order to force Jonah to carry out God's command.

Dücker offers a different interpretation of the allusion to the biblical Jonah in Camus's short story. For him, the biblical Jonah is what Camus's Jonas aspires to be. Although Jonah's assertion of his will against God is costly – he is tossed overboard – he struggles to maintain his reputation (as a prophet), and the people of Nineveh believe him because of his unblemished reputation. In a sense, after his 'rebirth' as he fell from the loft, Jonas has taken over Jonah's role and function (Dücker 2011: 360–362).

The Romanian poet, playwright, and novelist Marin Sorescu (1936–1996 CE) wrote the one-person play *Jonah: A Tragedy in Four Scenes* (*Iona*) (1968).[4] In this drama, Jonah represents the condition of human existence. He finds himself swallowed by a huge fish. Thinking that he has made his escape from it by hacking through its stomach, he finds himself inside a bigger fish, and yet another even bigger one. At the end of the drama, Jonah realizes that he can never escape this prison that constitutes his life. He then takes the knife and cuts open his own stomach.

The American poet, literary critic, and art historian David Shapiro (1947–) has written a long poem called 'In a Blind Garden', published in 1988, about the experiences of loss and lack of answers for the future, using Jonah in the fish as the leading metaphor.

6. Let the Fish Speak!

A few retellings give the fish a voice. The German poet Günter Eich (1907–1972 CE), in his short text 'Jonas', looks at the Jonah narrative from the perspective of the fish (Eich 1999: 90–91). He stresses the obedient character of the fish, which harkens to God's voice and does his bidding. From the Hebrides off the west coast of Scotland via the Sargasso Sea to Tierra del Fuego at the very bottom of South America and on to the Antarctic, the fish is looking for Jonah so that he can fulfil God's command. The fish mourns that it has had to leave its own offspring near the Hebrides and doubts that it will ever find Jonah. In the end, the fish ponders whether it will devour Jonah or whether the prophet will devour it (see further Wiegmann 2005: 326; Kühlmann 2011: 320–321). While the story never intersects with the biblical account chronologically, it nonetheless contrasts Jonah's disobedience with the obedience of the fish. It further parallels Jonah's journey with that of the fish through the themes of futility, exile, and lack of resolution (see further Jonah 4:4).

The modern choral work *Jonah: A Musical Morality* by William Mathias likewise gives the fish a voice, having it call out and look for Jonah:

> Narrator: And the great fish called,
>
> Choir: Jonah! Jonah! Where are you, Jonah? Where are you, Jonah? Jonah, are you there?
>
> [Bar-rest]
>
> Narrator: And the Lord commanded the great fish,
> Choir: Swallow up Jonah! Swallow up Jonah! Swallow, swallow, swallow!

On the same topic of obedience, Elie Wiesel questions whether the whale really had to be that obedient (Wiesel 1981: 142):

> Does the whale really have to obey God? Could it not ask God what evil it has committed to be forced to inflict such suffering 'onto this man who is His and His alone?' True, the whale saves Jonah, but why only after three days and three nights? Why not have it spit him back ashore right away?

Later in the same chapter, Wiesel revises his estimation of the whale as he stresses that he, in parallel, swallows 'the suicidal prophet but it also saves him; it could stifle him; it does not. It could keep him prisoner longer; instead, it sets him ashore safe and sound' (Wiesel 1981: 147).

Focusing on the fact that 'God appointed' the fish, Barnes's retelling in his book *A History of the World in 10½ Chapters* highlights not only the lack of free will of the fish but God's bullying behaviour towards it (cf. also Jonah 1:3):

> [T]he beast is evidently as much of a pawn as Jonah […] the great fish is casually dismissed from the story the moment its narrative function has been fulfilled […] God finger-flips the blubbery jail hither and thither like a war-game admiral nudging his fleet across maps of the sea. (p. 177)

In a very different manner, *The Journey with Jonah*, a novella for children written by the American author Madeleine L'Engle (1918–2007 CE), is populated with talking animals who offer a running commentary on the Jonah narrative. Several of them, among them the whale, fill the role of God. As expressed by the whale (p. 41):

> How else should God speak
> Except through his own creation?
> All creatures great or weak
> Live through his contemplation.
> He will not lose sight of anyone whom
> he may seek.

At first, the whale is humorously explaining the situation to a little fish that he has swallowed (by mistake) at the same time as he swallowed Jonah (p. 36):

> Little fish, we are three days' journey from dry land. At the end of that time I shall vomit forth this prophet, and I only hope my digestion isn't ruined before then. If you aren't careful, I shall vomit you forth upon the dry land, too.

He later takes on God's role and encourages Jonah to reflect on this situation (p. 37):

> Attend, prophet, without arrogance or condescension
> Nineveh is waiting for your utterance
> [...]
> Take your fingers out of your ears, O prophet, and attend.
> Your flight is useless. Let your disobedience end.
> God has prepared me simply to confound you.
> And you are accustomed to God: this should not astound you.

The tragedy *Jona: Trauerspiel in fünf Akten*, composed in 1988 by the German playwright and author Peter Hacks (1928–2003 CE), provides a different perspective (see further Doms 2011: 379–381). When the Assyrian army general Eskar conveys his compassion for Jonah's experience in the fish, Jonah retorts that the fish had it much worse (my translation):

> Eskar: Then you obviously suffered more than ever a person did.
> Jonah: Do you think so?
> Eskar: Three days in the belly of a whale.
> Jonah: For my part, I wonder whether the whale has not suffered more than ever a fish did. I prayed, of course, during the whole three days. Imagine yourself, with a praying herring inside you.

7. Jonah and Pinocchio

As we have already seen, many works of fiction allude to the biblical Book of Jonah. Yet, the book *Le avventure di Pinocchio* (*Pinocchio: The Tale of a Puppet*), written by the Italian author Carlo Collodi (1826–1890 CE) in 1883, has a special place in the reception history of Jonah due to its sustained interaction with the Jonah narrative. *Pinocchio* tells of the woodcarver Geppetto who creates a wooden puppet and names him Pinocchio. The puppet dreams of becoming a real boy. Pinocchio, however, is not particularly nice. When he is born, he laughs derisively in his creator's face and steals his wig, he frequently gets carried away by bad company, and he often lies (and when he does, or is under stress, his nose becomes longer). After struggling and weeping over his deformed nose, the Blue Fairy summons woodpeckers to peck it back to normal. Pinocchio's bad behaviour, rather than being charming or endearing, is meant to serve as a warning. Collodi originally intended the story to be a tragedy. He chastises Pinocchio for his lack of moral fibre and his persistent rejection of responsibility and desire for fun: Pinocchio ought to work, be good, and study.

The story of Pinocchio and the story of Jonah converge in their respective protagonists' meeting with a sea creature. In the book *Pinocchio*, Pinocchio finds his father in the belly of the terrible 'dog fish' (*pesce-cane*), later referred to as a shark (but never as a whale [*balena*]). (In contrast, the animated film Pinocchio (1940), produced by Walt Disney Productions, features a whale.) Pinocchio says 'Oh father, dear father! Have I found you at last? Now I shall never, never leave you again'. Geppetto has been living on his ship inside the shark for two years, reduced to a compartment in the shark's stomach, eating the food from the ship. Now he is down to his last crumbs and his last candle. Pinocchio asks, 'What will happen when this last candle burns out?' to which Geppetto answers, 'And then, my dear, we'll find ourselves in darkness'. Faced with this prospect, Pinocchio suggests that they must attempt to run out of the shark's mouth and dive into the sea. As Geppetto cannot swim, Pinocchio asks his father to climb onto his shoulders so that he can carry him safely to shore. Geppetto queries how a marionette will have that strength, whereupon Pinocchio responds that if they die, they shall at least die together. Pinocchio swims away with his old father on his back and they are saved. Throughout the novel, Pinocchio undergoes a series of 'conversions'. Pinocchio's act of saving his father, as well as his willingness to provide for him and his decision to devote himself to work, study, and being good, helps transforming him into a real boy.

Jonah and *Pinocchio* share several similarities. First, God and Geppetto (and also The Fairy with Turquoise Hair) seek to help their 'boy' to change. They both, in a sense, send the fish. Second, the rebellious prophet/the rebellious puppet both end up getting swallowed by a sea creature after failing to follow the instructions of their 'father'. Third, Jonah and Pinocchio both find redemption in the belly of a whale. Jonah can only become a real prophet if he saves the people of Nineveh/ Pinocchio can only become a real boy if he saves his father. The way they carry out this task is different, however. Jonah asks God for a second chance to prove that he is worthy to fulfil God's plan, no matter where it leads him. Pinocchio proves that he is brave, truthful, and selfless (and thus earns the right to become a real boy) by risking his life to travel into the depths of the ocean to save his father. The endings are also different: whereas *Jonah* depicts a prophet who has not really changed at all, *Pinocchio* concludes with a 'Happy Ending' and a truly transformed boy. In this sense, Collodi de-problematizes the Jonah narrative to make it fit the genre of children's literature (see further Föcking 2011: 429–440; cf. also Gale, 'Pinocchio and Religion'). He also aligns it with the Christian appropriation of the book by turning Jonah into a story about ultimate redemption.

The encounter between Jonah and Pinocchio is also the butt of several jokes. The first season of the Israeli television programme 'The Jews are Coming' (2014), consisting of satire sketches, features a scene where Pinocchio and Jonah, sitting inside the fish and eating out of cans, are discussing whether 'everything that is written in the book *Pinocchio* / the Bible happened in reality'. As Jonah insists that 'all that is written in the Bible happened in reality' (כל מה שכתוב בתנ"ך קרה באמת), his nose grows longer.

8. What did the Fish Really Look Like?

There are many depictions of Jonah's fish, ranging from a relatively fish-like creature to a huge sea monster. The range of the depictions further stretches from graffiti to masterpieces now hanging in national museums of art.

In the Patriarchal Basilica (Friuli Venezia Giulia), Aquileia (Italy), a mosaic from the fourth-century CE depicts Jonah being swallowed by some kind of (sea) creature (see Figure 6).

The Kennicott Bible, a mediaeval Spanish manuscript of the Hebrew Bible that is currently stored in the Bodleian Library in Oxford, offers another depiction of Jonah's fish (folio 305r [1476]). The artist, Joseph Ibn Hayyim, provides the reader with highly stylized figures in rich colours.

A very different image is preserved in the graffiti inscription in the nave of Norwich Cathedral (England) from the fifteenth century. It features a ship about to be swallowed by an enormous open-mouthed whale. The graffiti is accompanied by a prayer for a fisherman or mariner. It is very likely that the whale is Jonah's whale (Gye 2013).

A fourteenth-century illustration from Jami al-Tavarikh (Compendium of Chronicles), 'Jonah and the Whale', currently in the Metropolitan Museum of Art in New York, contains a surprisingly 'fish-like' fish (see Figure 7). This image is also noteworthy in that it contains the common motif of the angel Gabriel bringing clothes to Jonah (see below, Jonah 2:11).

Hundreds of other depictions can be cited alongside these four representative examples.

9. Did It Really Happen?

So far, we have explored the *depiction* of the fish in the biblical text and beyond. Here, we shall look more closely at those retellings that, in some form or

114 *Jonah Through the Centuries*

Figure 6 Patriarchal Basilica (Friuli Venezia Giulia), Aquileia (Italy) – a mosaic from the fourth-century CE depicts Jonah. Aquileia – Basilica – Mosaic with Jonah thrown on the beach. Source: YukioSanjo. Licensed under CC BY-SA 3.0.

Figure 7 A fourteenth-century illustration from Jami al-Tavarikh. Jonah and the Whale. Source: Metropolitan Museum of Art. Public Domain.

another, make the claim that Jonah, the historical human being, really survived inside a large sea creature. These explanations may be naturalistic insofar as they point to physical evidence, and they may be anecdotal inasmuch as they appeal to comparable stories. To set the stage, Luther's words on Jonah 1:17 in his German commentary are apt:

> Who would believe this story and not regard it a lie and a fairy tale if it were not recorded in Scripture?

9.1 Naturalistic Explanations

Beginning with those explanations that focus on physical evidence, Augustine's discussion, found in his 'Letter 102', Question VI.31 from 409 CE is noteworthy. Augustine draws attention to a skeleton, the huge ribs of which were on display in a public place in Carthage and 'well known to all men there'. He argues that those who have seen this ribcage should not doubt the possibility that Jonah could have entered through its mouth and had enough space within its wide cavern.

Many scholars in the nineteenth century followed suit, as they explored (natural) ways in which Jonah might have survived inside the fish. Many of these suggestions were collated (and ultimately rejected) in John Kitto's *Cyclopeida of Biblical Literature* (pp. 142–143):

> Less, in his tract, *Vom Historischen Styl der Urwelt*, supposed that all difficulty might be removed by imagining that Jonah, when thrown into the sea, was taken up by a ship having a large fish for a figure-head – a theory somewhat more pleasing than the rancid hypothesis of Anton, who fancied that the prophet took refuge in the interior of a dead whale, floating near the spot where he was cast overboard (Rosen. Prolegom. in Jon. p. 328). Not unlike the opinion of Less is that of Charles Taylor, in his Fragments affixed to Calmet's Dictionary, No. cxlv., that it signifies a life-preserver, a notion which, as his manner is, he endeavours to support by mythological metamorphoses founded on the form and names of the famous fish-god of Philistia.
>
> [...] There is little ground for the supposition of Bishop Jebb, that the asylum of Jonah was not in the stomach of a whale, but in a cavity of its throat, which, according to naturalists, is a very capacious receptacle, sufficiently large, as Captain Scoresby asserts, to contain a merchant ship's jolly-boat full of men (Bishop Jebb, Sacred Literature, p. 178).
>
> [...] Granting all these facts as proof of what is termed the economy of miracles, still must we say, in reference to the supernatural preservation of Jonah, Is anything too hard for the Lord?

These types of views are alluded to, yet likewise also discarded, in Melville's *Moby-Dick* (Chapter 83, 'Jonah Historically Regarded'). In this chapter, the narrator

Ishmael discusses the historicity of the Book of Jonah and highlights that many people in Nantucket doubt that Jonah stayed alive inside a whale. One man especially, Sag-Harbor, voices several reasons why Jonah would never have survived:

> Another reason which Sag-Harbor (he went by that name) urged for his want of faith in this matter of the prophet, was something obscurely in reference to his incarcerated body and the whale's gastric juices. But this objection likewise falls to the ground, because a German exegetist supposes that Jonah must have taken refuge in the floating body of a dead whale – even as the French soldiers in the Russian campaign turned their dead horses into tents, and crawled into them. Besides, it has been divined by other continental commentators, that when Jonah was thrown overboard from the Joppa ship, he straightway effected his escape to another vessel nearby, some vessel with a whale for a figure-head; and, I would add, possibly called 'The Whale', as some craft are nowadays christened the 'Shark', the 'Gull', the 'Eagle'. Nor have there been wanting learned exegetists who have opined that the whale mentioned in the book of Jonah merely meant a life-preserver – an inflated bag of wind – which the endangered prophet swam to, and so was saved from a watery doom. (Herman 1851 / Richard Bentley / Public domain)

As shown convincingly by Pardes, Melville – though the voice of Sag-Harbor – is here offering a parody of the scholarly opinions quoted in John Kitto's *Cyclopeida of Biblical Literature*, as well as many other conservative critical scholars of the time who sought to defend the historicity of Jonah's sojourn inside the fish by appealing to naturalistic explanations (Pardes 2005: 141–144; Sprang 2011: 449–450). In response, the narrator Ishmael rejects these arguments ('foolish arguments of old Sag-Harbor only evinced his foolish pride of reason'), and readers of *Moby-Dick* are given the distinct impression that the book as a whole rejects both the (orthodox) historical interpretation of Jonah's sojourn inside the fish, as well as any (liberal) attempt at explaining its miraculous aspects naturalistically (New 1998: 281–303).

9.2 Anecdotal Evidence

Turning to anecdotal evidence, many stories of purportedly true incidents narrate how human beings, sometimes together with their vessels, have been swallowed by a whale and survived to tell the tale. Here, it suffices to name but a few (see further Ziolkowski 2007: 65–92). Lucian of Samosata (a city on the Euphrates in today's Turkey) (second century CE) wrote a parody of travel tales, called *A True Story*. Among many fantastic adventures, it narrates how Lucian, his companions, and their ship were swallowed and trapped within a giant whale (Book I, section 30) (Ziolkowski 2007: 76–77):

> But it seems that a turn for the better often means the start of worse troubles. We'd been sailing for just two days in good weather, and the third dawn

was breaking, when towards the east we suddenly saw a large number of sea-monsters and whales. One of them in particular, the largest of all, was about one hundred and seventy miles long. He came up on us with gaping mouth, lashing up the sea to a surge of foam far in advance of him, and showing teeth much larger than human phalluses, all of them sharp as stakes and white as ivory. We embraced and bade one another a last farewell, and waited. In no time he was on us, and with one gulp swallowed us down, ship and all. However, he didn't manage to crush us first with his teeth, as the ship slipped through the gaps into his interior.

The tenth-century French monk Letaldus composed a poem which has been called 'About a Certain Fisherman Whom a Whale Swallowed'. The poem has survived in two manuscripts: a twelfth-century and an eleventh-century manuscript (Ziolkowski 1984: 107–118). The poem tells of a humble English fisherman who, together with his boat, was swallowed by a whale. He survived for four days inside the whale and ultimately succeeded in killing the animal by setting fire to his vessel (cf. the Disney version of *Pinocchio*, above), as well as damaging its flank from the inside with his sword (cf. *La meva Cristina*, below). The whale washes ashore and the fisherman is freed from the carcass by the townspeople of Rochester. The fisherman survives but his hair has fallen out, he is blind, and his skin is partly eaten away, yet he is soon restored to full health. As Ziolkowski has argued, this story is unlikely to be an independent witness of the survival of a man inside a whale but instead a reworking of earlier mythical whale lore, among them the Book of Jonah (Ziolkowski 2007: 67–69). This narrative is thus not evidence of the historical veracity of the Jonah narrative; it rather shows the literary impact of the same narrative and thus falls into the category of 'retellings'.

Moreover, as noted earlier, the Jonah narrative can be read as a myth. These types of retellings form, in a sense, a continuation of such myths. The idea of human beings being swallowed and later disgorged by sea beasts is attested in stories worldwide, of which the aforementioned myths of Heracles and Perseus are early European examples. Letaldus's poem thus stands in the combined tradition of the widely spread folk story motif of a man trapped inside a whale and the biblical tradition of the Book of Jonah (Ziolkowski 2007: 73–82). In fact, the concluding part of the poem 'About a Certain Fisherman Whom a Whale Swallowed' makes an explicit reference to the sailor being 'like another Jonah' (*Ionas uelut alter*, line 185) (Eng. transl. Ziolkowski 2007: 243–248; original Latin, see Bisanti, lines 185–186):

And then the shipwrecked man, like another Jonah, in the middle of the city apprises the astonished people about the miracle of life restored.

In more recent times, several stories report how humans allegedly have survived inside sea creatures. At times, these reports have been appealed to as proof of the historical veracity of the biblical Jonah narrative. For instance, a man named James Bartley (1870–1909 CE) is the protagonist of a nineteenth-century story. Bartley recalls how he in 1891 was swallowed by a sperm whale and found alive, four days later, after that the whale had died of constipation. When Bartley came out of the whale, he was blind, and his skin was bleached white from the stomach fluids of the whale (Wilson 1927: 635–638). The authenticity of this story has, however, been thoroughly refuted (see further Davis 1991: 224–237).

'And Jonah was in the belly of the fish for three days and three nights'

The statement in Jonah 2:1b [Eng. 1:17b] that Jonah was in the fish for three days and three nights has given rise to a prevalent New Testament typology, namely, that Jonah's ordeal in the fish is a type for Jesus's time in the realm of the dead between his death on Good Friday and his resurrection on Easter Sunday. The origin of this typology is found in Matt 12:39 – 'But none will be given it except the sign of the prophet Jonah' and Luke 11:30 – 'For as Jonah was a sign to the Ninevites'. It is, however, not immediately evident from the context what this sign constitutes. There are three common explanations:

  i. Genitive of apposition: *Jonah himself is the sign*. Jonah is the old preacher of repentance; Jesus is the new preacher. This interpretation is based on the above-mentioned typology of Jonah as a type for Christ.
  ii. Objective genitive: *the sign that Jonah experienced*. The sign is the three nights and days that Jonah experienced in the realm of death.
  iii. Subjective genitive: *the sign that Jonah gave*. The sign is Jonah's sermon to the people of Nineveh and, as such, his call to repentance.

As noted by Chow, it is also not clear that the same meaning of the sign applies to both the Lukan and the Matthaean traditions; rather, we must remain open to the possibility that the same words meant different things to particular readers in their different situations (Chow 1995: 18–19). In the ensuing discussion, we shall explore how all three interpretations play a role in the reception history of Jonah 2:1b.

1. Jonah's Three Days as a Type for Jesus's Death and Resurrection

The Church Fathers agree that the three days and the three nights in Jonah 2:1b point to Jesus's death and resurrection. There is, nonetheless, a very practical problem with this interpretation, namely, that it is difficult to arrive at 'three days and three nights' between Friday afternoon and Sunday pre-dawn. Jerome, for example, discusses at length what is involved when counting the days. Using the example of a man who leaves the house at nine o'clock one day and arrives at his other house at three o'clock the next day, Jerome maintains that it is correct to state that he has been travelling for two days even though he has not used all the hours of the two days. In the same way, it is three days between Jesus's death and his resurrection. Augustine, following suit, argues that parts of the first day, the whole of the second day, and parts of the third day should together count as three days. He finds further support for the Jonah/Jesus typology in Jonah's willingness to die so that the sailors might live ('Letter 102': *Question VI.32*):

> Just as Jonah passed from the ship to the belly of the whale, so Christ passed from the cross to the sepulchre, or into the abyss of death. And as Jonah suffered this for the sake of those who were endangered by the storm, so Christ suffered for the sake of those who are tossed on the waves of this world.

Cyril of Jerusalem likewise emphasizes the similarities between Jesus and Jonah: both were sent to preach repentance, both slept on board a boat, both went voluntarily towards their death, and both returned to life ('Catechetical Lecture 14:17–20'). Cyril of Alexandria too sees the mystery of Christ as foreshadowed and somehow represented in the story of the divinely inspired Jonah. He alludes to Jonah being tossed overboard to still the storm as he notes that Jesus willingly went to his death to make the storm abate; thus by his death we were saved:

> The tempest abated, the rains passed, and waves settled down, the force of the winds diminished, deep peace then prevailed, and we enjoyed fair weather of a spiritual kind, since Christ has suffered for us.

In parallel, many of the Church Fathers stress the distinction between Jonah and Jesus. Earlier, in the Introduction to his commentary, Cyril of Alexandria highlights that not everything which befell Jonah should be understood as relevant and applicable to the process of seeing Jonah as a type for Christ. In particular, the fact that he tries to flee from God's command is different from Jesus, who neither displayed any reluctance or lack of enthusiasm for his ministry nor tried to flee from the face of God. Further, while Jonah was disappointed in God's compassion, Jesus was not disappointed to see the nations saved. Theodoret of Cyrus likewise notes in his commentary to Jonah 2:3 that whereas Jesus faced both death and resurrection voluntarily, Jonah had no control over his life. That is, in fact, why Jonah calls the fish 'the belly of hell': the beast is deadly, and Jonah is already presumed dead. Jonah is alive only because *God* wills it so.

2. Jonah/Jesus Typology and the Arts

The understanding of Jonah as a prefiguration of Jesus's resurrection is a common trope in Christian art.

One of the most powerful examples is surely Michelangelo's depiction of Jonah in the Sistine Chapel (see Figure 8), in the row of colossal prophets and sibyls that line the walls of the ceiling. Their positioning is not chronological but hierarchical, with Jonah being positioned alone in the centre of the short wall. As the ceiling curves inwards, Jonah appears to be leaning forward, yet at the same time he is depicted as leaning backwards, creating a powerful image of a sculpture. His central position, as well as the fact that he is the only prophet without any form of scribal tool, emphasizes that Jonah himself, rather than any prophecy of his, is the sign that points towards Jesus's resurrection (see further Abrahams 2015: 12–13; Quint 2015: 416; Dotson 1979a: 227, 247).

The picture contains several features laden with Christian symbolism. Through the image of the fish, which appears behind him, Jonah clearly

FIGURE 8 Michelangelo's depiction of Jonah in the Sistine Chapel. Source: Sistine Chapel. Public Domain.

represents Jesus's resurrection. Furthermore, the plant in the background may be the *qiqayyon* that – understood by especially Augustine to be a symbol for the Old Covenant – was destroyed by the worm, alias Jesus, and thus also represents the salvation of the Gentiles (see further Jonah 4:7) (Dotson 1979b: 408–409).

Inherent in many of the typological interpretations of the three days is the sense that Jonah is an *imperfect* type of Christ, ultimately to be replaced by the perfect 'true Jonah', namely Jesus. This kind of anti-Jewish replacement theology is expressed clearly in a short reflection on Jonah (17,188, stanza 11), written by Adam of St Victor, a French poet and composer (d. 1146) (Eng. transl. Friedman 1981: 103–104, 127 endnote 10):

> In the story of the whale
> Jonah fugitive
> Figures forth the True Jonah;
> After three days he came live
> From the whale's narrow belly.
> The flowr of Synagoga withers
> And that of Ecclesia blooms.

3. Jonah's Time inside the Fish as Punishment for His Sins

In parallel with the typological interpretation, many Christian interpretations of the Jonah narrative portray the fish, as well as Jonah's time inside the fish, as God's punishment for Jonah's sin of disobedience. Jonah sinned by disobeying God's command in Jonah 1:3, and he is now being punished. This idea reaches prominence in the writings of the Church Fathers. The so-called *Constitutions of the Holy Apostles*, an early Christian text that sought to offer authoritative prescriptions and guidance on moral conduct for clergy and possibly also for laity, positions Jonah next to David, who repented of his sin (with Bathsheba), and Hezekiah, who remitted his offence (of boasting). It states that God caused Jonah, upon his refusal to preach to the Ninevites, to be swallowed up by the whale. Yet, upon praying to God, Jonah retrieved his life from corruption (2.3.22). Thus, in contrast to the biblical narrative where the fish is God's tool for saving Jonah, this treatise conceives Jonah's sojourn inside the fish as punishment for his disobedience.

Luther's views, expressed in his German commentary, may also fall into this category. At first, Luther envisages Jonah's incarceration inside the fish as an experience akin to torture:

> Jonah must have thought these the longest days and nights ever lived under the sun. It must have seemed an interminably long time that he sat there in the dark.

Yes, I suppose, that he occasionally lay down and stood up. He saw neither sun nor moon and was unable to compute the passage of time. Nor did he know where in the sea he was travelling about with the fish. How often lung and liver must have pained him! How strange his abode must have been among the intestines and the huge ribs!

As his commentary progresses through the psalm in Jonah 2 (vv. 3, 4), Luther comments that much of it speaks of God and his wrath. Notably, the references to waves in Jonah 2:4 [Eng. 2:3] and Jonah's claim of being cast away from God's presence in Jonah 2:5 [Eng. 2:4] are all aspects of Jonah's penance.

The same sense of punishment is attested also in the Geneva Bible note to Jonah 1:17. The Lord sent the fish to chastise the prophet 'with a most terrible spectacle of death', yet this act would in parallel also strengthen and encourage him, showing that God was standing by him when he sought to carry out his duty that God had commanded him.

Along similar lines, Father Mapple, in his sermon in *Moby-Dick* ch. 9, expands on Jonah's realization that he has been swallowed by the fish because of his sins:

> He feels that his dreadful punishment is just. He leaves all his deliverance to God, contenting himself with this, that in spite of all his pains and pangs, he will still look towards his holy temple. And here, shipmates, is true and faithful repentance; not clamorous for pardon, but grateful for punishment. And how pleasing to God was this conduct in Jonah, is shown in the eventual deliverance of him from the sea and the whale. Shipmates, I do not place Jonah before you to be copied for his sin, but I do place him before you as a model for repentance. Sin not; but if you do, take heed to repent of it like Jonah. (Herman 1851 / Richard Bentley / Public domain)

In being swallowed by the fish, Jonah is made aware that he is totally corrupt. His punishment is deserved and an expression of God's justice (Herbert Jr 1969: 1614; Sprang 2011: 447). In this manner, the sermon transforms Jonah, rather than the people of Nineveh (who never make an appearance in Father Mapple's sermon), into a symbol of the true penitent sinner whom everyone should emulate.

As we have noted, in Christian retellings, Jonah's major sin is that of *disobedience*. In Muslim tradition, however, Jonah's major sin is that of *anger*. Q21:87 states that 'And remember when he (*Jonah*) went off in *anger*'. This outburst takes place early in the Muslim version of the Jonah narrative: Jonah preached to the people of Nineveh, but they refused to listen. As a result of the Ninevites' lack of repentance, Jonah became angry and fled to the sea. This retelling reads Jonah 4:1–4 back into the narrative of Jonah's flight. It also aligns Jonah's mission with that of Muhammad: just as Jonah initially preached to the non-repentant Nineveh and fled, so Muhammad initially preached to the recalcitrant Mecca (cf. Jonah 1:3).

Finally, a few Jewish interpreters also connect Jonah's time in the fish with punishment for sin. Ibn Ezra, in his commentary to Jonah 2:2, asking for the ultimate reason why Jonah was swallowed by a fish, responds that Jonah was inside the fish so that God could save him from sin.

4. Jonah's Survival inside the Fish as a Miracle

Alongside the notion that Jonah's time inside the fish was a punishment for his sins, exegetes also stress that his actual survival of the ordeal was truly miraculous. Many Jewish retellings compare Jonah's survival inside the fish with other miraculous events in Israel's history. The Hellenistic-Jewish sermon *On Jonah* 25:2–4, for example, depicts Jonah praying to God and describing his marvellous salvation as being on a par with three other miracles: the three men's endurance in the fiery furnace (Dan 3:19–30), Daniel's survival in the lions' den (Dan 6), and the Israelites' crossing of the Red Sea (Exod 14:21–22, 29). *Gen. Rab.* 5:5 preserves the same tradition.

These types of comparisons are also found among Christian interpreters. Jerome, for instance, in his commentary to Jonah 2:2, discusses the objections of people around him to the biblical claim that Jonah survived inside the fish. Jerome points out in response that God has performed greater miracles than that, such as the survival of the three men in the fiery furnace, the Exodus out of Egypt, and Daniel's survival in the lion's den. Jerome further compares the Book of Jonah with Greek and Roman mythologies and with Ovid's *Metamorphoses*. Why would Jonah's sojourn inside the fish be considered more incredible than, say, Daphne's change into a bay tree and Jupiter's transformation into a swan? If these stories are widely believed, so the argument goes, then what is so problematic with the story of Jonah? From a similar perspective, Cyril of Alexandria likens Jonah's survival inside the fish with the Greek tales about Hercules and how he was first swallowed and then regurgitated by a sea monster (see further Hill 2008: 160–161). He also highlights the miracle that an unborn child is able to live immersed in natural moisture in the womb of a pregnant woman, yet still is alive and well-nourished.

Adding to the list of comparative examples, the early Church Father and Bishop of Lugdunum (modern day Lyon) Irenaeus (died 202 CE) likens Jonah's survival inside the fish not only to the survival of the three men in the fiery furnace, but also to the fact that Elijah's flesh was not consumed in the chariot of fire (2 Kgs 2:11) (*Against Heresies*, 5.5.2). Appealing more to material in the New Testament, Augustine argues in his 'Letter 102' that Jonah's three days in the fish must have been a miracle on a par with Jesus's resurrection on the third day or Lazarus's resurrection on the fourth day (John 11:44). He asks with perfect logic whether the pagan who ridicules the story of Jonah whether 'he thinks it is easier for a dead man to be raised in life from his sepulchre, than for a living man to be kept in life in the spacious belly of a sea monster' (*Question VI*.31). Later in the same letter (*Question VI*.32), Augustine, as Jerome, compares Jonah's survival in the fish with the miracle of the three young men in the furnace (Dan 3). Turning the same argument upside down in his 'Catechetical Lecture 4:12', Cyril of Jerusalem uses the miracle of Jonah's survival as the means of convincing those Jews who doubt the veracity of Jesus's resurrection. If they can believe that Jonah came forth from the whale on the third day, so the argument goes, cannot Christ likewise have risen on the third day?

Ibn Ezra, looking at Jonah's survival from a more scientific perspective, points out that no person has the strength to survive inside a fish for an hour, let alone for three days. Thus, he concludes, the events in Jonah 2:1 must truly constitute a miracle.

5. Unique Interpretations of Jonah's Three Days inside the Fish

Some of the interpretations of Jonah's time inside the fish are unique insofar as they do not fall into any of the above-mentioned chief categories. Theodore of Mopsuestia's understanding of Jonah's time inside the fish as a quiet time of reflection and prayer is quite exceptional. He writes that

> […] in his belly the prophet passed three days and nights quite unaffected. The result was that he marvelled at being kept unharmed and quite unaffected in the sea monster, as though finding himself in some small room in complete security; and he turned to prayer, which he directed to God.

Cyril of Alexandria's interpretation leans in the same direction:

> Coming to no harm, using the sea monster as a home, thinking clearly, and suffering no kind of ill effects of body or mind, he sensed divine assistance, knowing God is benevolent.

The symbolic interpretation of the Jonah narrative as a treatise of a person's walk through life, as suggested by the Christian bishop and martyr St Methodius of Olympus (died c. 311 CE), is also distinctive (cf. also *the Zohar* above). For St Methodius, Jonah's three days in the fish function as a symbol of our three stages in life: past, present, and future ('Fragment on Jonah').

6. Poetic Renderings of Jonah's Time inside the Fish

Several poets have sought to capture Jonah's time inside the fish. In this category, Aldous Huxley's (1894–1963 CE) contrapuntal sonnet 'Jonah' from 1917 stands out due to its fantastic imagery:

> A cream of phosphorescent light
> Floats on the wash that to and fro
> Slides round his feet – enough to show
> Many a pendulous stalactite
> Of naked mucus, whorls and wreaths
> And huge festoons of mottled tripes
> And smaller palpitating pipes
> Through which a yeasty liquor seethes
> [...].

The poem ends not with Jonah's deliverance from the fish but with the prophet still trapped inside it, making the fish spout 'music as he swims'. According to Meckier, Jonah in this poem is no prototype for Christ; on the contrary, he is a symbol for 'both the futility of art and the irrelevance of a philosophical mind'. Jonah is thus 'another clueless poet-philosopher, isolated and ineffectual', who sings in a grotesque floating cathedral (Meckier 2012: 121).

7. Symbolic Renderings of Jonah's Time inside the Fish

The notion of being 'inside the whale' has often been treated as symbolic of a certain kind of existence. Several contemporary biblical scholars, for example, understand Jonah's existence inside the fish as a figurative expression of Israel in exile (see, e.g. Wright 1886: 55–56; Smith 1898: 50; Smart 1956: 872–873; Ackroyd 1968: 244–245; Rogerson 1994: 239–244; Smith-Christopher 2002: 133). Authors and poets have likewise often employed the image of Jonah trapped inside the fish or even Jonah safely ensconced in the womb of the fish symbolically (cf. also above). The English novelist George Orwell (1903–1950 CE) uses this picture in his essay 'Inside the Whale' as a metaphor for accepting life as it is rather than trying to change it. Sitting inside the fish, a person is protected from the dangers of the outside world (Orwell 1961: 151–152):

> For the fact is that being inside a whale is a very comfortable, cosy, homelike thought. The historical Jonah, if he can be so called, was glad enough to escape, but in imagination, in day-dream, countless people have envied him. It is, of course, quite obvious why. The whale's belly is simply a womb big enough for an adult. There you are, in the dark, cushioned space that exactly fits you, with yards of blubber between yourself and reality, able to keep up an attitude of the completest indifference, no matter what happens. A storm that would sink all the battleships in the world would hardly reach you as an echo. Even the whale's own movements would probably be imperceptible to you. He might be wallowing among the surface waves or shooting down into the blackness of the middle seas (a mile deep, according to Herman Melville), but you would never notice the difference. Short of being dead, it is the final, unsurpassable stage of irresponsibility.

In the hands of the Nobel Prize laureate in literature (1999) Günter Grass (1927–2015 CE), Jonah's time inside the fish becomes a time of contemplation of his existence. In his book *The Tin Drum* (*Die Blechtrommel*, 1959), the protagonist Oskar is hiding under a stage from the Nazis. Oskar waits out the situation in his place of hiding, understood both as hell and as the netherworld, comparing himself with Jonah inside the whale (p. 110) (see further Arnds 2004: 114–116; Kühlmann 2011: 325):

> Things finally grew quiet in the wooden labyrinth, which was about the size of the whale in which Jonah sat in oily lethargy. But Oskar was no prophet, he was feeling hungry. There was no Lord to say, 'Arise, go unto Nineveh, that great city, and preach unto it'. Nor did the Lord have to grow a gourd for me that a worm would then destroy at the Lord's command. I didn't bewail that biblical gourd, nor Nineveh, even one called Danzig. I had affairs of my own to attend to, tucked my non-biblical drum under my seater, and without hitting my head or scratching myself on a nail, emerged from the bowels of a grandstand that, meant for meetings and rallies of all sorts, had the proportions of a prophet-swallowing whale merely by chance.

In his poem 'Jonah', found in his collection of poems *Parables and Portraits*, the American poet Stephen Mitchell (1943) likewise envisages Jonah's time inside the fish as a rather comfortable place of contemplation:

> After the first few hours he came to feel quite at ease inside the belly of the whale [...] Everything – the warmth, the darkness, the odour of the sea – stirred in him memories of an earlier comfort. His mother's womb? Or was it even before that, at the beginning of the circle which death would, perhaps soon, complete? He had known of God's mercy, but he had never suspected God's sense of humour. With nothing to do now until the next instalment, he leaned back against the rib and let his mind rock back and forth [...]

In a very different manner, in his play *The Burden of Nineveh*, Laurence Housman has Jonah tell the story of his survival twice. The first time, he tells it 'as it really happened' to his interlocutor Shemmel (who to a certain extent represents God). Jonah describes how the sailors cast him into the sea (Scene 2):

> So they took, and made ready to cast me forth into the sea. But because they wished not my death, they made a cross-beam of wood, and bound me to it, and therewith they cast me from the ship; and it passed on, and I saw it no more. And the raging of the sea was round me, and the roaring of its waves went over me. But the beam bore me up through the midst of it; and the Hand of the Lord held me so that I did not die.

As Jonah explained, this experience made him realize that God had indeed called him to Nineveh. When he later comes to Nineveh, he transforms this event into a story about how God sent a great fish to swallow him. The people listen astonished to him and, as a result, they stay and listen to his message of God's coming destruction on Nineveh (Scene 3).

8. The Number Three

Last but not least, a few commentators have focused their interpretations of the number 'three' in the 'three days and three nights', three often being used as a symbolic number. *Gen.Rab.* 56:1, for instance, provides a long list of seven other things that also happened on the third day: Abraham saw Mt Moriah on the third day of walking (Gen 22:4); God will restore his people on the third day (Hos 6:2); Joseph's brothers spent three days in prison (Gen 42:18); Israel encountered God near Mt Sinai on the third day (Exod 19:16); the spies hid near Jericho for three days (Josh 2:16); Ezra and his companions stayed in Jerusalem for three days upon their arrival in Yehud (Ezra 8:32); and Esther appealed to King Xerxes on the third day (Est 5:1).

Jonah 2:2 [Eng. 2:1]

> And Jonah prayed to Yhwh, his God, from the womb of the fish.

Whence Did Jonah Pray?

Verse 2 states clearly that Jonah prayed to Yhwh from the womb/belly of the fish. Nevertheless, three factors have made commentators problematize this statement. First, the perceived difficulty in praying while inside a fish makes it likely that Jonah prayed only *after* his release. Second, the use of verbs indicating past/completed actions in the prayer suggests that Jonah only prayed once he had been vomited out. Third, the content of the prayer, i.e. the fact that Jonah refers to God's response (Jonah 2:3 [Eng. 2:2]), indicates that Jonah already had experienced deliverance at the time of praying.

On the one hand, many interpreters insist that Jonah prayed while inside the fish, and they draw lessons from this fact. Beginning with the Church Fathers, Basil of Caesarea (also known as Basil the Great) (329–379 CE) interprets the fact that Jonah prayed while still in the fish as a sign that he did not despair of his life. As such, he is a model to be emulated ('Letter 242', section 1). His contemporary, Gregory of Nazianzus, likewise praises Jonah's courage, alongside that of other biblical heroes (as well as that of Basil of Caesarea) in his 'Oration 43.74: On Basil the Great':

> Do you praise the courage of Elijah (2 Kgs 1:1) in the presence of tyrants, and his fiery translation? Or the fair inheritance of Elisha, the sheepskin mantle, accompanied by the spirit of Elijah? You must also praise the life of Basil, spent in the fire. I mean in the multitude of temptations, and his escape through fire, which burnt, but did not consume, the mystery of the bush (Exodus 3:1), and the fair cloak of skin from on high, his indifference to the flesh. I pass by the rest, the three young men bedewed in the fire (Daniel 3:5), the fugitive prophet praying in the whale's belly (Jonah 2:1) and coming forth from the creature, as from a chamber; the just man in the den, restraining the lions' rage (Daniel 6:22) and the struggle of the seven Maccabees (2 Maccabees 7:1), who were perfected with their father and mother in blood, and in all kinds of tortures. Their endurance he rivalled, and won their glory.

Turning to the mediaeval Jewish exegetes, Ibn Ezra is also of the firm opinion that Jonah prayed when still inside the fish. Noting the *qatal* and the *wayyiqtol* forms of the verbs in the prayers, forms that would normally indicate an action in the past, Ibn Ezra cites several passages where one of these verbal forms conveys an event that, from the perspective of the speaker, is yet to happen (e.g. Gen 48:22; 49:15; Num 24:17). Ibn Ezra also notes that other statements in the psalm point towards a future fulfilment, for instance, the statement in Jonah 2:5 where Jonah anticipates that he will see the temple again. From a different perspective, Radak highlights that it was an additional miracle (in addition to Jonah's survival inside the fish) that Jonah was not in shock but remained in control of his thoughts and knowledge and was thus able to pray.

On the other hand, many other scholars reject this interpretation as impossible. Luther, for example, claims in his German commentary that Jonah did not pray the very words of the prayer written in Jonah 2 while inside the fish, as 'his mood when surrounded by this horrible death was not so cheerful as to compose a fine song'. Instead, at that point he merely indicated how he felt, unaware as he was of his future delivery. What we have here in Jonah 2 is rather a poem that Jonah wrote *after* his delivery, written retrospectively as a way of glorifying God. Calvin concurs. The prayer that Jonah prayed inside the fish did not consist of the very words that we now have in Jonah 2; at most, as he was in a state of distress, the words in Jonah 2 reflect the thoughts that the prophet dwelt on (Lecture 76).

How Did Jonah Pray?

Whereas Luther and Calvin assume that Jonah at most thought or muttered his prayer, other interpreters have explored the practical issue of Jonah *voicing* it. The Hellenistic-Jewish sermon *On Jonah* 18:1–3 goes the furthest in responding to this issue. When Jonah prayed to God inside the fish, so the sermon states, Jonah used the mouth of the fish to utter the prayer, 'as a musician (his) instrument'. For an onlooker, it would thus have seemed as if the fish were the intercessor for the prophet's salvation (cf. Siegert 1980: 20).

> Now, since the prophet was seemingly sheltered in the belly of the huge fish but was actually protected by the Arm of God, he prayed [while he was]. As we have said, inside the huge fish and subjugated the beast's mouth to his prayer. And one could see the huge fish turned into an amazing newly made defender of the prophet's salvation; it opened its mouth to let the prayer out, it lent [him] its tongue for the pronunciation of words. Touched by the prophet as a musical instrument, [it played] a melody by the musician's finger.

The sermon further claims that Jonah prayed for two things: that he would escape from the teeth of the huge fish that carried him, and that he would be safe inside the fish from all the other sea creatures around (*On Jonah* 22:2).

What Did Jonah Pray?

The psalm in Jonah 2 falls roughly into the category of psalms of thanksgiving, i.e. a genre where the psalmist not only describes his/her calamities but also thanks God for his/her opportune delivery. Even so, several interpreters view the psalm as a confession of sins.

1. Jewish Retellings: The Day of Atonement

The link between the Book of Jonah and confession of sins is made most explicitly in Jewish liturgy, where the Book of Jonah is one of the prescribed readings for the Day of Atonement/Yom Kippur (*b.Meg.* 4:6).

> On Yom Kippur one reads '... after the death ...' (Lev 16:1) and one concludes with 'for thus said the high and exalted one' (Isa 57:15) and at the afternoon service, one reads about forbidden marriages (Lev 18); and one concludes with Jonah.

More specifically, the Book of Jonah is the *Haftarah* (reading from the prophets) for the *Minhah* (the afternoon service) service (whereas Isa 57:15–58:14 is the *Haftarah* for *Shaharit* [the morning service]) (Stökl Ben Ezra 2003: 55). The Rabbis hint at the reason why the Book of Jonah is selected for the Day of Atonement. According to the Mishnah (*m.Tan.* 2:1), the people of Nineveh are held up as a paradigm for fasting and repentance:

> Our brothers, concerning the people of Nineveh it is not said, 'And God saw their sackcloth and their fasting', but 'and God saw their deeds, for they repented from their evil way' (Jonah 3:10).

The Mishnah (*m.Tan.* 2:4) continues by stating that:

> For the sixth he says, 'He who answered Jonah in the belly of the fish will answer you and hear the sound of your cry this day. Blessed are you, O Lord, who answers prayer in a time of trouble'.

The Jerusalem Talmud (*y.Tan.* 2:9) on the same passage emphasizes this interpretation, as does the Babylonian Talmud (*b.Tan.* 2:9).

The significance, as well as its force of imagination, of the Book of Jonah is well illustrated by the micrography found in BL Add 21160, f. 292. Alongside the Hebrew text of the Book of Jonah, the scribe has 'drawn' Jonah and the fish in Aramaic (see Figure 9).

The example of Jonah praying in the fish is thus often used as an example of how God hears the prayers of his people. Even if the biblical narrative never explicitly states that God answered Jonah or that he heard his prayer, the very fact that God commanded the fish to vomit out Jonah (2:11 [Eng. 2:10]) is a sign that God listened to Jonah and responded favourably to his prayer.

The Israeli Nobel Prize laureate in literature (1966) S. Y. Agnon (1888–1970 CE) elaborates on this topic in his *Days of Awe* (pp. 262–263):

> For the prophetic portion, the Book of Jonah is read from beginning to end, in order to teach us that no man can flee away from God [...]
>
> Another reason why we read the Book of Jonah is because it informs us that God pardons and forgives those who turn in Teshuvah [repentance], as we are told in the case of Nineveh.
>
> Another reason for reading the book of Jonah is because the prophecy of Jonah purposes to teach us that the compassions of God extend over all that He has made, even idolators – then how much more do they extend over Israel!

2. Christian Retellings

The notion that Jonah confessed his sins while inside the fish is also prevalent among Christian interpreters. Most vividly, the fourteenth-century English homiletic poem 'Patience' features Jonah pouring out his guilt throughout his prayer (lines 281–288):

> And there he dwelled at last, and to the Lord called:
> 'Now Prince, have pity on your prophet!
> Though I be foul and fickle, and false of my heart,
> Take away now your vengeance, through virtue of pity;
> Though I be guilty of guile, the shame of prophets.
> Thou art God, and all goods are truly your own;
> Have now mercy of your man and his misdeeds,
> And easily prove you are Lord, on land and in water'.

Figure 9 Jonah and the fish in Aramaic.

Yet, as shown by Brooke Davis, Jonah's prayer in 'Patience' is not a humble petition that arose from Jonah's spiritual poverty; rather it reveals a calculating spirit as Jonah encouraged God to show his power (line 288) (Davis 1991: 276).

Dominick Argento's choral work *Jonah and the Whale*, based in part on 'Patience', nuances the depiction of Jonah and renders him truly contrite:

> Narrator:
> So in the belly of that beast he abided in full.
> Three days and three nights, ever thinking on the Lord;
> He who in happiness had hidden from his God,
> Now, in sorrow and suffering, sought him.
> At last, stillness descended and in the silence he prayed.

Argento arranges Jonah's prayers masterfully. A tenor, representing Jonah, sings an aria, where the text is taken from the Authorized Version of Jonah 2. In parallel, the chorus sings Ps 130 in Latin, the opening words of which are *De profundis clamavi ad te* ('Out of the depths have I cried unto thee, O Yhwh'). Together, both prayers create a sense of true penitence and trust in God's mercy and forgiveness.

3. Islamic Retellings

Islamic retellings likewise often assume that Jonah's prayer (to Allah) was a confession of sins. In fact, it is often understood to constitute the very peak of the Jonah narrative. Qur'an 37:142–144 reads:

> Then the big Fish did swallow him, and he had done acts worthy of blame. Had it not been that he (repented and) glorified Allah,
> He would certainly have remained inside the Fish till the Day of Resurrection.

The penitent element of Jonah's prayer is also stressed in later qur'anic commentaries. In his *tafsīr* to Q37:139–148, the Sunni scholar Ibn Kathīr (1300–1373 CE) accentuates Jonah's contrite attitude by mentioning the tradition that the sound of Jonah worshipping God in the fish reached the angels in heaven, who then approached God (see further McAuliffe 1988: 46–62). The *tafsīr* further stresses Jonah's righteousness, his charitable deeds, and his truly penitent, prayerful, and grateful attitude towards God (Eng. transl. http://www.qtafsir.com/index.php?option=com_content&task=view&id=1927):

> When it occurred to the Prophet Yunus, upon him be peace, to call
> upon Allah in these words when he was in the belly of the great
> fish, he said,
> 'La ilaha illa Anta, You are glorified! Truly, I have been of the
> wrongdoers'.
> This call went and hovered around the (mighty) Throne, and the
> angels said, 'O Lord, this is the voice of one who is weak but
> known, in a faraway strange land'.
> Allah, may He be exalted, said, 'How do you know this?'
> They said, 'O Lord, who is he?'
> Allah, may He be exalted, said, 'My servant Yunus'.
> They said, 'Your servant Yunus, from whom there kept coming
> acceptable deeds and supplications which were answered!'
> They said, 'O Lord, will You not have mercy on him for what he did
> during his time of ease, and save him from this trial and tribulation?'
> He said, 'Of course'.
> So, He commanded the great fish, and it cast him forth on the
> naked shore.

In his *tafsīr* to Q21:87–88, Ibn Kathīr writes further (Eng. transl. Reynolds 2010: 121–122):

'That is my servant Jonah. He rebelled against me and so I have enclosed him in the belly of the fish'. They asked: 'You mean the virtuous servant from whom good work ascended to You every day and night?' He replied, 'Yes'. At this the angels interceded for Jonah and God commanded the fish to cast him on the shore.

In parallel, Q68:48–50 encourages Muhammad not to be like Jonah who cried out while in distress:

So wait patiently for the judgment of your Lord, and be not like the companion of the fish, when he cried while he was in distress. Were it not that favour from his Lord had overtaken him, he would certainly have been cast down upon the naked shore while he was blamed. Then his Lord chose him, and He made him of the good.

In this manner, the Qur'an calls attention to both the similarities and the differences between Jonah and Muhammad. Both prophets felt rejected by the people to whom they were sent to preach. Muhammad should not, however, imitate Jonah's enraged departure; he should rather wait patiently for God to sort things out.

It is furthermore possible that Q21:87–88 speaks of Jonah's time in the fish:

And Yunus, when he went away in wrath, so he thought that We would not straiten him, so he called out among afflictions: There is no god but Thou, glory be to Thee; surely I am of those who make themselves to suffer loss. So We responded to him and delivered him from the grief and thus do We deliver the believers.

The focus of the passage is on Jonah's prayer inside the fish. Jonah is the prophet whose call is directly answered by Allah. Although Jonah is trapped in the triple darkness of fish, sea, and night, he is nevertheless able to proclaim that *'There is no God but Thou, glory be to Thee'*.

4. Artistic Retellings: Music

Carissimi's oration *Jonas* from 1650 offers a long and most pious retelling of Jonah's prayer inside the fish. Jonah, sung in Latin by a tenor, asks God to remember his mercy. Each section of the tripartite prayer ends with Jonah's plea to God 'to be appeased, to forgive, and to have mercy'.

John Beckwith's *Jonah: Chamber Cantata for Chorus, Four Soloists, and Instruments* in four movements from 1963 conveys a different mood. As noted by Dowling Long and Sawyer, Jonah's prayer is marked 'angry' (forte) and 'sarcastic' to express his anger and resentment towards God for sending him to Nineveh. The concluding chorale, sung *a cappella*, ends, however, on a more reconciliatory note: 'The Lord who made both sea and shore [...] Hates nothing he has made, his mercy is our shade' (Dowling Long and Sawyer 2015: 124).

The 1980's pop group *Burning Sensation* produced a song called 'Belly of the Whale' (1982). The singer likens himself to Jonah and expresses sentiments such as 'I feel so lonely in the belly of the whale'. The singer, stuck in a party inside the whale, is longing to escape the loneliness of the crowd (Dowling Long and Sawyer 2015: 29; https://en.wikipedia.org/wiki/Burning_Sensations).

'from the womb'

The biblical narrative specifies that Jonah prayed 'from the belly/womb of the fish'. The Hebrew term *me'eim* can denote either 'womb' or 'belly', i.e. the innermost parts. The meaning 'womb' has given rise to an intriguing set of interpretations. The Hellenistic-Jewish sermon *On Jonah* makes a repeated connection between Jonah's time in the fish and the time that a foetus spends in its mother's womb (16:1):

> […] and while the prophet was swimming, the huge fish drew him inside like breath and conceived him alive in its belly.

The fish thus 'conceives' Jonah. The same image of the fish as a mother appears later in the sermon in the context of Jonah's prayer, where Jonah likens his time inside the fish to that of a foetus in its mother's womb and how this experience taught him about natural labour (25:7–8):

> This is incredible childbirth, for no one else is present here and no doctor controls the life-giving process; it is vivified inside [the fish] with the help of your Holy Hand and will be accomplished through us, for there is no obstacle to your power herein. Thus, the huge fish's pregnancy with me shows how natural labour takes place.

Turning to the Church Fathers, Ambrose (340–397 CE), Bishop of Milan, applies the womb imagery in Jonah 2:2 to the Christian life (*Seven Exegetical Works*, p. 408):

> 'From my mother's womb you are my God', since once I was in the womb, I never departed from You. I was with You; like Jonah when he was in the belly of the fish, I prayed to You on behalf of the people. And truly, Christ was with God from His mother's womb, according to what is written.

In his 'Poem 24', Paulinus of Nola describes how a man named Martinianus experienced something akin to Jonah. After having tumbled from the boat into the sea, the boat met him, like the fish met Jonah, and took him in. In this description, the boat is likened to a 'womb', in this way bringing his description into dialogue with the 'womb language' in Jonah 2:2:

> Throughout the night it bore him faithfully in its safe womb till it could take him back to harbour.

Far less comforting, the poem 'Patience' depicts Jonah's situation most vividly as it refers to him speaking 'from hell's womb' (line 306).

From a different perspective, Radak suggests that the Hebrew expression 'from the womb' does not refer to the womb of the fish; instead, it is an idiom that denotes Jonah's state of mind. To reach this interpretation, Radak conflates the imagery of verses 2 ('from the womb') and 3 ('from Sheol') and argues that both verses depict Jonah praying from the midst of his difficulty. In further support, Radak cites Pss 130:1 and 118:5, where, in both cases, the preposition *me* ('from') conveys the petitioner's state of mind rather than any specific location (cf. Bob 2013: 53).

'the fish'

The term used to denote the fish in Jonah 2:2 [Eng. 2:1] has a slightly different form compared to that used elsewhere in the book. The form in Jonah 2:2 appears to be a feminine noun (*dagah*) (דגה), in contrast to Jonah 2:1 [Eng. 1:17] and 2:11 [Eng. 2:10], where the customary masculine noun (*dag*) (דג) is attested. As the defining adjective 'big' (m.sg.) in verse 2:1 and the defining verb 'and he vomited' (3 m.sg.) in 2:11 make clear, the fish is definitely male. The careful reader is thus led to believe that the fish has had a sex change halfway through the narrative or, as Sherwood tongue in cheek claims, that the Hebrew text is a paragon of political correctness (Sherwood 1998: 55). This intricate textual situation has led to a wide range of weird and wonderful interpretations.[5]

Most translations are unable to reflect the shift from *dag* to *dagah* and then back to *dag* again. For instance, the LXX and the Vulgate do not reflect this change, given that neither Greek nor Latin can differentiate between male and female fish when using only a noun form. As a result, few Christian exegetes were troubled by (or even aware of) this textual problem. In contrast, the Aramaic of Targum Jonathan, following the MT closely, employs the m.sg. form to denote the fish in Jonah 2:1, while using the f.sg. form in the following verse 2. Verse 11 then speaks of a m.sg. entity again (reading based on Sperber 1962: 3:437–438). The visibility of this difference in the Hebrew text and its Aramaic translation caused Jewish commentators to spend considerable ink on this intriguing matter.

Several Jewish interpreters opt to see this discrepancy as the result of multiple fish. In the Babylonian Talmud (*b.Ned.* 4:3), for example, Rabbi Pappa explains the difference as one between a big fish (*dag*) and a small fish (*dagah*), using Exod 7:21, which speaks of a shoal of fish, in support. In the particular case of Jonah, Rabbi Pappa argues that Jonah was vomited out by the big fish and swallowed by a little one. Providing more details, Rashi (commentary to Jonah 2:1) maintains that Jonah was first swallowed by a male fish. While inside the fish, Jonah had enough space to stand up comfortably. Jonah, as a result, was not sufficiently troubled to pray for relief. As this situation was unsatisfactory from God's perspective, God directed the male fish to spit out Jonah. Jonah was subsequently swallowed by a female fish. Because she carried embryos (which pressed against the belly), Jonah was cramped and thus stressed, which in turn motivated him to pray. This midrashic interpretation of two fish is given further attention in the nineteenth-century commentary by Malbim. Like Rashi, Malbim maintains that Jonah was stirred to pray only in the narrow belly of the female fish. In support of his interpretation, Malbim refers to the fact that the word *dag/dagah* belongs to a small collection of nouns where the feminine form is used collectively to denote a *group* of items. In Gen 1:26, 28; Exod 7:18; Isa 50:2; and Ezek 47:10, the feminine noun *dagah* denotes a shoal of fish (BDB 185). Malbim develops this thought further in a new direction: the female fish in Jonah 2:2 was collective in the sense that she, appearing during the time of reproduction, contained multitudes of eggs. Thus, she represented a shoal of fish (cf. earlier also Radak).

As noted earlier, the biblical text testifies to a shift from *dag* to *dagah* and then back to *dag*. The commentators surveyed so far, however, have postulated only two fish. The little-known Midrash of the Repentance of Jonah the Prophet (MRJP), attested in only three manuscripts, rectifies this omission as it describes how Jonah was swallowed by three fish. Following MS Warsaw 258, the beginning of the midrash follows the above-mentioned midrashic trajectory until the moment when God commanded the *dagah* to spew out Jonah. At that point, God summoned a male fish bigger than all the others to swallow up Jonah and the female fish (Kadari 2016: 111–113).

This tradition resurfaces later in the Islamic retelling of the Jonah story in the writings of Al-Tha'labī. In his *Lives of the Prophets*, God commanded a fish to swallow Jonah. Another fish later swallowed that fish and dived down to his dwelling place in the sea. Later, yet another fish swallowed the second fish and brought all of them up the Tigris to Nineveh, where he delivered Jonah. This retelling further incorporates the tradition, found in the Hellenistic-Jewish sermon *On Jonah* 17:1–4 and in *PRE* 10, that the fish took Jonah on a sight-seeing tour of the sea (see below) (Kadari 2016: 114–116).

Other Jewish scholars reject this interpretation as pure nonsense. Ibn Ezra, for instance, argues that like the noun 'righteousness' that appears in two different forms in Hebrew (*tsedek/ts^edaka*), the noun 'fish' has one masculine and one feminine grammatical form. The two forms can be used interchangeably, and there is accordingly no need to postulate two different fish. Ibn Ezra's comparison with *tsedek/ts^edaka* is not fully apt, however, in that the word *ts^edaka* is not a feminine form of the masculine *tsedek* (Sasson 1990: 155).

Turning to modern scholars, the change from *dag* to *dagah* has often been understood as an indication of the genre of the Jonah narrative. According to McKenzie, the sex change of the fish is one of the many deliberately farcical or nonsensical features of the story that alert the readers to the fact that they are reading a *satire*: 'the whole story is intended to be preposterous because its very purpose is to make fun of Jonah and his attitude' (McKenzie 2005: 7).

For others, the blurring of the biological sex of the fish is a narrative issue. According to Sasson, a story can use either sex (or both at once) for an animal in such cases where its biological sex is of no importance for the story. In support of his theory, Sasson cites two letters written in Akkadian, composed by the same person and describing the same incident. One letter uses the Akkadian m.sg. term for 'lion', and the other employs the Akkadian f.sg. term for 'lioness' (Sasson 1990: 156).

From a different perspective, Trible connects the apparent feminine fish with the grammatical feminine gender of 'the ship' (*'oniah*), evident also in the possessive suffix in the expression 'its fare' (*shecharah*) in Jonah 1:3. In her view, this nuance, alongside the female fish in Jonah 2:2, contributes to the feminine imagery of the story (Trible 1994: 130, fn 27). Along similar lines, Ackerman argues that the gender change is a focusing device which serves to parallel Jonah's experience on board the ship and inside the fish. He moves from the 'innermost of the ship' (f.) (1:5) to the innermost of the fish (f.) (2:2) (Ackerman 1981: 232). Taking the female imagery in a different direction, Almbladh connects the feminine fish with the womb imagery in Jonah 2:1, 2 [Eng. 2:2, 3]. Both the Hebrew word *me'eim* (v. 1) and *beten* (v. 2) can refer to the womb (e.g. Gen 25:23; Ps 139:13). According to her, these 'womb-like' connotations of Jonah's temporary place of respite may have contributed to the 'feminization' of Jonah's fish (Almbladh 1986: 25, fn. 52). Finally, I have argued that the *he* of the term *dagah* is not a f.sg. suffix at all, but instead signifies a lengthened nominal form that is sometimes used to emphasize a narrative pause (cf. Job 34:13; 37:12; Ezek 8:2) (Tiemeyer 2016).

Jonah 2:3 [Eng. 2:2]

> And he said: 'I called out in my distress to Yʜᴡʜ and he answered me. I cried out from the belly of Sheol; you heard my voice'.

Jonah's Time in the Fish – —The Overarching Story

Many retellings of the Jonah narrative depict Jonah's time inside the fish. There are three main retellings: the fabulous, the scary, and the lethal. We have already dealt with the latter two[6] and shall therefore focus only on the first category here. This set of retellings interacts with the prayer in verses 3–10 (Eng. vv. 2–9), in the sense that it understands and transforms several of its metaphorical statements into literal descriptions of Jonah's journey with the fish.

The Hellenistic-Jewish sermon *On Jonah* 17:1–4 recounts Jonah's relative comfort inside the fish:

> The belly of the huge fish became the house of the drowning prophet, its eyes the mirror of the external visible things, and the movement of its flippers similar to a king's chariot. O prophet, you were given great honour when you moved at a chariot's speed, just as when the huge fish swam toward you! Did any ruler ever have the opportunity to look as deep into the world's abyss as you? Invisible things have become visible to you! To whom among humans were the ends of the earth seen as clearly as to you, and [to whom] was the abyss of the sea shown as a view? For whom else have the crafts ever rendered such a perfect machine possible, so that you are there and observe everything, but no one sees you, the observer?

There is a clear affinity between the imagery in this sermon and the descriptions of Jonah's time inside the fish in *PRE*. *PRE* 10 narrates how, after Jonah has been swallowed by the fish, the fish tells Jonah about its destiny, namely, to be devoured by the Leviathan. In response, Jonah asks the fish to take him to meet the Leviathan, claiming that the true reason for his descent to the deep sea is really to deal with the Leviathan. Jonah states his intention to kill it in the future. But for now, he shows the Seal of the Covenant of Abraham to the Leviathan, whereupon the latter flees.

> The fish said to Jonah: 'Do you not know that my day had arrived to be devoured in the midst of Leviathan's mouth?' Jonah replied: 'Take me beside it, and I will deliver you and myself from its mouth'. It brought him next to the Leviathan. (Jonah) said to the Leviathan, 'On your account have I descended to see your abode in the sea, for, moreover, in the future will I descend and put a rope in thy tongue, and I will bring thee up and prepare thee for the great feast of the righteous'. (Jonah) showed it the seal of our father Abraham (saying), Look at the Covenant (seal), and Leviathan saw it and fled before Jonah a distance of two days' journey. (Jonah) said to [the fish]: 'Behold, I have saved you from the mouth of Leviathan, show me what is in the sea and in the depths'.

As a reward for saving the fish, Jonah demands that the fish shows him the marvels of the sea and the depths. The fish then takes Jonah to the places of wonder from Israelite history (among them the place where Israel crossed the Re(e)d Sea), as well as the foundation of the earth, Sheol, and the place beneath Yhwh's temple. Every scene or new adventure is inspired by the metaphorical description in the biblical text:

> It showed him the great river of the waters of the Ocean, as it is said, 'The deep was round about me' (Jonah 2:5), and it showed him the paths of the Reed Sea through which Israel passed, as it is said, 'The reeds were tapped about my head' (Jonah 2:5); and it showed him the place whence the waves of the sea and its billows flow, as it is said, 'All thy waves and thy billows passed over me' (Jonah 2:3); and it showed him the pillars of the earth in its foundations, as it is said, 'The earth with her bars for the world were by me' (Jonah 2:6); and it showed him the lowest Sheol, as it is said, 'Yet hast thou brought up my life from destruction, O Lord, my God' (Jonah 2:6); and it showed him Gehinnom, as it is said, 'Out of the belly of Sheol I cried, and thou didst hear my voice' (Jonah 2:2); and it showed him (what was) beneath the Temple of God, as it is said, '(I went down) to the bottom of the mountains' (Jonah 2:6).

During his time in the fish, Jonah has light and he can, in relative contentment, use the eyes of the fish to look out at the wonders of the sea:

> He entered its mouth just as a man enters the great synagogue, and he stood (therein). The two eyes of the fish were like windows of glass giving light to Jonah. Rabbi Meir said: One pearl was suspended inside the belly of the fish and it gave illumination to Jonah, like this sun which shines with its might at noon; and it showed to Jonah all that was in the sea and in the depths, as it is said, 'Light is sown for the righteous' (Ps 97:11).

Thus, not unlike Professor Pierre Aronnax in Jules Verne's *Twenty Thousand Leagues Under the Seas: A World Tour Underwater* (1870), Jonah is on a forced sight-seeing tour of the wonders of the great deep, which he is able to see through the eyes of the fish/the windows of the Nautilus.

When the fish is below the Temple, Jonah commands the fish to stand still, and Jonah prays to God. Yet, God responds only when Jonah vows to kill the Leviathan:

> Forthwith Jonah said to the fish: 'Stand in the place where you are standing, because I need to pray'. The fish stood (still), and Jonah began to pray before the Holy One, blessed be He, and he said: 'Sovereign of all the Universe! Thou art called "the One who kills" and "the One who makes alive", behold, my soul has reached unto death, now restore me to life'. He was not answered until this word came forth from his mouth, 'What I have vowed I will perform' (Jonah 2:9), namely, I vowed to draw up Leviathan and to prepare it before Thee, I will

perform (this) on the day of the Salvation of Israel, as it is said, 'But I will sacrifice unto thee with the voice of thanksgiving' (Jonah 2:9).

In a sense, *PRE* 10 likens Jonah's journey in the fish to an inverted ascent narrative: in contrast to the other prophets who ascend to catch a glimpse of the heavenly throne room (e.g. Isa 6; Zech 3), Jonah descends into the netherworld. At the end of his journey, Jonah asks, or rather commands God: 'I have reached death, now raise me up, bring me back to life!' As phrased by Adelman, 'the prophet essentially undergoes a resurrection; he has been privy to a kind of mystical afterlife experience and returns to his body an exalted soul' (Adelman 2009: 213). After this prayer, the fish spits Jonah out upon the dry land.

'I called out'

Verse 3 employs a set of three verbs in the so-called *qatal* forms: 'I cried, I called, you heard'. These forms normally denote past actions. Jonah thus appears to speak of his salvation as having already taken place. Jerome consequently comments on Jonah's surety and lauds him for his faith. Rather than despairing of God's mercy, Jonah focuses completely on praising him. In his praise, Jonah gives thanks for God's past actions on his behalf rather than asking God for future acts of salvation. In fact, Jonah 2:3 depicts how Jonah remembered God and cried out to him the minute he saw the fish (rather than only when inside the fish). Somewhat differently, Radak argues that Jonah, even though he was still trapped inside the fish, rested in the knowledge that he would leave the belly of the fish in peace.

In his commentary to Jonah, the reformer Bugenhagen applied Jonah's call for help to God to his own situation in Wittenberg. The Christian Reformers, in their fight against Catholic plots (real or imagined), called out to God for help. In Bugenhagen's writing, Jonah's call is transformed into a model for all faithful people who live in fear and uncertainty to cry out to God, as well as an expression of faith in God's mercy (as quoted in Lohrmann 2012: 98–99).

'The Belly of Sheol'

Jonah 2:3 uses the term 'the belly of Sheol'. The phrase 'Sheol', although strictly denoting the realm of the dead (see Jonah 2:1), is often understood in Christian tradition to be synonymous with hell. Jerome offers a dual interpretation of the statement: on the one hand, the text speaks about Jonah the man; on the other hand, every statement is also applicable to Christ. Speaking about the man, the belly of Sheol clearly refers to the great size of the belly of the fish; speaking about Christ, Jerome compares this verse with Ps 16:10, where the psalmist declares that God will not abandon his/her soul in Sheol. From a different angle, Cyril of Alexandria maintains that Jonah here compares the fish to Hades and death in that it knew how to kill and savagely consume its prey (even if Jonah himself suffered no harm).

Turning to Jewish interpretations, a few Sages appeal to Jonah 2:3 in their attempt to understand Gehenna. In the Babylonian Talmud (*B.Erub.* 2:1–3), Rabbi Jeremiah ben Eleazar states that Gehenna has three gates: one in the wilderness, one in the sea, and one in Jerusalem. In support, he cites Num 16:33 (wilderness), Jonah 2:3 (sea), and Isa 31:9 (Jerusalem). He further declares that Gehenna has seven different names: Sheol/netherworld (Jonah 2:3), destruction (Ps 88:12), pit (Ps 16:10), tumultuous pit (Ps 40:3), miry clay (Ps 40:3), shadow of death (Ps 107:10), and underworld (Ps 107:10).

In general, however, most Jewish interpreters reject the literal interpretation of Sheol in Jonah 2:3 and instead argue for a metaphorical understanding. TJ paraphrases the verse so that the reference to Sheol disappears. Instead, the translation reads 'from the bottom of the deep I pleaded', thus replacing the Hebrew word *sheol* with the Aramaic concept of *tehoma* ('primeval ocean', 'deep'), i.e. the same word that appears in Gen 1:2. Many mediaeval Jewish exegetes follow suit. Rashi clarifies that Jonah is not in Sheol but that the belly of the fish is *like* Sheol to him. Ibn Ezra likewise notes that Sheol is a deep, dark place which is the very opposite of heaven; i.e. Jonah is as far away from God as one can possibly be. A metaphorical interpretation is also advocated by Luther, who claims in his German commentary to Jonah 2:2 that when Jonah writes 'the belly of Sheol', what he means is the belly of the fish: the time that he spent there was as dreadful as hell to him, as he suffered the agonies of death. Jonah is thus not describing the fish itself but his emotions inside the fish.

Ingeniously, Abarbanel connects this statement in Jonah 2:3 with the identification of Jonah with the son of the women of Zarephath (1 Kgs 17:17–24). Jonah's outcry here is thus a reference to his resurrection by Elijah (see also Jonah 1:1). This interpretation 'solves' the temporal problem that faces interpreters of the prayer in Jonah 2, namely, how Jonah could speak in the past tense about his salvation from Sheol.

God's Response – Jonah's Surety of Salvation
Many Christian poetic retellings of the Jonah narrative have used Jonah's prayer as a model for a faithful response to calamities. The Elizabethan poet Michael

Drayton (1563–1631 CE) offers the following moving contemplation of Jonah's time in the fish in 'The Song of Jonah in the Whales Bellie':

> In grief and anguish of my heart, my voice I did extend,
> Unto the Lord, and he thereto, a willing ear did lend:
> Even from the deep and darkest pit, and the infernal lake,
> To me he hath bowed down his ear, for his great mercies' sake.
> For thou into the middest, of surging seas so deep
> Hath cast me forth: whose bottom is so low and wondrous steep.
> Whose mighty wallowing waves, which from the floods do flow,
> Have with their power up swallowed me, and overwhelmed me though.
> Then said I, lo, I am exiled, from presence of thy face,
> Yet will I once again behold, thy house and dwelling place.
> Waters have encompassed me, the floods enclosed me round,
> The weeds have sore encumbered me, which in the seas abound.
> Unto the valleys down I went, beneath the hills which stand,
> The earth hath there environed me, with force of all the land.
> Yet hast thou still preserved me, from all these dangers here,
> And brought my life out of the pit, oh Lord my God so dear.
> My soul consuming thus with care, I prayed unto the Lord,
> And he from out his holy place, heard me with one accord.
> Who to vain lying vanities doth wholly him betake,
> Doth err also, God's mercy he doth utterly forsake.
> But I will offer unto him the sacrifice of praise,
> And pay my vows, ascribing thanks unto the Lord always.

Jonah 2:4 [Eng. 2:3]

> For you have cast me into the deep of the heart of the sea, and a stream surrounds me; all your breakers and your waves have passed over me.

Modern scholars often emphasize the remarkable number of textual allusions and even direct quotes from several psalms in the psalm in Jonah 2 (see, e.g. Brenner 1993: 184–186; Dell 1996: 93–95; Ben Zvi 2003: 47–48). These features were noted also by earlier scholars. As Luther points out in his German commentary to 2:3, this verse bears a striking resemblance to Ps 42:8 [Eng. 42:7]. Luther thus suggests that Jonah borrowed his speech from that psalm.

> Deep calls to deep in the roar of your waterfalls; all your waves and breakers have swept over me.

Jerome offers a dual commentary of many verses in the Book of Jonah: one that applies to the character of Jonah and one that applies to Christ as foreshadowed by Jonah. Regarding Jonah 2:4a [Eng. 2:3a], for Jonah, this verse reflects the moment when he was ensconced in the stomach of the whale. Read typologically, Jonah 2:4a and Ps 69:3 (Eng. 69:2), where the psalmist declares how he had sunk in deep mire, without a foothold, and how the water engulfed him, together foreshadow the same moment in Christ's life (i.e. his death, as referred to in Matt 12:40). Turning to Jonah 2:4b [Eng. 2:3b], Jerome understands the breakers and waves to refer metaphorically to temptations in (the Christian) life (cf. Job 7:1; 1 Cor 10:13; Heb 4:15).

Modern readers have often commented on the discrepancy between the content of the psalm and the surrounding narrative (see also below). The reader already knows that it was the sailors who reluctantly threw Jonah into the sea (Jonah 1:15), yet here Jonah claims that God did so. When reading the final form of the MT, this lack of cohesion reflects Jonah's twisted view of reality (cf. Barrett 2012: 244).

Jonah 2:5 [Eng. 2:4]

> And I said, I am cast out from before your eyes, yet I will surely gaze again at your holy temple.

'And I said, I am cast out from before your eyes'

Jonah 2:5 [Eng. 2:4] is problematic within its present literary context. There is a tension between Jonah's claim in verse 5a that he has been *driven away* from God's presence and what the reader knows to be true from the narrative in Jonah 1:2–3, namely, that Jonah *actively fled* from before God's presence. Many mediaeval Jewish exegetes therefore seek ways to reconcile the statement in Jonah 2:5 with the narrative in Jonah 1. Among them, Rashi suggests that Jonah's words in verse 5 express Jonah's *feelings* (rather than being an impartial assessment of the *facts*) when he was thrown into the sea. Radak argues along similar lines that verse 5 conveys Jonah's perspective on the events. Although God kept his eyes on Jonah at all times, Jonah himself thought that he had died when he was tossed into the water and that God had hidden his face and eyes from him. The Reformers follow suit. In his German commentary, Luther understands Jonah's statement in verse 5 both in a physical and a spiritual sense. Jonah's heart may have told him that he was going to die, and he may have despaired of ever returning to the land of the living. In parallel, Jonah may have felt that due to his disobedience he was eternally cast out from God's presence like one of the damned. Calvin likewise emphasizes that Jonah here articulates his feelings of total alienation from God (Lecture 76).

'yet I will surely gaze again at your holy temple'

Our understanding of this half-verse pivots on the precise translation/interpretation of the opening conjunction *ach*. Calvin argues that this conjunction conveys the sense of 'truly' and 'nevertheless'. As such, so Calvin, verse 5b expresses either Jonah's certainty or alternatively his wish that he will, at one point in the future, again see the temple (Lecture 76). Earlier, Jerome had suggested that Jonah showed his desire and confidence in the future. Moreover, being endowed with a prophetic spirit, Jonah was able to focus on things beyond his present predicament. Turning to its typological meaning, Jerome maintains that verse 5b speaks about the relationship of Jesus the son with the Father. For Jesus, the Father is the temple, and Jesus states how he will be one with the Father again (cf. John 1:1; 10:38; 14:10–11; 17:21).

Looking at verse 5b from a more mundane perspective, a few Jewish interpreters are concerned with its practical aspects (cf. also below Jonah 2:8 [Eng. 2:7]). What does it really mean to 'gaze at [God's] holy temple'? Radak clarifies that Jonah here expresses the wish to 'pray'. From a different perspective, this reference to the 'temple' complicates matters when we read the Book of Jonah as a story about the prophet with the same name from Gath-Hepher in the Northern Kingdom (see Jonah 1:1) (Ben Zvi 2003: 47–51). If Jonah is indeed a northern prophet, why would he wish to see the temple (in Jerusalem)?

Jonah 2:6 [Eng. 2:5]

> The abyss encompassed me even to my soul; the abyss surrounded me; seaweed was wrapped around my head.

Interpreters continue to seek spiritual insights in the various statements in the psalm. Jerome notes that the term 'abyss' may refer to God's judgement, as it does in Pss 36:7 [Eng. 36:6] and 42:8 [Eng. 42:7]. For Calvin, this verse, as well as the following one, reveals that Jonah knows that the present calamity has happened to him on account of his sins (Lecture 76).

Turning to the expression 'seaweed was wrapped around my head', the consonantal Hebrew form *samekh, waw, pe* can be read either as 'reeds' (*suf*) or as 'end' (*sof*). This ambiguity is picked up by the LXX as it translates the phrase as 'last my head went down'. Yet other translators note the allusion inherent in the word 'reeds' to the 'Red Sea' or, as it is in Hebrew, the 'Reed Sea' (*yam suf*). TJ thus translates 'the Reed Sea was suspended above' Jonah's head. TJ is possibly the source of the midrash, attested later in *PRE* 10 (above), where the fish shows Jonah the place where the children of Israel were able to pass across the Reed Sea at the time of the Exodus (see further Smolar and Aberbach 1983: 123; Sasson 1990: 185). This line of exegesis is also advocated by Rashi, who states, in line with *PRE* 10, that Jonah was able to *see* this place through the two eyes of the fish that were like two windows.

Looking at the issue from a more pragmatic perspective, Radak asks perceptively how seaweed could be around Jonah's head when he is *inside* the fish. He offers the solution that the seaweed was really wrapped around the head of the fish (not the head of Jonah). Even more matter-of-factly, Luther argues that all that this expression means is that reeds and cane grow in abundance on the shores of the sea or great lakes or even ponds. Anyone who is submerged in the ocean will thus inevitably be covered by reeds (German commentary). In contrast, Calvin argues that this phrase is surely a metaphorical description. It is, in fact, improper to take the text here literally and to argue that it speaks of the head of the fish (Lecture 76).

Jonah 2:7 [Eng. 2:6]

> To the bases of the mountains I descended; the earth, its bars are behind me forever. You have brought up from the pit my life, o Yhwh, my God.

'To the bases of the mountains I descended'

A few commentators take the statement in Jonah 2:7a [Eng. 2:6a] that Jonah descended to the bases of the mountains literally. Cyril of Alexandria, for example, understands it to mean that the sea monster, in whose belly Jonah was, 'probably lurked in rocks and in sea caves'. In other words, Jonah descends because the fish descends. Other commentators offer metaphorical interpretations. Among them, Cyril of Jerusalem likens the mountains with Jesus's sepulchre hewn out of rock ('Catechetical Lecture' 14:17–20):

> And after a few words, he says, in the person of Christ, prophesying most clearly, My head went down to the chasms of the mountains; and yet he was in the belly of the whale. What mountains then encompass thee? I know, he says, that I am a type of Him, who is to be laid in the Sepulchre hewn out of the rock.

The Sages compare Jonah 2:7 with other biblical texts. In Midrash Tanhuma (Buber), *Wayyetse*, Rabbi Eleazar ben Azariah connects the verse with Jacob's dream about the ladder in Gen 28:12. When Jacob saw the ladder placed on earth, God in fact showed him Jonah. The connection between the two passages is likely to be the shared use of the Hebrew verb 'descend' (*yarad*), although this is not made explicit: as the angels in Gen 28:12 ascended and descended on the ladder between heaven and earth, so Jonah descended to the bases of the mountains and then later ascended back to earth.

J.R.R. Tolkien may have been influenced by Jonah 2:7 when he described Gollum's first glimpse of what was going to be his home under the Misty Mountains in *The Fellowship of the Ring* (1954, ch. 2, 'The Shadow of the Past') (Wolfe 2014: 22):

> It would be cool and shady under those mountains. The Sun could not watch me there. The roots of those mountains must be roots indeed; there must be great secrets buried there which have not been discovered since the beginning.

Later, in 1957, Tolkien translated the Book of Jonah for the English Jerusalem Bible, using the French translation *Bible de Jérusalem* as his source text.

'the earth, its bars are behind me forever'

In the next line, Jonah speaks of the earth and how 'its bars' are 'behind him forever'. Much has been written on the nature of these bars. In general, commentators have detected a metaphor in this expression that articulates Jonah's feelings of being buried for the rest of his life. Cyril of Alexandria, focusing on the term 'everlasting', argues that the enormity of the danger and the gravity of the events led Jonah to think that he was dead and had arrived at Hades itself, from where none emerges or in any other way returns once having been entrapped. Many mediaeval Jewish commentators, among them Rashi and Ibn Ezra, also interpret this verse as an expression of Jonah's despair of ever returning to dry land again. Luther (German commentary) likewise maintains that this statement mirrors Jonah's fear of having to remain in the fish forever, like a person confined to a dungeon or prison with doors and windows barred. A person sinking down to the depth of the ocean is doomed to remain there. In this way, Jonah gives no thought to anything else but death, having lost hope entirely and given himself over to death.

'You have brought up from the pit my life, o Yhwh, my God'

A problem with the above-mentioned interpretation is, however, that its expressed sense of ultimate despair, emphasized by the word 'forever', seemingly negates the immediately following proclamation of trust in God's salvation in verse 7b [Eng. v. 6b]. The chronology of events is another problematic issue. In Jonah 2:7b, the speaker proclaims how God *lifted* him up from the pit, thus apparently referring to an act that, from the speaker's perspective, God has already accomplished. In other words, Jonah speaks of his salvation *prior* to the fish spitting him out in verse 11 [Eng. v. 10].

The discrepancy between Jonah's despair and his subsequent confidence in God's redemption is addressed by Radak as he imagines what Jonah might have thought: in the beginning, I thought that I would never reach the dry land again, i.e. that it had closed its bars against me, and that the sea would be my grave. Now, however, being inside the fish I know it will not be my grave but that I will escape from it alive and return to the dry land. Along similar lines, Luther maintains that verse 7b marks the change in Jonah. Different thoughts come to his mind and 'faith again raises its head and strives to win the victory' (German commentary). Seeking to solve the chronological conundrum, Rashi suggests a two-stage ascent. Jonah had actually been even deeper down in the sea where he saw the 'pit'. It is accordingly from this deeper place that God has now (already) lifted him.

Looking more at the imagery itself, Jerome compares this verse with both Ps 75:4 [Eng. 75:3], where God declares that he has set firm the pillars of the earth, and the divine statement (to Cyrus) in Isa 45:2, where God promises that he will shatter the doors of bronze. Jerome further discusses the reference to the 'pit' in light of Ps 16:10, where the psalmist declares that God will not abandon his soul in Sheol; Ps 103:3–4, where the psalmist praises God for redeeming him from the pit; and Rom 7:24, where Paul lamentingly asks who will set him free from this body of death. Jerome concludes by stating that Jonah, while inside the fish, must have been forced to corrupt his body by eating the food of animals and drinking from veins and arteries, yet somehow also had managed to remain safe and sound.

Jonah 2:8 [Eng. 2:7]

> When my soul fainted, I remembered Yhwh; may my prayer come before you to your holy temple.

'When my soul fainted, I remembered Yhwh'

Jonah 2:8a [Eng 2:7a] contains the rather unusual *hithpael* infinitive verb *hith'atef*. To explain its meaning here, Rashi draws on Lam 2:11, where the same root, also in *hithpael*, means 'to faint'. Similarly, Ibn Ezra appeals to Ps 102:1, where the *Paal* form of the same root means 'to be faint'. Going one step further, Radak argues that this verb conveys 'to die': when Jonah was first swallowed by the fish, he thought that he was going to die. Later, when Jonah realized that he was still alive in the belly of the fish, he began to believe that his prayers would reach God.

Jerome compares the subsequent statement that Jonah 'remembered YHWH' with Ps 77:6 [Eng. 77:5], where the psalmist remembered former days and days of eternity. Jonah had at this point lost all hope of ever finding a way out of the fish, instead seeing himself imprisoned in its intestines for the remainder of his days. His final hope was God himself. Looking at the expression typologically, it presages Jesus's plea in the garden of Gethsemane, when his soul is overwhelmed with sorrow to the point of death, for the cup to pass him by (Matt 26:38–39; Mark 14:34). Jonah's statement also foreshadows the time of the cross when Jesus commends his spirit into God's hand (Luke 23:46, cf. Ps 31:6 [Eng. 31:5]).

'may my prayer come before you to your holy temple'

Turning to Jonah's supplication in verse 8b that his prayer would come before God in his holy temple, Cyril of Alexandria praises Jonah for his resolve not to give in to depression in the face of hardship but instead to seek the Lord in prayer. Hardship is, after all, according to Cyril, character building (cf. Rom 5:3–5).

Speaking more specifically about the reference to the 'temple' in this verse (cf. above, Jonah 2:5 [Eng. 2:4]), two distinct lines of exegesis can be observed: this verse refers either to the actual physical temple (in Jerusalem) or it is another word for heaven. Opting for the first interpretation, *PRE* 10, followed by Rashi, tells how the fish took Jonah to the very place underneath the temple. Opting for the second interpretation, Radak argues that Jonah here is referring to heaven, citing Ps 114:4 and 2 Chron 30:27 in support. Calvin, aware of both possibilities, argues that this is indeed a reference to the physical temple, as it was the custom under the law to pray in the temple. Although the word 'temple' may sometimes refer to heaven, this is not the sense meant here. Jonah perceived that he was far away from the temple, yet God was near him (Lecture 76).

Jonah 2:9 [Eng. 2:8]

> Those who observe the vapours of vanity forsake their goodness.

'Those who observe the vapours of vanity'

The rare Hebrew term *hevel* conveys a sense of uselessness and meaninglessness. Most famously, it appears five times in Ecc 1:2, where it is translated as 'vanity'. Here, in Jonah 2:9, the word appears in a construct chain (*havlei shav*) where its plural form expresses the 'breathiness' of vanity (*shav*). It is also the name of Adam and Eve's second son Abel (Gen 4:2). Given the sustained allusion to Cain (see 1:3; 4:4) in the Book of Jonah, as well as the allusions to the flood narrative (see 1:1, 2; 4:11), a few modern scholars have suggested that the use of the term *hevel* here is an oblique reference to Abel and wider to Gen 1–11 (e.g. Hesse and Kikawada 1984: 8).

'forsake their goodness'

The notion of divine *hesed* ('goodness', 'loving-kindness') forges a link between the Book of Jonah and the Book of Ruth (see also Jonah 4:4), where the word appears twice. In Ruth 1:8, Naomi expresses the hope that God will show her 'loving-kindness' in the same way as Ruth and Orpha showed her 'loving-kindness'. In Ruth 3:10, Boaz commends Ruth for having shown him 'loving-kindness' by not pursuing a younger man. What 'loving-kindness' does, in this understanding, is to cleave to someone rather than abandoning him or her. For the modern exegete Cary, Jonah is a person who, by fleeing from God, forsakes God's 'loving-kindness' (Cary 2008: 100–101). His behaviour may thus be contrasted with Ruth's, who cleaves in faithfulness to both Naomi and Boaz and so, by extension, also to the God of Israel.

The Identification of the Subject

The meaning of Jonah 2:9 [Eng. 2:8] is uncertain, and the translator is faced with a series of questions. To what group of people does the psalmist refer, what are they doing, and what is 'their goodness' (*hasdam*) that they are forsaking? Two main lines of exegesis prevail: while Jewish interpreters tend to identify the people referred to with the (Gentile) sailors in Jonah 1, many Christian interpreters classify them as the Jews.[7]

The Sailors

In traditional Jewish interpretation, the word *shav* ('vanity') is understood as a euphemism for 'idols'. In Jonah 2:9, the category of 'those who observe the vapours of vanity' is parallel with the ones who 'abandon their goodness'. In other words, 'to abandon their goodness' is to say that they worshipped idols.

If one reads Jonah 2 in isolation, this interpretation is straightforward and in line with sentiments expressed elsewhere in the Bible. If, however, one reads Jonah 2:9 as an integral part of the surrounding Jonah narrative, this interpretation becomes problematic. The only people in the Book of Jonah who are explicitly described as worshipping gods other than Yhwh are the (Gentile) sailors (Jonah 1:5), yet overall, they are depicted in a very favourable light throughout Jonah 1. The sentiment here in Jonah 2:9, interpreted in its wider context of the Book of Jonah, is thus incongruous with the portrayal of the sailors in Jonah 1 (Ackerman 1981: 243). Alternatively, it does refer to the sailors who, from Jonah's perspective, still worship idols. The reader knows, however, that this situation is no longer true (Timmer 2008: 165–166).

TJ emphasizes the connection between vanity and Gentile idol worship by translating the opening statement of Jonah 2:9 as 'I am not like the nations, who worship idols', thus making an explicit connection back to Jonah 1:5. Many Jewish exegetes follow suit. Rashi, among them, argues that this verse speaks about idol worshippers. First, Rashi has Jonah state, in line with TJ, that he is different from the sailors who have turned away from God, as he instead brings offerings of thanksgiving to God. Second, following *PRE* 10, Rashi understands the term *ḥasdam* ('their goodness') as referring to the sailors' past acts of kindness towards their idols. Now, however, they have abandoned such folly and turned to follow the God of Israel. Ibn Ezra likewise identifies these idol worshippers with the sailors of Jonah 1. In contrast to Rashi, Ibn Ezra maintains that the term *ḥasdam* refers to the sailors' act of throwing Jonah into the sea, which they perceived to be an act of kindness. Radak, offering a third interpretative variant, envisages Jonah reflecting upon the sailors. The sailors believed in Y HWH for only a brief time, i.e. immediately after their survival on board the ship. Later, they failed to fulfil their vows (cf. Jonah 1:16) and chose instead to return to their idolatry. A few Church Fathers also identify the worshippers of idols here with the sailors in Jonah 1. Theodore of Mopsuestia, for example, states:

> Those working as sailors, although attached to idols and devoted to that false belief, wanted to spare me; but overcome by the calamities, they abandoned that view, realizing they had no chance of life unless they were rid of my company.

The Jews
Many other Christian interpreters, however, have used this verse in their anti-Jewish polemic by identifying the worshippers of vanity with the Jews. For Jerome, Jonah 2:9 raises a philosophical matter, namely worship of vanity. According to Jerome, Jonah speaks prophetically about such Jews who endeavour to observe the precepts of humankind and the commandments of the Pharisees, all of which is vanity. In addition, the very fact that Jonah makes this observation tells us something positive about Jonah himself: in the midst of his calamity, surrounded by eternal night in the intestines of a great beast, the prophet is not thoughtful of his danger but instead has the presence of mind to

philosophize on the question of nature! Jonah's pondering thus emphasizes the greatness of the prophet's spirit. In his German commentary, Luther likewise associates the adherents of vanity with the people of Israel. In his view, Jonah rebukes 'the foolish work-righteous and hypocrites, who do not rely solely on God's grace but on their own work'. In this way, Jonah alludes to his own people 'who relied on the Law and on works and who not only snubbed the Gospel of God's grace but also persecuted it'.

Jonah 2:10 [Eng. 2:9]

> 'But I will sacrifice to you with a voice of thanksgiving; that which I have vowed I will pay. Salvation to Y<small>HWH</small>'.

Many Christian exegetes continue to combine Christological readings and anti-Jewish polemic in their interpretations of Jonah 2:10 [Eng. 2:9]. Jerome links the claim that Jonah 'will sacrifice' with Jesus's sacrificial death of the cross (1 Cor 5:7). In stronger terms, Luther conflates Jonah 2:10 with Ps 50:13, where God asks rhetorically whether he would eat the flesh of bulls or drink the blood of goats. In this way, Luther manages to re-conceptualize Jonah 2:10 as a statement of condemnation against the Jews, their sacrifices, and their works: Jonah, although knowing about God's grace, is here nevertheless 'steeped in the delusion that God esteemed the person and his works, particularly that of the people of Israel. Even now he has not entirely divested himself of this' (German commentary).

Jonah further promises that what '[he] has vowed, [he] will pay'. Jerome connects the notion of vows here with the references in John 6:39; 10:28; and 17:12, where Jesus declares that it was his father's will to send him (Jesus) so that others, through him, would be safe. Centuries later, Calvin turns this phrase into an example of anti-Catholic polemic. Discussing the character of Jonah's vow, Calvin emphasizes that this was an act of thanksgiving or a testimony of gratitude. This type of vow should not be confused with what the 'Papists' (of his days) are doing, namely, attempting to pacify God by 'frivolous practices' such as abstaining from meat for a particular amount of time or wearing sackcloth, or undertaking a pilgrimage (Lecture 77).

Jonah 2:11 [Eng. 2:10]

> And Y<small>HWH</small> spoke to the fish and it vomited Jonah upon the dry land.

'And Yhwh spoke to the fish'

According to Jonah 2:11 [Eng. 2:10], God spoke to the fish. This claim raises the (somewhat obvious) question to what extent God speaks with animals and to what extent animals can hear God. In his customary matter-of-fact manner, Ibn Ezra clarifies that God *did not* actually speak to the fish; this is rather a metaphor which conveys that God compelled the fish to fulfil God's command. Along similar lines, Radak elucidates that God here made his desire known to the fish so that it would know to spew Jonah out. Even so, a few Rabbis used the fact that God spoke with the fish in Jonah 2:11 as a proof text in other contexts. Notably, *Gen.Rab.* 20:3 appeals to this divine-piscine communication as part of its argument as to why only humans, snakes, and fish have sexual intercourse face-to-face, while all other creatures have sexual relations 'dog style'. The former category contains only those creatures to whom God communicates verbally: God obviously speaks with humans (Gen 3:17), he also spoke with the snake (Gen 3:17), and here in Jonah he spoke with the fish (Jonah 2:11).

'and it vomited Jonah upon the dry land'

Turning to the execution of the divine command, the fish vomits Jonah upon the dry land. The Hebrew word for vomiting, the *hiphil* of the root *koph, yod, aleph*, is a relatively rare but strong word (cf. below Jonah 4:6). It is elsewhere used in Lev 18:25, 28; 20:22 to denote the action of the land/earth to spew out its inhabitants due to their pollution. The LXX here offers a less graphic reading by using the more sanitized verb ἐξέβαλεν, meaning 'he cast out'.

We shall explore three different aspects of this action. First, what is the theological significance of this act of vomiting? Second, how did Jonah look when he emerged from the fish? Third, where did Jonah end up when he had been spewed out?

1. The Theological Significance of Vomiting

Jonah's emergence from the fish has been understood symbolically as an act of redemption and rebirth in both Christian and Jewish interpretation.

1.1 Jewish Interpretations

Beginning with Jewish interpretations of Jonah's rescue from the fish, the Jerusalem Talmud (*y.Ber.* 9:1, cf. also *Gen.Rab.* 5:5, above) refers to Jonah 2:11 within the context of discussing God's relationship with and faithfulness to his people Israel, using the fact that God saved Jonah from the belly of the fish as an example. Another Talmudic passage (*y.Ber.* 10:1) highlights God's power to save his prophets (cf. above Jonah 2:1) by comparing God's rescue of Jonah with his rescue of Daniel from the lions' den (Dan 6) and of the three men in the fiery furnace (Dan 3):

> He saved Moses from the sword of Pharaoh. He saved Jonah from the belly of the whale, Shadrach, Meshach and Abednego from the fiery furnace, and Daniel from the lions' den.

In more modern times, the Russian-Israeli Jewish painter Eugene Zalmanovich Abeshaus (1939–2008 CE) used the emergence of Jonah from the fish to express the sense of rebirth of (Russian) Diaspora Jewry when making *aliyah*. In his painting 'Jonah and the Whale in Haifa Port' from 1978, currently in the Sherwin Miller Museum of Jewish Art, Tulsa, Oklahoma, Jonah steps out of the mouth of the fish as he arrives as a new immigrant (*'ole ḥadash*) to Israel.

1.2 Christian Interpretations

Turning to Christian interpretations, several Church Fathers refer to Jonah's release from the fish as proof of the tenet of bodily resurrection. Tertullian, in ch. 58 of his discussion 'On the Resurrection of the Flesh', mentions Jonah being vomited out from the fish, safe and sound. For him, this fact, alongside the fact that Daniel's three friends survived (as did their clothing) the furnace of Babylon, shows the resurrection of the physical body.

> That the fires of Babylon injured not either the mitres or the trousers of the three brethren, however foreign such dress might be to the Jews (Daniel 3:27), that Jonah was swallowed by the monster of the deep, in whose belly whole ships were devoured, and after three days was vomited out again safe and sound […] to what faith do these notable facts bear witness, if not to that which ought to inspire in us the belief that they are proofs and documents of our own future integrity and perfect resurrection?

Methodius likewise appeals to the fact that Jonah's flesh was not dissolved after three days in the fish as support of the belief in bodily resurrection ('Fragment on Jonah'):

> Moreover, Jonah having spent three days and three nights in the belly of the whale, was not destroyed by his flesh being dissolved, as is the case with that natural decomposition which takes place in the belly, in the case of those meats which enter into it, on account of the greater heat in the liquids, that it might be shown that these bodies of ours may remain undestroyed. […] Whence also the Word descended into our world, and was incarnate of our body, in order that, having fashioned it to

a more divine image, He might raise it incorrupt, although it had been dissolved by time. And, indeed, when we trace out the dispensation which was figuratively set forth by the prophet, we shall find the whole discourse visibly extending to this.

Jerome stresses the Christological aspects of Jonah 2:11. Seeing Jonah as a type for Christ, Jerome emphasizes that the great fish, hell, and the deep, were forced to give back the Lord to the land of the living so that he in turn can free others from the chains of death. Jerome argues that the verb 'to vomit' speaks in a very emphatic way of the triumphant life which emerges from the deepest and most impenetrable parts of death. The Christological aspects of Jonah 2:11 are also captured in art. A set of two stained glass windows in Cologne Cathedral, Germany, from about 1280 testifies to the significance of Jonah's salvation from the fish as a prototype for Jesus's resurrection by depicting the two events side by side.

2. Jonah's Appearance after Leaving the Fish

Turning to the second issue, namely, Jonah's appearance once the fish had vomited him out, the Reformers especially stress the wondrous fact that Jonah was still alive after three days inside the fish. Luther (German commentary) notes that the fish obviously was kept from digesting Jonah and accordingly concludes that the natural digestive process of the fish must have been momentarily suspended. The fish would also have had to vomit the food out again in order to be able to return Jonah to land unharmed:

> The fish who was but recently the tool of death must now be life's implement; it must be a gateway to life.

Calvin likewise emphasizes the miraculous aspects of Jonah's salvation. As a fish continuously draws water, Jonah would not have been able to breathe while in the fish; he must, therefore, have been preserved beyond the power of nature (Lecture 77).

Jonah's emergence from the fish has been the subject of many paintings. Most famously, perhaps, is the ceiling composition in the Sala Superiore (Upper Hall) of the Scuola Grande di San Rocco in Venice of Jonah leaving the whale's body, painted by the Venetian painter Tintoretto (1518–1594 CE) between 1575 and 1578. It expresses the sheer force and brutality of the event.

Another famous image is the painting 'Jonah and the Whale' by the Dutch painter Pieter Lastman (1583–1633), presently in the Kunstpalast, Düsseldorf, Germany (see Figure 10).

Other retellings of Jonah 2:10 explore how Jonah looked when he came ashore. There are three main interpretative lines: (1) Jonah unchanged; (2) Jonah naked; and (3) Jonah hairless and beardless.

2.1 Jonah Unchanged

According to most stories about people who have been swallowed by a fish, the survivors emerge from their ordeal blind, without hair, and bleached by stomach fluids of the fish (see above, Jonah 2:1). In conscious opposition to these stories, several Christian sources underline that Jonah had not been physically harmed by his time inside the fish. Among them, the pseudepigraphical text *Acts of Paul* (preserved in Coptic and written approximately 160 CE), in the part that is known as Paul's third letter to the Corinthians, states explicitly that Jonah was not physically altered:

> [29]ye know how Jonas the son of Amathi, when he would not preach to them of Nineveh, but fled, was swallowed by the sea-monster; [30]and after three days and three nights God heard the prayer of Jonas out of the lowest hell, and no part of him was consumed, not even a hair nor an eyelash (3 Cor 3:29–30).

As noted by Ziolkowski, Jonah's unaltered appearance was important for the understanding of Jonah as a precursor of Christ and his release from the fish as a prefiguration of Jesus's resurrection (Ziolkowski 1984: 114).

FIGURE 10   'Jonah and the Whale' by Pieter Lastman, Kunstpalast, Düsseldorf. Source: Dr. M. J. Binder, Museum Kunstpalast. Public Domain.

2.2 Jonah Naked

In contrast, it is a common trope in art to depict Jonah reaching the shore *naked*. Friedman has traced the development of this motif and argues that its origin can be found in Christian traditions. It combines the notion of Jonah as a sign for Jesus's Passion with the idea of Jonah's exit from the fish as a sign of rebirth (Friedman 1988: 132–133).

In the Carrow Psalter, for example, a manuscript from East Anglia dating from the mid-thirteenth-century (see Figure 11), we can clearly see that Jonah is thrown into the fish fully dressed and later emerges naked, although with his hair intact (Walters Manuscript W.34, fol. 131 r detail, cf. below).

In other depictions, Jonah (also) enters the water naked. Jonah's nakedness prior to being swallowed by the fish may be an allusion to the tradition that the catechumen took off their old clothes prior to being baptized. This phenomenon can be observed on the fourth-century Brescia Casket, presently found in Museo di Santa Giulia (see Figure 12) (Friedman 1988: 133).

2.3 Jonah Hairless and Beardless

In several rabbinic stories, Jonah is portrayed not only as naked but also as hairless and beardless. Ginzberg mentions that the intense heat in the belly of the fish had consumed Jonah's garments and made his hair fall out. He does not list an exact reference to this tradition, however (Ginzberg 1913: 4:252). One of the few textual sources is *Midrash Tanhuma* (par. *Toledot*, section 12). In the context of Jonah 4:6 (below), this midrash states that Jonah's hair was plucked along with his beard (citation and translation, see Ziolkowski 1984: 115; idem 2007: 85–86; cf. *Yalqut Shim'oni* (Salonika, 1527), 129b, Eng. transl. James L. Kugel):

> And Jonah rose up to flee to Tarshish from before the Lord and he went down to Joppa. Finally, He caused him to endure all the hardships and the fish swallowed him and he called to the Lord from the entrails of the fish, and finally the hair of his head was plucked along with his beard from the heat that he received in the entrails of the fish; and afterward he went off [on a mission] that was still not to his advantage.

Similarly, *Yalqut Shim'oni*, in a comment on Jonah 4:8, reports a comparable situation (quote taken from Ziolkowski 1984: 115, fn. 38, cf. Kadari 2016: 116–118):

> His clothes had been burned and his coat and his hair.

FIGURE 11   Carrow Psalter. Walters Manuscript W.34, fol. 131r detail. The Walters Art Museum, Baltimore.

A few artistic depictions of Jonah also portray him as bald and lacking a beard. Friedman argues that baldness was often associated with rebirth in mediaeval sources, as well as with judgement. Thus, the depiction of Jonah without hair conveys the dual notions of Jonah being judged (and thus condemned to time in hell in the fish), yet subsequently also being reborn (when the fish vomited him out) (Friedman 1988: 134–135). For example, the statue of Jonah in Bamberg cathedral (Germany) from 1210s features Jonah without hair.

Jonah's baldness may also stem from his association with the prophet Elisha (see Jonah 1:1). Both men were scorned and suffered torment at the hands of

FIGURE 12   Brescia Casket, Museo di Santa Giulia, Brescia, Italy. Lipsanoteca di Brescia. Source: RobyBS89. Public Domain.

men: Elisha was famously mocked and called 'baldhead' in 2 Kgs 2:23, and Jonah was thrown into the water. Through their suffering, both men are precursors for Jesus's passion. We have already mentioned the typological significance of Jonah being thrown into the sea (Jonah 1:15); Elisha's tormentors were likewise understood to foreshadow Jesus's tormentors at the crucifixion. In addition, pictorial evidence suggests that in the Middle Ages, Jesus was envisaged to have had his beard and his hair pulled out prior to his crucifixion. The reference to shaving in the fourth Servant Song (Isa 53:7), understood by the Church to speak about Jesus's death, may also have contributed to the depiction of bald Jonah (Friedman 1988: 137–141).

Alternatively, Ziolkowski suggests that the origin of the Christian depiction of Jonah being bald comes from the writing of John the Deacon/Johannes Hymonides (825–880 CE) (see further Modesto 1992: 212). In his adaptation of the biblical parody *Cena Cypriani* 2.166, John the Deacon makes the following pun: 'Jesus was drinking raisin wine, bald Jonah Marsian wine'. Later in 2.235, he refers to 'Bald Jonah was naked and shipwrecked at sea' (see John the Deacon, *Cena Cypriani*, as cited in Ziolkowski 2007: 87).

The tradition of a hairless and beardless Jonah appears also in Letaldus's poem 'About a Certain Fisherman Whom a Whale Swallowed' (Ziolkowski 2007: 243–248 (lines 156–159, 165–169)):

> Out of the whale Within comes forth filthy into the open air. […] baldness, eating away, had scrubbed smooth the whole head of the Englishman, as he looks at the light restored from the sea. The burnt-off skin had left his nails protruding, and his eyelids in growing had brought in thick shadows; and the new light, as it returns, injures his eyes.

The mediaeval German-Swedish painter Albrekt Målare decorated several churches, predominantly around Lake Mälaren. A common motif in his paintings is the prophet Jonah entering the whale clothed, with hair and beard, and emerging from it naked and without hair and beard. His depiction of Jonah draws from motifs elsewhere associated with the prophet Elisha, who is envisaged as being bald (2 Kgs 2:23) (Friedman 1988: 126–129). In Härkeberga Church (near Enköping, Sweden), for example, Albrekt Målare depicts Jonah entering into the fish (to the right) and emerging out of the fish (to the left) (see Jonah 1:13 with picture). A similar image is found in the ceiling of Täby Church, near Stockholm.

2.4 Islamic Depictions of Jonah

In Islamic retellings, Jonah leaves the fish naked (see also Jonah 4:6). In much Islamic iconography, Jonah is depicted halfway emerged from the fish. He is being met by the archangel Gabriel, who assists him out of the fish and offers him a cloak and a turban to cover himself. Jonah's new garments are signs of honour that symbolize God's acceptance of his repentance and prayers. Jonah is also portrayed with a halo in the form of flames in order to emphasize his prophetic identity. A good example of this type of iconography is found in a copy of Al-Tha'labi's *Lives of the Prophets* (1575–1576, TSMK, H. 1227, 122b.) (for more examples, see Haral 2019).

2.5 Miscellaneous Depictions of Jonah

A few depictions of Jonah's return to dry land do not fit into these four categories. Rather prosaically, the fourteenth-century English homiletic poem 'Patience' states that 'Jonah drifted to the shore in muddy clothes' (line 341).

The short story 'Mr. Jonas' by the English novelist Henry Green (1905–1973 CE) offers a unique take on Jonah's exit from the fish. During a fire, a man is discovered sitting in the burning building. The rescue team manages to rescue him amid smoke, fire, and water. The man, identified as a Mr Jonas, emerges 'bone dry' but saying nothing. The story ends with the following words (p. 20) (Russell 1983).

> I saw a bald head, then khaki shoulders. He was not coughing. He was getting up alone. Then I saw he was smothered in dust. He was bone dry. It was Mr. Jonas. As he came up and out, almost without assistance, we all began talking to him, telling him where to tread. He said absolutely nothing. He climbed right into that archway and disappeared. [...] When the other crew took over we had fought our way back to exactly the same spot above that hole out of which, unassisted once he had been released, out of unreality into something temporarily worse, apparently unhurt, but now in all probability suffering from shock, had risen, to live again whoever he might be, this Mr. Jonas.

Mr Jonas, like the biblical Jonah, is rescued from his limbo state in the burning house/the fish by the help of water and outside help (the rescue team/God), and his rescue is likened to being born anew and given new life.

3. Where Did Jonah End Up after the Fish Had Vomited Him Out?

This question highlights a potential difficulty in the Jonah narrative: Jonah was presumably swallowed by the fish in the Mediterranean. When the fish spat him out, Jonah would have ended up nowhere near Nineveh (situated on the eastern bank of the Tigris river); he would thus have been forced to travel quite a distance by land before reaching the city. This problem is highlighted in a rather ironic manner in *Moby-Dick* (Chapter 83), where the old whaler Sag-Harbor makes fun of the Jonah story (see further Pardes 2005: 141–142):

> Poor Sag-Harbor, therefore, seems worsted all round. But he had still another reason for his want of faith. It was this, if I remember right: Jonah was swallowed by the whale in the Mediterranean Sea, and after three days he was vomited up somewhere within three days' journey of Nineveh, a city on the Tigris, very much more than three days' journey across from the nearest point of the Mediterranean coast. How is that? But was there no other way for the whale to land the prophet within that short distance of Nineveh? Yes. He might have carried him round by the way of the Cape of Good Hope. But not to speak of the passage through the whole length of the Mediterranean, and another passage up the Persian Gulf and Red Sea, such a supposition would involve the complete circumnavigation of all Africa in three days, not to speak of the Tigris waters, near the site of Nineveh, being too shallow for any whale to swim in. Besides, this idea of Jonah's weathering the Cape of Good Hope at so early a day would wrest the honour of the discovery of that great headland from Bartholomew Diaz, its reputed discoverer, and so make modern history a liar. (Herman 1851 / Richard Bentley / Public domain)

It should be mentioned in this context that there is evidence of repeated ancient attempts to build a canal that joined the Nile with the Red Sea.

In a similar manner, Peter Hacks describes in his tragedy *Jona* how it was uncomfortable for the fish not only to have Jonah inside but also to have to navigate the sandbanks of the Tigris River (p. 15) (my translation):

> Jonah: Exactly. It did not matter to me, up or down, but it must have been terrible for the whale. And then up the Tigris, between all the sandbanks. I can only guess how one feels, being a whale in the Tigris and with a priest on board.

In contrast, in his *Lives of the Prophets*, the Muslim scholar Al-Tha'labī maintains in all seriousness that the fish brought Jonah all the way up the Tigris to Nineveh (Kadari 2016: 114).

Other retellings solve the issue differently. Dominick Argento's choral work *Jonah and the Whale*, for example, has the fish vomit Jonah out at the exact same spot as where it had all started, presumably back in Israel, to parallel and contrast Jonah 1:1–3 with Jonah 3:1–3:

> Narrator:
> Then our Father firmly commanded the fish
> To spit up the sinner on some dry shore.
> Jonah looked at the land that lay before him:
> It was the very same spot where his journey had started.
> Once again the wind of God's word whirled about him:
> The voice of God:
> Will you never go to Nineveh, not by any means?
>
> Jonah:
> Yes, I shall go, Lord: grant me your grace.

What Happened to the Fish?

After vomiting out Jonah, the fish had fulfilled his God-given task. What happened to the fish then? The Israeli poet Dan Pagis (1930–1986 CE) offers a chilling retelling of the Jonah story in his poem 'Tidings' where the fish, no longer required by God, is left to die (see further Sherwood 2000: 175–176):

> The great fish that vomited out Jonah
> swallowed nothing more.
> Without any prophecy in his guts, he pined away.
> The great fish died and the sea vomited him out onto dry land,
> three hundred cubits of disappointed and forsaken flesh
> in the light of the end of day.
> [...]

The End?

John Tavener's dramatic cantata *The Whale: A Biblical Fantasy* is tightly focused on the fish. Its eighth and final section, called 'The Vomiting', ends, as its title suggests, in Jonah 2:11 where the fish vomits out Jonah and thereafter disappears from the biblical narrative.

Notes

1 I have published much of the material discussed here as a separate article (Tiemeyer 2017c).
2 For the Leviathan traditions in the Bible and the ancient Near East, as well as the lexical connections between the Leviathan, the *tannin*, and the Ugaritic Litan, see Barker 2014: 129–167. See also Heider 1999: 834–836, who helpfully summarizes the biblical occurrences and states that 'what emerges from a review of the OT references is the portrait of a sea monster (or dragon) who served in various texts as a personification of chaos or those evil, historical forces opposed to Yahweh and his people' (p. 836).
3 I am very grateful to Lars Öberg, who not only shared this photo with me but also granted me the right to use it in this book.
4 I wish to thank my student Elias-Claudius Sautiut for drawing my attention to this work.
5 Much of the material here has been published earlier in Tiemeyer 2016.
6 See above, 'The fish as a monster' and 'The fish as death'.
7 Parts of this discussion are published in Tiemeyer 2019b.

Jonah 3

The third chapter of the Book of Jonah introduces the reader to the people of Nineveh. They hear Jonah's message, they understand it as a conditional prophecy, and they repent. We shall look at how exegetes through the ages have wrestled with the theological questions that Nineveh's repentance and God's change of mind raise, and we shall note how comparisons between the Ninevites and the people of Israel often resulted in anti-Jewish interpretations.

Jonah Through the Centuries, First Edition. Lena-Sofia Tiemeyer.
© 2022 John Wiley & Sons, Ltd. Published 2022 by John Wiley & Sons, Ltd.

Jonah 3:1

And the word of Yhwh came to Jonah a second time, saying:

'A second time'

The statement in Jonah 3:1 that God spoke to Jonah 'a second time' raised questions for especially the rabbis and the mediaeval Jewish commentators. As clarified above (Jonah 1:1), Jonah is traditionally identified with Jonah, son of Amittai, in 2 Kgs 14:25. As God now speaks to him again in Jonah 3:1, is this only the *second* time that Jonah received divine communication (rather than, say, the third or even the fourth time)?

The Babylonian Talmud (*b.Yeb.* 11:2) clarifies that the phrase 'a second time' in Jonah 3:1 refers only to God's words to Jonah regarding Nineveh. There is, however, a potential similarity between Jonah's mission to Nineveh and his previous one in the time of Jeroboam, son of Joash: just as Jonah's attitude towards Nineveh turned from bad to good, so in the time of Jeroboam, son of Joash, his attitude towards Israel turned from bad to good. Radak concurs, explaining that although God may have spoken to Jonah several times prior to the command to go to Nineveh, the reference in 3:1 concerns only the matter of Nineveh.

Looking at God's twofold calling to Jonah from a Christological perspective, many of the Church Fathers associate Jonah's ultimate obedience this second time with events in the Gospels when Jesus initially hesitated but eventually acquiesced to do God's will. Jerome, for example, compares Jonah's initial refusal to go to Nineveh and his subsequent compliance with God's command, on the one hand, with Jesus's initial wish to let the cup (of suffering) pass him by (Matt 26:39) and his subsequent submission to his father's will on the cross, on the other. Jerome further likens Jonah's surrender in Jonah 3:3 to that of Jesus who, after three days in hell, announces the mission command in Matt 28:19 to spread the Gospel. Cyril of Alexandria likewise connects Jonah's reluctance to go to Nineveh prior to his stay inside the fish with Jesus's initial reluctance to spread the Gospel beyond the borders of Israel (Matt 15:24; 10:5–6). After having been to Hades, however, Jesus, like Jonah, preached the Gospel to everyone.

Jonah 3:2

Rise, go to Nineveh the great city and call out to it the message that I am speaking to you.

God's second command to Jonah is sometimes associated with Jonah being newborn and even re-baptized. Notably, Francis Quarles writes in his poem 'A Feast for Worms' from 1620 (section VIII):

> Once more the voice of Heavens high Commander
> (Like horrid claps of Heavens dividing thunder,
> Or like the fall of waters breach [the noise
> Being heard far distant off)] such was the voice)
> Came down from Heav'n to Jonah, new-born Man,
> To re-baptized Jonah, and thus began.
> […]
> Arise; let all thy assembled pow'rs agree
> […]
> Arise, and go to Nineveh (the great)

There is a difference in the Hebrew between Jonah 1:2 and Jonah 3:2. Whereas Jonah 1:2 features the preposition '*l* (על), which is often rendered 'speak *against* Nineveh', Jonah 3:2 features the preposition '*l* (אל), which often conveys a less harsh 'speak *to* Nineveh'. The change may reveal a softening of God's attitude towards Nineveh (Lindsay 2016), or towards Jonah (Sutskover 2014: 211). The modern choral work *Jonah: A Musical Morality* by William Mathias thus offers a counterintuitive reading. In this retelling, God's initial command, prior to Jonah's flight, was to preach repentance and God's forgiveness, whereas his second command, following Jonah's time in the fish, is to preach vengeance:

> Jonah, arise. Go now to Nineveh, Nineveh the wicked. Prophesy woe, prophesy vengeance. Warn them of the harvest of unrighteousness. Speak only the words I shall place in your mouth. Preach to the people the word of the Lord.

Jonah 3:3

> And Jonah rose and went to Nineveh in accordance with YHWH's word, and Nineveh was a great city to God, a journey of three days.

'And Jonah rose and went to Nineveh'

The Hellenistic-Jewish sermon *On Jonah* speaks of Jonah's manner of getting to Nineveh. Notably, *On Jonah* 26:3–5 likens Jonah to a horse that, after being tamed, is now so eager to obey his master that he runs to Nineveh!

> I think that just as a wild horse frequently rears before it is forcefully tamed (for it is unwilling to accept the bridle), likewise the prophet became humble and calm after many wanderings and after having understood that God, to whom his words were addressed, is inescapable. He not only hastened but [it was] as if [he] himself was transformed into the message; he turned the three-day journey into one day's simple task with the sole concern of imparting the message from the voice of God to the Ninevites, so that the time determined for [curing] the Ninevites' illness

should not be sluggishly wasted on the journey. Soaked in sweat, in a hurry and in complete obedience, he reached the people.

Jerome conveys a similar sense as he states that Jonah reached Nineveh in one day although this journey would normally have taken three days (cf. Jonah 3:3b).

As hinted at in the sermon *On Jonah*, many exegetes perceive a change in Jonah, brought about by his time in the fish. Jonah is now more willing to obey God than he was back in Jonah 1:1–3. Cyril of Alexandria, in his commentary to Jonah 2:11, states that the fish 'releases the prophet from his innards, who had profited from the ordeal or, rather, was given heart by the experience and gained a clear knowledge that it is risky to resist the divine decrees'. Calvin concurs, arguing that Jonah has improved under God's scourges. He has been severely chastised, to the point that his current behaviour shows that he has been subdued and led to obey God. Moreover, the fact that he began preaching promptly on the first day (Jonah 3:4) proves him to be a changed man (Lecture 77).

The End?

A few retellings end here. Most intriguingly, Father Mapple (*Moby-Dick*, ch. 9) concludes his sermon with the words:

> Yet even then beyond the reach of any plummet – 'out of the belly of hell' – when the whale grounded upon the ocean's utmost bones, even then, God heard the engulphed, repenting prophet when he cried. Then God spake unto the fish; and from the shuddering cold and blackness of the sea, the whale came breeching up towards the warm and pleasant sun, and all the delights of air and earth; and 'vomited out Jonah upon the dry land'; when the word of the Lord came a second time; and Jonah, bruised and beaten – his ears, like two sea-shells, still multitudinously murmuring of the ocean – Jonah did the Almighty's bidding. And what was that, shipmates? To preach the Truth to the face of Falsehood! That was it! 'This, shipmates, is that other lesson; and woe to that pilot of the living God who slights it. Woe to him whom this world charms from Gospel duty! Woe to him who seeks to pour oil upon the waters when God has brewed them into a gale! Woe to him who seeks to please rather than to appal! Woe to him whose good name is more to him than goodness! Woe to him who, in this world, courts not dishonour! Woe to him who would not be true, even though to be false were salvation! Yea, woe to him who, as the great Pilot Paul has it, while preaching to others is himself a castaway!' (Herman 1851 / Richard Bentley / Public domain)

Father Mapple transforms the biblical narrative into a story about Jonah's (personal) salvation: from hard-heartedness, fear, and punishment, to penitence and redemption expressed by Jonah's joy in his obedience to God. For Father Mapple, the fate of the people of Nineveh – their repentance and their survival – plays no role. As noted earlier (Jonah 1), Jonah in Father Mapple's preaching symbolizes a man who repents, an image that stands in sharp relief against the portrayal of Jonah in the (omitted) biblical Chapter 4. This focus on Jonah's repentance furthermore subverts the emphasis in the biblical narrative on God's patience and compassion (see further Holstein 1985: 13–20).

'a great city to God'

Jonah 3:3 repeats the statement in Jonah 1:2 that Nineveh was a 'great city to God'. *Gen.Rab.* 37:4 uses the reference to Nineveh in Jonah 3:3 to clarify the syntax of Gen 10:12, which talks about a city called Resen. As its syntax is ambiguous, however, the reader does not know whether the city of Resen or the city of Nineveh is 'great'; Jonah 3:3 sheds light upon the conundrum and clarifies that it is Nineveh that is the great city.

The notion that Nineveh is great 'to God' in this clause is unclear. Looking at the issue from a linguistic perspective, Radak argues that when the Bible wants to emphasize that something is exceedingly big, it connects it with God. For example, Ps 36:7 [Eng. v. 6]; Ps 80:11 [Eng. v. 10]; SoS 8:6; and Jer 2:31, all contain a reference 'to God'/'to YHWH', yet this word is not necessarily translated. In contrast, looking at it from a theological angle, Luther argues in his German commentary that Nineveh was thus called because God had befriended the city, that he was loath to destroy it, and that he is also the God of the Gentiles. The appellation 'a city to God' is furthermore prophetic: God knew that they were going to accept the prophetic word and repent and thus truly become a 'city to God'.

'a journey of three days'

According to Jonah 3:3b, the city is 'a journey of three days'. This statement is problematic in two respects.

First, it potentially creates a problem when we compare it with the following verse 4, which speaks of Jonah's entering the city in terms of 'a journey of a single day'. Cyril of Alexandria, in his commentary to Jonah 3:1–2, explains the matter ingeniously: it would normally take three days for anyone visiting the city to cross it, but it took Jonah only one day due to 'his irresistible enthusiasm'. Along similar lines, Theodore of Mopsuestia argues that Jonah, upon entering the city, began to walk around part by part and spent a day preaching.

Second, the notion of Nineveh being 'a journey of three days' implies that Nineveh must have been incredibly large, even by modern standards, for it to take three whole days to walk across it. Therefore, several scholars, among them

Ibn Ezra, explain that the three-day journey refers to the circumference of the city. It would take but one day to walk from one side to the other. Along similar lines, Luther states in his German commentary that what is really meant here is the time it takes to stroll around it in a leisurely gait. Calvin rejects these types of explanations, however, instead claiming that the city was very great indeed. In support, the fact that there were 120 000 children in the city (Jonah 4:11, cf. below) shows its enormous size (Lecture 77). Using a contemporary comparison (albeit weakened by the difference in density), it takes approximately 8 ½ hours to walk across London (from Enfield to Croydon, located about 21 miles apart), a city of more than 8 000 000 inhabitants.[1]

Jonah 3:4

> And Jonah began to come to the city, a distance of one day, and he called and said: 'In 40 days Nineveh will be overturned'.

'And Jonah began to come to the city'

Ibn Ezra, commenting on the phrase 'and he began', points out that some commentators appeal to this verb in support of their claim that the people of Nineveh had already begun to repent from their evil deeds prior to Jonah's arrival (cf. Jonah 3:3). Ibn Ezra himself, however, argues that this is *derash* (the meaning of the text as informed by midrash). Instead, this phrase simply means that Jonah began to speak. From a modern perspective, Havea asks why Jonah waited a whole day to call out his message. He speculates that Jonah may have disregarded the poor people living at the outskirts of the city as less important and unworthy of his proclamation and thus expendable (Havea 2020: 35–54).

What Did Jonah Really Say?

Jonah's statement that Nineveh would be 'overturned' (*neh^epachet*) in 40 days raises several issues. Whereas Christian interpreters tend to explore the actual content of Jonah's preaching, Jewish interpreters focus more on the exact meaning of the verb *neh^epachet*.

The Content of Jonah's Sermon

Did Jonah simply declare – in one single, short sentence on one single occasion – Nineveh's imminent fate or did he rather preach repentance (and possibly on more than one occasion)? This issue is intertwined with the message and genre of the Book of Jonah, as well as with Jonah's attitude to God and the people of Nineveh.

While the biblical narrative implies that Jonah said nothing more than the exact sentence 'in 40 days Nineveh will be overturned' (after all, Jonah did not want Nineveh to repent [see Jonah 4:2]), many (predominantly Christian) interpreters do not want to go down this route. Instead, they assume that the biblical text does not record Jonah's complete message. Cyril of Alexandria, for example, argues that the prophets often did not write down for us all the words that came to them from God. In more detail, Theodore of Mopsuestia, following the reading of the LXX (below), states that the whole point of Jonah disclosing to the people that the city would be destroyed in three days was to inspire them to repentance:

> It would have been futile for him to threaten destruction if it absolutely had to happen, since there would have been no point in the threat; so the result was that they either reformed and averted the punishment, or they did not reform and it was justly imposed on them.

Theodore further states that the people of Nineveh would clearly never have believed in God on the basis of the single remark 'three days more and Nineveh will be destroyed' alone, uttered by a completely unknown foreigner and without any word about the one who had sent him. Therefore, 'it is obvious that he also mentioned God, the Lord of all, and said he had been sent by him; and he delivered the message of destruction, calling them to repentance'. As Hill notes, Theodore in this way undermines what the author of the Book of Jonah actually wanted to say (Hill 2013: 202 n. 31).

Along the same lines, the fifth-century poem *Hymnus Ieiunantium* ('Hymn for those who fast') by the Christian poet Prudentius elaborates on Jonah's message and transforms it into a call to belief (lines 131–136):

> Thus turned again to duty's path
> To Nineveh he swiftly came,
> Their lusts rebuked and boldly preached
> God's judgment on their sin and shame;
> 'Believe!' he cried, 'the Judge draws nigh
> Whose wrath shall wrap your streets in flame'.

The Reformers offer similar interpretations. Luther maintains in his German commentary that it is not known how many days Jonah spent in Nineveh before he had conveyed his message to the entire city. We may nonetheless assume that he did not confine himself to the words written in verse 4, but expounded on the theme of why such wrath would come upon them, what kind of sins they had committed, how one should be a godly person, etc. Calvin likewise states that, since the people of Nineveh ended up believing in God (Jonah 3:5), Jonah's preaching cannot have been as concise as Jonah 3:4

reports. Rather, Jonah would have introduced his discourse by declaring that he was God's prophet and thus made his pronunciations with God's authority. He would also have referred explicitly to the Ninevites' particular sins, how grievous these sins were to God, and therefore how God's impending punishment of them was just. Furthermore, the Ninevites must have derived something more than terror from Jonah: they must have been informed that if they submitted to God, they might be pardoned. In other words, they must have conceived some hope of grace (Lecture 77). More succinctly, the Geneva Bible notes to Jonah 3:4 claim that Jonah went into the city and preached until the city was converted. The notes to Jonah 3:5 further state that Jonah declared to the people of Nineveh that he was a prophet sent to them from God, to make known his judgement against them.

Later preachers followed suit. The Congregationalist pastor of the South Church in Boston, Massachusetts, Joseph Sewall (1688–1769 CE), preached in his sermon 'Nineveh's Repentance and Deliverance' that Jonah, like Noah(!), declared to the people of Nineveh:

> We may suppose that Jonah declared to them the Grace and Mercy of the God of Israel and show'd them the Way of Salvation thro' the then promised Messiah; so tho' their Bodies should be destroy'd, their Souls might be sav'd in the Day of the Lord'. (pp. 4–5)

Sewall's interpretation is noteworthy in that it distinguishes between physical and spiritual redemption. It furthermore turns Jonah's message of doom to the Ninevites into a message of hope of deliverance on the Day of Judgement. Sewall's audience should emulate the people of Nineveh to save their soul and thus obtain life after death.

What Does the Verb neh^{e}pachet *Mean?*
The verb *neh^{e}pachet* can be translated literally as 'overturned', yet this 'overturning' can be understood in two ways: it can denote either physical destruction or spiritual transformation (from evil to good). Is one or the other or even both meanings inherent in Jonah's prophecy? It is common, especially among Jewish commentators, to highlight the dual meaning of this verb: whereas Jonah understood the verb to have only the first meaning (and thus acted the way that he did), it later, in retrospect, became clear that God had intended the second meaning all along. As a result, Jonah's prediction turned out to be correct after all: Jonah accurately foretold Nineveh's (spiritual) overturning. In other words, the use of the specific verb *neh^{e}pachet* enabled the reversal of the decree while staying true to the prophetic prediction. It also provided the people involved

with the free will to choose the outcome. Rashi, for example, describes a positive Catch-22: if the people of Nineveh had not repented, then the first meaning (destruction) would have turned out to be correct; if they did repent, however, then the second meaning (turning from bad to good) would have been meant. In contrast, Radak, noting that the verb *neh^{e}pachet* appears elsewhere in the context of the destruction of a city in Gen 19:25 (cf. also Deut 29:22), argues that this verb emphasized the severity of their situation and thus spurred the Ninevites on.

Exploring the dual meaning of the verb *neh^{e}pachet* from a different perspective, the Babylonian Talmud (*b.San.* 89b) questions how Jonah 3:4 can be read coherently with Amos 3:7, which states that God does nothing without first revealing his secret to the prophets. As the prophecy in Jonah was really about repentance, however, rather than about physical destruction, God did not have to reveal its exact meaning to Jonah:

> A tanna recited before R. Hisda: 'He who suppresses his prophecy is flogged'. To which he retorted: 'One who eats dates out of a sieve is flogged'! Who then warned him? Abaye answered: 'His fellow prophets'. Whence do they know? – Said Abaye: 'For it is written, Surely the Lord will do nothing but that he reveals his secret [unto his servant the prophets]'. But perhaps they [the Heavenly Court] repented thereof? – Had they repented, all prophets would have been informed – Jonah was originally told that Nineveh would be turned, but did not know whether for good or for evil.

Why Did God Tell the People of Nineveh of the Planned Destruction Beforehand?

The above-mentioned comparison between Jonah and Amos highlights the ultimate purpose of (ancient Near Eastern) prophecy. The point of a prophecy of doom is, in fact, its own cancellation: the foretelling of God's planned punishment aims to make sure that people repent so that the predicted punishment will not take place (Tiemeyer 2005: 329–350). The intended audience of the Book of Jonah would thus have understood Jonah's call here as an implicit call to repentance rather than as a statement conveying information. The verdict is still open, and the people have a chance to cancel the prediction. John Chrysostom, in his Homily 5.4, 'On Repentance and Almsgiving', goes directly to the centre of this issue, as he states that God sent Jonah to Nineveh for the very purpose of annulling the prophecy:

> This is why he threatened with hell: so He would not lead anyone away to hell.

Equally poignantly, the early Christian theologian and ascetic Origen (184–253 CE) asks whether God deceived the people of Nineveh (*Homilies on Jeremiah and 1 Kgs 28*, Jer 19:7):

> Yet three days and Nineveh shall be destroyed', speaking as one who speaks truly or not? Or as one who deceives by a deceit that converts?

The Gaulish Church leader Caesarius of Arles (468/470–542 CE) goes beyond the text of Jonah and links Jonah's call to repentance in Nineveh to the situation in his own days. Just as the people of Nineveh repented in three days, so let all those who listen to God today likewise repent. There will, however, be a time when it is too late to repent (Sermon 133.5). Many Jewish interpreters advocate the same view. As Malbim suggests, the people of Nineveh intuitively understood Jonah's message to be conditional. God would not have sent Jonah to them unless he intended them to use the forty days of grace to change their behaviour.

In How Many Days Would Nineveh Be Destroyed?

The MT stipulates that Nineveh would be destroyed in 'forty days'. In contrast, the LXX speaks of 'three days'. Many interpreters through the centuries, Jewish and Christian alike, have preferred the reading of the LXX. The Hellenistic-Jewish sermon *On Jonah* 27:2 speaks of 'three days' here as do many of the Church Fathers. John Chrysostom, in his Homily 5.4, 'On Repentance and Almsgiving', makes a case that three days are enough even for barbarians to annul God's anger at sin. God was likewise satisfied with a mere three days of repentance before he forgave them.

A few interpreters debate the difference between the MT and the LXX. Jerome ultimately settles in favour of the MT as he compares the forty days in Jonah with Moses's forty-day fast in the wilderness (Exod 34:28), Elijah's forty-day fast during his flight from Jezebel (1 Kgs 19:8), and Jesus's forty-day fast in the wilderness (Matt 4:2). Augustine explains in ch. 44 of his *City of God* the difference between the MT and the LXX in an ingenious matter: while the three days in the LXX prefigure the time between Jesus's death and resurrection, the forty days in the MT prefigure the time between Jesus's resurrection and his ascension (cf. the *Glossa Ordinaria* for the same interpretation):

> So that, if the reader desires nothing else than to adhere to the history of events, he may be aroused from his sleep by the Septuagint interpreters, as well as the prophets, to search into the depth of the prophecy, as if they had said, In the forty days seek Him in whom thou mayest also find the three days, – the one thou wilt find in His ascension, the other in His resurrection.

Looking more at the implication of the forty days delay between the proclamation of destruction and the execution of said destruction, Havea emphasizes that at least the rich people of Nineveh would have had time to evacuate the city. They could pack and leisurely move with several days to spare. In contrast, the poor people may have found evacuating from Nineveh difficult even with a forty-day deadline. This long time between threat and execution may furthermore suggest that God was not serious about overthrowing Nineveh, which in turn suggests that Jonah, rather than the people of Nineveh, was the target of God's actions (Havea 2020: 35–54).

How Would Nineveh Be Destroyed?

A few retellings of the Jonah narrative wonder about the specific method by which Nineveh would be destroyed. As suggested by the shared use of the root *hapach* ('destroy'/'overturn') in Gen 19:25 and Jonah 3:4, it is commonly assumed that Nineveh, had it not repented, would have been destroyed in a manner akin to that of Sodom and Gomorrah, i.e. through fire and brimstone (Gen 19:24). The fourth-century poem *De Jona et Nineveh*, attributed to Tertullian, opens with a reference to the fires of Sodom and Gomorrah (line 2) and then continues to refer to Nineveh in the context of fire (lines 9–12):

> A city-Nineveh-by stepping o'er
> The path of justice and of equity,
> On her own head had well-nigh shaken down
> More fires of rain supernal.

Prudentius' aforementioned *Hymnus Ieiunantium* follows suit. The reference to fire and smoke-cloud in lines 136–138 seems to envisage something akin to the destruction of Sodom and Gomorrah:

> Whose wrath shall wrap your streets in flame'
> Thence to the lofty mount withdrew,
> Where he might watch the smoke-cloud lower.

In contrast, the Middle English poem *Patience* (line 506) appears to understand the verb *neh^epachet* to convey an earthquake, presumably due to its inherent meaning of 'turning over' (Lee 1982: 202–203):

And overthrow yonder town when it has turned.

Later preachers also took a certain delight in exploring various means by which God might have destroyed Nineveh, had it turned out to be needed. Thomas Bradbury, in his sermon from 1720, asks his audience to imagine a 'rage of pestilence' or 'Convulsions of a Civil War' or 'the Deluge of a foreign Invasion' ('The Repentance of Nineveh', 13–14).

Jonah 3:5

> And the people of Nineveh believed in God and they called a fast and they put on sackcloth, from the big ones to the small ones.

The reference to the repentance of the Ninevites in Jonah 3:5–8 may have been picked up by Judith 4:9–14, given that it reports a very similar procedure (Ueberschaer 2020).

> [9]All the men of Israel cried most fervently to God and humbled themselves before him. [10]They, their wives, their children, their cattle, all their resident aliens, hired or slave, wrapped sackcloth round their loins. [11]All the Israelites in Jerusalem, including women and children, lay prostrate in front of the Temple, and with ashes on their heads stretched out their hands before the Lord. [12]They draped the altar itself in sackcloth and fervently joined together in begging the God of Israel not to let their children be carried off, their wives distributed as booty, the towns of their heritage destroyed, the Temple profaned and desecrated for the heathen to gloat over. [13]The Lord heard them and looked kindly on their distress. The people fasted for many days throughout Judaea as well as in Jerusalem before the sanctuary of the Lord Almighty. [14]Joakim the high priest and all who stood before the Lord, the Lord's priests and ministers, wore sackcloth round their loins as they offered the perpetual burnt offering and the votive and voluntary offerings of the people. (New Jerusalem Bible)

The Hellenistic-Jewish sermon *On Jonah* 28:4 contains a unique interpretation of this verse as it depicts how the Ninevites summoned men and women, elders and princes, servants, kings, and lords together into one sorrowful assembly and gave a long speech wherein they outlined their programme of repentance. This interpretation disagrees in part with the biblical narrative in the following 3:6 where the king (sg.) takes an active role (see also Muradyan and Topchyan 2013: 790, fn. to 28:4–36:3). Later on in the same sermon (36:1–3), the speakers invite Jonah to serve as their intercessor.

There are relatively few depictions of the Ninevites' repentance. One of the exceptions is the stained glass windows in Ely Cathedral from 1858 by George Hedgeland (see Figure 13). The middle panel features Jonah preaching repentance, whereas the surrounding right panel depicts the Ninevites' repentance.

FIGURE 13   Stained glass windows at Ely Cathedral, England. Source: Hatns A. Rosbach. Licensed under CC BY-SA 3.0.

Nineveh is depicted as an Assyrian city, emphasized by the appearance of the winged figure in the background of the right panel.

'And the people of Nineveh believed in God'

Jonah 3:5 claims that all the people of Nineveh 'believed in God'. What exactly did this belief entail, though? Did it merely mean fasting and putting on sackcloth, as the rest of the verse specifies, or did it involve something else such as performing good deeds and/or worshipping the God of Israel? In response, Abarbanel states that the phrase 'they believed in God' must mean that they believed in God's *executive power* to accomplish matters (including destroying their city Nineveh).

Turning the attention to Jonah's role in the Ninevites' new-found faith, Luther, in the Preface to his German commentary, holds Jonah in the highest esteem and argues that he should serve as a model for all ministers involved in administering the Word:

> Jonah is also an object of comfort for all who administer the Word. It teaches them not to despair of the fruit of the Gospel, no matter how badly it appears to be devoid of fruit and profit. For here a single man, Jonah, is dispatched to the mightiest king and the greatest kingdom of that day. When we compare the two, Jonah and this king, it impresses us as ridiculous and completely impossible that such a mighty king and such a mighty kingdom should be moved, converted, and frightened by the words of one weak individual, a stranger to boot, and by a message which the king himself did not even hear – he heard it only as a report. In view of this, I am tempted to say that no apostle or prophet, not even Christ himself, performed and accomplished with a single sermon the great things Jonah did.

Other interpreters have sought to isolate the exact factor which made the people of Nineveh believe Jonah. In short, what did Jonah do to inspire such faith in his word and to trigger such repentance? Ibn Ezra, citing Rabbi Joshua, claims that the sailors (from Chapter 1) went to Nineveh prior to Jonah's arrival and spoke the word of God to the people. This exegetical move explains, in turn, why the Ninevites had faith (when Jonah himself arrived). Radak likewise suggests that the sailors (who had cast Jonah into the sea) had gone ahead to Nineveh to tell of God's miraculous rescue of Jonah through the big fish. This miracle showed God's power and the trustworthiness of his message through his prophet.

This interpretation resurfaces in Thomas Bradbury's sermon on Jonah from 1720. According to Bradbury, the Ninevites believed in Jonah because the rumour of his survival at sea and in the fish had gone before him ('The Repentance of Nineveh', pp. 20–21):

> It is probable he told the Ninevites what a Course of Danger and Deliverance he had gone through. Perhaps they might hear some part of the Story from the Mariners [...] Now to find that this Man was yet alive, and hear him telling the rest of the Story, that God had appointed a great Fish to be his preserver; and that, after three days in the Belly of that Creature, he was returned to Land and Daylight: This could not fail to strike the Wonder of all who hear it; and 'tis not unlikely they might know his Case from our Lord's way of giving us the Passage, that Jonah was a Sign to the Ninevites.

Along similar lines, the modern animated film *Jonah: A VeggieTales Movie* features the three pirates having turned up in Nineveh ahead of Jonah's own arrival. When Jonah later appears and begins to preach, his reference to his survival inside the fish provides the turning point when the people of Nineveh decide to believe his message.

The notion that someone had arrived in Nineveh prior to Jonah is turned into a joke in the Israeli television programme *The Jews are Coming*. One episode depicts Jonah arriving in Nineveh, only to realize that due to his delay in the fish, someone has already preached in Nineveh 'three or four weeks ago'. To quote the guard with whom Jonah is speaking, 'we listened to him; now everything is better'. As Jonah cries out in despair to God, the Ninevite guard realizes that he is Jonah and conveys a new divine message, this time that the wickedness of Assur has risen before God. Unsurprisingly, at that point Jonah loses it completely (https://www.youtube.com/watch?v=QDUBIZMVZYs).

'and they called a fast'

Verse 5b claims that the people of Nineveh called a fast and wore sackcloth. This statement contradicts the content of verses 6–8, where the King of Nineveh calls a fast and commands his people to wear sackcloth. This discrepancy in the biblical narrative caused Ibn Ezra (commentary to Jonah 3:7) to argue that verse 5b is out of order. Jonah's word reached the king, and he proclaimed a fast, etc. (vv. 6–9) *before* the people of Nineveh believed (v. 5). In contrast, Radak upholds the view that the people of Nineveh made their own repentance (v. 5) before the warning reached the king (v. 6).

To Fast or Not to Fast

Many Church Fathers emphasize the merit of the Ninevites' fasting. Ambrose, in his 'Letter 44', argues that a person who does not fast is naked. Thus, had Adam fasted he would not have become naked (Gen 3:7). He continues by stating that 'Nineveh freed herself from death by fasting'. John Chrysostom likewise declares that 'fasting snatched the city from these gates of death and returned Nineveh to life' (Homily 5.4, 'On Repentance and Almsgiving'). Jerome compares the individual benefit of fasting versus wearing sackcloth. In his view, the former is superior since it is visible only to God, whereas the latter involves also the penitent's fellow men. So, if there were a choice between the two options, then fasting would be preferable, yet both options combined constitute the ultimate response to God.

In sharp contrast, Luther, in his German commentary, points out that the people of Nineveh 'do some things that God does not command them', namely fasting and putting on sackcloth. For Luther, God is uninterested in these superficial things; he wants the heart. Luther further likens the Ninevites' behaviour to that of monks, who in their cowls perform their customary actions in cloisters and churches especially during Lent and Holy Week: 'these are indeed found to be sheer buffoonery'. Although Luther concedes that 'a fearful heart, a humble and frightful conscience, may of course also do foolish things to evidence its intense seriousness', he declares unequivocally that outer actions are unnecessary at best and may even be harmful.

Encouragement to Be like the People of Nineveh

In much Christian reception, the Ninevites' penitence has often been praised as an outstanding example that we all should emulate. Gregory of Nazianzus, for instance, encourages his audience to be like Nineveh and not like Sodom (Gen 19:17, 23), i.e. to be people who repent of their wickedness lest they be consumed by it ('Oration 16.14'). In harsher words, John Chrysostom seeks to shame his audience by comparing them to the people of Nineveh (Homily 20, section 21, 'Homilies Concerning the Statues'):

> After this are we not ashamed, must we not blush, if it turns out that in three days only the barbarians laid aside all their wickedness, but that we, who have been urged and taught during so many days, have not got the better of one bad habit?

Chrysostom later also encourages his audience not only to fast but, like the people of Nineveh, also to change their lives and abandon the evil ways completely (Homily 4 on 'Second Corinthians: 2 Corinthians 2:11'):

> God, says He, saw that they turned everyone from his evil way, and He repented of the evil that He had said He would do unto them (Jonah 3:10). He said not, He saw [their] fasting and sackcloth and ashes. And I say not this to overturn fasting, (God forbid!) but to exhort you that with fasting ye do that which is better than fasting, the abstaining from all evil.

Anti-Jewish Comparisons

Many Christian writers have employed the Ninevites' penitence in their anti-Jewish polemic (Urbach 1949: 118–122; Golka 1986: 51–61). In his *Dialogue with Trypho*, ch. 108, Justin Martyr offers a comparison to the detriment of the Jews:

> And though all the men of your nation knew the incidents in the life of Jonah, and though Christ said amongst you that He would give the sign of Jonah, exhorting you to repent of your wicked deeds at least after He rose again from the dead, and to mourn before God as did the Ninevites, in order that your nation and city might not be taken and destroyed, as they have been destroyed; yet you

not only have not repented, after you learned that He rose from the dead, but, as I said before you have sent chosen and ordained men throughout all the world to proclaim that a godless and lawless heresy had sprung from one Jesus, a Galilean deceiver, whom we crucified, but his disciples stole him by night from the tomb, where he was laid when unfastened from the cross, and now deceive men by asserting that he has risen from the dead and ascended to heaven.

Jerome comments more briefly but not less scathingly that 'Nineveh believed but not Israel; the foreskin believed, but circumcision remained without faith'. Cyril of Alexandria likewise compares the behaviour of the people of Nineveh with that of Israel:

> While this was the situation of the Ninevites, however, Israel in its stupidity did not obey the Law, mocking the provisions of Moses and setting no store by the statements of the prophets. Why do I make this claim? They also turned killers of the Lord, not even believing Christ himself, Saviour of us all.

Ephraem the Syrian (303–373 CE) wrote a long metrical homily called *The Repentance of Nineveh* which, as the title suggests, focuses completely on the Ninevites' repentance. Throughout the homily, the people of Israel are compared unfavourably with the people of Nineveh, given the latters' exemplary behaviour, in a manner that is full of anti-Jewish sentiments. In Chapter 5 of the homily, Ephraem elaborates on Jonah's amazement at the reformation of the Ninevites and how it compares with the sinful behaviour of his own people. Chapter 6 continues in the same vein, as Jonah enumerates the crimes of Israel (lines 64–85):

> When Jonah looked on Nineveh,
> She gathered her sons together as a Church.
> All Nineveh was purified;
> The fast in the midst of her was held in honour;
> But the holy temple in Zion,
> They had made a den of robbers.[2]
> He looked on Nineveh, and the King
> Paid adoration unto God;
> He looked on Jeroboam,
> And he was worshipping the calves.
> The sins of the Ninevites made them tremble,
> With loud crying before God;
> The Hebrews sacrificed their sons,
> And offered up their daughters to devils.
> In their fasting, the Ninevites
> Poured out their wines.
> From the Ninevites there was perceived

> The fair savour of mourning;
> But in the midst of Zion there breathed
> The perfume and incense of idols.

In Chapter 7 of the homily, God responds to the Ninevites' repentance and decides not to overthrow Nineveh. At first, Jonah is displeased but, as the Ninevites praise him for pleading their case, Jonah relents (Chapter 8). In gratitude, the people of Nineveh accompany Jonah to the borders of Israel and wish to enter the land. Jonah, however, deters them as he fears that they would be shocked by the Israelites' iniquities (Chapter 9). A compromise is reached (Chapter 10): from a high hill the Ninevites observe Israel's multiple sins, among them the high places (lines 9–11), their idols (lines 13–19), the calves of Jeroboam (lines 27–30), the depravity of the Israelites, such as oppression, prodigality, intemperance, lasciviousness, fornication, falsehood, robbery, incantation, magic, 'chaldaeism', soothsaying, injustice, and wickedness (lines 37–50) – the list goes on and on.

The final Chapter 11 of his homily opens with the words:

> Having seen the wickedness of the Israelites, the Ninevites resolved to return to their own country. While honouring Jonah, they condemn his countrymen, who boast themselves of their relation to Abraham, while they are idolaters.

The rest of Chapter 11 of the homily continues in the same vein:

> The sins they had approved, but now
> repented of,
> The Hebrews had clothed themselves with;
> The idolatry which the heathen had cast off,
> This abominable nation had taken up
> (lines 9–12).
> […]
> Perhaps this people is about to be extirpated
> In place of Nineveh which has not been overthrown (lines 19–20)

Ephraem concludes by exhorting his own audience to follow in the footsteps of the people of Nineveh.

This type of anti-Jewish comparison persists in the writings of the Reformers. Luther compares Nineveh's behaviour favourably with that of Jerusalem at the time of Jesus. To emphasize his point, Luther draws attention to Jesus's words to the centurion in Matt 8:10 of not having encountered such faith in all of Israel (German commentary). Bugenhagen, in the Preface to his Jonah commentary, follows suit and compares the repentance among the people of Nineveh with the 'unbelieving and obstinate impenitence of the Jews, who repented neither at the preaching of Jonah nor at the preaching of the Messiah, God's Son' (as quoted in Lohrmann 2012: 77). The English congregational minister Thomas Bradbury likewise brings Matt 12:41 into his sermon 'The Repentance of Nineveh' to underscore the contrast: whereas the people of Nineveh believed Jonah, a mere messenger, and repented of their sins, the people of Israel neither believed nor repented despite hearing Jesus, the son of God, in person (pp. 22–24). A similar type of anti-Jewish polemic is attested in Joseph Sewall' sermon 'Nineveh's Repentance and Deliverance', preached in Boston in 1740. Sewell writes (p. 18):

> Notwithstanding this, God said to his People, If ye will not be reformed, but will walk contrary to me, then will I also walk contrary to you, and will punish you seven Times for your sins [...] Jerusalem and the Temple were destroyed by Fire, and God's People led into Captivity to Babylon. And after their merciful Restoration, when they had filled up the measure of their Sins by disobeying and crucifying the Lord of Glory, and then by rejecting the Offers of the Gospel made to them by His Apostles; the Wrath of God came upon them to the uttermost by the Romans, and they are made an Execration and a Curse unto this Day.

'and they put on sackcloth'

The comment that the people of Nineveh put on sackcloth has given rise to some embellishment in select retellings of the Jonah narrative. Yet, what has possibly intrigued even more commentators is what they did *not* wear. Prudentius' *Hymnus Ieiunantium*, for example, spends a lot of ink (lines 148–150) describing the kind of clothes that the fine ladies put aside for the occasion:

> each haughty dame
> Puts silken robes and gems away,
> In sable garbed, and ashes casts
> Upon her tresses' disarray.

Later in the same poem (lines 156–158), the clothes that the king removed are described as equally rich and opulent. In this way, Prudentius highlights the trappings of wealth of the Ninevites (Lee 1982: 204–205).

Jonah 3:6

> And the matter reached the king of Nineveh and he rose from his throne and removed his cloak from upon him and donned sackcloth and sat in the dust.

'And the matter reached the king of Nineveh'

Jonah 3:6 speaks of an anonymous 'king of Nineveh'. At this point, the identification of Jonah with the prophet in 2 Kgs 14:25 who lived during the reign of Jeroboam II (r. 786–746 BCE) becomes problematic. If we adhere to this identification, the most fitting monarch would be either Ashurnasirpal II (r. 883–859 BCE) or Shalmaneser III (r. 859–824 BCE). It was, however, only Sennacherib (r. 705–681 BCE) who around 700 BCE turned Nineveh into a truly great city (cf. 2 Kgs 19:36–37), i.e. at least 40 years after Jonah's supposed visit to the city. Until the modern study of Assyriology, knowledge of the Neo-Assyrian monarchs was limited to those mentioned in the Hebrew Bible. Exegetes thus had to make do with their very limited (and often factually faulty) knowledge when seeking to identify the 'king of Nineveh'. In *Midrash Jonah* 99–100, for example, the King of Nineveh is equated with King Osnappar of Assyria (i.e. Ashurbanipal (r. 668–627), cf. Ezra 4:10) (Ginzberg 1913: 4:250, cf. *Yalkut Shimoni* 550:3).

The most intriguing identification is found in a note in Codex Reuchlinianus of Targum Jonathan, namely, that the King of Nineveh (of the Book of Jonah) was none other than Pharaoh (of the Exodus tradition): 'the Pharaoh who was king in those days in Nineveh' (Cathcart and Gordon 1989: 108, fn. 8). This tradition recurs in *PRE* 43. The King of Nineveh was Pharaoh of Egypt, who, according to *PRE*, was the sole survivor of the incident at the Red Sea when God drowned the Egyptian army in order to save the people of Israel. Pharaoh repented and subsequently went to rule in Nineveh. Having learnt his lesson at the Red Sea, upon hearing Jonah's message he was quick to repent and to order his subjects to do likewise.

Speaking more generally about what Jonah 3:6 can teach us about government, Augustine points out that a king needs to serve God in two capacities: as a man and as a leader who exerts the necessary strength to sanction laws that command goodness and that prohibit its opposite. In the case of the King of Nineveh, he performed his royal duties well by compelling the whole city to appease the Lord ('Letter 185', Chapter 5, section 19). Likewise, Jacob of Serug emphasizes the leadership of the King of Nineveh after whom all leaders should pattern themselves (56. 459.6–460:21). Along slightly different lines, the *Glossa Ordinaria* comments on the difficulty for the powerful of this world to convert to the humility of Christ.

Later retellings have allowed the King of Nineveh to serve as a symbol of a contemporaneous monarch. The first oratorio ever composed in the New World is probably the oratorio and accompanying libretto *Jonah* by Samuel Felsted (?1743–1802 CE) (Dox 1991: 37–46). The oratorio itself, as well as the illustrations on the manuscript, suggests that the choice of Jonah as its subject matter probably reflects the growing tension between Britain and its struggling

American colonies. Read this way, the British monarch George III, like the King of Nineveh, was threatened with God's imminent destruction due to royal hubris. Unless Britain repented, God would obliterate it (Marks 1997: 131).

'and he rose from his throne and removed his cloak from upon him'

The king, upon hearing the news of Jonah's message, rose from his throne and 'removed' something that belonged to him 'from upon him'. The meaning of the Hebrew word *adarto* is uncertain, yet the context suggests that it is a piece of his royal clothing. The word *aderet* elsewhere denotes (a prophet's) 'mantle' (cf. 1 Kgs 19:19; 2 Kgs 2:8). TJ adds adjectives to its translation, in this way seeking to clarify that the king rose from 'his *royal* throne' and removed 'his *precious* clothes'. Radak follows suit, explaining that this word refers to the royal robe that the king was wearing. The *Glossa Ordinaria* goes into further detail as it specifies that the king exchanged his purple-dyed clothes for sackcloth, his perfume for mud, and his purity for filth.

The Hellenistic-Jewish sermon *On Jonah* 37 inserts more high-level officials, together with office-appropriate actions, to this verse. In addition to the king who 'replaced the throne of his power with sackcloth', the sermon specifies that the judges put down the sceptre and their authority, the masters granted freedom to their slaves, the elders scattered ashes over their grey hair, and the old women pulled out their hair. There were no more weddings and all that was heard was lament and mourning.

The king's removal of his cloak recalls Esth 4:1, where Mordechai's response to the decree of destruction is to tear his clothes, put on sackcloth and ashes, and go out wailing into the city. Later, in Esth 4:3, all the Jews in the province fasted, wept, and lay on sackcloth and ashes. As noted by Seidler, the Book of Esther narrative probably invokes the earlier Jonah narrative in order to emphasize the aspects of sin, remorse, and redemption (Seidler 2019).

Jonah 3:7

> And he proclaimed and said in Nineveh: 'By the decree of the king and his nobles, saying: let neither man nor animal, cattle, nor sheep eat anything, let them not feed, and let them not drink water'.

As already mentioned above, the king's proclamation is problematic insofar as the people of Nineveh are already fasting (Jonah 3:5). In view of this apparent redundancy, Radak ponders whether the royal proclamation referred to in

Jonah 3:7 contained any additional information. Seeing that the *people* were already repenting, Radak suggests that the king's proclamation managed to encourage the repentance of the *animals*.

The fact that the animals were not allowed to feed has been the source of much rabbinic discussion.[3] Many rabbis deem the decision not to give animals sustenance to be a sign of the Ninevites' inherent insincerity and cruelty. As stated in the Jerusalem Talmud (*y.Tan*. 2:1, cf. *Pesiqta deRab Kahana* xxiv: xi), the Ninevites acted cruelly towards their animals so as to force the animals to cry out (thus explaining Jonah 3:8):

> III.A. S-Y. Said R. Simeon b. Laqish: 'The repentance that the men of Nineveh carried out was deceitful.'
>
> What did they do?
>
> R. Hunah in the name of R. Simeon b. Halaputa: 'They set up calves inside, with the mothers outside, lambs inside, with the mothers outside, and these bellowed from here, and those bellowed from there'.
>
> 'They said, "If we are not shown mercy, we shall not have mercy on them".'
>
> 'This is in line with that which is written: "How the beasts groan! The herds of cattle are perplexed because there is no pasture for them; even the flocks of sheep are dismayed"' (Joel 1:18)
>
> Said R. Aha: 'In Arabia that is how they act [toward their beasts, treating them cruelly].'
>
> 'But let man and beast be covered with sackcloth, and let them cry mightily to God; [yes, let everyone turn from his evil way and from the violence which is in his hands]' (Jonah 3:8).

The Babylonian Talmud (*b.Tan*. 2:1–11) concurs as it repeats the accusation of cruelty towards animals and children and emphasizes how the people of Nineveh began to bargain with God, saying that unless God had mercy on them, they would not have mercy on the animals:

> 'Let them be covered with sackcloth, both man and beast' (Jon 3:8).
> What did they do?
> They set beasts by themselves and children by themselves and said before him, 'Lord of the world, if you don't have mercy on us, we shall not have mercy on these'.

In contrast to the rabbis, many Church Fathers laud the Ninevites' actions regarding their animals. John Chrysostom, for example, states that animals, as well as humans, were included in the fast, 'so that all living things would abstain from evil practices. This total response won the favour of the Lord of all' (Homilies on Genesis 1.7). Others, among them Cyril of Alexandria, consider the reference to the animals to be a case of hyperbole:

> It did not necessarily happen, God's requiring hardship on the part of the animals. Instead, the sacred text suggested it as well to bring out the extraordinary degree of the Ninevites' repentance.

The fifth-century poem *Hymnus Ieiunantium* ('Hymn for those who fast') by the Christian poet Prudentius conveys an almost tender picture of the Ninevites' care for their animals (lines 166–170):

> The very flocks are closely penned
> By careful hands, lest they should gain
> Sweet water from the babbling stream
> Or wandering crop the dewy plain;
> And bleating sheep and lowing kine
> Within their barren stalls complain.

Following suit, the fourteenth-century English homiletic poem 'Patience' states (lines 392–395):

> Let no beast graze on heath, or on grassy plain.
> Nor pass to any pasture, nor pick any herbs,
> Nor any ox to hay, nor any horse to water;
> All shall cry starving, with all our
> manifest strength.

Bradbury is rather more sceptical concerning what he deems to have been a 'Spectacle'. On the one hand:

> to go through a City of three Days Journey, and see a vast multitude of Men and Cattle, urged with the Pains of hunger, in every Street [...] Children shrieking, crying, mourning; the Cattle lowing, yelling, howling; and this Clang of Sounds continued through all Parts of the City. Perhaps never did such a mixture of Groans go up to Heaven.

On the other hand, Bradbury also states that 'We are told, that those Eastern Countries used to run their Devotion into Extremities', and that 'They knew no better'. Thus, his audience should realize that the sacrifice of a broken and contrite Spirit is preferable to God ('Repentance of Nineveh', pp. 33–35).

The Geneva Bible notes to Jonah 3:7 highlight the fact that the animals should be regarded as collateral damage. They had clearly done nothing wrong yet were nonetheless going to suffer for the sins of humanity as God's wrath hung over all creatures. As the animals fasted, man should be astonished by their example.

A few commentators interpret the statement less literally and see the four categories man, animal, cattle, and sheep as four different types of humans. According to the interlinear glosses in the *Glossa Ordinaria*, for example, the men are the reasonable ones, whereas the animals are the foolish ones, the oxen the wise ones, and the sheep the simple ones.

Jonah 3:8

> But let man and beast cover themselves with sackcloth, and let them call out mightily to God, and let each one of them turn from his evil way and from the violence that is in their hands.

'But let man and beast cover themselves with sackcloth'

Jonah 3:8 continues to speak of both humans and animals. The Hellenistic-Jewish sermon *On Jonah* 37 discusses at length the inclusion of animals in this decree, suggesting that they were included because they would have suffered alongside humanity in the destruction of Nineveh even though they were innocent of any wrongdoing and unable to reason or understand human intentions.

In contrast, Calvin states that it is both strange and ridiculous that the king should bid animals to repent; such acts are for human beings alone. The king accordingly acted foolishly and contrary to all reason. Neither oxen nor sheep can pacify the wrath of God. Yet, there may nonetheless be a deeper aspect to the king's behaviour: as the people of Nineveh saw the suffering of the innocent animals, they would have realized their own need for penitence and recognized the validity of their own punishment. In fact, seeing the suffering of the innocent animals may have roused them to acknowledge their own sins. Calvin continues to argue that although the matter of wearing sackcloth, fasting, and other outer signs of penitence have no value, on this occasion these actions were sanctioned by God; even so we should nowadays refrain from following the example of the people of Nineveh. Later in the same lecture, Calvin highlights that even though both humans and animals are required to wear sackcloth according to the beginning of this verse, the ensuing command to call out to God must surely refer to humans alone. He concludes by emphasizing that prayer is the only remedy in affliction (Lecture 78).

The poem 'A Feast for Worms', written from a Calvinist perspective by Francis Quarles in 1620, is likewise highly critical of the Ninevites' outward show of repentance (Meditation 9):

> Can Sackcloth clothe a fault, or hide a shame?
> Can ashes cleanse thy blot? Or purge thy offence?
> [...]
> Such holy madness God rejects, and loaths,
> That sinks no deeper, than the skin, or cloaths:
> 'Tis not thine eyes which (taught to weep by art)
> Look red with tears, (not guilty of thy heart)
> 'Tis not the holding of thy hands so high,
> Nor yet the purer squinting of thine eye,
> 'Tis not your mimick mouth, your antick faces,
> Your Scripture phrases, or affected Graces,
> Nor prodigal up-banding of thine eyes,
> Whose gashful Balls do seem to pelt the skies.

As pointed out by Steere, these lines need to be situated within the context of the controversies between the Calvinists (followers of the French Reformed theologian John Calvin) and the Arminians (followers of the Dutch Reformed theologian Jacobus Arminius) concerning the place and function of the altar in worship. They form part of Quarles's polemic against the Arminians: 'The false repentance of the Ninevites is configured in terms that would have resonated directly with a Protestant readership in 1620: each piece of criticism levelled at the Ninevites is a common contemporary accusation made by Calvinists, moderate and militant alike, against the perceived false outward Arminian worship' (Streete 2009: section 16).

In the following section of the same poem, Francis Quarles stresses the necessary combination of faith and work exemplified by Ninevites' repentance (section 10):

> Because their faith and works went both together;
> He saw their faith, because their faith abounded;
> He saw their works, because on faith they grounded:
> He saw their faith, their works, and so relented;

The Hellenistic-Jewish sermon *On Jonah* 38 also explores the quality of the Ninevites' repentance, offering a unique perspective. It is, in fact, difficult to ascertain whether the sermon fully approves of the actions of the people of Nineveh. It states that they did not take care of their children and their animals, husbands and wives lived separately, no table was properly set, and everyone slept and ate on the ground. In parallel, the people dressed up in their best clothes, with the rationale that if Nineveh was destroyed, this would be their burial dress; if Nineveh was spared, this would be a fitting garment to celebrate God's mercy. This depiction of people 'eating' and 'wearing their best clothes' contradicts, of course, the plain sense of the biblical text that claims that the people of Nineveh fasted and wore sackcloth!

Jerome advocates an alternative, non-literal interpretation of the reference to sackcloth. In his view, the act of wearing sackcloth denotes mourning, worry, and sadness. In support for this metaphorical interpretation, Jerome draws from Joel 2:10 where the sun and moon are darkened, and Isa 50:3 where God will cover the heaven with sackcloth.

'and let them call out mightily to God'

The people of Nineveh are commanded 'to cry out mightily' to God. Hebrew has very few proper adverbs, instead using the preposition 'with' followed by a noun to convey an adverbial sense. Here in Jonah 3:8, the expression 'with might' (*bᵉḥazkah*) is best rendered in English as 'mightily'. Rashi, however, takes the statement *bᵉḥazkah* literally to mean 'with force', and argues that the men of Nineveh separated children from their mothers 'with force' and stated to God that 'if you do not show us mercy, we will not show mercy to these hostages'.

A few retellings provide the exact words that the people of Nineveh called out to God, lacking in the biblical text. Powerfully, albeit anachronistically, Dominick Argento's choral work *Jonah and the Whale* depicts the people of Nineveh (sung by the chorus) crying out climactically (marked as *con urgenza*) *Kyrie eleison/Christie eleison/Kyrie eleison* (see further McGaghie 2010: 11).

'and let each one of them turn from his evil way and from the violence that is in their hands'

Turning to the acts of violence from which the people of Nineveh should refrain, the Babylonian Talmud (*b.Tan.* 1:2) records that, according to Rabbi Ammi, the second half of verse 8 refers specifically to violent robbery. Later, in the same section of the Babylonian Talmud, Samuel is quoted as having said that the expression 'to turn from the violence of their hands' really means to undo the wrong that has been done, even if that would entail tearing down one's house to give back a beam that one has stolen:

> Even if someone stole a beam and built it into his villa, he should tear down the entire villa to the ground and restore the beam to the original owner.

A few retellings explicitly enumerate Nineveh's sins. The Hellenistic-Jewish sermon *On Jonah* 27:3–4, for example, contains an extensive list of all the wicked things that the people of Nineveh did, among them perverting justice, worshipping ill-gotten wealth, seeking lawless fleshly pleasures, defiling marriage, robbing corpses, etc. Cyril of Alexandria, in his commentary to Jonah 3:5, likewise itemizes Nineveh's sins. He maintains that the city had innumerable shrines to idols, unspeakable practices were popular among the population, the inhabitants showed respect to soothsaying and false prophecy, astrologers were considered wise, and anyone with a facility for any kind of vice enjoyed great renown.

On a rather more humorous note, the pop cantata *Jonah-Man Jazz* (1967) by Michael John Hurd (1928–2006 CE) construes Nineveh's sins in terms of partying (song 1), where the 'jazzin'' and the jivin'' made a terrible din'. Because the people danced all night, there was little time for work and prayers, causing God to draw the conclusion that 'Well this ain't right!'

Anti-Jewish Polemic

Like the preceding verses, Jonah 3:8 has also been exploited in anti-Jewish polemic. Cyril of Alexandria compares the behaviour of the people of Nineveh with that of Israel in his commentary to Jonah 3:5:

> Now, the Ninevites were very wise, devoting themselves to an abandonment of depravity by means of fasting, this being the single authentic and blameless form of repentance. Since Israel by contrast did not possess a facility for it, and sometimes gave evidence of a fasting that was ill-considered and profane, God ordered the prophet to raise his voice and proclaim to them 'This is not the fasting that I wanted, says the Lord […]' (Isa 58:3–5).

Jonah's Reaction to the Ninevites' Penitence

Whereas the biblical narrative focuses on the Ninevites' actions of remorse and repentance, a few retellings have explored Jonah's reaction to these endeavours. The American poet and literary critic Judson Jerome (1927–1991 CE) draws an interesting portrait of the prophet in his poem 'Jonah'. His Jonah is a most righteous man who is thoroughly disgusted by the sins that he sees around him. His reasons for not obeying God's command to preach repentance stem from his contempt for sinners and their desire for economic profit, his doubts that they would heed his word, and his overall lack of desire to associate with them:

> Who will publish Your truth, Lord? Who will be editor?
> Will they soil me with celebration? Will they award me a prize?
> And feast me, and the women come and bring me wine?
> (p. 10)

To his disdain, the people of Nineveh repent and become paragons of virtue and obedience:

> Thrift has descended upon you as a kind of paralysis.
> The merchants put up modest notices. The police take no bribes.
> Yea, those of high place are returning money to the public coffers.
> How tedious such virtue! How docile! How conventional!
> Have I chastised your stagnation that you have discovered complacency?
> Ah, with what relief you avoid error!
>
> (p. 17)

Jonah thus abhors the people's repentance as much as he abhorred their previous sins. For him, their repentance is as conventional as their sins, and he finds their obedience to be motivated not by true fear of God but by economic gain and wish for safety: it has merely turned out to be more profitable to obey God and to be 'good'. The poem ends with God's speech to Jonah, where the deity highlights his own free will and his freedom to establish the kind of justice that he sees fit.

Jonah 3:9

> 'Who knows, God may turn and change his mind and turn from his fierce anger so that we will not perish'.

Verse 9 has a potentially ambiguous opening, depending on how one divides the verse. There are two different possible translations, as pointed out by, among others, Radak. The prevalent way of reading the verse is to pause between 'who knows' and 'God may turn and change his mind and turn from his fierce anger', with the result that 'we will not perish' (as reflected in the translation above). According to this reading, God is solely responsible for the 'turning'. The alternative way of reading the text is to position a pause after the first 'turn', and to translate: 'whoever knows [and] returns, (and) God will change his mind and turn from his anger', etc. According to this reading, the people of Nineveh do the first 'turning'.

TJ opts for the second reading, presumably to avoid the notion that God changes his mind:

> Whoever knows that there are sins on his conscience let him repent of them and we will be pitied before the Lord, and he will turn back from the vehemence of his anger, and we will not perish.

In this way, TJ avoids the notion of God 'changing his mind' (*niphal* of the Hebrew root *niḥam*), as well as the open-ended statement 'who knows' (see further below). In parallel, it emphasizes the efficacy of repentance (Cathcart and Gordon 1989: 108, fn. 11). The sinner is the subject of the first occurrence of the Aramaic verb *yatuv* ('turn back'//Heb. *yashuv*); only because of the sinner's 'turning' will God 'hold back' his anger. The same verb is used also in TJ Jonah 3:10 with the same effect: 'And the Lord "turned" from the evil he had threatened to do to them'. Probably in response to this type of interpretation, Ibn Ezra clarifies that God is the subject of the verb 'and he will turn'.

From a different perspective, modern scholarship has noted the use of the root 'turn' (*shuv*) both in Jonah 3:8 with the people of Nineveh as its subject and in Jonah 3:9 with God as its subject. Thus, as the people turn from their evil ways, so God turns (twice) from his plans and his anger (Sutskover 2014: 312).

'who knows'

The marginal gloss to 3:9 in the *Glossa Ordinaria* claims that the expressed ambiguity inherent in the statement 'who knows' encourages people to obey God. If people doubt their salvation, they may be more prone to doing penance and, in turn, provoke God to mercy.

Jacob of Serug offers an interesting take on the Ninevite king's decision to encourage citywide repentance. Although, according to Jacob, Jonah preached repentance and judgement but left little room for redemption and salvation, the king detected Jonah's proclivity for Nineveh's destruction and – in view of his knowledge that God had the authority to redeem Nineveh should he so wish – sought to circumvent it (Eng. transl. Kitchen 2011: 38–39):

> See, the Hebrew threatens and warns
> concerning our destruction
> Let us devise a way so he does not rejoice over
> us when he defeats us.
> [...]
> He is not convinced that it is not his [right] to
> refute his words
> His Lord has authority over him to reverse lest he
> destroy us.
> (51. 450:7–14)

The reformer Bugenhagen spends much ink in his Jonah commentary on the statement 'who knows'. This expression had gained significance in the discourse between the Reformers and the Catholics regarding 'certainty of faith'. At the Council of Trent (1545–1563), the Catholics condemned the Lutheran dogma that by confession and absolution, Christians know through faith that they have received total forgiveness of sins. Instead, although no pious person ought to doubt God's mercy, it befits people to be apprehensive about their own state of grace. In response, Bugenhagen argues that Jonah 3:9 supports exactly the opposite standpoint, namely the doctrine of 'certainty of faith' (Lohrmann 2012: 73–75).

'and God will change his mind'

The key interpretative crux in Jonah 3:9 concerns the meaning of the verb *niḥam* (in *niphal*), a verb that most neutrally can be translated as 'to change one's mind' (cf. Jeremias 1975; Parunak 1975: 512–532). It is also commonly translated as 'to repent' (e.g. AV) or 'to relent' (e.g. NIV). This verse is reminiscent of the captain's statement in Jonah 1:6bβ 'Perhaps God will consider us so that we will not perish'.[4] Exegetes have spent much ink on the topic of God's (im)mutability and his ability to change his mind in response to human actions. This issue has two aspects, one ontological and one textual: (1) does God change his mind, and (2) does the Bible describe God as changing his mind? While we may strive to differentiate between these two aspects, many commentators through the ages have conflated them.

Jewish Views

The Hellenistic-Jewish sermon *On Jonah* reveals that the issue of God's mutability was debated quite early on. It comments on God's prerogative to change his mind yet upholds in parallel his omniscience. God is likened to a physician who sometimes must cure a person 'with fire and water'. He may threaten an ill city with death to protect it and keep it alive (Chapter 2). The sermon declares that God is his own Lord and thus free to change a death sentence should he so wish. Such a change, however, is not done capriciously and without cause. In the case of Nineveh, it was God's plan to destroy the city, but it was also his right to annul this decision when the circumstances changed (Chapter 46:7–8) the German translation in Siegert 1980: 42, is clearer on this point):

> You proclaimed not what you wished but what you were entrusted with; it is me, the Autocrat, who issued the threat to them. I possess the power to apply or change laws and to annul a death sentence; having sent the proclamation with veracity, I then transformed it into philanthropy.

The sermon thus claims that God has the authority to change laws. In this manner, God's mutability is fully compatible with his omnipotence (Siegert 1992: 210). It is also in line with his omniscience, as God had knowledge of Nineveh's future actions all along (Chapter 3). How could he not, so the logic goes, given that he gives his prophets foreknowledge (cf. Dan 2:21) (Siegert 1980: 10;

Muradyan and Topchyan 2013: 777 [3:1–2]). The sermon ends on a more definite note, whereby God asks rhetorically how it would have been possible for him to maintain his verdict of death when the people of Nineveh changed their lives (Chapter 53):

> How can I keep unchanged the announced death sentence for those who have changed their character? [...] Just as for the former way of life they deserved a cruel proclamation, likewise for their repentance, on the contrary, they are worthy of humanity.

This sermon also interacts with the aforementioned rabbinical notion that Jonah's message was indeed fulfilled, only in a way that he did not foresee (Jonah 3:4). God's speech to Jonah alludes to the idea of 'overturning' (3:4, *neh^{e}pachet*). Nineveh was indeed 'overturned' in the sense that their hearts and their lives, rather than their physical city walls, were changed. This 'overturning' was, furthermore, the work of God's hand alone (rather than Jonah's work) (Siegert 1980: sections 191–196).

There is overall little evidence to suggest that the Sages perceived God's change of mind as a major theological obstacle. The Babylonian Talmud quotes Rabbi Isaac who mentions four things that may cancel the judgement against a person: charity, crying out, change of name, and change of character. In the case of Jonah 3:10, it was the Ninevites' change of character that caused God to revoke his planned judgement (*b.Rosh hashana* 1:2). Many of the mediaeval Jewish exegetes likewise spend relatively few words on this perceived theological difficulty. Radak, in his commentary to Jonah 3:10, brings to the readers' attention the similar passage in Exod 34:7 which lists God's ability to change his mind among his 'thirteen attributes of mercy'. He further refers to God's desire to adjust his plans in accordance with the actions of humanity, as spelled out in Jer 18:7–8, as well as in the passage in Ezek 18:27–28 of the wicked man who may turn back from his evil ways. Showing more awareness of a potential theological problem, Abarbanel states that God's word remains forever (Isa 40:8b) and accordingly asks whether God's proclamation of Nineveh's destruction should be understood as definite or conditional. Even if the text does not explicitly mention any conditions, according to Abarbanel, such conditions are nevertheless implied as we can learn from Jer 18:7–8. Thus, the main point of Jonah's prophecy was to teach the Gentiles forgiveness (commentary to Jonah 3:4). God's decision is thus contingent on human behaviour. In contrast, Ibn Ezra objects to the notion of God 'changing his mind', claiming that this is a human endeavour and not to be associated with God. The Torah is merely speaking the 'language of people'; it is an example of anthropomorphism (commentary to Jonah 3:10).

Christian Views

While most rabbinic interpreters detect no major theological issue in Jonah 3:9, most of the Church Fathers do. In general, the Church Fathers view God to be impassible and not subject to anger and other emotions that would cause him to change his mind.

Jerome's view on God's change of mind, expressed in his commentary to Jonah 3:10, adheres closely to the rabbinic tradition insofar as he alludes to Jer 18:7–8 and God's ability to alter his plans if his people alter their behaviour. In support, he also refers to Ezek 33:11, which clarifies that God prefers a sinner's repentance to his death. At the same time, Jerome hints at the possibility that God, being merciful to the core, planned to pity the people of Nineveh all along. Such a prior decision is evidenced by the very fact that God *pronounced* his threat: someone who is intent on punishing someone does not actually *threaten* to do so (but, as implied, just goes ahead and does it to make sure that nothing comes between the plan and its execution). The *Glossa Ordinaria* likewise states that God's decision to spare the Ninevites had been God's purpose all along.

Tertullian speaks of God immutability in his *Against Marcion* II 24. His main problem is not so much God's ability to change his mind (he can), however, but God's alleged lack of foresight combined with the (misconceived) notion that God could err. According to Tertullian, his opponent Marcion (ca 85–160 CE) has misunderstood the Hebrew verb *niḥam* (Greek μετανοέω). It has nothing to do with caprice or with a recollection of God's wrongdoing or confession of some evil act or with a mistake. It is also not a lack of foresight as, according to Tertullian, Marcion and he agree that foresight is an essential divine quality. In the case of Jonah 3:9–10; 4:2, Tertullian postulates that Marcion would claim that it refers to God's admission of error. In response, Tertullian argues that as error cannot coexist with God's supreme goodness, abundant kindness, and mercy, so the Book of Jonah *cannot* refer to a divine confession of wrongdoing. As Marcion would agree, a good tree cannot bring forth evil fruits (Matt 7:18). Thus, the reference to 'evil' in Jonah 3:10 and 4:2 cannot speak of God's nature but instead of his judicial authority. When God states that 'he creates evil' (Isa 45:7) and that 'he sends evil' against his people (Jer 18:11), what is meant is the evils of vengeance. These types of evils befit a judge and do not bring him into disrepute. In the specific case of Jonah, the 'evil' is God's right and legal judgement upon a city that deserved to be so judged. As such, God's change of mind should not be put on a par with a human being's change of mind. Instead, the notion is to be understood 'as neither more nor less than a simple reversal of a previous decision, such as can be brought about without any adverse judgement upon that other'.

At the other end of the scale, Augustine states clearly that, unlike human beings, God does not change his mind about anything that he does. 'His view of absolutely everything is fixed, just as his foreknowledge is certain'. What we encounter in Jonah rather are words that seek to communicate with all kinds of people (*City of God*, 15.25, cf. Ibn Ezra above).

Turning to later Christian writings, Haimo of Auxerre appears to be happily unconcerned with God's change of mind. He writes in his commentary to Jonah 3:10: 'For if the world is converted, the Lord is converted; and when the sinners change their life, He will change His sentence'.

In the case of the Protestant Reformers, there is a sharp distinction between Calvin and his followers, who really struggle with this issue, and Luther and his followers, who dismiss it as a matter of little significance. To quote the latter in his German commentary on Jonah 3:9:

> It is superfluous to enter on the subtle question here how God can repent, turn from and regret His anger, since He is unchangeable. Some people are deeply concerned about this; they complicate the matter for themselves unnecessarily!

Rather, for Luther, what is of real import in Jonah 3:9 is God's grace that hovers in the background, ready to forgive. In his German commentary, Luther focuses instead on the opening question of the verse 'who knows' and asks to what extent it reflects the Ninevites' faith (or lack thereof) in God's salvation. In his Latin commentary to the same verse, Luther claims that the people of Nineveh *believed* God's word and that is why God looked favourably on their acts. Acts alone would not have brought about God's favour. As to the notion of God '*niḥam* concerning the evil' in Jonah 4:2, Luther zooms in on the word 'evil' and states that God rises above evil. Luther's German commentary to Jonah 3:9 documents the same interest in the Ninevites' faith. Although the king talks as if he were in doubt, the fact that he calls a fast, etc. reveals his faith in God. This faith is not yet strong but trembles in fear. The people's faith is also to be commended. Even though they had had no promise of salvation from Jonah, they humbled themselves and repented. Moreover, despite the lack of a promise of mercy, they did not despair in fear and fright. Through their behaviour, they are putting both Jews and Christians to shame, who have had access to the comfort of God's word.

Calvin, as can be expected, is much more intent on defending the tenet of God's immutability and absolute foreknowledge. In his comments to Jonah 4:2, he emphasizes that there is no inherent link between human repentance and divine pardon, as God offers his pardon freely. The fact that his pardon is nevertheless conditional upon repentance is merely to make sure that people do not abuse his indulgence and forbearance. Speaking more directly about the statement that God changed his mind, Calvin emphasizes that God is ever the same and consistent with himself. From his perspective, there is no change of mind; it is only we who perceive him to have done so. When we repent, it appears as if God has changed from wrath to mercy, and it is this human perspective that is visible in the Book of Jonah. The Bible, aimed at us, accommodates our perspective when it states that God was angry and later pacified, yet we need to be clear that God is always like himself and subject to none of our feelings (Lecture 79).

Somewhat surprisingly, the Geneva Bible notes to Jonah 3:10 do not comment on the matter of God's change of mind but simply point the reader to Jer 18:8 (cf. above).

Francis Quarles, described by Streete as 'always a staunch middle-of-the-road Calvinist Anglican' (Streete 2009: section 7), comments on God's change of mind in his poem 'A Feast for Worms' from 1620 as following (Meditation 8):

> When he repents from ill,
> He wills a Change; he changes not his Will;
> The Subject's chang'd, which secret was to us,
> But not the mind that did dispose it thus;
> Denounced Judgment God doth oft prevent,
> Be neither changes counsel, nor intent;
> The voice of Heaven doth seldom threat perdition,
> But with express, or an impli'd Condition,
> So that, if Niniveh return from ill,
> God turns his hand, he doth not turn his Will.

According to Streete, we need to 'compare the picture given here of an immutable God who resists destroying Nineveh with the comments throughout the poem on the perils of interfering in the affairs of foreign nations. The omnipotent Calvinist God whose decrees are absolute and, in this case, irenic, could also be read as an affirmation of Jacobean monarchical absolutism with a pacific bent' (Streete 2009: section 14).

Muslim Views
Sura 10:98 (part of the so-called Sura *Yunus*) states that Allah, in His mercy and kindness, removed from [the people of Nineveh] their punishment, which was going to befall them. For this reason, Allah said, 'Was there any town that believed [after seeing the punishment] and its faith [at that moment] saved it [from the punishment]?' The sura proclaims further that 'Except the people of Yunus when they believed, We removed from them the punishment of disgrace in the life of the world and We gave them the enjoyment for a life-time'.

As explained by the Persian scholar, historian, and qur'anic exegete Al-Ṭabarī in his historical chronicle *Tarikh al-Rusul wa al-Muluk* ('History of the Prophets and Kings'), Nineveh was unique among all cities in the world as

God 'removed from them the chastisement of degradation' when they believed, that is, it was pardoned by God after he had decided to destroy it (Eng. transl. Perlmann 1987: 4:160, 163). Al-Ṭabarī further tells of a tradition (according to al-Ḥārith) that Jonah's message, which the angel Gabriel originally had commanded him to deliver, was to announce how God would keep his chastisement from the people of Nineveh so that they might repent. In other words, the conditional character of the message was intended from the very beginning and, as such, the message was more of a warning than a prediction. Another tradition (according to Ibn Ḥumayd) maintains that God encouraged Jonah to leave Nineveh, as he was going to send the chastisement upon the city. The people realized this and, as they saw Jonah leave, they followed him, lamented, and repented, with the result that their chastisement was averted. In yet another tradition (according to al-Ḥusayn), the people of Nineveh, upon hearing the threat that Jonah delivered, asked God for forgiveness, and God withheld the chastisement from them (Eng. transl. Perlmann 1987: 4:161–165). The qur'anic material thus disputes whether God's word is an unchanging decree or whether it can be changed because of God's compassion and grace (Steffen 1994: 122). In contrast, later Islamic texts, for instance, the ḥadīth heard from Wahb ibn Munabbih, no longer discussed the question of God's changeability: mainstream Islam did not consider God's mutability to be a serious option, as it would contradict his omniscience (Rubin 1984; Saeedimehr 2018). This theological consensus, in turn, forced Muslim commentators to explain Jonah's reluctance to go to Nineveh in non-theological ways (e.g. being too weak or too afraid of carrying out his mission, see Jonah 1:3) (Steffen 1994: 122–124).

Jonah 3:10

> And God saw their deeds – that they turned from their evil way – and God changed his mind concerning the evil which he had planned to do to them, and he did not do [it].

'And God saw their deeds'

The statement in verse 10a that 'God saw their deeds' raises, naturally one might say, the question as to what deeds God is referring. While a straightforward reading of the text suggests that the intended deeds are the fasting and the donning of sackcloth mentioned in Jonah 3:5, it is possible, at least hypothetically, that the deeds are those referred to in Jonah 3:8 instead, namely the evil ways and acts of violence. Thus, the Mishnah (*m.Tan.* 2:1) argues that the wording of verse 10, i.e. that 'God saw their deeds' rather than 'God saw their sackcloth and their fasting', is in fact an indication that the straightforward interpretation is anything but straightforward: God saw not their outer acts of penitence (vv. 5–8); instead he saw that they repented from their evil. The Babylonian Talmud on the same passage (*b.Tan.* 2:1) elaborates further on this matter:

> Our brethren, it is not the wearing of sackcloth and the fasting that make the difference, but repentance and good deeds make the difference.

This interpretation stands in contradiction with the above-mentioned interpretation in the Jerusalem Talmud (*y.Tan.* 2:1) that the Ninevites' repentance was deceitful (Jonah 3:7).

Gen.Rab. 44:12 puts Jonah 3:9–10 to a different use. Rabbi Huna in the name of Rabbi Joseph teaches that three matters can annul an evil decree: prayer, acts of charity, and repentance. To prove the third point, Rabbi Huna argues that good deeds made a difference in the case of the people of Nineveh (cf. also *Pesiqta deRab Kahana* 28:3). The Babylonian Talmud (*b.Rosh.* 1:2) makes the same point, although it mentions four things: charity, crying out (in supplication), change of name, and change of character. The case of the people of Nineveh falls into the fourth category.

Christian interpreters also discuss the deeds of the Ninevites. Jerome, for example, emphasizes that God sees actual deeds (rather than potentially empty words). He contrasts the real deeds of the people of Nineveh with the 'vain promises' that Israel was in the habit of making (e.g. Exod 24:3, 7, 'and they said: "all that God spoke we will do and we will hear/obey"'). Much later, Calvin, speaking against 'the Papists', warns that the 'deeds' here were neither the wearing of sackcloth, nor the ashes and the fasting. Rather, what is meant is that they turned from their evil ways (Lecture 78). By contrast, several modern scholars have argued the very opposite, namely, that the focus on 'deeds' here is intentional: God saw neither their faith nor that they stopped worshipping their idols and turned to him wholeheartedly; what God saw was instead (merely) their deeds. The Ninevites' response constituted a far cry from a full conversion to Yhwh (e.g. Walton 1992: 54).

By all accounts, the repentance of the people of Nineveh was astonishing. Early Christian exegetes lauded the Ninevites for the fact that they 'turned from their evil ways' after hearing Jonah's (very short) message. John Chrysostom, for example, is impressed by the fact that the people of Nineveh repented with due carefulness, even though they did not know the issue. (In contrast to Israel), the people of Nineveh had neither read the prophets nor heard the patriarchs, and they had not had another Nineveh as an example to emulate ('Homily 5 Concerning the Statues', section 17). In contrast, the Reformers show more scepticism. Luther returns to his hobby horse (grace rather than works) and repeats in his German commentary to Jonah 3:10 what he said regarding Jonah 3:5, namely that:

> 'To turn from one's evil way' is not a trivial work; it does not involve fasting and wearing sackcloth, but believing in God with all one's heart and loving the neighbour as one's self; that is, it demands piety and righteousness in one's whole being, both inwardly and outwardly, in body and soul. God wants the entire person. He has an aversion to shilly-shallying and hypocritical people.

Calvin is even more unconvinced. In his commentary to Jonah 1:1–2 (Lecture 72), Calvin sees little reason to believe that the Ninevites had truly repented from the heart, given that the city soon afterwards became exceedingly hostile towards Jerusalem and the Jews (as evidenced by, e.g., 2 Kgs 18–19).

'and God changed his mind concerning the evil which he had planned to do to them, and he did not do [it]'

Jonah 3:10b affirms the hope that God would change his mind in response to the Ninevites' repentance. This statement, in Rashi's view, confirms that a prophecy that foretells suffering upon people is always conditional and can always be revoked by repentance (cf. Exod 32:14; Jer 18:7; Ezek 33:19). Other scholars ponder what the 'evil' that God had lined up for the Ninevites would have been, had they *not* repented. Cyril of Alexandria, for example, suggests, in line with Ezek 18:31–32, that the evil here would have been divine wrath.

The people of Nineveh are never explicitly told that their city will be spared. After Jonah 3:10, the narrative focus shifts back to Jonah. Jonah certainly does not tell the citizens of Nineveh about God's change of mind, but instead leaves the city to watch the fate of its inhabitants from a distance. Thus, the Book of Jonah leaves the people of Nineveh perpetually wondering when or if Jonah's message would become reality (Lindsay 2016). Seeking to fill this narrative gap, Jacob of Serug states explicitly that the people of Nineveh expressed their joy and showed their gratitude to the king (who had guided them through their repentance), even though the statement that 'the morning came and brought the Gospel' is still rather vague from a practical perspective! (Eng. transl. Kitchen 2011: 40)

> The morning came and brought the Gospel to the sons of the city and brought to an end the evil which was threatened against its walls.
>
> [...]
>
> They saw one another as departed ones after resurrection, and they shouted prudently to the one who resurrects the day. (63. 475:20–576:1, 8–9)

The Bible is silent about the Ninevites' reaction to God sparing them – presuming that they eventually realized that their city was not going to be destroyed. Seeking to fill this lacuna, the Hellenistic-Jewish sermon *On Jonah* 39 states that when the people of Nineveh realized that God had decided to spare their city, they summoned a second assembly and thanked God.

The End?

Interestingly, many retellings end with Jonah 3:10. Josephus's retelling in *Ant.* 9:10 finishes abruptly with the words:

> It is also reported that Jonah was swallowed down by a whale, and that when he had been there three days, and as many nights, he was vomited out upon the Euxine Sea, and this alive, and without any hurt upon his body; and there, on his prayer to God, he obtained pardon for his sins, and went to the city Nineveh, where he stood so as to be heard, and preached, that in a very little time they should lose the dominion of Asia. And when he had published this, he returned. Now I have given this account about him as I found it written [in our books.]

Josephus is thus remarkably uninterested in the outcome of Jonah's preaching to Nineveh. For all the reader of his account can figure, Nineveh was destroyed (cf. above). It is possible that this end seeks to align Josephus's account with the fate of Nineveh known from history: the city was destroyed in 612 BCE.

From a purely dramatic viewpoint, the dialogue between God and Jonah in Jonah 4 is rather a let-down. The fifth-century poem *Hymnus Ieiunantium* ('Hymn for those who fast') written by the Christian poet Prudentius, for example, concludes the Jonah section of the poem (lines 171–176) with

> Moved by such penitence, full soon
> God's grace repealed the stern decree
> And curbed His righteous wrath; for aye,
> When man repents, His clemency
> Is swift to pardon and to hear
> His children weeping bitterly.

The fourth-century poem *De Jona et Nineveh*, attributed to Tertullian, also ends with Jonah 3. Although the final lines in the poem describe Jonah sitting inside the fish, they point forward to Nineveh's salvation (lines 20–29):

> Rousing with mind august presaging seers.
> For to the merits of the Ninevites

> The Lord had bidden Jonah to foretell
> Destruction; but he, conscious that He spare;
> The subject, and remits to suppliants
> The dues of penalty, and is to good
> Ever inclinable, was loth to face
> That errand; lest he sing his seerly strain
> In vain, and peaceful issue of his threats
> Ensue.

Carissimi's oratorio *Jonas* from 1650 likewise comes to a close with the Ninevites confessing their sins, asking for forgiveness, and pleading with God to save them: 'We have sinned, Lord, we have sinned, and we have not walked in your ways, but turn to us, Lord, and we will turn, let your face shine upon us and we will be saved'.

The Elizabethan morality stage play *A Looking Glass for London and England* culminates with Jonah 3:10. The focus of the play, however, is less on Nineveh's new-found piety and more on its (past) sins. To quote Sager, 'penance and repentance do not make good theatre, whereas sex and violence have an enduring appeal' (Sager 2013: 56). The concluding scene (lines 2388–2394) features Jonah alone on the stage, where he applies the lesson of Nineveh to the people of London and England, warning them to fear and repent before it is too late:

> O London, maiden of the mistress isle,
> Wrapt in the folds and swathing clouts of shame:
> In thee more sins then [sic] Nineveh contains,
> Contempt of, despite of reverend age,
> Neglect of law, desire to wrong the poor,
> Corruption, whoredom, drunkenness, and pride,
> Swollen are thy brow with impudence and shame.

Several modern retellings for children also finish here. Peter Mills's picture book *Jonah's Adventure with the Big Fish*, for instance, ends somewhat abruptly. After Jonah's prolonged adventure with the fish (being the focus of the story as implied by the title), the last page tells how God called Jonah again, Jonah obeyed, and the people of Nineveh repented. Thus, due to Jonah's obedience, God did not have to punish them after all. The pictures accentuate this happy ending: the last image of the book depicts Jonah walking happily and contentedly towards Nineveh.

The modern pop cantata *Jonah-Man Jazz* (1967) by Michael John Hurd likewise omits all of Jonah 4 and instead closes on a cheery note by having all the people of Nineveh sing God's praise.

Notes

1 For the estimate, see http://www.kgbanswers.co.uk/how-long-does-it-take-to-walk-from-one-side-of-london-to-the-other/3281558.
2 Clearly influenced by Matt 21:13.
3 Part of this discussion appears in Tiemeyer 2019b.
4 A different version of this discussion is published in Tiemeyer 2018: 125–146.

Jonah 4

The final chapter of the Book of Jonah features a dialogue between Jonah and God, where Jonah expresses his anger at God's compassion, and God responds with a series of actions aimed at helping Jonah to understand the reasons for his compassion. We shall explore how interpreters throughout the last 2000 years have struggled not only with Jonah's seemingly uncharitable behaviour but also with God's apparent failure to be unmerciful, and how they have sought to comprehend the tension between divine justice and divine mercy.

Jonah Through the Centuries, First Edition. Lena-Sofia Tiemeyer.
© 2022 John Wiley & Sons, Ltd. Published 2022 by John Wiley & Sons, Ltd.

Jonah 4:1

This displeased Jonah greatly and it grieved him.

Why Did Jonah Become Angry?

As already noted in Chapter 1, many theories abound as to why Jonah was so greatly displeased by the Ninevites' repentance. The explanations tend to fall into one of five categories.

1. Jonah Was Upset Because He Feared Being Considered a False Prophet

This first category, namely, that Jonah feared being considered a false prophet, is by far the most prevalent explanation, and it is advocated by Jewish and Christian interpreters alike. Beginning with the latter, Jerome states that Jonah was indignant because, at God's command, he had spoken falsely. Yet he would rather speak the truth and have a countless multitude perish than speak falsely and have them saved (*Against the Pelagians*, book 3, section 6). Theodore of Mopsuestia likewise maintains that Jonah felt distressed because he was now likely to gain the reputation of being a sham and a charlatan for threatening destruction that in the end did not happen. Cyril of Alexandria also adopts this line of thinking, stating explicitly that

> It was not because the city had escaped destruction – the attitude of a wicked and envious man, unbecoming a saint – but because he gave the impression of being a liar and a braggart, idly alarming them, speaking his own mind and not at all what came from the mouth of the lord, as Scripture says.

The same sentiment is also conveyed in the fourteenth-century English homiletic poem 'Patience'. In lines 427–428, Jonah states that 'For it would be sweeter to die soon, as I think, than to preach thy lore longer, that thus makes me a liar'. The Reformer Calvin likewise adheres to this interpretation, but also adds that Jonah was influenced by false zeal when he could not bear with resignation that the city of Nineveh had been saved from destruction. In the beginning, Jonah's attitude would not have been wrong, yet his excess here in Chapter 4 is sinful. Even so, Jonah should be commended in that he was not willing to allow God's name to be profaned but instead sought to uphold its honour (Lecture 79). The same sentiments are also voiced in the Geneva Bible notes to Jonah 4:1, 3.

Turning to Jewish exegetes, Rashi argues that Jonah was displeased because now the nations would see him as a false prophet. Radal explains further that Jonah's anguish was not motivated by his pride (as that would have been out of character for a prophet of God) but instead feared that the whole institution of prophecy would be discredited. This, in turn, would lead to God's name being profaned (as quoted in Zlotowitz 1978: 132).

2. Jonah Was Upset Because the Neo-Assyrians Would Destroy Israel

The second line of interpretation is that Jonah was upset because he realized that the Neo-Assyrians would ultimately destroy the Northern Kingdom of Israel (in 721 BCE, cf. 2 Kgs 17). It is voiced predominantly by Jewish scholars. Ibn Ezra, for instance, in his commentary to Jonah 4:3, states that Jonah, fearing that Israel would not repent and thus that evil might come upon her, behaved in the manner of Elisha. Ibn Ezra thus compares Jonah's statement that God should take his life (Jonah 4:3) with the narrative about Elijah, Elisha, and the Aramean monarch Hazael (1–2 Kings). In 1 Kgs 19:15–18, God commanded Elijah to go to Damascus to anoint Hazael King of the Arameans. Elijah did so, even though being a prophet he realized that Hazael would later bring suffering upon the Israelites. Likewise, his disciple Elisha foresaw Hazael's ascent to the throne, yet in parallel lamented the destruction that this king would cause Israel (2 Kgs 8:7–12) (see further Bob 2013: 38).

Along similar lines, Abarbanel (commentary to Jonah 4:1–2, cf. also Malbim) focuses on the Neo-Assyrian threat to Israel. He argues that Jonah's grief stemmed from his realization, brought about by his prophetic foreknowledge, that Assyria would become the rod of God's anger and the instrument of God's punishment of Israel. According to Abarbanel, Jonah's anger is predominantly directed at God: Jonah's anger at God is a result of God's seemingly unfair treatment of Israel: while God was prepared to forgive Nineveh despite their continued idolatry, he used a different yardstick for Israel and upheld his wrath against Israel. In contrast, according to the Italian Jewish Bible commentator Ovadia ben Jacob Sforno (1475–1550 CE), Jonah's anger is mainly directed at Israel: he knew that Israel, unlike the people of Nineveh, would fail to listen to the prophet's call. This, in turn, would lead to the Neo-Assyrian destruction of Israel (as quoted in Zlotowitz 1978: 131). Radak's interpretation (Jonah 4:1, 2) follows suit yet is more vague, simply stating that Jonah was afraid that the people of Nineveh would repent and that their repentance would cause evil to Israel. He further argues that Jonah was sad because Israel would not repent.

3. Jonah Was Upset Because the Gentiles' Salvation Would Mean the Jews' Death

Jerome, adding a New Testament perspective to the debate, argues that Jonah despaired of Israel's safety because the Gentiles would turn to God (Rom 11:25) and therefore ultimately bring about the Jews' death. Jerome stresses God's primary commitment to his people Israel: Jesus cried over Jerusalem and refused to take the bread that belongs to the Jewish people (Matt 15:26; Mark 7:27), and the apostles always began their ministry in the synagogue (Act 13:46). Jonah, aware of this future, is saddened and pleads that Israel would not be destroyed forever after the conversion of such a multitude of Gentiles (commentary to Jonah 4:2–3). Jonah's sadness is thus not strictly because of the Gentiles' safety; rather it is due to Israel's unbelief. Like Jesus, Jonah weeps for Jerusalem, wishing that although they die refusing him, they will rise again to confess the Son of God (commentary to Jonah 4:9).

4. Jonah Was Upset Because He Begrudged the Gentiles the Possibility of Becoming Children of God

Offering a much more critical evaluation of Jonah, Luther states unequivocally that Jonah, as a representative of the Jews in general, begrudged the Gentiles the privilege of becoming Christians. Jonah would have deplored the notion that Judaism was unnecessary and their laws useless – according to Luther, the logical conclusion of the Ninevites' salvation – as he would have understood it to deprecate and disparage his fellow countrymen (German commentary).

5. Being Upset, Jonah Reflects on His Journey So Far

The Hellenistic-Jewish sermon *On Jonah* surely advocates the most unusual take on Jonah's reaction to the repentance of Nineveh. When Jonah saw the Ninevites' reaction to his message – how they faithfully repented and how their sorrow turned to gladness – Jonah began to ponder his reasons for fleeing from his mission in the first place (ch. 40). Jonah muses that he sought to escape God for the sake of protecting God's name and honour (ch. 41). He then offers an alternative reason, namely, that he fled to be able to speak not only about 'the humanity of God on earth' (i.e. his mercy and forgiveness) but also about God's 'might on the sea'. Had Jonah not fled, so the argument goes, he would never have ended up inside the fish and, as a result, he would never have had the opportunity to experience the wonders of the deep:

> With my tiny eyes, I saw the abyss: the rocks that have taken root amid the waves, the light that gushes forth for the enjoyment of the marine animals, the agitation of the waves, the playfulness of the aquatics, and the various forms of animals. After fleeing from this human world, I received a new, different one instead: I became a swimmer among the aquatic animals; I was fed in the deep like a marine beast; I inhaled wet, not dry, air to survive; I drew breath from the fish's windpipe; I danced with the playful beasts and moved along with swimmers […] I [saw] how terrible the sea monsters' appearance is how it resembles that of the terrestrials, [the former] having got four times more savage nature; how sometimes they are amiable and friendly but sometimes show teeth to one another – I saw all this during my wanderings. (42:2–3, 7–8)

When Did Jonah Become Angry?

The timeline envisaged by Jonah 3–4 is not fully clear. Above all, what is the chronological relationship between God's change of mind (Jonah 3:10), Jonah becoming angry (Jonah 4:1), and Jonah leaving the city (Jonah 4:5)? In short, did Jonah leave the city after spending 40 days there, or did he spend merely one day there before leaving the city to wait outside for its demise? This conundrum has caused several retellings to rewrite the sequence of events with the aim of making them progress more logically.

The first option is to position Jonah's departure from the city *before* the Ninevites even have begun to repent, so that when God decides to spare them, Jonah is already outside the city. The Hellenistic-Jewish sermon *On Jonah* 40, for instance, maintains that Jonah had already left the city prior to God's decision to spare Nineveh in Jonah 3:10. Along slightly different lines yet reaching more or less the same results, Ibn Ezra, in his commentary to Jonah 4:5, argues that the reference to Jonah leaving Nineveh in verse 5 teaches us about something that happened earlier *during* these 40 days, whereas verses 1–4 speak about an event which happened *after* those same 40 days. In contrast, Radak maintains that Jonah 4 depicts the correct chronological sequence. Thus, Jonah learnt already during the 40 days that God would not destroy Nineveh, because God told him so in the spirit of prophecy (commentary to Jonah 4:1). His expression of grief in verses 1–4 thus takes place while he is still in Nineveh. He then leaves the city in verse 5 to anticipate further events, hoping that the repentance would wear itself out and that the Ninevites would relapse to their wicked ways before the end of the 40-day period of grace (commentary to Jonah 4:5).

The second option is to envisage that Jonah left Nineveh only after 40 days, i.e. on the day that the destruction was scheduled to take place. Calvin, for example, argues that Jonah abandoned the city only after 40 days had passed. At that point, he was not yet sure about the effects of his proclamation (Lecture 80, comment on Jonah 4:5). The same idea is expressed by the Geneva Bible notes to Jonah 4:5.

Jonah 4:2

> And he prayed to Yhwh and said: 'O Yhwh, is this not what I said when I was in my country? Therefore, I made haste[1] to flee to Tarshish, because I knew that you are a gracious and compassionate God, slow to anger and abounding in love, and willing to change your mind regarding evil'.

Jonah's Behaviour

Jonah 4:2 brings out what many later interpreters have considered to be Jonah's worst side: his displeasure in God's decision to have mercy on the people of Nineveh. Despite trying to speak highly of Jonah, Cyril of Alexandria states that 'humanly speaking, [Jonah] was mean-spirited [...] His attitude was unstable, unworthy of a saintly mind' (commentary to Jonah 4:3).

Turning to the Reformers, Luther, in his German commentary to Jonah 1:3, states that Jonah was loath to see God spare the city, with the rationale that such sinners did not deserve mercy, especially since they did not have the Law and divine worship. In Luther's view, God's decision to spare Nineveh does, in fact, render the Jews' laws and divine worship 'forever a useless and unnecessary burden for people'. Luther continues by claiming that God does not accord the people of Israel any special privileges because of their divine worship. *Vice versa*, God does not need to withhold his grace from the people of Nineveh because they do not possess such worship. Grace extends to all (cf. Rom 4:4–5). If Jonah had but realized that, he like Abraham would have remained obedient to God. Luther's exegesis is inspired by the parable of the labourers in the vineyard in Matt 20:12 where the latecomers (identified by Luther with the Gentiles) earn the same as those who have laboured since the morning (identified by Luther with the Jews).

The same critical attitude towards Jonah persists among modern writers, where Jonah has come to represent the narrow-minded, nationalistic Jew who rejects the rights of the 'Other'. Here, it suffices to quote Ruether and Ruether, who use the Jonah narrative as a lens through which to comment on the modern Israeli-Palestinian conflict (Ruether and Ruether 1993: xxi; for an apt criticism, see Sherwood 1998: 58):

> God then tried to instruct his angry, chauvinist prophet in the true nature and ways of God. God is not the God of one people only. God created and loves all nations; all are the work of God's hand. God does not wish for the destruction of any nation, but rather that all repent and should be saved.

In parallel, speaking about the dialogue between God and Jonah, Luther notes in his German commentary to Jonah 4:1–2 that although Jonah clearly is in the wrong here, there is something admirable in the way that he confides his problems in God as in a father: 'He chats so uninhibitedly with God as though he were not in the least afraid of Him'. In this way, Luther notes, God allows his children to blunder and err greatly and grossly, yet is forever kind, paternal, and amicable when he deals with his children. Calvin likewise emphasizes Jonah's honesty. Although Jonah boasts of his flight and thus holds on to his obstinacy, he nevertheless also shows willingness to submit to God. Jonah's behaviour here, according to Calvin, is an example of the faithful praying in a disturbed mind and offering up confused prayers. This type of behaviour, however, should not be understood as a sign of hypocrisy (Lecture 79).

Abraham, Moses, Joel, and Jonah

The dialogue between God and Jonah throughout Chapter 4 forms a lengthy and to some extent also open-ended treatise on divine justice and mercy. It recalls in many ways the similar dialogue between God and Abraham in Gen 18 (cf. Jonah 1:2) (cf. Band 1990: 181). Rather than arguing about God's planned *destruction* like Abraham, however, Jonah argues about God's planned act of *mercy*. The topic – God's justice and God's mercy – is the same; the outcome, however, is (probably) the opposite (but see Jonah 4:11).

Early in this discussion (v. 2), Jonah enumerates God's so-called 'thirteen attributes of mercy', a list that also appears in slightly different versions in other places in the Hebrew Bible. The first instance, canonically speaking, is attested in Exod 34:6–7, where God declares his attributes to Moses (cf. Num 14:18; Mic 7:18; Nah 1:3; Pss 86:15; 103:8; 145:8; and Neh 9:17). Joel 2:13 and Jonah 4:2 contain a longer version that emphasizes God's ability to 'change his mind' (*niphal* of the root *nḥm*). This intertextual web creates a comparison between Israel and Nineveh, where both are subject to God's mercy and where the divine mercy to the former cannot be completely isolated from God's mercy to the latter. It also encourages a comparison between Moses, Joel, and Jonah, where the first two prophets actively sought to prevent Israel's annihilation whereas Jonah passively sought to accomplish Nineveh's demise (but possibly also actively sought to ensure Israel's survival; cf. above) (see further Scoralick 2002: 182–185; eadem 2020; Kamp 2003: 217–223; Timmer 2013). As Dozeman suggests, both Joel 2:13 and Jonah 4:2 explore the implications of Exod 34:6–7 within the context of God's covenant with Israel and the nations (Dozeman 1989; cf. Day 1990: 46–47, *contra* Kelly 2013).

God's Failure to Be Unmerciful

The explicit reason for Jonah's flight is, according to Jonah 4:2, God's tendency to show mercy or, viewed negatively, God's failure to withhold mercy (see also above, Jonah 1:3). Several literary retellings of the Jonah narrative ponder the notion of God's lack of desire to punish the guilty. The pivotal issue is the balance between mercy and justice. Can true mercy exist in the absence of true justice? Put aptly by the British literary theorist Terry Eagleton (1943–), Jonah refused to obey God because there did not seem to be any point in obeying him (Eagleton 1990: 232):

> God is a spineless liberal given to hollow authoritarian threats, who would never have the guts to perform what he promises [...] the point of Jonah's getting himself thrown overboard is to force God to save him, thus dramatically demonstrating to him that he's too soft-hearted to punish those who disobey him [...] Jonah doesn't believe for a moment that Nineveh's suspiciously sudden repentance is anything of his own doing: it has been brought about by God, to save himself the mess, unpleasantness and damage to his credibility as a nice chap consequent on having to put his threats into practice [...] God would have spared the city even if Jonah had stayed at home; it's just that he needs some excuse to do so. [...] And if God just goes around forgiving everybody all the time, what's the point of doing anything? If disobedience on the scale of a Nineveh goes cavalierly unpunished, then the idea of obedience also ceases to have meaning. God's mercy simply makes a mockery of human effort.

'A Masque of Mercy'
Several modern retellings have elaborated on this issue. Robert Frost's play *A Masque of Mercy* from 1947 is a case in point. In this retelling, the central figure Jonah Dove is described as a fugitive, not from justice but from what he believes is God's failure to uphold divine justice. In his view, God is obliged to punish the wicked; he must do so in his role as the supreme and just deity. God, however, has failed to carry out this task (see further Irwin 1969: 308–309; Timmerman 2002: 86). Jonah states poignantly:

> I've lost my faith in God to carry out
> The threats He makes against the city evil.
> I can't trust God to be unmerciful.
> (pp. 393–394)

Later in the same play, Jonah Dove continues:

> I refuse to be the bearer of an empty threat.
> He may be God, but me, I'm only human:
> I shrink from being publicly let down.
> [...]
> His very weakness for mankind's endearing.
> I love and fear Him. Yes, but I fear for Him.
> I don't see how it can be to His interest
> This modern tendency I find in Him
> To take the punishment out of all failure

> To be strong, careful, thrifty, diligent,
> Anything we once thought we had to be.
> (p. 401)

For Jonah, God's mercy absolves the consequences of human sin. Paul, Jonah's interlocutor throughout this play, serves as Jonah's exegete, teacher, and therapist. He naturally represents the New Testament author and theologian bearing the same name (Timmerman 2002: 86). Paul endeavours to show Jonah that he is not running from God himself but from God's mercy-justice contradiction (see further Fagan 2007: 211). Justice, he states, matters little:

> Jonah, I am glad, not sad to hear you say
> You can't trust God to be unmerciful.
> There you have the beginning of all wisdom.
> (p. 397)

Paul continues to highlight the message of mercy in the Book of Jonah:

> You should be an authority on Mercy
> That book of yours in the Old Testament
> Is the first place in literature I think
> Where Mercy is explicitly the subject.
> I say you should be proud of having beaten
> The Gospels to it.
> (p. 404)

Paul encourages Jonah to go through the door to the cellar, an action that would symbolize that Jonah gives up his clinging to justice and his own logic and instead willingly embraces God's mercy. After some hesitation, where Jonah declares that

> I am your convert. Tell me what I think.
> My trouble has been with my sense of justice.
> And you say justice doesn't really matter.
> (p. 413)

Jonah decides to go down, yet as he does, the door slams in his face (and presumably kills him). This incident is ambiguous and can be understood in several ways. As voiced by the character Paul, the door kills Jonah because he was reluctant to give up his old self: 'Some lingering objection holds you back' (p. 413) (Juhnke 1964: 161). Alternatively, the audience may wonder: could it be that not only is there no justice, there is also no true mercy? (Fagan 2007: 213) The play ends with Jonah's death. Jonah realizes that what he had, namely justice, was all he ever had. He utters his final plea, 'mercy on me for having thought I knew', before he fades, i.e. dies. Throughout the play, humanity's view of God's justice is corrected and seeks to bring about the realization that God's mercy is freely given (Loreto 1999: 29). Jonah's dead body is placed before the cross:

> Nothing can make injustice just but mercy.
>
> (p. 417)

This ending can be understood in two ways. Either Jonah dies, crumpled by justice and untouched by mercy, or mercy has overcome the justice upon which he built his life, and Jonah dies a transformed man (Timmerman 2002: 88).

'Jonas zum Beispiel'

The idea of divine mercy and divine justice is also raised in the adaptation of the Jonah narrative called 'Jonas zum Beispiel' ('Jonah as Example') by the German writer, editor, and scholar Uwe Johnson (1934–1984 CE). This title raises the obvious question: in what aspect is Jonah – as a book and as a character – an example? Discussing the connotations of the term *Beispiel* ('example'), Reinhard suggests that the Book of Jonah in its entirety is about being an example. Jonah wants Nineveh's destruction to be a (negative) example of God's justice, yet he knows all along that this is not God's intention (Jonah 4:2). The reason why Jonah tries to flee from carrying out God's command further reflects his own reluctance to be an example of God's mercy. There are other such examples. In fact, Jonah might argue that his salvation by God through the fish is a positive example of God's mercy; what is now needed – to create symmetry and balance – is a negative example of God's constancy and justice (Reinhard 2011: 341–342).

Jonah's Foresight

The notion that Jonah was able to foresee the course of events and thus to modify his own behaviour in view of this foresight is an interesting notion that several literary texts have picked up. In the poem 'Tom Fool at Jamaica' by the American poet Marianne Moore (1887–1972 CE), Jonah's rigidity, as well as his attempt to impose a system upon events even when he is confronted with the need to revise his course of action, is effectively contrasted by a small boy who drew a picture of 'a mule and a jockey' who were willing to alter their course out of respect for a tiny obstacle (see further Borroff 1956: 466–469):

> Look at Jonah embarking from Joppa, deterred by
> the whale; hard going for a statesman whom nothing could detain,

although one who would not rather die than repent.
Be infallible at your peril, for your system will fail,
and select as a model the schoolboy in Spain
who, at the age of six, portrayed a mule and a jockey who had
pulled up for a snail.

Jonah 4:3

'And now, Yhwh, take my life from me because my death is preferable to my life'.

Realizing that God was really going through with his plans of compassion for Nineveh, Jonah expresses a desire to die. Scholars have tried to explain Jonah's death wish. The rabbis offer the most benevolent interpretations. Radak, for example, puts Jonah's plea to God here on a par with that of Moses's pleas during the wandering in the wilderness. On the one hand, for the sake of saving Israel, Moses asks God to blot him out of his book unless God forgives Israel (Exod 32:32). On the other hand, for entirely different reasons, Moses responds to the Israelites' complaints about the manna by asking to die so that he would not have to hear their grumbles (Num 11:15).

In contrast, many Christian interpreters underscore that wishing to die is akin to despair (and thus an affront to God). Calvin, for instance, argues that whoever wishes to die before his/her appointed time is struggling against God. It is not up to humanity to determine when to quit this world. We ought instead, with submissive minds, to continue in life for as long as God decides to keep us in the station in which we are placed. In short, death is not to be desired because of a state of mind caused by the weariness of life. We should love life in such a way so that we are prepared to lay it down whenever the Lord pleases (Lecture 79).

Jonah 4:4

And Yhwh said: 'Is it good for you to be so angry?'

In Jonah 4:4, God asks Jonah a question. Several predominantly Christian exegetes find the notion that God asks a question to be theologically problematic, as a question can, from their point of view, be mistakenly understood as a sign that God is not omniscient. Their starting point is thus that God knows everything. A divine question cannot, therefore, be a mere quest for information; instead it seeks to help or rebuke the human interlocutor.

According to Jerome, God's query to Jonah here is an attempt to push Jonah to articulate the reason behind his anger.

In sharp contrast, Calvin rejects Jerome's interpretation outright as a distortion of the plain sense of Scripture, as God is clearly rebuking Jonah here (Lecture 79). Furthermore, according to Calvin, any attempt to explain Jonah's anger as part of the prophet's concern with the future fate of his people Israel (cf. Jonah 4:1 above) is misguided. Rather, Jonah should be held accountable for his failure to care for the fate of such a large city as Nineveh (Lecture 80, Commentary on Jonah 4:10–11).

God's Mercy for Strangers

Several retellings comment on Jonah's lack of willingness to extend God's mercy to people outside of Israel. The modern choral work *Jonah: A Musical Morality* by William Mathias, for example, inserts a long speech at this point in the Jonah narrative to emphasize God's universal mercy:

> Jonah: Therefore I accuse you, Lord, I accuse you of mercy, of mercy.
> Sopranos and Tenors: My mercy is kept for thousands, for all people, Jonah. (For all the people – the brown, the black, the white, and those who are the colour of the pale moonlight.) God's providence and mercy is for all the people, Jonah. […]
> Jonah: Why does my God offer salvation to a world of strangers, to a world of strangers?
> Sopranos and Tenors: Let no man be a stranger, Jonah. See him with understanding. Gaze into his eyes that you may meet your own. Now rest, Jonah. Rest, that you may see how things shall be with Nineveh, with Nineveh, with Nineveh, with Nineveh, with Nineveh.

Nonetheless, Jonah continues to insist on his right to be angry, whereupon God (sung by the full choir) points to the tree and the worm (Jonah 4:6–10).

In modern scholarship, Jonah's attitude has often been (unfavourably) contrasted with the inclusive attitude attested in the Book of Ruth: whereas Jonah wishes to preserve God's mercy to the people of Israel, the overarching message of the latter book is to show God's universal love. Recently, Howe Gaines has highlighted how the prophet Jonah's wariness of foreigners is countered in the Hebrew canon by the message of the Book of Ruth. In parallel, Gaines stresses the danger that such a comparison entails, as it often slides into anti-Jewish polemic where 'Jonah symbolizes benighted Judaism, while repentant Nineveh represents enlightened Christianity'. Instead, the *Book* of Jonah is a Jewish book, the overarching message of which is a form of self-criticism of the very attitude displayed by the *character* of Jonah (Gaines 2003: 9, 14, 53, 95, 131–133).

Jonah's Anger and Cain's Anger

Several Jewish exegetes, among them the Vilna Gaon, have noted the affinity between, on the one hand, the description of Jonah's anger and God's questioning of the reason behind that anger in Jonah 4:1, 4, 9 and, on the other hand, the dialogue between Cain and God in Gen 4:5–6. The comparison is triggered by the shared use of the Hebrew verb *ḥarah* = 'to be angry' (see further Shapiro 1997: 93; cf. also Downs 2009: 41), as well as by the shared rare expression *milifne Adonai* = 'from before the Lord' (Jonah 1:3, 10; Gen 4:14a, 16a) (Vanoni 1978: 143). Together, these instances of common vocabulary create an impression of Jonah as a man fleeing from and also being banished from God's presence (Tiemeyer 2019a: 265–266). Among modern scholars, Berger offers a thought-provoking reading of Jonah as a man who, like Cain, longs for Eden. Both Jonah and Cain decline the opportunity that repentance signifies, and both men ultimately fail to reach their goal of a return to the paradisiacal existence of Eden (Berger 2016: 13–14).

La meva Cristina

In parallel, the notion of Jonah as a perpetual exile and as a type for the 'wandering Jew' is picked up in several fictional retellings of the Jonah narrative.

In her short story 'My Christina' ('La meva Cristina'), the Catalan novelist Mercè Rodoreda (1908–1983 CE) uses the Jonah narrative as a template for exploring the notion of marginalization and estrangement that are the companions of exile. A shipwrecked sailor is swallowed and thus saved by a whale. At first, the sailor is grateful towards the whale and names her 'Cristina' after his shipwrecked boat. Half-way through the narrative, the sailor sees green land and manages to leave the whale. As he is swimming towards land, however, the whale catches up with him and swallows him anew. At this point, the relationship between the sailor and his saviour turns bitter. The sailor remains inside the whale for years and slowly becomes one with her through eating her flesh. When the whale dies, the sailor finally escapes but finds that he is unable to reintegrate into society. He is transformed by his sojourn in the whale and, as a result, regarded as a freak by his former compatriots. Most poignantly, the sailor arrives in a village where he is met by a woman who calls him 'her husband'. The sailor, however, cannot recognize her. The reader is left wondering whether this actually was the sailor's home but that he now has become so attuned to his exilic existence that he cannot acknowledge it as such. Even stronger, the sailor can no longer go home, because home as he remembers it no longer exists and because he himself is no longer the same man that he was before he left (Nichols 1986: 405–417). Life in exile/in the fish, first perceived to be a haven and then transformed into a prison, has altered him beyond recognition; the fish/personified Exile has turned the sailor into something less foreign and instead part of herself (Tiemeyer 2019a: 266–268).

A estranha nação de Rafael Mendes
The same tradition of Jonah as a fugitive appears in the novel *The Strange Nation of Rafael Mendes* by Moacyr Scliar (cf. Jonah 1:15). The present-day character Rafael Mendes explores the lives of his ancestors, going all the way back to Jonah (pp. 39, 69–70, 75–83). The Jonah narrative lends structure to the novel with the help of repeated allusions to it and through references to rootlessness, sea journeys, and (near) death by drowning.

> I was able to track down someone named Jonah as the most distant of my known ancestors. [...] Throughout the ages, they fled from place to place, from country to country; they crossed oceans, they scaled mountains, living strange adventures, sensing a disturbing summons. (p. 75).

As the novel progresses, the reader encounters a long sequence of Jonah's descendants, each of them characterized by their rootlessness that is caused by a combination of being persecuted and of searching for the golden tree. Habacuc – a Jonah/Rafael Mendes reincarnation living in the first century CE – flees from the Romans to Yafo, boards a ship, and ends up in Spain (presumably an allusion to Tarshish in the Jonah narrative). As his flight coincides with the death of Jesus, Habacuc's descendants are doomed to be rootless:

> 'Your crime didn't go unnoticed', replied the voice. 'Because of the sins you and others have committed, a god has died, Habacuc. As punishment, your descendants will wander the earth until they finally hark to the word of the children of light. Have I made myself understood?' (p. 93).

Another Jonah/Rafael Mendes incarnation aspires to become a sailor. In a clear allusion to Jonah's encounter with the sailors (Jonah 1), Rafael mistakes the other sailors for Hebrews, only to be disappointed (pp. 185–190). In the penultimate incarnation, Rafael Mendes seeks to return to Spain to fight with the Republicans (p. 259). He never reaches Spain, however, but instead dies on board the ship and his body, like that of Jonah, is thrown into the sea:

> During a brief moment of lucidity, he announced that he would be dying soon; he asked that his body be cast into the sea so that like Jonah (to use his own words) he could reach his destination. (p. 259).

Scliar's novel, evoking the Book of Jonah, creates in Rafael Mendes an alternative type of Jonah. In Scliar's hands, Rafael, like Jonah has a mission, but unlike Jonah, he does not know exactly what that mission is. Furthermore, Rafael, like Jonah, flees; but whereas Jonah's flight is an active rebellion, Rafael's flight is rather passive, undertaken in response to the events that befall him (Barr 1996: 42–45). Finally, Rafael, like Jonah, wishes to reach Spain (i.e. Tarshish), but neither man arrives at his destination, instead either dying at sea or being forced to reroute to Nineveh. The lasting impression of Jonah and of his alter ego, Rafael, is that of the eternal exile who, haunted by his God, has no home and never makes it to his promised land.

Jonah 4:5

> And Jonah left from the city and sat east of the city and made himself there a sukkah and he sat under it in the shade so that he would see what would happen in the city.

This verse connects backwards to Jonah 4:1. As already discussed (Jonah 4:1), the chronological relationship between Jonah's anger in Jonah 4:1–4 and his action in Jonah 4:5 is unclear.

'And Jonah left from the city and sat east of the city'

The statement that Jonah sat down 'east of the city' has caused a few scholars, among them Jerome (cf. the *Glossa Ordinaria*), to note the similarity to Gen 4:16–17, which speaks about the city of Enoch that Cain built 'east of Eden'. While Jerome does not identify Jonah with Cain in any salient way, it is possible that Scliar made such a link in his novel *The Strange Nation of Rafael Mendes* (see Jonah 4:4) (Berger 2016: 14; Tiemeyer 2019a: 260–261).

'and made himself there a sukkah'

Cyril of Alexandria makes a pertinent comparison between Nineveh and Jonah's shelter: '[Jonah] expected, in fact, that [the city] would perhaps be shaken and collapse or, be burnt to the ground like Sodom. Instead, it was his house that was ruined, the shelter he had built himself'. The *Glossa Ordinaria*, commenting on the word 'himself', states that Jonah stayed in Nineveh alone, as no inhabitant in Nineveh would have been able to live with the prophet.

'so that he would see what would happen in the city'

Several commentators note that Jonah here must have expected the city to be destroyed. He thus sat down to watch an anticipated spectacle of mass destruction. Cyril of Alexandria, for example, states that Jonah presumed that Nineveh would fall as he deemed it impossible that their repentance during such a relatively short time span (three days, following the LXX) would be sufficient to atone for a life of sin: 'After all, why should three days' effort benefit people who were buried in every form of wrongdoing and guilty of such dreadful sins?'

Other commentators read this verse with an awareness of Nineveh's eventual destruction in 612 BCE, as narrated in, among other places, the Book of Nahum. Notably, Targum Jonathan adds the word 'in the end' to its translation of Jonah 4:5, a reading which probably reflects not only the translator's awareness of Nahum's prophecy of Nineveh's destruction, but also his historical knowledge of Nineveh's ultimate demise (Cathcart and Gordon 1989: 109, fn. 7). This latter insight is expanded on in a few later, literary retellings of the Jonah narrative. In the poem 'Jonah', the Jewish South African poet Lewis Sowden (1903–1974 CE) writes (see further Liptzin 1985a: 248):

> It took a hundred years or more,
> while Heaven's patience held,
> to fetch a sword for Nineveh
> as Jonah had forespelled.
> Then was that city ripped with flood
> and raked with hammer and hood.
> The only monument to stand
> is Jonah and his book.

Jonah 4:6

And God appointed a qiqayyon and it grew up over Jonah to be a shelter for his head [and] to save him from its evil, and Jonah rejoiced greatly over the qiqayyon.

'And God appointed a qiqayyon'

Jonah 4:6 tells us that God appointed a plant, with the purpose of giving shade to Jonah. Exegetes over the ages have been confounded by four key issues. First, what type of plant was it? Second, why did God perceive that Jonah needed a plant for shade when Jonah already had built a shelter for himself (v. 5)? Third, from what 'evil' would the plant save Jonah? Fourth, what is the symbolic significance of the plant?

1. What Type of Plant Are We Talking About?

The identity of the *qiqayyon* has troubled many exegetes through the ages. In fact, the translation of this word may even have caused a riot in Oea, a city in Libya, as mentioned in a letter from Augustine to Jerome (Augustine, *Epistles* 71, 5) (Bazzana 2010: 311)! In parallel, many of these same translators have confessed that this matter is overall relatively unimportant and need not be discussed!

Beginning with the ancient versions, the LXX (κολοκύνθα) denotes some form of gourd plant (*Cucurbita*). This understanding is often reflected in art. For example, the statue 'Jonah Under the Gourd Vine' (280–290 CE) from Roman Asia Minor, currently in the Cleveland Museum of Art, shows Jonah reclining under a gourd-like vegetable (see Figure 14). Aquila and Theodotion, in contrast, opted to transliterate the Hebrew word (κικεῶνα), whereas Symmachus chose to render it as 'ivy' (κισσός).

Turning to the Jewish commentators, the Babylonian Talmud (*b.Shab.* 2:1) records a discussion between Rabbi Isaac ben Rabbi Judah and Rabbi Simeon ben Laqish concerning the exact identification of the plant, whether it is a gourd plant or a castor oil plant (*ricinus communis*):

> Rabbi Isaac ben Rabbi Judah said: 'It is cotton seed oil'. Rabbi Simeon ben Laqish said: 'It is oil from the gourd of the kind that Jonah planted'. Said Rabbah bar Hannah: 'I myself saw the type of gourd that Jonah planted; it is like a ricinus tree and grows in ditches. It is planted at the entrance of stores; from its pits they make oil; under its branches all the sick people in the West take a rest'.

The mediaeval Jewish commentators followed suit. Ibn Ezra cites the sages of Spain who think that the *qiqayyon* is either a type of *dala'at* ('pumpkin') or a type of *qarah* ([another kind of] 'pumpkin'), yet ultimately concedes that we really do not need to know the exact answer! Radak goes into more detail as he seeks to uncover the type of plant to which Jonah 4:6 is referring. He states that the plant is tall, beautiful, and provides shade. He cites the above-mentioned *b.Shab.* 2:1 and notes that Rabeinu Shmuel ben Hafni identifies it with what in

FIGURE 14 'Jonah Under the Gourd Vine', Cleveland Museum of Art, United States. Source: Wmpearl. Licensed under CC0 1.0.

Arabic is called *aloe vera*, and he comments that it is to be compared to a plant, mentioned in the geonim's *responsas*, that has kernels and from which cold drinks are made.

Many Christian readings of Jonah 4:6 also envisaged a gourd, as can be observed in much early Christian art (see also below). Against this background, Jerome's translation of the term *qiqayyon* as *hedera* ('ivy') in his Vulgate in accordance with Symmachus (above), rather than adhering to the traditional understanding of the LXX, was a controversial change (Bazzana 2010: 310–313, 317–321). In his commentary to Jonah, Jerome elaborates further. He notes with surprise how many people reacted very negatively – even accusing him of sacrilege – to his decision to translate the term *qiqayyon* as 'ivy'. Notably, his translation was heavily criticized by the monk and theologian Tyrannius Rufinus (344/345–411 CE) in his *Apology Against Jerome* 2, 39:

> Now therefore after four hundred years the truth of the law comes forth for us, it has been bought with money from the Synagogue. When the world has grown old and all things are hastening to their end, let us change the inscriptions upon the tombs of the ancients, so that it may be known by those who had read the

story otherwise, that it was not a gourd but an ivy plant under whose shade Jonah rested; and that, when our legislator pleases, it will no longer be the shade of ivy but of some other plant.

Jerome continues to argue that although the appearance of the plant near Jonah was a miracle, it grew according to its nature (i.e. its growth was not miraculous, cf. below). Turning to its symbolic meaning, Jerome argues that the *qiqayyon* here in Jonah was the fulfilment the prophecy in Zech 6:12 about the 'shoot' (commentary to Jonah 4:5).

The Reformers continue to debate the best translation of the term *qiqayyon*. In his German commentary, Luther opts for the *vitis abla* plant, which in German is *Wildrübe*, and argues the matter at great length, only to conclude eventually that 'this question is not so vital, and we need not squabble so vehemently about the words, so long as we are sure about the facts'. Calvin likewise spends what may be considered a disproportionate amount of time on the subject, given that he himself states that it is a 'thing of no moment'. He rejects the translation 'ivy' in the Vulgate and instead – lest he cause any disturbance – favours the older translation 'gourd'. Nevertheless, he acknowledges that he has 'spoken more than [he] intended'. Calvin brings his discussion to a close by emphasizing the miraculous growth of the plant (Lecture 80).

The identity of the plant is also the topic of the qur'anic discussion in sura 37:146–148:

> We cast him forth on the naked shore in a state
>   of sickness,
> And We caused to grow, over him, a spreading
>   plant of the gourd kind.

The fact that the Qur'an speaks about a 'gourd' (a kurbis-plant rather than the ricin plant) in its retelling of Jonah 4:6 suggests that it probably received the story via the LXX and not via the MT (Steffen 1994: 120–121).

In Islamic art, the sixteenth-century miniature found in the Zubdat-al Tawarikh manuscript, presently in the Museum of Turkish and Islamic Arts in Istanbul, depicts Jonah hiding in the gourd tree (see Figure 15).

A few modern scholars have opted not to identify the *qiqayyon* with a specific plant but instead to see the name as part of a wordplay. For Halpern and Friedman, the choice of the *qiqayyon* has nothing to do with its biological classification; it is selected due to its phonetic similarity with the terms for 'innocent' (*naqiʾ*) in Jonah 1:14 and 'vomit' (*wayyaqeʾ*) in Jonah 2:11 [Eng. 2:10] (Halpern and Friedman 1980: 85–86). Going one step further, Strawn suggests that the final part of the word *qiqayyon* can be read as a form of the

Figure 15 The Zubdat-al Tawarikh manuscript, Museum of Turkish and Islamic Arts, Istanbul. Jonah and the fish, Jeremiah in wilderness. Source: Painters of Sultan Murad III, Zubdat-al Tawarikh. Public Domain.

name 'Jonah', resulting in the meaning 'Jonah has certainly vomited' or, in his view more plausible, 'he/it has certainly vomited Jonah', the subject being either God or the fish (Strawn 2012: 455–457).

2. Why a Plant when Jonah Already Has a Shelter (Sukkah)?

A potentially more significant issue, at least from literary and exegetical perspectives, concerns God's reason for assigning a plant for shelter to Jonah in the first place (v. 6), given that Jonah had already built himself a sukkah that, so we may assume, would have given him sufficient shelter (v. 5). There are two main lines of exegesis: conflation and succession. The Hellenistic-Jewish sermon *On Jonah* 40:3 solves the conundrum by conflating the shelter with the plant: Jonah sat under a shelter covered with the branches of the *qiqayyon*. Likewise, Theodore of Mopsuestia states that God let the plant grow so that it would give shelter to the tent that Jonah had already built. He further envisages fruits hanging down on all sides to give Jonah considerable comfort. Along similar lines, Jerome argues that the *qiqayyon* gave additional shade, thus supplementing the shade that the sukkah provided. In contrast, other exegetes maintain that the *qiqayyon* replaced the shelter. Radak, for instance, speculates that the branches of the sukkah had maybe dried out, as Jonah had already lived in the sukkah for 40 days.

More modern scholars have highlighted the affinity between Jonah 4:5 and the narrative in 1 Kgs 19:4–5, where another prophet, Elijah, sat under another tree and wished to die (Frahm 2016: 434). This comparison is to the detriment of Jonah: the contrast turns Jonah into an 'anti-prophet' or a person of ridicule and parody. Elijah wished to die because he felt inadequate to fight Jezebel and her prophets of Baal, whereas Jonah wished to die because of the death of a plant which had caused him personal discomfort (Vawter 1983: 113–114; Band 1990: 187; Dell 1996: 89; Schellenberg 2015: 357; for a different take, see Halpern and Friedman 1980: 90).

3. What Was the 'Evil' from which God Wanted to Save Jonah?

The most common (and most straightforward) explanation of the 'evil' from which God wanted to save Jonah is to see it as a reference to potentially harmful sunrays. We find, for example, this explanation among the mediaeval Jewish exegetes: Rashi explains that the evil here is the heat of the sun, as do Ibn Ezra and Radak.

The Islamic treatment of the plant – its kind, *raison d'être*, and ramifications – is most interesting in that God's decision to grow the plant has nothing to do with teaching Jonah a lesson (*contra* Jonah 4:10). Rather, God lets it grow out of compassion so that Jonah's skin would be able to heal. His skin was so sore after being inside the fish, that any small amount of sunshine would be torture for him (see, e.g. al-Ṭabarī 1987: 166; al-Kisai 1997: 324; Al-Tha'labī 2002: 687). This Islamic tradition is strongly reminiscent of that found in Midrash Yonah 102 and in MRJP (see also above, Jonah 2:11), suggesting that the two are linked (Kadari 2016: 116–120). According to the midrash, when Jonah saw that Nineveh was spared, he felt encouraged to ask God to forgive his own flight from God's command. God forgave him and, moreover, seeing that Jonah was sore from his time within the fish, decided to let the *qiqayyon* grow to protect him from the sun and from the insects that plagued him (Eng. transl. Ziolkowski 2007: 86):

> And because of the great heat that Jonah had in the entrails of the fish, his clothes were burned and all the hair of his body and his head, along with his beard, and flies and insects and ants and fleas were spread upon him and tortured him on all sides until he asked his soul to die, as it is said. 'And he asked his soul to die'. Hence the sages said: anyone who has it within his power to seek mercy on his fellow and does not so seek, or to bring him to repent and does not so bring him, will eventually come into great suffering.

This tradition was clearly widespread. Ibn Ezra, for example, continues his discussion of Jonah 4:6 by referring to some people who claim that Jonah needed shade because his body was sore from being in the fish for so long.

4. The Symbolic Value of the Plant

The plant has not been neglected as interpreters have sought to interpret the Book of Jonah symbolically.

On the one hand, the *Glossa Ordinaria* makes the anti-Jewish identification of the *qiqayyon* (identified as 'ivy') with Israel. It grows quickly but has little in terms of roots and is unequal in stature to the cedar and the cypress. It is also like Israel in its temporality: it provided Jonah with shade for a limited time, lacking a sure foundation, only to be replaced.

On the other hand, Elie Wiesel argues poignantly that the real hero of the Jonah narrative is the *qiqayyon*. It is brought into the world merely to die. Its life is created only to serve as an example with its quick death. God does not really care for it; only Jonah does (Jonah 4:10). Jonah, who has seen so much, has pity on the small plant that offers him protection. Such a man would not lack compassion for Nineveh, but he loves Israel more (cf. Jonah 1:2) (Wiesel 1981: 153–154):

> He does not wish Nineveh to die, yet he does not wish Nineveh to live at the expense of Israel. To love mankind is honourable; to love it against Israel is not. Is that the reason for Jonah's death wish? Does he wish to die because of the inner moral conflict of reconciling his love of man with his incommensurate love of his people? Does God show him the tragic fate of the plant to provide the ultimate illustration that all things are related, that one must feel pity for both Nineveh and the Kikayon, that one must love other people through one's own – and never outside one's own?

The Reclining Jonah

In early Christian art, Jonah is often depicted as a reclining nude under the plant. In fact, 'Jonah reclining' is the third key image in the so-called Jonah cycle (cf. Jonah 1:15). We can observe this phenomenon in the third-century sarcophagus from the Church of Santa Maria Antiqua, c. 275 CE. There has been much scholarly discussion on the interpretation of this image. It probably borrowed elements from the early Christian Greco-Roman context and is likely to reflect depictions of Endymion (Davis 2000: 79–81). As Jensen has shown, viewers familiar with both the biblical Jonah narrative and the Roman story of the youth who was cursed with perpetual youth and perpetual sleep (and the unconscious progenitor of Elene's 40 children) would have inferred a secondary Christian meaning to the Jonah story, namely, that Jonah awaits the resurrection 'in a state of blissful repose' (Jensen 2000: 72–73). Jensen further argues that this kind of symbolism would have been suitable in funeral contexts. For Jonah, in contrast to Endymion, sleep would have been an interim state. As such, the reclining Jonah figure would have reminded the audience of the resurrection (Jensen 2000: 173). As to Jonah's nudity, Jensen argues that it symbolizes the nudity of the baptismal candidates who without clothes were dipped and reborn 'from the womblike waters of the baptismal font' (Jensen 2000: 173, including fn. 55–56, 65). From a different perspective, Davis argues that the reclining Jonah is a visual sign of the physical resurrection. The Early Church (e.g. Tertullian) understood Jonah to have left the fish physically unscathed (cf. discussion Jonah 2:11). The reclining Jonah/Endymion here symbolizes the body's preservation after death and by extension also the bodily resurrection. The depiction of Jonah reclining under the plant would thus be an example of a new allegorical reading of the Jonah narrative that sought to visualize the resurrection of the flesh (Davis 2000: 80; *contra* Bazzana 2010: 321–322).

Jonah's Happiness

Jonah 4:6 further states that 'Jonah rejoiced greatly over the *qiqayyon*'. Cyril of Alexandria compares Jonah to an infant and an unsophisticated mind, both being very easily disposed to both distress and satisfaction. They quickly change from distress to joy, sometimes under the influence of a thing of no consequence.

Poetic Retellings

The novel *Jonah's Gourd Vine* (1934) by the African-American novelist and Baptist preacher Zora Neale Hurston (1891–1960 CE) is a semi-autobiographical novel the title of which is derived from Jonah 4:6–8. The protagonist, the preacher John Buddy Pearson, is just like the plant in Jonah 4:6–8. First, he flourishes in his role, but ultimately, he also withers. His ultimate decline is due to his failure to interpret the signs in his own life correctly. John detects divine messages in the events around him, most pertinently in his encounter with a train at the beginning of the novel. He expresses his inability to decipher their messages, yet he simultaneously perceives that there is a message to discern if only he had the tools to do so. Accordingly, he dedicates himself to learning this mystical language and also to communicating it to his fellow human beings. The novel further expresses the potential conflict between the spoken and the written word. In a sense, Lucy (John's love and later also his wife) represents not only the gift of writing, which initially allows John to prosper but also the worm, which threatens to kill John's own oral tradition. In the end, John is killed by a train, the same sign that first set his journey in motion, without having reached full understanding.

The links between Hurston's novel and the Book of Jonah are manifold. First, John, like Jonah, lives at odds with God's word; both are involved in a type of hermeneutical struggle to understand God's speech and to allow it to influence their lives. Second, both are prophets insofar as they are commissioned by God to speak not their own words but God's. Third, both men initially resist God's words before ultimately accepting the divine command to preach. Finally, both men fail to internalize God's message in their own life. Just as Jonah never really changes throughout the narrative, so John fails to achieve his own change of heart, and his life does not reflect the teaching of God's word. Thus, both narratives end without their protagonists having reached anything akin to an understanding of God's ways (Ciuba 2000: 126–127, 130).

Jonah 4:7

> And God appointed a worm when the dawn rose the next morning and it attacked the qiqayyon and it withered.

'And God appointed a worm when the dawn rose the next morning'

Just as God 'appointed' a fish (2:1 [Eng. 1:17]) and a *qiqayyon* (4:6), now he 'appoints' a worm. Later, in Jonah 4:8, he will finally also 'appoint' an eastern wind (4:8). Throughout the Book of Jonah, God mobilizes and manipulates nature to instruct Jonah (cf. Trible 1990: 194–195).

God's appointment of the worm has given rise to what may be one of the most peculiar – and also one of the most anti-Jewish – interpretations in the reception history of the Book of Jonah, namely, that the worm is a type for either Christ or the Gospel, while the *qiqayyon* represents the Old Covenant. The impetus for this interpretation is Ps 22:6, where the psalmist states 'I am a worm and not a man'. This interpretation is advocated by many of the Church

Fathers. Augustine, for example, speaks of the 'morning worm' that caused the Old Covenant to wither away by the coming of Jesus and the forging of the New Covenant ('Letter 102'):

> Wherefore the shadow of that gourd over his head prefigured the promises of the Old Testament, or rather the privileges already enjoyed in it in which there was, as the apostle says, a shadow of things to come (Colossians 2:17), furnishing, as it were, a refuge from the heat of temporal calamities in the land of promise. Moreover, in that morning-worm, which by its gnawing tooth made the gourd wither away, Christ Himself is again prefigured, forasmuch as, by the publication of the gospel from His mouth, all those things which flourished among the Israelites for a time, or with a shadowy symbolic meaning in that earlier dispensation, are now deprived of their significance, and have withered away. And now that nation, having lost the kingdom, the priesthood, and the sacrifices formerly established in Jerusalem, all which privileges were a shadow of things to come, is burned with grievous heat of tribulation in its condition of dispersion and captivity, as Jonah was, according to the history, scorched with the heat of the sun, and is overwhelmed with sorrow; and notwithstanding, the salvation of the Gentiles and of the penitent is of more importance in the sight of God than this sorrow of Israel and the shadow of which the Jewish nation was so glad.

This interpretation is taken up by none other than Luther, who argues that Jesus is the worm that God appoints. Jesus attacks the plant which is the Law and abolishes it through the Holy Spirit. As a result, 'Judaism withered and decayed in all the world, and thus we see it today. Its verdure is gone, it flourishes no longer, nor is there a saint or a prophet sitting in its shade today. Its day is spent'. In support of this interpretation, Luther cites Ps 22:6. The fall of Judaism took place at dawn 'on the day of Grace, of the New Testament' (German commentary, 'Concluding Remarks').

'and it attacked the qiqayyon and it withered'

Jewish scholars tend to focus on the practical aspects of the verse: how exactly did the worm 'attack' the plant so that it withered? Radak, for example, comments that the verb 'attack' is used here to denote how the worm devoured the lower part of the plant so that it could not receive water from the ground and thus withered and died.

In his play *The Burden of Nineveh*, Act 5, Housman has the plant die on the 40th day. Thus the *qiqayyon* dies instead of Nineveh:

> On the day, and at the hour, when Nineveh should have perished, there came a blight upon the gourd, so that all its leaves withered; and after the blight came a

strong wind, and tore it, and broke it – the only thing in the land that had been kind to me – making it useless! Then came the sun and smote me, and spake to me the Word of the Lord, 'Behold, thou are nothing!' that is what has come to me from God, after all that I did for Him.

Jonah's interlocutor in the play, Shemmel, manages to convince Jonah that this is neither a sign of God's displeasure nor a sign that Jonah did not speak God's words in Nineveh. Rather, the whole point of Jonah's preaching to the people of Nineveh was their repentance. As such, Jonah achieved what God wanted from him.

Jonah 4:8

And when the sun rose, God appointed an eastern, sultry wind, and the sun hit Jonah's head, and he grew faint, and he desired to die, and he said: 'My death is better than my life'.

'God appointed an eastern, sultry wind'

A few commentators have understood God's appointment of the 'eastern sultry wind' symbolically. Jerome, for instance, in his commentary to Jonah 4:7, suggests that the wind here in Jonah 4:8 is the Roman generals who destroyed Israel completely after the resurrection of Christ.

The American poet Marianne Moore alludes to Jonah 4:8a in her poem 'Is Your Town Nineveh':

> Is it Nineveh
> and are you Jonah
> in the sweltering east wind of your wishes?
> I myself, have stood
> there by the aquarium, looking
> at the Statue of Liberty.

In Moore's hands, Nineveh becomes a symbol of New York, a city that evokes not only feelings of depression, isolation, and disgust but also connotations of freedom and opportunity. Moore, seeing herself as a kind of Jonah, maintains that she, being a poet, has moral and social obligations towards the city: she is to argue against what she considers to be America's increasing self-centredness and commercialism and to point the reader towards personal freedom. In her endeavours, she understands herself to be guided by both the scientific delights of the aquarium and the freedom epitomized by the Statue of Liberty (Miller 2000: 351–152).

In another of Marianne Moore's poems, 'Sojourn in the Whale', Moore portrays Ireland and, by extension, also herself as a kind of female Jonah who is offered freedom and opportunity when arriving in New York. Her main goal becomes not to be swallowed by the whale, i.e. she is not to lose her own identity among the powerful institutions already established there; rather, she is to succeed on her own terms. For Moore, Jonah is a positive hero: he not only seeks to stay free, but he also has to transform Nineveh (i.e. New York), not by threatening it with its imminent destruction but by offering it aesthetic leadership (Miller 2000: 351–354).

'and he grew faint'

When the sun hit Jonah's head, Jonah 'grew faint' (*it'alaf*). The *hithpael* form of the root *ayin, lamed, pe* is attested only three times in the Hebrew Bible. In Gen 38:14, it means literally 'to wrap', whereas here in Jonah and Amos 8:13, it takes the metaphoric meaning 'to grow faint' and 'to wither'. Ibn Ezra combines all three instances as he claims that Jonah grew faint wrapped in his clothes.

Turning to modern scholars, Muldoon has noted that a different form of the same root appears in Ezek 31:15 within an oracle about Assyria. In the wider oracle in Ezek 31:3–18, Assyria/the king of Assyria is likened to a majestic tree that is the envy of all the trees in Eden. As it dies, 'all the trees of the field withered away because of it'. For Muldoon, the *qiqayyon* in Jonah 4 stands for the rise and fall of Assyria; Jonah 4:8 thus hints forward towards the fall of Nineveh (Muldoon 2010: 129–143; cf. Berger 2016: 75).

Jonah 4:9

> And God said to Jonah: 'Is it pleasing to you to be angry with the qiqayyon?' And Jonah said: 'It is pleasing to me to be angry; even until death'.

In Jonah 4:9, God asks Jonah if it is 'pleasing to him to be angry' and Jonah responds affirmatively that it is. This expression is very difficult to translate into English. In this dialogue, the word choice in the Hebrew text conveys the impression that Jonah somehow takes a certain morbid pleasure in expressing his anger.

In his anger, Jonah expresses a wish to die (cf. also Jonah 4:3). Many exegetes criticize Jonah for this wish. Calvin, for example, remarks that Jonah was overwhelmed by grief and rushed headlong into a state of despair, in this way boiling over with displeasure beyond all due limits (Lecture 80). It should be noted, however, that Calvin fails to point out the rather overt ridiculous aspects of Jonah's grief.

Looking at the matter from a modern ecological perspective, Havea criticizes God, rather than Jonah, for his attitude and actions towards the plant. Whereas Jonah clearly did care about the plant, God's statement in Jonah 4:9 implies that the plant was not worth much in his eyes (Havea 2020: 68–79).

Jonah 4:10

> And YHWH said: 'You pitied the qiqayyon for whose sake you did not labour and that you did not cultivate, that lived for one night and perished after one night'.

In the biblical text, the *qiqayyon* functions as a symbol of ephemerality and inconsequence: how can Jonah care for something for which he had not invested time or labour and something that was there only for a brief period? By implication, Jonah should rather care about things that are lasting and of significance (such as the people of the city of Nineveh, v. 11). The divine statement about the *qiqayyon* in verse 10 and that about Nineveh in verse 11 form parallels. If we read verse 11 as a rhetorical question (see Jonah 4:11), this shared use of the verb 'pity' serves both to compare and contrast Jonah's and God's behaviour. Jonah pities the plant, and God pities Nineveh. There is a difference in their care, however: whereas Jonah has never worked to take care of the one-day-old plant, God has invested both time and labour in the city, and its destruction would accordingly grieve him. Therefore, God has decided to spare the city. In this comparison, the worm is God's alter ego but also his counterpoint: the worm destroyed the *qiqayyon*, which was transient and unimportant; God will not destroy Nineveh, which has existed for a long time and is important.

Julian Barnes puts a different spin on the *qiqayyon* in his book *A History of the World in 10½ Chapters*. Calling the whole incident an example of street theatre, he claims that the moral of the story is: 'you didn't punish the gourd when it failed you, did you; and in the same way I'm not going to punish Nineveh' (p. 176). Phrased differently, the issue is less that of Jonah's anger at God for destroying the gourd and more about Jonah's lack of consequence: if he wanted God to be angry with the Ninevites when they failed to live a righteous life, Jonah should have been angry at the *qiqayyon* when it failed in its duty to provide him shade.

The comparison in verses 10–11 between the destruction of the *qiqayyon* by God/the worm and the non-destruction of Nineveh by God is also the underlying topic of Peter Hacks's tragedy *Jona: Trauerspiel in fünf Akten* from 1988. The play was performed for the first time in 2009 in Wuppertal, Germany. In this play, Jonah's task, different from that which is in the biblical narrative, is to determine whether Nineveh, ruled by Queen Semiramis (cf. Jonah 1:1), deserves to be destroyed. Jonah's initial reaction, however, is that *every* city deserves to be destroyed (translation mine; see further Doms 2011: 381–382):

> What an imposition to condemn a city to doom, in case it deserves it. Of course, the case is given. Of course, it deserves it. I would not know of any city, which did not deserve it. (p. 13)

Jonah agrees, however, to go and 'check Nineveh out' since God has so commanded. The notion that all cities are bad is expanded upon in a dialogue between the character Eskar and Jonah, where the former asks for Jonah's estimation of Nineveh. Jonah responds that, yes, bad things are taking place in the city (such as rubbish in the streets, children hitting their teachers, even Queen Semiramis's murder of her husband), yet it is not so different from the city of his own king Jeroboam. In fact, Nineveh reminds Jonah of Jerusalem (p. 54) (cf. Doms 2011: 383–384).

Yet when Jonah realizes that the queen has banished her daughter, Nineveh ceases to be an average city and instead becomes the essence of a rejected city, and Jonah becomes prepared to inform God to destroy it (cf. Doms 2011: 384–385):

> God, hear me, Jonah is speaking, it concerns Nineveh. You were of course right, as always; the city in question ... (p. 62)

After this exclamation, Jonah declares his wish to withdraw to his *qiqayyon* (here *Kürbis*, ['pumpkin']), only to find that it has withered.

Although God is referred to in the drama, he is no *dramatis persona* and thus does not speak. God's silence becomes germane to the retelling of Jonah 4, as the dialogue in the biblical text between God and Jonah is transformed into a prophetic monologue. In his speech, Jonah first assumes that God sent the worm to teach him about his care for Nineveh. As Jonah continues to speak, however, he becomes open to the possibility that he may have misunderstood the situation:

> Forgive my presumptuous and impious rejection, God; it was due to my feelings and the sun. Lord, I thank you for sending this worm into this pumpkin; should you by chance not have sent it, I thank the worm. (p. 63)

It is thus possible that Jonah has read too much into the sequence of events; they may really be pure coincidences. Even so, the incident with the *qiqayyon* and the worm helped Jonah make his final decision that Nineveh should, after all, be spared destruction (Doms 2011: 386–388):

> I should not whine about a withered pot plant and at the same time demand the downfall of a city, that is the teaching. (p. 63)

Thus, what stops Jonah from destroying Nineveh is, to quote Profitlich and Stucke, 'a superior historical philosophical insight'. Jonah knows that it is possible for something positive to grow out of a negative present. The play ends with Jonah's declaration that he wishes to maintain uprightness and refuses to serve Nineveh's own aims:

> Nineveh wants to fall; am I Nineveh's marionette, that I should want what Nineveh wants? (p. 96)

In Hacks's hands, the Book of Jonah is used to critique the long, gradual decline of the German Democratic Republic as a state and as a society. Nineveh is a city-state that has lost all purpose except the preservation of power. In Jonah's words, the city is characterized by 'state smart-aleckiness: self-satisfied, smirking lies; tolerating anything and so hurting everything; doing this and doing that and none of it thoroughly' (p. 87) (Profitlich and Stucke 1995: 59). The main antagonist, Queen Semiramis, plays off her neighbouring states Babel and Ararat against each other. Nineveh survives, 'defiled and disgraced'.

Jonah 4:11

> 'And I, should I not/I should not pity Nineveh, the great city, in which there are 120 000 people who do not know their right [hand] from their left [hand] and many cattle'.

A Rhetorical Question or a Declarative Statement?

In nearly all interpretative traditions, the statement in Jonah 4:11 is understood as a rhetorical question, yet no grammatical or syntactical issue pre-empts an asseverative reading where God's words convey a statement of facts. As discussed by Ben Zvi, a rhetorical reading is firmly embedded in the text of Jonah itself, where God's willingness to revoke his planned destruction is a clear expectation. Turning from text to authors, the *literati* responsible for creating the text would have been familiar with rhetorical questions, and the image of a deity who has pity on repentant sinners would have been fully in line with their own worldviews. Yet, as they were also familiar with Nineveh's ultimate demise, they would not have wanted to rule out reading v. 11 as a declaration of facts. Moreover, a declarative statement would have been consonant with other theological viewpoints that were prevalent among them. Thus, they allowed the inherent ambiguity of God's statement in Jonah 4:11 in order to ensure a multivalent text. This double reading creates an open-ended text (cf. below) or a book with 'two endings': the literary one where God repents and the historical one where God destroys Nineveh (Ben Zvi 2009; Tiemeyer 2017b; cf. Guillaume 2006; idem 2009).

'120 000 people'

The text of Jonah 4:11 makes clear that Nineveh contained more than '120 000 people'. The term here for 'people' is *'adam'*, i.e. 'man' in singular. Radak explains that this masculine term does not refer only to *male* humans, but that the sum of 120 000 includes women as well.

The Hellenistic-Jewish sermon *On Jonah* 46–53 transforms God's speech in Jonah 4:10–11 into two long speeches that together proclaim God's reasons for his compassion for Nineveh. They bring home the message that through God's decision to show mercy, children kept their parents and parents kept their children (50:2).

'who do not know their right [hand] from their left [hand]'

These people are described as unable to differentiate between their right hand and their left hand. Many traditional exegetes have taken this expression literally and accordingly have argued that Nineveh contained more than 120 000 *infants*, the rationale behind their interpretation being that only infants are unable to distinguish between left and right. If this interpretation is correct, it would, in turn, mean that the total population of Nineveh must have been enormous. Among the Church Fathers, Theodore of Mopsuestia maintains that Jonah 4:11 here speaks of infants. They are singled out in the text in order to underscore the vast number of inhabitants in Nineveh, as well as to stress that such young children have not had the opportunity to sin yet and would thus have constituted innocent victims had the city been destroyed. Cyril of Alexandria likewise maintains that the people referred to in Jonah 4:11 cannot distinguish between left and right because of their (young) age. Looking at the situation from a somewhat different perspective, the fifth-century Christian writer Salvian the Presbyter suggests that these infants constituted the main reason for God's compassion: God was appeased when he heard the crying of the little children, i.e. the innocent victims. 'He thereby declared that because of the purity of the innocent ones, he was also sparing the faults of the guilty ones' (Letter 4). This interpretation also appears among the Reformers (e.g. Calvin, Lecture 80; the Geneva Bible notes to Jonah 4:11). In seventeenth-century England, Francis Quarles refers to infants in his poem 'A Feast for Worms' (Section xiii), in the line 'whose infants are in number so amounting'. This interpretation persists well into the nineteenth century as it appears (and is accepted) in Kitto's *Cyclopedia of Biblical Literature* (p. 422).

Several Jewish commentators follow suit (e.g. Radak, Rashi). Ibn Ezra explicitly argues that the 120 000 people in Jonah 4:11 denoted only a part of Nineveh's population, namely the children who had *not* sinned. The presence of these children in Nineveh, as well as that of the innocent animals, is indeed what saved the city. Had God chosen to destroy Nineveh, its destruction would have been complete like that of Sodom. Such an all-embracing destruction, Ibn Ezra implies, would, from God's perspective, not have been just (cf. Gen 18:22–33).

In contrast, Luther disagrees with this literal interpretation. In his view, the reference to 'not knowing their right hand from their left' in Jonah 4:11 refers to the Ninevites' specific lack of knowledge of the God of Israel. Not being Jews, they were not conversant with divine matters; unlike the Jews, they did not have the Law of Moses, and they had not had any prophets who would have taught them how to conduct themselves before God (German commentary).

'and many cattle'

The last two Hebrew words of God's speech (and the last two words of the Book of Jonah) mention 'many cattle'. Several interpreters have interpreted these 'cattle' symbolically. Cyril of Alexandria, for example, appears to understand the 'cattle' as standing for foolish people: 'this is the way Christ saved everyone, giving himself as a ransom for small and great, wise and foolish, rich and poor, Jew and Greek'. In contrast, Rashi, in his commentary to Jonah 4:7, interprets the 'cattle' as a reference to adult humans (i.e. in contrast to the children in the immediately preceding clause). Other interpreters take the reference at face value and maintain that God really is speaking about animals here. Theodore of Mopsuestia, very matter-of-factly, comments that the animals must be kept unharmed for those of the citizens who were being saved, presumably so that the survivors would have something to eat.

Modern scholars, in contrast, have often understood this reference to animals as a sign that God cares about the animal world. Trible, for example, states that (Trible 1990: 198; cf. eadem 1996: 525)

> [A]n ecology of pity becomes the paradigm for a theology of pity, and that pity embraces not just the human population of Nineveh but also its animals.

Along similar lines, Limburg compares Jonah 4:11 with Jesus's statement about God's care for the sparrows of Jerusalem (Matt 10:29–31). The story of Jonah thus 'acknowledges a solidarity between humans and the animals' (Limburg 1993: 97–98). Simon likewise sees Jonah 4:11 as an example of how God's grace encompasses not only repentant (human) sinners but all living creatures (cf. Ps 36:7) (Simon 1994: 141), Person Jr. suggests that the Book of Jonah as a whole criticizes the readers' anthropocentrism (Person Jr 2008), and Havea argues that it is the vulnerable beasts of Nineveh that made God change his mind about destroying the city (Havea 2020: 55–67). From a more practical angle, Bolin argues that these views are anachronistic; the animals here are sacrificial animals and as such serve to stabilize and maintain the divine–human relationship (Bolin 2010).

Other modern scholars, among them Greenstein and Kamp, have highlighted the contrasting connections between the flood story in Gen 6–9 and the Book of Jonah. In the flood story, God sends a flood that will destroy the animals although they have done nothing wrong. Likewise, Noah does not seem to care about the death of the innocent children and animals that the flood will cause; he only saves his immediate family and a fraction of all the animals. In contrast, in the Book of Jonah, God cares a lot about both innocent children and innocent animals and is willing to abandon his destructive plans to save them. This contrast is highlighted in the shared use of the *Niphal* root of *nḥm*: in Gen 6:6, God changed his mind regarding his creation of humanity; in Jonah 3:10, God changed his mind regarding his plans of destruction [regarding both humanity and the animal world] (Kamp 2003: 209–217; Greenstein 2016).

And All the Creatures Lived Happily Ever After?

How did Jonah, the fish, and the people of Nineveh fare after Jonah 4:11? The book ends on an open note, but its open-endedness demands a continuation, and ancient and modern readers alike have picked up the challenge and written 'sequels'. The direction of these 'sequels' is not a foregone conclusion, however. The question of the place and appropriateness of compassion in verses 10–11 is really addressed to the readers (Abusch 2013), and as these readers, we can choose to accept either God's or Jonah's perspective. Unlike the Book of Job, where Job accedes to God's perspective, Jonah's voice never acquiesces to and merges with that of God (Dell 1996: 98–100; Sherwood 1998: 56–58, 63).

The Ultimate Fate of the People of Nineveh

What happened to the people of Nineveh after their reprieve? Did their repentance endure, or did they relapse and return to their former wicked behaviour? Also, did God continue to spare the people of Nineveh or did he ultimately decide to destroy them? When reading the Book of Jonah within the Book of the Twelve, as well as with an awareness of world history, it is obvious that the ending of the Book of Jonah is not the real ending, insofar as Nineveh was destroyed in 612 BCE (Ben Zvi 2003: 17–30; Timmer 2013; Tiemeyer 2017b). According to Guillaume, reading Jonah 4:11 as a declarative sentence solves the 'unnecessary clash' between Jonah and Nahum (and history) (cf. above). Rather than leaving the book open-ended, this reading has God announce that, no, he will *not* spare Nineveh. According to this reading, Nineveh's destruction takes place after 40 days: just as God killed the *qiqayyon*, so he destroyed Nineveh (Guillaume 2009). Looking at the issue from a slightly different perspective, Trible points out that God did not show compassion because the people of Nineveh repented, but because God had pity, as Jonah had pity on the *qiqayyon*. Maybe God's pity is another instance of divine caprice? (Trible 1990: 199; cf. also Vermeulen 2017: 243)

Most commentators read Jonah 4:11 as a rhetorical question, however, and postpone Nineveh's ultimate demise to a future time. Several commentators refer to the Book of Jonah in their commentaries to Nahum, a book that speaks of Nineveh's destruction. Theodore of Mopsuestia, for example, opens his commentary to Nahum with a brief recapitulation of the content of the Book of Jonah. After the events divulged in Jonah, God allowed the people of Nineveh to show their true colours, whereupon they adopted such 'depraved attitudes' and such 'ferocity and vicious behaviour' that they attacked the Northern Kingdom and even advanced on Jerusalem, showing no respect for the temple and the worship of God conducted there. For Theodore, the people of Nineveh can be compared with the people in Egypt at the time of Joseph. At first, the Egyptians were welcoming to Joseph and his family; later, they enslaved the people of Israel.

The idea that the Ninevites' repentance was insincere or at least not long-lasting is also a prevalent feature in many Jewish interpretations of the Jonah story (cf. Jonah 3:7). *PRE* 43 stands out in this respect, as it states unequivocally that the repentance of the inhabitants of Nineveh lasted exactly 40 years (Eng. transl. Adelman 2011: 84):

> For forty years the Holy One, blessed be He, was slow to anger with them, corresponding to the forty days, which He said to Jonah: 'In another forty days, Nineveh shall be overthrown!' (Jonah 3:4). After forty years, they returned to their many evil deeds, more so than their former ones, and they were swallowed up like the dead in the lowest Sheol, as says: 'Men groan in the city; (the souls of the dead cry out)' (Job 24:12).

As argued by Adelman, this passage may be understood as a polemic against the concept of the 'sign of Jonah' as found in Matt 12:39–41 and Luke 11:29–32. According to these two passages, the people of Nineveh will rise up and judge the Jews at the time of Jesus. Following *PRE*, the repentance of the people of Nineveh was short-lived, and rather than serving as judges, they can be found in the deepest level of Sheol (Adelman 2011: 84–85).

The Ultimate Fate of Jonah

Other interpreters look at the subsequent fate of Jonah. The reader of the Book of Jonah leaves the prophet sitting east of Nineveh. What happened to him afterwards?

What Happened Next?
The text known as *The Lives of the Prophets* (*Vitae Prophetarum*), a document of Jewish origin written most likely in Jerusalem in Greek around the turn of the first century (Schwemer 2020: 423–425), continues the story of Jonah (Eng. transl. Torrey):

> [2]After he had been cast on shore by the whale and had made his journey to Nineveh, on his return he did not stay in his own land, but took his mother and settled in Tyre, a country of foreign peoples. [3]For he said, 'In this way I will take away my reproach that I prophesied falsely against the great city Nineveh'.
>
> [4]Elijah was at that time rebuking the house of Ahab and having called a famine upon the land he fled. Coming to the region of Tyre he found the widow and her son, for he himself could not lodge with the uncircumcised. [5]He brought her a blessing; and when her child died, God raised him from the dead through Elijah, for he wished to show him that it is not possible to flee from God.
>
> [6]After the famine was over, Jonah came into the land of Judea. On the way thither his mother died, and he buried her beside the oak of Deborah. [7]Thereafter having

settled in the land of Seir, he died there and was buried in the tomb of the Kenizzite, the first who became judge in the days when there was no king.

⁸He gave a sign to Jerusalem and to all the land: When they should see a stone crying aloud in distress, the end would be at hand; and when they should see all the Gentiles gathered in Jerusalem, the city would be razed to its foundations.

According to this piece of 'fan-fiction', Jonah, born near Ashdod, did not return home after his journey to Nineveh but instead settled in Tyre, where he later died. After having been resurrected by Elijah (and thus identified with the son of the widow from Zarephath [1 Kgs 17], cf. Jonah 1:1), he travelled to Judah, where he later died (again) in Saraar (Tiemeyer 2019a: 261). Speaking more specifically of Jonah's burial place, the Prologue of the *Glossa Ordinaria* also assumes that Jonah went back to the land of Israel after his journey to Nineveh. According to the glossator, Jonah is buried in one of the cities of Gath, 'in a hamlet that is at the second milestone on the road to Sepphoris, on the road by which one goes to Tiberias' (Eng. transl. McDermott 2013).

Other traditions maintain that Jonah died near Nineveh. On the second of the two mounds covering Nineveh's ruins (the hill of Kuyunjik and the hill of Nabi Yunus), there was until recently an Islamic shrine called the Mosque of the Prophet Jonah. This mosque traditionally replaced an Assyrian church that commemorated Jonah's burial place. It was blown up by the Islamic State on 24 July 2014.

Jonah's Silence
The Book of Jonah ends with silence. God is given the last word, and the reader is left wondering whether Jonah ultimately acceded to God's perspective of mercy, or whether he continued to challenge God's right to forgive the people of Nineveh. The Bible leaves this question open, but later retellings provide diverse answers.

In several literary retellings, Jonah accepts God's perspective or at least shows that he is not opposed to it. Lodge and Greene, for example, end their Elizabethan play *A Looking Glass for London and England* with Jonah alone on the stage. After having encouraged the audience to heed the message of the play (cf. Jonah 2:1), Jonah expresses his renewed sense of wonder at God's greatness (lines 2220–2221):

> Oh who can tell the wonders of my God
> or talk his praises with a servant's tongue.

The message of the play is thus that there are limits to humanity's understanding of God and that consequently it is humanity's condition to be in a state of perpetual wonder (Sager 2013: 69). Housman's play *The Burden of Nineveh* likewise ends with Jonah acknowledging the wisdom of God's standpoint, as expressed by his interlocutor Shemmel:

> Jonah: You are a greater prophet than I, Shemmel, for in you is more understanding of God, and of His ways.

Uwe Johnson's adaptation of the Jonah narrative in his 'Jonas zum Beispiel' ends with a series of rhetorical questions. Did Jonah remain outside Nineveh more than 40 days to see what would ultimately happen? Did Jonah die as he wished to? Did Jonah get up and continue his life in Nineveh? Who knows? This retelling emphasizes the openness of the biblical account, and its final question 'Who knows?' echoes the key passage in Jonah 3:9, where the King of Nineveh orders the people to repent on the off-chance that God might change his decree. In Johnson's hands, this question suggests that just as God may do what he fancies, so Jonah's future could be different from what we expect. Who knows? (see further Salzmann 2006: 139–150).

Madeleine L'Engle's retelling *The Journey with Jonah* has an interesting ending that tentatively suggests that Jonah eventually would come to share God's point of view or at least cease to resist it. After the worm has eaten the vine, Jay, Jonah's faithful companion (a bird) suggests eating the worm. After a conversation between Jonah, the bird, and the worm, Jonah ends up having pity on the worm and asking the bird not to eat it, after which he and the bird return to Gath-Hepher:

> Let him go, O foolish fowl.
> I am shaken by pity,
> And it is more terrible than anger.
> What God does or does not do in Nineveh
> Is out of my hands
> As well as my comprehension,
> But I will spare this worm.
>
> (p. 61)

Other retellings are less optimistic and envisage Jonah ultimately rejecting God's perspective. The film *Jonah: A VeggieTales Movie* from 2003, for example, offers a thought-provoking take on the ending of the Jonah narrative. Rather than leaving it open-ended as the book does, the film (and the two supporting characters, the caterpillar Khalil and the camel Reginald) abandons Jonah to his sulking. In this manner, the film implies that Jonah has chosen not to accept God's stance on Nineveh but instead to remain unconvinced by God's right to show compassion. In line with the Christian outlook of *VeggieTales*, Jonah's continued rebellion against God is viewed negatively, and the overall tone of the film condemns Jonah.

Judson Jerome's Jonah also continues to resist God's viewpoint. In response to God's final speech to Jonah that he should continue to preach to the people of Nineveh, because their repentant attitude appears to be wearing off, Jonah is silent. In the words of the narrator:

> And now would you choose to die? Would my
>   lecturer die?
> Nay, speak to the people a sequel. Say God is
>   no computer.
> Complain of that in the tavern, for already the
>   tavern is opening.
> Jonah went, thirsting for unreason, and his heart
>   was not at peace.
>   ('Jonah', p. 20)

Otto Erich Hartleben's paraphrase 'Der Prophet Jona' problematizes all easy answers. In this retelling, Jonah is given a voice and he responds to God's last statement in Jonah 4:11 (my translation):

> You are God, the Lord of eternities,
> who gives life and takes life,
> who remains in the self-determination of your creation,
> untouched during the change of all times.
> However, I am only entirely human of the earth,
> who passes like the green of nature,
> who wilts like the pumpkin plant –
> and I rage justly to the death.

Being a human, who withers like the *qiqayyon*, Jonah cannot share God's eternal perspective and cannot participate in his capricious decision-making, untouched by mortal life. Instead, Jonah defends his right to be angry, even unto death.

On a more critical note, the musical rendering of the Jonah narrative *Der Mann ohne Toleranz* ('The Man Without Tolerance') from 2004, created by the Jewish composer Samuel Adler (1928–) and sung in German and Hebrew, depicts Jonah's inability to accept God's decision to pardon Nineveh. In powerful language, Adler conveys Jonah's refusal to hear God in the storm and his refusal to contemplate the suffering that the innocent of Nineveh would have had to endure had God not relented. Jonah walks away from the situation, unable and unwilling to relent (Eng. transl. Andreas Tiemeyer):

> And Jonah went. And the burden of Nineveh that he had seen hung over his head, but he walked with a darkened mind. It howled in the storm and it cried in the wind and a voice cried out. For the sake of those, for the sake of those, for the sake

of those, for the sake of those animals, clean and unclean. And the messenger of the Lord was stunned and looked but there was only darkness, and he heard nothing but an unrelenting howling and blowing that gripped his coat and pulled at it and shook it, like a pleader's hand [pulls] the garment of one unmercifully running away, but he did not relent; he strode and held his coat.

In yet other retellings, Jonah's envisaged ultimate non-acceptance of God's perspective is described as a positive development. In the Danish novel *Profeten Jonas Privat* (written in 1935), the author Harald Tandrup (1874–1964 CE) uses the Jonah narrative as an open satire of Nazi Germany and its hatred of the Jews. Jonah is described as harmless, lacking both physical and moral courage. To quote from the dust-jacket of the English translation:

> [...] in the city of Tyre, in Phoenicia, where Jonah, a poor little Hebrew, is living as a lodger in a low-class boarding house as the prospective husband of his landlady. The voice of the Lord suddenly commands him to go to Nineveh.

Upon receiving God's command to go to Nineveh, he flees in utter terror. When he ultimately ends up in Nineveh, he is used by the Assyrian monarch to prophesy against the priestly establishment. The king is later poisoned by his priestly opponents, and the priests blame Jonah for having called down God's judgement upon Nineveh. To appease the priests, the new king Sennacherib promises to save the country by killing all the Jews, a decision that is applauded by all. Jonah manages to survive the looting and the slaughter, yet he is a changed man. Now, he has gained the courage to stand up to God and he questions the point of it all. What is the point when God does not punish the guilty? What is the point when the godless prosper while those who fear God and walk the path of righteousness receive at most a meagre reward? Never again will he be reckoned among those who praise his name; instead, Jonah has become one of the great doubters (accessed via the German translation Tandrup, *Der Prophet Jona – privat*, 362–366; see further Liptzin 1985a: 242–243).

Jonah also questions his future and his calling in James Bridie's play *Jonah and the Whale*, albeit in a different manner. Jonah is mortified as he realizes that nothing is going to happen to Nineveh and declares that he will never again prophesy, as he has come to realize that he is not in God's confidence. He thought that he alone heard God's voice; now he has learnt that God speaks to other creatures, such as the whale. In his final speech, Jonah declares:

> What am I to do? My whole life has given way beneath me. I thought I was a great prophet. Everything I did or said was on that understanding. And now I find I am nobody. I am only an ordinary man. (p. 61)

Modern scholarship has opted for other ways of interpreting Jonah's final silence. Ryu offers a postcolonial reading of Jonah, where Jonah's final silence is a legitimate response to God's mercy on Nineveh and in fact the only resistance left for the colonized and oppressed Jews in post-monarchic Yehud. According to Ryu, it is difficult for the oppressed to write a book the theme of which praises God's universal salvation towards their oppressors (Ryu 2009: 198). Along similar lines, Boase and Agnew read the ending of Jonah through the lens of trauma theory and argue that Jonah's anger represents the collapse of his worldview. Read against the background of the destruction of Jerusalem, Jonah embodies the survivors' shattered belief that God is unwaveringly on the side of Judah/Israel and against the nations. Silence is all that Jonah has left when the last vestige of his belief in a God who would bring recompense against the Persian colonisers has disappeared (Boase and Agnew 2016: 18–19).

The Ultimate Fate of the Fish

Very few retellings concern themselves with the ultimate fate of the fish. One exception is Dominick Argento's choral work *Jonah and the Whale*, which holds up the fish as an example of obedience to God that we should all follow (and Jonah ultimately does so as well):

> Narrator:
> Far faring afloat on swirls of pure waters.
> A great fish frolicked, filled with heavenly grace.
> For unlike the petulant prophet who faltered.
> The whale never wavered – God's will it obeyed.
>
> So should we all, if we wish to be wise,
> Tread patiently the path appointed by God.
>
> Jonah:
> Salvation is of the Lord.
> Amen.

Modern Jonahs?

Several modern authors have used the character of Jonah to contrast him with modern humanity. In the poem 'Jonah' by the Polish poet Zbigniew Herbert (1924–1998 CE), the biblical Jonah is contrasted with a person in modern society. A modern Jonah is more sensible: in contrast to the fantastical biblical narrative where God is omnipresent and omniscient, a modern Jonah 'puts on a false moustache, opens an antique shop, keeps his head down, lives a quiet life' (Sherwood 2000: 174).

> [...]
> the second time he does not take on
> a dangerous mission
> he grows a beard
> and far from the sea
> far from Nineveh
> under an assumed name
> deals in cattle and antiques
> [...]

At the same time, while the biblical Jonah had a clear fate, determined by God, modern humanity appears to live in the domain of blind chance. A modern Jonah would disappear without a trace when he fled, rather than being rescued by a fish. Moreover, in contrast to Jonah, modern humanity has no sense of destiny and has no comprehension of the meaning of existence or death. A modern Jonah may as well die of something as senseless as cancer. He will never become the hero or even an anti-hero of a myth that will lend meaning to his existence or preserve his memory for posterity (Barańczak 1987: 19–20).

Note

1 The Hebrew verb *kiddamti* here is difficult to translate. Literally it means 'to meet, to confront'. There are two main lines of exegesis: (1) Jonah 'made haste' to flee, and (2) Jonah anticipated [God's decision] and thus fled.

Conclusion

Before I began this project five years ago, I thought I knew exactly what the message of the Book of Jonah was: it was about God's grace to repentant sinners. Now, five years down the road, I am significantly less sure. Although my present uncertainty may be viewed as a negative consequence of my research, I do not share that view. Having spent the last five years in Jonah's company, I have come to treasure and respect this most recalcitrant, stubborn, tiresome, and (to be honest) not very palatable prophet, as well as the profound and often disturbing message of the book bearing his name. I have

Jonah Through the Centuries, First Edition. Lena-Sofia Tiemeyer.
© 2022 John Wiley & Sons, Ltd. Published 2022 by John Wiley & Sons, Ltd.

encountered so many different and mutually opposing ways of reading the book that I have been forced to observe my own preconceived ideas being turned upside down, and I have allowed the interpreters to change my way of thinking. As a result, my journey with Jonah has been tremendously enriching. So, thank you, Jonah!

My re-evaluation of the Book of Jonah can be aptly called 'reception exegesis', a term coined by Paul Joyce and Diana Lipton in their Wiley Blackwell Commentary to Lamentations. Whereas 'reception history' and *Wirkungsgeschichte* ('impact history') focus on the ways that the biblical text has been conceptualized and interpreted and how these interpretations have had an impact on our way of thinking and acting, 'reception exegesis' puts the focus squarely on the biblical text. It explores how its history of reception helps us to see aspects of the text that are present in the text, yet often hidden from plain view due to our own predetermined ideas of what the text ought to be about. For me, reception exegesis has altered my way of approaching the Book of Jonah and has (hopefully) made me a far more perceptive reader than I was before.

My first re-evaluation concerns the prophet Jonah himself. A surface-reading of the Book of Jonah reveals a mean-spirited, disobedient, and sulking man who thinks far more about his own comfort than others' well-being. This image is indeed also prevalent in the history of interpretation. Many of the Church Fathers perceive the prophet Jonah in exactly this manner and have unfortunately also appealed to this image in their anti-Jewish polemic, with disastrous results. Alongside this negative portrayal, however, many other Jonahs exist. The very same Church Fathers detected in Jonah a type for Christ, and they highlighted his sacrificial symbolic death that saved the sailors from shipwreck and an ensuing watery grave. Many Jewish rabbis (as well as a few Church Fathers) saw yet another Jonah. For them, Jonah was a hero and a martyr who ran away from God's command in order to save Israel's reputation or even its very existence. Reading the Book of Jonah in light of the Neo-Assyrian destruction of the Northern Kingdom of Israel in 721 BCE, they regarded Jonah's attempt to vouchsafe Nineveh's destruction as an honourable endeavour to ensure that Israel would survive as a nation. They also discovered a Jonah who, like Moses in Exod 32:10–14, 32, was prepared to die for the well-being of his fellow Israelites.

Modern retellings of the Jonah narrative made me discover yet other aspects of Jonah. I came to see a man who, overwhelmed by God's calling to carry out a seemingly impossible mission, sought to escape his God-given destiny. In his struggle with God, Jonah becomes a champion of free will and of a person's right to determine his/her own fate. I have also found in Jonah a fellow human being who dares to object to God's seemingly random and cavalier way of dispensing justice. How can Jonah work with God when God does not obey the rules of sin and punishment? How can Jonah be God's partner when God cannot be relied on to punish the wicked, but instead demonstrates a tendency to show undeserved mercy?

Last but not least, I have realized that I am more similar to Jonah than I find comfortable. Working through 2500 years of reception history, I have been forced to face up to the fact that I can easily identify with the sulking prophet who, like the elder brother of the prodigal son in Luke 15:25–32, wished to deny his fellow sinners the right to repent and receive God's grace. Reading and re-reading the Book of Jonah highlights our own shortcomings in the face of God's undeserving and lavish mercy.

My second re-evaluation concerns the fish. Before my five-year-long journey with the Book of Jonah, the fish was merely a physically huge but theologically small character in the book. I now know better. I have learnt of the 'fall of the fish', where the fish is transformed from being God's helpful servant who, in contrast to Jonah, obeys God's command, into an image of hell incarnate in whom Jonah suffers the punishment for his disobedience. The New Testament and the Church Fathers emphasize the lethal aspects of the fish, where Jonah's time inside the fish is akin to Jesus's time between his death on Good Friday and his resurrection on Easter morning. Mythic retellings likewise stress how the fish is a symbol of death: Jonah dies when he is swallowed by the fish and is reborn three days later when the fish vomits him out. Other retellings highlight how Jonah's time inside the fish embodies the exilic experience, where the fish represents an enforced diaspora existence. Yet all along the fish is doing God's bidding: he is Jonah's saviour who saves him from drowning, keeps him alive and secure for three days, and transports him safely back to the shore. Not only that, the fish in *Pirqe de-Rabbi Eliezer* is an ancient Nautilus in which Jonah travels comfortably on a sight-seeing cruise through Israel's history twenty thousand leagues under the sea. For me, the fish will henceforth be the unsung and often underrated hero of the Book of Jonah, who without a thought to its own comfort, heeded God's commands and harboured and nurtured Jonah for three days in its very womb.

My third re-evaluation concerns the people and animals of Nineveh. Until my sustained encounter with 2500 years of reception history, I had unquestionably accepted the Ninevites as the true penitent sinners, who turned from their wicked ways and received divine pardon. My interaction with midrashic retellings changed my mind. Following their lead and beginning to read the Book of Jonah in dialogue with the Book of Nahum, I started to question the sincerity of the Ninevites' repentance. Given the destruction of Nineveh in 612 BCE, their remorse cannot have been heartfelt, or at least not long-lasting.

This insight shifted my focus from the humans to the animals, another group of literary personas that I confess to have hitherto largely overlooked. Why did the animals have to fast and wear sackcloth? Did the Ninevites really deny their animals water to drink? If so, that would have been an act of cruelty towards animals rather than an expression of their piety. Furthermore, who would be responsible for the animals' predicted demise? Given their innocence, why would they have had to suffer the consequences of the Ninevites' sins had God decided to go ahead with his punitive plans? I began to see the animals of Nineveh as collateral damage, both to the devices of God and those of the people of Nineveh. This insight, in turn, cast God's final words in Jonah 4:11 into a new light. God *does care* for the innocent, and his mercy towards the Ninevites may ultimately have had less to do with their repentance, sincere or otherwise, and more with God's own sense of justice towards all his creation.

My fourth re-evaluation concerns the sailors. More than two millennia of interaction with the Book of Jonah put the spotlight anew on both their virtues and their shortcomings. Are they good men who put Jonah's safety above their own as they hesitated to throw him overboard, or are they rather to blame for ultimately sacrificing the lone man to save the many? The sailors' identity metamorphoses before our very eyes as we browse the reception history of the Book of Jonah. Some Church Fathers liken the sailors to Pontius Pilate. For modern readers, this analogy depicts the sailors as men who wash their hands of responsibility for Jonah's death. When the sailors decided to toss Jonah into the sea, they committed murder as they had no way of foreseeing Jonah's salvation through the fish. Other Christian retellings transform the Gentile sailors into symbols of the Jews (!), who were willing to sacrifice Jesus for their own survival (cf. John 11:50). In contrast, Jewish retellings alternate between lauding the sailors' conversion to Judaism after seeing God's salvation of Jonah through the fish and castigating them for transgressing all rules of hospitality by killing the Jewish fugitive who sought refuge on board their ship.

My fifth and final re-evaluation concerns the character of God. As hinted at already, God's decision to spare the city of Nineveh challenges our sense of justice to the core. Five years ago, I read the Book of Jonah as a simple tale of God's mercy and his invitation to sinners to repent and receive his grace. Now I am less sure about the simplicity of this message. On one level, I still adhere to the aforementioned straightforward theological understanding of the book: God is always willing to forgive a penitent heart. On another level, however, I have come to see the Book of Jonah as a wisdom tale or even a philosophical treatise of divine justice: how can we relate to a God who is willing to forgive a ruthless Gentile nation because of one single act of repentance, while he in parallel chooses to ignore the plight of his own people who have already (and repeatedly) suffered the punishment for their sins? The concluding dialogue between God and Jonah in Chapter 4 is remarkable in many ways. The views of God and Jonah are given equal narrative space, and the open-ended conclusion of their discussion leaves it up to the reader to decide whether to side with God or with Jonah.

I am hopeful that this book has taken you on a similar journey. I have endeavoured to present the material in an open-ended and value-free manner to enable you to be challenged by the Book of Jonah and to reach your own conclusions regarding its message(s). These conclusions may differ widely from mine, yet it is my hope that you have come to love and treasure the book as I have done.

Biography

Brief Biographies of Jewish, Christian, and Muslim Interpreters

Abarbanel (1437–1508), Portuguese Jewish statesman and philosopher.
Abbot, George (1562–1633), English Calvinist Archbishop and Chancellor of Trinity College, Dublin.
Abeshaus, Eugene Zalmanovich (1939–2008), Russian-Jewish painter.
Albrekt Målare (Latinized as Albertus Pictor) (1440/45–1509), German-Swedish painter known for his wall paintings in churches in southern Sweden.

Jonah Through the Centuries, First Edition. Lena-Sofia Tiemeyer.
© 2022 John Wiley & Sons, Ltd. Published 2022 by John Wiley & Sons, Ltd.

Ambrose (340–397), Bishop of Milan.
Arminius, Jacobus (1560–1609), Dutch Reformed theologian.
Augustine (354–430), theologian and philosopher, Bishop of Hippo Regius in North Africa.
Basil of Caesarea (329–379), Greek Bishop of Caesarea Mazaca in Cappadocia, Asia Minor.
al-Baṣrī, Abu Sa'id Abi Al-Ḥasan (642–728), early Muslim preacher, ascetic, theologian, exegete, judge, and mystic.
Brenz, Johannes (Latinized as John Brentius) (1499–1570), German theologian and Protestant reformer.
Bugenhagen, Johannes (1485–1558), theologian and Protestant reformer from the Duchy of Pomerania.
Caesarius of Arles (468/470–542), church leader in Gaul and promoter of ascetic elements in the Western Church.
Calvin, John (1509–1564), French theologian, pastor, and reformer during the Protestant Reformation.
Carissimi, Giacomo (1605–1674), Italian composer.
Cassiodorus (485–585), Roman statesman serving in the administration of Theodoric the Great.
Chrysostom, John (349–407), Archbishop of Constantinople.
St Columba/Colm Cille (521–597), Irish abbot and missionary.
Cyril of Alexandria (376–444), Patriarch of Alexandria.
Cyril of Jerusalem (313–386), Bishop of Jerusalem.
Drayton, Michael (1563–1631), English Elizabethan poet.
Ephrem the Syrian (303–373), Syriac Christian deacon and a prolific Syriac-language hymnographer and theologian.
Gregory of Nazianzus (329–390), Archbishop of Constantinople and a theologian.
Haimo of Auxerre, long considered to have been the Bishop of Halberstadt (d. 853); however, more recent research suggests instead that he was a Benedictine monk at the Abbey of Saint-Germain in Auxerre (d. 875).
Hedgeland, George (1825–1898), British designer of stained glass windows.
Hooper, John (1495–1555). English Protestant reformer, Bishop of Gloucester and Worcester, and later martyr (during the reign of Mary I).
Ibn ʿAbbās, Abd Allah (619–687), an uncle of the Prophet Muhammad, known for his knowledge of tradition and critical interpretation of the Qur'an.
Ibn Ezra, Abraham ben Meir (1089–1167), Spanish-Jewish biblical commentator.
Ibn Kathīr, Imād al-Dīn Ismāʾil (1300–1373), Muslim Sunni scholar, historian, and expert on tafsir (Qur'anic exegesis) and faqīh (jurisprudence).
Irenaeus (died 202), early Church Father and apologist, Bishop of Lugdunum in Gaul.
Jacob of Serug (451–521), Syrian poet and theologian, the author of 700 verse homilies (*mêmrê*).
Jarrell, Randall (1914–1965), American poet and literary critic.
Jerome (347–420), priest, theologian, and historian.
John the Deacon/Johannes Hymonides (825–880), deacon in the Roman church.

Josephus (37–100), Roman-Jewish scholar and historian.
Justin Martyr (100–165), early Christian apologist and martyr.
Kimhi, David (Radak) (1160–1235), rabbi, biblical commentator, philosopher, and grammarian from Provence.
Lastman, Pieter (1583–1633), Dutch painter.
Luther, Martin (1483–1546), German professor of theology, priest, monk, and reformer during the Protestant Reformation.
Malbim = Meir Leibush ben Yehiel Michel Wisser (1809–1879), Russian Jewish rabbi, grammarian, and biblical commentator.
Marcion of Sinope (ca. 85–160), early Christian thinker most famous for arguing that the teaching of Jesus was incompatible with the God of the Hebrew Bible.
St Methodius of Olympus (died ca. 311), Christian bishop and martyr.
Michelangelo (1475–1564), Italian sculptor, painter, architect, and poet.
Origen (184–253), early Christian theologian and ascetic.
Paulinus of Nola (354–431), Roman poet, writer, and senator.
Al-Qummī, Humannad ibn 'Ali ibn Babawaih (923–991), Persian Shi'ite Islamic scholar.
Rabinowitz, Chaim Dov (1909–2001), Lithuanian Jewish historian and biblical commentator (author of the *Daat Soferim*).
Radal = Rav David Luria (1798–1855), Russian rabbi, Kabbalist, commentator, and linguist from Bechov. He wrote commentaries on the Babylonian Talmud and *PRE*.
Rashi (Rabbi Shlomo ben Itzchak) (1040–1105), French rabbi, biblical commentator, and Talmudist from Troyes.
Rufinus, Tyrannius (344/345–411), Roman monk and theologian.
Sa'adia HaGaon (882/892–942), Egyptian rabbi, philosopher, and biblical commentator during the Geonic period in the Abbasid Caliphate.
Salvian the Presbyter (400–490), Christian writer living in Gaul (modern France).
Sforno, Ovadia ben Jacob (1475–1550), Italian Jewish biblical commentator.
Al-Ṭabarī, Huhammad ibn Jarir (839–923), prominent Persian scholar, historian, and exegete of the Qur'an.
Tertullian (160–220), early Christian apologist from Carthage.
Theodore of Mopsuestia (350–428), Bishop of Mopsuestia, part of the Patriarchate of Antioch, in the province of Cilicia (modern-day Turkey).
Theodoret of Cyrus (393–466), Antiochian theologian, bishop, and controversial Church Father.
Tintoretto (Jacopo Comin) (1518–1594), Venetian painter.
Vilna Gaon (Elijah ben Solomon Zalman or HaGra) (1720–1797), Lithuanian Jewish Talmudist, Halakhist, Kabbalist, and leader of the Misnagdic (i.e. non-Hasidic) Jewry from Vilna.
Yosef Kara (1065–1135), French Jewish biblical commentator from Troyes.
Al-Zamakhsharī, abu al-Qawim Mahmud ibn Umar (1075–1144), mediaeval Persian scholar, follower of the Mu'tazilite theological doctrine.
Zeno of Verona (300–371), Christian martyr and thought to be Bishop of Verona.

Bibliography

Ancient Near Eastern Texts

Inanna's Descent to the Netherworld. A Mesopotamian myth preserved in a Sumerian and an Akkadian version. For an English translation of the Sumerian version, see http://etcsl.orinst.ox.ac.uk/section1/tr141.htm.

Jonah Through the Centuries, First Edition. Lena-Sofia Tiemeyer.
© 2022 John Wiley & Sons, Ltd. Published 2022 by John Wiley & Sons, Ltd.

Early Jewish/Christian Writings

Joseph and Aseneth. Its date is unknown but was probably composed before the sixth century CE. Its origin, whether Jewish or Christian, is debated. English translation by David Cook, 'Joseph and Aseneth'. In H. F. D. Sparks (ed.), 1984. *The Apocryphal Old Testament*. Oxford: Oxford University Press, pp. 465–503 (485). On-line access: http://www.markgoodacre.org/aseneth/translat.htm.

Hellenistic Synagogal Prayers. A group of sixteen prayers that may be remnants of Jewish synagogal prayers. English translation by D. R. Darnell and D. A. Fiensy, in James H. Charlesworth (ed.), 1985. *The Old Testament Pseudepigrapha*, Vol. 2: *Expansions of the Old Testament and Legends, Wisdom and Philosophical Literature, Prayers, Psalms, and Odes, Fragments of Lost Judeo-Hellenistic works*. Garden City, NY: Doubleday, pp. 2:677–697.

Josephus, *Antiquities of the Jews*. Unless otherwise stated, the English translations are taken from William Whiston, 1987. *The Works of Josephus*. Complete and Unabridged. New Updated Version; Peabody, MA: Hendrickson. See http://penelope.uchicago.edu/josephus/index.html. For the Greek text and the translation by Christopher T. Begg and Paul Spilsbury, see https://pace.webhosting.rug.nl/york/york/showText?text=anti.

Lives of the Prophets (*Vitae prophetarum*). Transl. William M. Brinner, 2002. *Lives of the Prophets*. Leiden: Brill, pp. 681–688. See also the English translations by Charles Cutler Torrey, 1946): http://www.summascriptura.com/html/Lives_of_the_Prophets_Torrey.html.

On Jona. A sermon attributed to Philo (i.e. Pseudo-Philo), preserved only in a sixth century Armenian translation which, in turn, is translated into German and into Latin. Siegert suggests a historical setting in the synagogue in Alexandria at the time of Philo (25 BCE–c. 50 CE) (Siegert 1996: 191–192). Transl. Aram Muradyan and Gohar Topchyan, 'Pseudo-Philo, On Samson and On Jonah'. In Feldman, Louis H., James L. Kugel, and Lawrence H. Schiffman (eds), 2013. *Outside the Bible: Ancient Jewish Writings Related to Scripture*. 3 Vols. Philadelphia, PA: Jewish Publication Society/ Lincoln, NE: University of Nebraska Press.

Testament of the Twelve Patriarchs. Preserved in Greek as a Christian work but it may potentially be based on an earlier Jewish text in Hebrew. Transl. Harm W. Hollander and Marinus de Jonge, 1985. *The Testament of the Twelve Patriarchs: A Commentary*. Studia in Veteris Testamenti Pseudepigrapha 8. Leiden: E.J. Brill.

3 Corinthians. A Greek pseudo-epigraphical work dedicated to the apostle Paul. The earliest extant copy is Papyrus Bodmer X, dating to the third century. Transl. M. R. James. Accessed via http://pages.uoregon.edu/sshoemak/321/texts/3_corinthians.htm.

3 Maccabees. A book, written in Greek, about the persecution of the Jews during the reign of Ptolemy IV Philopator (222–205 BCE). It was probably written sometimes between 100–30 BCE, although a significant minority argues for a Roman date. English translation: H. Anderson, in James H. Charlesworth (ed.), 1985. *The Old Testament Pseudepigrapha*, Vol. 2: *Expansions of the Old Testament and Legends*,

Wisdom and Philosophical Literature, Prayers, Psalms, and Odes, Fragments of Lost Judeo-Hellenistic works. Garden City, NY: Doubleday, pp. 509–530. For an in-depth discussion, see Sara Raup Johnson, 2004. *Historical Fictions and Hellenistic Jewish Identity: Third Maccabees in its Cultural Context*. Berkeley, CA: University of California Press, pp. 129–141.

Rabbinical Texts

Ecclesiastes Rabbah/Der Midrasch Kohelet: Zum Ersten Male ins Deutsche Übertragen. Transl. Aug. Wünsche, 1880. Leipzig: Otto Schulze. Accessed via http://sammlungen.ub.uni-frankfurt.de/freimann/content/pageview/3614757.

Genesis Rabbah. A compilation of midrashoth on Genesis, composed between 300–500 CE. Accessed in Hebrew via www.daat.ac.il/daat/tanach/raba1/shaar-2.htm. Translated into English with Notes, Glossary and Indices by Rabbi H. Freedman and Maurice Simon, 1939. London: Concino Press. Accessed via https://archive.org/stream/RabbaGenesis/midrashrabbahgen027557mbp_djvu.txt.

Mishnah and Tosefta. Unless otherwise stated, the English translations are taken from the edition by Herbert Danby, 1919. London: The Macmillan Company.

Herr, Moshe David. 'Midrashim, Smaller'. In *Encyclopaedia Judaica*. Access online via http://www.jewishvirtuallibrary.org/jsource/judaica/ejud_0002_0014_0_13849.html.

Midrash Tanhuma, Buber. Eng. transl. *Midrash Tanhuma English*. Vol. 1 Genesis, 1989. Hoboken, NJ: Ktav.

Midrash Tehilim. Transl. A. Wünsche, 1892. Trier: Sigmund Mayer, p. 233. Accessed via https://archive.org/stream/MidraschTehillim/Midrasch_Tehillim#page/n7/mode/2up.

Pirqe de Rabbi Eliezer (PRE). A Jewish midrash that is traditionally attributed to the tanna Rabbi Eliezer ben Hyrcanus. There is no consensus about its date, but it was probably not written prior to the eighth century CE. Unless otherwise stated, the English translations are by Gerald Friedlander, 1916. *Pirqe de Rabbi Eliezer: (The chapters of Rabbi Eliezer the Great) according to the Text of the Manuscript Belonging to Abraham Epstein of Vienna*. London: Kegan Paul, Trench, Trubner & Co./New York: Bloch. See further https://archive.org/stream/pirkderabbieli00frieuoft/pirkderabbieli00frieuoft_djvu.txt.

Seder Olam Rabbah. This rabbinic work, probably composed in the second century CE, offers a chronology from the creation to the conquest of Persia by Alexander the Great. For the Hebrew text, see https://www.sefaria.org/Seder_Olam_Rabbah.18?lang=bi. Eng.transl. http://www.betemunah.org/sederolam.html.

Shapiro, Rabbi Moshe, 1997. *The Book of Jonah: 'Journey of the Soul'. An Allegorical Commentary adapted from the Vilna Gaon's Aderes Eliyahu*. Artscroll Judaica Classics. New York: Mesorah Publications.

Targum Jonathan. The official Eastern Aramaic translation of the Prophets. For a critical edition of the Aramaic text, see Sperber, Alexander, 1962. *The Bible in Aramaic*, III.

The Latter Prophets According to Targum Jonathan. Leiden: E.J. Brill. For an English translation, see Cathcart, Kevin J., and Robert P. Gordon, 1989. *The Targum of the Minor Prophets: Translated, with a Critical Introduction, Apparatus, and Notes*. Aramaic Bible 14. Edinburgh: T&T Clark.

Yalkut Shimoni or 'the *Yalkut*' of Simon of Frankfurt. A midrashic anthology compiled in the thirteenth century. The compiler sought to gather all rabbinical sayings that he had at his disposal in one work which followed the order of the biblical books. He often but not always noted the source in the margins. For a discussion of the extant manuscripts, see further Jacob Elbaum, 'Yalkut Shimoni', in *Encyclopaedia Judaica*. Access on-line via http://www.jewishvirtuallibrary.org/jsource/judaica/ejud_0002_0021_0_21181.html.

Midrash Yonah is a late aggadic work that is traditionally read in the synagogue on the Day of Atonement. Its author drew mainly from *Pirkê de Rabbi Eliezer* and reworked it in his own (Hebrew) words. It was written no earlier than the eighth century. For more information, see Moshe David Herr, 'Midrashim, Smaller'. In *Encyclopaedia Judaica*. Access on-line via http://www.jewishvirtuallibrary.org/jsource/judaica/ejud_0002_0014_0_13849.html.

The Zohar. A work of Jewish mysticism. First published in Spain in the thirteenth century CE by a Jewish writer named Moses de León but attributed to a Rabbi who presumably lived in the second century CE. It is composed in a form of Aramaic.

The Babylonian Talmud. A work comprising the Mishnah and the Gemara. The latter consists of lengthy analyses of the Mishnah, the result of the rabbinic discussions that took place in the Academies in Babylon.

Mediaeval and Modern Jewish Commentators

Abarbanel, *Commentary on Jonah*.
Chaim Dov Rabinowitz, *Daat Soferim* (*Commentary to Trei Assar*, 'Commentary to Jonah').
Ibn Ezra, Avraham, *Rabbinic Bible*.
Malbim, *Mikra'ei Kodesh*, 'Commentary on Jonah'.
Radak (David Kimchi), *Rabbinic Bible*.
Radal (Rav David Luria), *Commentary on Pirkê de-Rabbi Eliezer*. For the Hebrew text, see http://www.hebrewbooks.org/21858. Note, however, that page 24 is missing from this website.
Rashi, *Rabbinic Bible*, 2 Kings 9:1. For an English translation of his commentary, see http://www.chabad.org/library/bible_cdo/aid/15915/jewish/Chapter-9.htm#showrashi=true.

Writings of the Early Church

Acts of Paul (preserved in Coptic and written approximately in 160 CE).

Constitutions of the Holy Apostles. The work can be dated from 375 to 380 CE. The provenance is usually regarded as Syria, probably Antioch. It forms eight treatises on Early Christian discipline, worship, and doctrine, intended to serve as a manual of guidance for the clergy, and to some extent for the laity. Accessed via http://www.ccel.org/ccel/schaff/anf07.ix.iii.iii.html.

Writings of the Church Fathers

Adomnán of Iona, 1995. *Life of St Columba*. Transl. Richard Sharpe. Harmondsworth: Penguin Books.

Ambrose, 1954. *Letters, 1–91*. Transl. Sister Mary Melchior Beyenka. Fathers of the Church 26. Washington, DC: Catholic University of America Press.

Ambrose, 1970. *Seven Exegetical Works*. Transl. Michael P. McHugh. Fathers of the Church 65. Washington, DC: Catholic University of America Press.

Augustine, 1887. 'Letter 102'. Transl. J. G. Cunningham. In *From Nicene and Post-Nicene Fathers*, First Series, Vol. 1. Buffalo, NY: Christian Literature Publishing Co. Accessed via http://www.newadvent.org/fathers/1102102.htm.

Augustine, 1887. 'Letter 185'. Transl. J. R. King. In *From Nicene and Post-Nicene Fathers*, First Series, Vol. 1. Buffalo, NY: Christian Literature Publishing Co. Accessed via http://www.newadvent.org/fathers/1102185.htm.

Augustine, *City of God*, chapter 44, in *St. Augustine's City of God and Christian Doctrine*. Transl. Philip Schaff; NPNF1-02. Accessed via https://www.ccel.org/ccel/schaff/npnf102.iv.XVIII.44.html.

Basil of Caesarea, 1895. 'Letter 242'. Transl. Blomfield Jackson. In *Nicene and Post-Nicene Fathers*, Second Series, Vol. 8. Buffalo, NY: Christian Literature Publishing Co. Accessed via http://www.newadvent.org/fathers/3202242.htm.

Caesarius of Arles, 2010. *Sermons*, Vol. 2 *(81–186)*. Transl. Mary Magdeleine Mueller. The Fathers of the Church 47. Washington, DC: Catholic University of America Press.

Cassiodorus, 1990–1991. *Explanation of the Psalms*, Vol. 3. Transl. Patrick Gerard Walsh. New York, NY: Paulist Press.

Chrysostom, John, 1889a. 'Homily 4 on Second Corinthians: 2 Corinthians 2:11'. Transl. Talbot W. Chambers. In *From Nicene and Post-Nicene Fathers*, First Series, Vol. 12. Buffalo, NY: Christian Literature Publishing Co. Accessed via http://www.newadvent.org/fathers/220204.htm.

Chrysostom, John, 1889b. 'Homily 5 Concerning the Statues', section 17. Transl. W. R. W. Stephens. In *From Nicene and Post-Nicene Fathers*, First Series, Vol. 9. Buffalo, NY: Christian Literature Publishing Co. Accessed via http://www.newadvent.org/fathers/190105.htm.

Chrysostom, John, 1889c. 'Homily 20 Concerning the Statues', section 21. Transl. W. R. W. Stephens. In *From Nicene and Post-Nicene Fathers*, First Series, Vol. 9. Buffalo, NY: Christian Literature Publishing Co. Accessed via http://www.newadvent.org/fathers/190120.htm.

Chrysostom, John, 1986. 'Homily 1'. In *Homilies on Genesis 1–17*. Transl. Robert C. Hill. Fathers of the Church 74. Washington, DC: Catholic University of America Press, pp. 20–28.

Chrysostom, John, 1998a. 'Homily 2: On Repentance, on the Melancholy of King Ahab, and on Jonah the Prophet'. In *On Repentance and Almsgiving*. Transl. Gus George Christo. The Fathers of the Church 96. Washington, DC: Catholic University of America Press, pp. 16–27.

Chrysostom, John, 1998b. 'Homily 3: Concerning Almsgiving and the Ten Virgins'. In *On Repentance and Almsgiving*. Transl. Gus George Christo. The Fathers of the Church 96. Washington, DC: Catholic University of America Press, pp. 28–42.

Chrysostom, John, 1998c. 'Homily 5: On Fasting and the Prophet Jonah, Daniel and the Three Youths'. Delivered on the Threshold of the Holy Fast'. In *On Repentance and Almsgiving*. Transl. Gus George Christo. The Fathers of the Church 96. Washington, DC: Catholic University of America Press, pp. 56–68.

Chrysostom, John. 'The Paschal Sermon'. Accessed via https://oca.org/fs/sermons/the-paschal-sermon.

Cyril of Alexandria, 2008. 'Commentary of Jonah'. In *Saint Cyril of Alexandria: Commentary on the Twelve Prophets*, Vol. 2. Transl. Robert C. Hill. Fathers of the Church 116. Washington, DC: Catholic University of America Press.

Cyril of Jerusalem. 'Catechetical Lecture 4:12, On the Ten Points of Doctrine'. Accessed via http://www.ccel.org/ccel/schaff/npnf207.ii.viii.html.

Cyril of Jerusalem. 'Catechetical Lecture 6:26, Concerning the Unity of God. On the Article, I Believe in One God. Also Concerning Heresies'. In *Nicene and Post-Nicene Fathers*, Series II, Vol. 7. Transl. Philip Schaff. Accessed via http://www.ccel.org/ccel/schaff/npnf207.ii.x.html.

Cyril of Jerusalem, 2003. 'Catechetical Lecture 14:7–20, on the Words, and Rose again from the Dead on the Third Day, and Ascended into the Heavens, and Sat on the Right Hand of the Father'. In Alberto Ferreiro (ed.), *ACCS. Old Testament XIV: The Twelve Prophets*. Downers Grove, IL: Intervarsity Press, p. 135. Accessed via http://www.ccel.org/ccel/schaff/npnf207.ii.xviii.html.

Ephraem the Syrian, 1853. *The Repentance of Nineveh*. Transl. Henry Burgess. London: Robert B. Blackader. For the full text in English translation and with a commentary by Henry Burgess, see https://books.google.co.uk/books/about/The_repentance_of_Nineveh_a_metrical_hom.html?id=GcICAAAAQAAJ&redir_esc=y.

Gregory of Nazianzus, 1894. 'Oration 2: In Defence of His Flight to Pontus, and His Return, after His Ordination to the Priesthood, with an Exposition of the Character of the Priestly Office'. Transl. Charles Gordon Browne and James Edward Swallow. In *From Nicene and Post-Nicene Fathers*, Second Series, Vol. 7. Buffalo, NY: Christian Literature Publishing Co. Accessed via www.newadvent.org/fathers/310202.htm.

Gregory of Nazianzus. 'Oration 16: On His Father's Silence, Because of the Plague of Hail'. Accessed via http://www.newadvent.org/fathers/310216.htm.

Gregory of Nazianzus. 'Oration 43: Funeral Oration on the Great S. Basil, Bishop of Cæsarea in Cappadocia'. Accessed via http://www.newadvent.org/fathers/310243.htm.

Haimo of Auxerre, 1993. *Commentary on the Book of Jonah*. Translated with an Introduction and Notes by Deborah Everhart. TEAMS Commentary Series. Kalamazoo, MI: Medieval Institute Publications.

Irenaeus of Lyons, *Against Heresies*, 5.5.2. Accessed via http://www.earlychristianwritings.com/text/irenaeus-book5.html.

Jerome, 1893. *Against the Pelagians*, book 3, section 6. Transl. W. H. Fremantle, G. Lewis, and W. G. Martley. *From Nicene and Post-Nicene Fathers*, Second Series, Vol. 6. Buffalo, NY: Christian Literature Publishing Co. Accessed via http://www.newadvent.org/fathers/30113.htm.

Jerome, 2014. In *Commentary on Jonah*. English Transl. Robin MacGregor. Edited by John Litteral. *Ancient Bible Commentary in English*. Ashland, KY: Litteral's Christian Library Publications.

Justin Martyr, 1885. *Dialogue with Trypho*, chapter 108. Transl. Alexander Roberts and James Donaldson. *The Ante-Nicene Fathers*, Vol. 1. Buffalo, NY: Christian Literature Publishing Co. Accessed via http://www.earlychristianwritings.com/text/justinmartyr-dialoguetrypho.html.

Origen, 2010. *Homilies on Jeremiah and 1 Kings 28*, Jer 19:7. Transl. John Clark Smith. Washington, DC: Catholic University of America Press.

Paulinus of Nola, 1975. *The Poems of St. Paulinus of Nola*. Transl. P. G. Wals. Ancient Christian Writers 40. New York, NY: Newman Press.

Rufinus, 1892. *Apology against Jerome*. Transl. W. H. Fremantle. *From Nicene and Post-Nicene Fathers*, Second Series, Vol. 3. Buffalo, NY: Christian Literature Publishing Co.

Salvian the Presbyter, 1947. 'Letter 4'. Transl. Jeremiah Francis O'Sullivan. In *The Writings of Salvian, the Presbyter*. Fathers of the Church 3. Washington, DC: Catholic University of America Press.

St Methodius, 'Fragment on Jonah'. Accessed via https://sites.google.com/site/aquinasstudybible/home/jonah/st-methodius-fragment-on-jonah.

Tertullian, 1885a. *De Jona et Nineveh*. Transl. S. Thelwall, *The Ante-Nicene Fathers*, Vol. 4. Buffalo, NY: Christian Literature Publishing Co. Accessed via http://www.tertullian.org/anf/anf04/anf04-26.htm.

Tertullian, 1885b. 'On Flight in Time of Persecution'. Transl. S. Thelwall. In *The Ante-Nicene Fathers*, Vol. 4. Buffalo, NY: Christian Literature Publishing Co. Accessed via http://www.newadvent.org/fathers/0409.htm.

Tertullian, 1885c. 'On the Resurrection of the Flesh.' Transl. Peter Holmes. In *The Ante-Nicene Fathers*, Vol. 3. Buffalo, NY: Christian Literature Publishing Co. Accessed via http://www.newadvent.org/fathers/0316.htm.

Tertullian, 1959. *On penitence and On purity*. Transl. William P. Le Saint. Ancient Christian Writers 28. Westminster, MD: Newman Press.

Tertullian, *Against Marcion*. Book II, chapter 24. Accessed via http://www.tertullian.org/articles/evans_marc/evans_marc_06book2_eng.htm.

Theodore of Mopsuestia, 2013. 'Commentary to Jonah', Introduction. Transl. Robert C. Hill. In *Commentary on the Twelve Prophets*. Fathers of the Church: A New Translation. Patristic Series. Washington, DC: The Catholic University of America Press.

Theodoret of Cyr, 2003. 'Commentary on Jonah', Jonah 2:3. In English translation, see Alberto Ferreiro (ed.), *ACCS. Old Testament XIV: The Twelve Prophets*. Downers Grove, IL: Intervarsity Press, p. 138.
Zeno of Verona, 1971. *Zenonis Veronensis Tractatus*. Corpus Christianorum. Series Latina 22. Ed. B. Löfstedt. Turnholti: Brepols, pp. 86–88.

Reform Commentaries

Bugenhagen, Johannes, 2012. Accessed via Lohrmann, Martin J. *Bugenhagen's Jonah: Biblical Interpretation as Public Theology*. Minneapolis, MN: Lutheran University Press.
Calvin, John, 1847. *Twelve Minor Prophets*, Vol. 3. Jonah, Micah, Nahum. Transl. John Owen. Calvin's Commentary. Edinburgh, Scotland: Calvin Translation Society.
Luther, Martin, 1974. *Jonah, Habakkuk*. Ed. H. C. Oswald. Luther's Work 19. St Louis, MO: Concordia Publishing House. The lectures on Jonah were originally printed in 1525.
1599 Geneva Bible Notes. Accessed via http://www.reformedreader.org/gbn/en.htm.

Muslim Authors

Al-Kisai, Muḥammad ibn Allah, 1997. *Tales of the Prophets*. Unless otherwise stated, the translations are by W. M. Thackston. Chicago, IL: Kazi Publications.
Al-Qummī, ʿAlī ibn Ibrāhīm, 2010. *Tafsir Qumi*. English translation by Reynolds, Gabriel Said. *The Qurʾān and Its Biblical Subtext*. Routledge Studies in the Qur'an. Abingdon: Routledge.
Al-Ṭabarī, Muhammad ibn Jarir, 1987. *History of al-Ṭabarī*. English translation by Moshe Perlmann, *The Ancient Kingdoms*. Albany, NY: State University of New York Press.
Al-Thaʿlabī, Aḥmad ibn Muḥammad, 2002. *Lives of the Prophets*. English Transl. William M. Brinner. Leiden: Brill, pp. 681–688.
Al-Zamakhsharī, Abū al-Qāsim Maḥmūd ibn Umar, 2019. *Al-Kashshaaf*. English Trans. Gabriel Said Reynolds, *The Qurʾān and Its Biblical Subtext*. Routledge Studies in the Qur'an. Abingdon, UK: Routledge.
Ibn Kathīr, Ismail, 2003. *Tafsīr al-Qurʾān al-ʿAẓīm*, Vol. 6 (Surat Al'Isra', Verse 39 to the end of Surat Al'Mu'minûn). Maktaba Dar-us-Salam. Accessed via http://www.quran4u.com/Tafsir%20Ibn%20Kathir/PDF/021%20Anbiya.pdf. See also http://www.qtafsir.com/index.php?option=com_content&task=view&id=1927.

Medieval Authored Texts

St Adomnán of Iona, 1995. *Life of St Columba*. Transl. Richard Sharpe. Harmondsworth: Penguin Books.

Apollodorus, 2008. *The Library of Greek Mythology*. Transl. Robin Hard. Oxford: Oxford University Press.

Cena Cypriani. This tale stems from the early middle ages and was later put in writing by, among other people, John the Deacon. It can be categorized as a combination of a parody, and allegory, and a satire of select passages in the Bible. For a discussion of its content, style, and manuscript tradition, see www.thefullwiki.org/Cena_Cypriani.

'Patience', a Middle English didactic, homiletic, and alliterative poem consisting of 530 lines. It was composed in the fourteenth century, written by an unknown author normally designated as the 'Pearl Poet' or the 'Gawain Poet'.

Letaldus (tenth century). 'About a Certain Fisherman Whom a Whale Swallowed' (*De quodam piscatore quem ballena absorbuit*). For the original Latin text, see Armando Bisanti, 'Il *Within piscator (De quodam piscatore quem ballena absorbuit)* di Letaldo di Micy'. Accessed via www.academia.edu/9265194/LETALDO_DI_MICY_-_Within_piscator_a_cura_di_A._Bisanti_.

De Jona et Nineveh, attributed to Tertullian. For a translation and discussion of authorship, see S. Thelwall, 1885. *Ante-Nicene Christian Library*, Vol. 18, in A. Roberts and J. Donaldson (eds), *The Writings of Tertullian*. Edinburgh: T&T Clark, pp. xviii–xix, 278–283. Accessed via http://www.tertullian.org/anf/anf04/anf04-26.htm

Vercelli Homilies, Anglo-Saxon collection.

The Whale, an Old English poem from the *Exeter Book*.

Prudentius, *Hymnus Ieiunantium*. For the original text as well as an English translation, see https://www.gutenberg.org/files/14959/14959-h/14959-h.htm#p07o.

Source Books/Critical Editions

Bertini, Ferruccio, 1995. *Letaldo di Micy: Within piscator*. Biblioteca del Medioevo latino. Florence: Giunti.

Brenton, *Septuagint Translation*. Accessed via ebible.org/eng-Brenton/JON01.htm.

Bob, Steven, 2013. *Go to Nineveh: Medieval Jewish Commentaries on the Book of Jonah Translated and Explained*. Eugene, OR: Pickwick Publications.

Danby, Herbert (transl.), 1919. *Tractate Sanhedrin: Mishnah and Tosefta*. London: The Macmillan Company.

Ferreiro, Alberto (ed.), 2003. *ACCS. Old Testament XIV: The Twelve Prophets*. Downers Grove, IL: Intervarsity Press.

Frieling, Simone (ed.), 1999. *Der rebellische Prophet: Jona in der modernen Literatur*. Göttingen: Vandenhoeck & Ruprech.

Ginzberg, Louis, 1913. *The Legends of the Jews*. Transl. Henrietta Szold. Philadelphia, PA: The Jewish Publication Society. English translation, see http://www.sacred-texts.com/jud/loj/loj409.htm.

Hard, Robin, 2004. *The Routledge Handbook of Greek Mythology: Based on H. J. Rose's Handbook of Greek Mythology*. London: Routledge.

Liddell, Henry George, and Robert Scott, 1889. *An Intermediate Greek-English Lexicon*. Oxford: Clarendon Press.
Lipiński, Edward, 2004. *Itineraria Phoenicia*. Leuven: Peeters.
Neusner, Jacob, 2007. *Habakkuk, Jonah, Nahum and Obadiah in Talmud and Midrash: A Source Book*. Studies in Judaism. Lanham, MD: University Press of America.
Pickthall, Marmaduke William, 1930. Translation of the Qur'an. Accessed via al-quran.info/?x=y#1.
Thorpe, Benjamin, 1842. *Codex Exoniensis: A Collection of Anglo-Saxon Poetry, from a Manuscript in the Library of the Dean and Chapter of Exeter, with an English Translation, Notes, and Indexes*. London: Society of Antiquaries of London.

Films/TV

Jonah: A VeggieTale Movie, 2002. American computer-animated comedy adventure musical film, produced by Big Idea Productions and it was released by Artisan Entertainment through its F.H.E. Pictures label. See further https://en.wikipedia.org/wiki/Jonah:_A_VeggieTales_Movie.
Pinocchio, 1940. American animated musical fantasy film produced by Walt Disney Productions. See further https://en.wikipedia.org/wiki/Pinocchio_(1940_film).
The Jews are Coming (org. Hebrew title: היהודים באים). Satire sketches, examining the history of the Jewish people since biblical times. Creators: Assaf Beiser, Yoav Gross, Natalie Marcus. See further http://www.imdb.com/title/tt4177454. Jonah and Pinocchio: See www.youtube.com/watch?v=XFCf9GGAIf8.

Secondary Literature

Abrahams, Simon, 2015. 'Michelangelo's Art through Michelangelo's Eyes', Part I, pp. 12–13. Accessed via http://everypainterpaintshimself.com/essay_pdfs/MLJ1.pdf.
Abusch, Tzvi, 2013. 'Jonah and God: Plants, Beasts, and Humans in the Book of Jonah (An Essay in Interpretation)'. *Journal of Ancient Near Eastern Religions* 13, pp. 146–152.
Ackerman, James S., 1981. 'Satire and Symbolism in the Song of Jonah'. In Baruch Halpern and Jon D. Levenson (eds.), *Traditions in Transformation: Turning Points in Biblical Faith*. Essays in Honor of F. M. Cross. Winona Lake, IN: Eisenbrauns, pp. 215–246.
Ackroyd, Peter, 1968. *Exile and Restoration: A Study of Hebrew Thought of the Sixth Century BC*. London: SCM Press.
Adelman, Rachel, 2009. *Return of the Repressed: Pirqe de-Rabbi Eliezer and the Pseudepigrapha*. Supplements to the Journal for the Study of Judaism 140. Leiden: Brill.
Adelman, Rachel, 2011. 'Jonah through the Looking Glass: Pirqe de-Rabbi Eliezer's Portrait of an Apocalyptic Prophet'. *The Journal of the Faculty of Religious Studies, McGill University* 39, pp. 79–92.

Amar, Itzhak, 2006/7. 'Similar [Motifs] in the Story of Jonah and the Story of Noah' [Hebrew]. *Megadim* 45, pp. 73–86.

Almbladh, Karin, 1986. *Studies in the Book of Jonah*. Studia Semitica Upsaliensia 7. Lund: Almqvist & Wiksell International.

Andrew, Malcom, 1973. 'Jonah and Christ in Patience'. *Modern Philology* 70, pp. 230–233.

Angel, Andrew R., 2006. *Chaos and the Son of Man: The Hebrew Chaoskampf Tradition in the Period 515 BCE to 200 CE*. Library of Second Temple Studies 60. London: T & T Clark.

Arnds, Peter O., 2004. *Representation, Subversion, and Eugenics in Günter Grass's The Tin Drum*. Studies in German Literature, Linguistics, and Culture. Rochester, NY and Woodbridge: Camden House.

Band, Arnold J., 1990. 'Swallowing Jonah: The Eclipse of Parody'. *Prooftexts* 10, pp. 177–195.

Barker, William D., 2014. *Isaiah's Kingship Polemic: An Exegetical Study in Isaiah 24–27*. Forschungen zum Alten Testament II/70. Tübingen: Mohr Siebeck.

Barr, Lois Baer, 1996. 'The Jonah Experience: The Jews of Brazil According to Scliar'. In David Sheinin and Lois Baer Barr (eds.), *The Jewish Diaspora in Latin America: New Studies on History and Literature*. London: Routledge, pp. 33–52.

Barrett, Rob, 2012. 'Meaning More than They Say: The Conflict between Yнwн and Jonah'. *Journal for the Study of the Old Testament* 37, pp. 237–257.

Bazzana, Giovanni B., 2010. '*Cucurbita super caput ionae*: Translation and Theology in the Old Latin Tradition'. *Vetus Testamentum* 60, pp. 310–311.

Ben-Chorin, Schalom, 1966. *Die Antwort des Jona: Zum Gestaltwandel Israels—Ein geschichts-theologischer Versuch*. Evangelische Zeitstimmen 25/26. Hamburg: Herbert Reich Evangelischer Verlag.

Ben Zvi, Ehud, 2003. *Signs of Jonah: Reading and Rereading in Ancient Yehud*. Journal for the Study of the Old Testament Supplement 367. Sheffield: Sheffield Academic Press.

Ben Zvi, Ehud, 2009. 'Jonah 4:11 and the Metaprophetic Character of the Book of Jonah'. *Journal of Hebrew Scripture* 9, Article 5. https://doi.org/10.5508/jhs.2009.v9.a5

Berger, Yitzhak, 2016. *Jonah in the Shadows of Eden*. Indiana Studies in Biblical Literature. Bloomington, IN and Indianapolis, IN: Indiana University Press.

Bickerman, Elias, 1967. *Four Strange Books of the Bible: Jonah/Daniel/Hoheleth/Esther*. New York, NY: Schocken.

Boase, Elizabeth, and Sarah Agnew, 2016. '"Whispering in the Sound of Silence": Traumatising the Book of Jonah'. *The Bible and Critical Theory* 12, pp. 4–17.

Bodkin, Maud, 1934. *Archetypal Patterns in Poetry: Psychological Studies of Imagination*. London: Oxford University Press.

Bolin, Thomas M., 1997. *Freedom beyond Forgiveness: The Book of Jonah Re-Examined*. Journal for the Study of the Old Testament Supplement 236/Copenhagen International Seminar 3. Sheffield: Sheffield University Press.

Bolin, Thomas M., 2010. 'Jonah 4,11 and the Problem of Exegetical Anachronism'. *Scandinavian Journal of the Old Testament* 24, pp. 99–109.

Borroff, Marie, 1956. '"Tom Fool at Jamaica" by Marianne Moore: Meaning and Structure'. *College English* 17, pp. 466–469.
Brenner, Athalya, 1993. 'Jonah's Poem Out of and Within Its Context'. In Philip R. Davies and David J. A. Clines (eds.), *Among the Prophets: Language, Image and Structure in the Prophetic Writings*. Journal for the Study of the Old Testament Supplement 144. Sheffield, England: JSOT Press, pp. 183–192.
Brinner, William M., 2002. *'Arā'is al-majālis fī qiṣaṣ al-anbiyā', or, 'Lives of the Prophets'*. Studies in Arabic Literature 24. Leiden: Brill.
Burge, Stephen R., 2017. 'Jonah (Book and Person): Islam'. In Constance M. Furey, Brian Matz, Steven L. McKenzie, Thomas Chr. Römer, Jens Schroeter, Barry Dov Walfish, and Eric Ziolkowski (eds.), *Encyclopaedia of the Bible and Its Reception 14*. Berlin: de Gruyter, pp. 587–588.
Calder, Norman, 1993. 'Tafsīr from Ṭabarī to Ibn Kathīr: Problems in the Description of a Genre, Illustrated with Reference to the Story of Abraham'. In G. R. Hawting and Abdul-Kader A. Shareef (eds.), *Approaches to the Qur'ān*. SOAS/Routledge Studies on the Middle East. London: Routledge, pp. 101–140.
Carden, Michael, 2006. 'The Book of Jonah'. In Deryn Guest (ed.), *The Queer Bible Commentary*. London: SCM Press, pp. 463–467.
Cary, Phillip, 2008. *Jonah*. SCM Theological Commentary on the Bible. London: CSM Press.
Cathcart, Kevin J., and Robert P. Gordon, 1989. *The Targum of the Minor Prophets: Translated, with a Critical Introduction, Apparatus, and Notes*. Aramaic Bible 14. Edinburgh: T&T Clark.
Cho, Paul Kang-kul, and Janling Fu, 2013. 'Death and Feasting in the Isaiah Apocalypse (Isaiah 25:6–8)'. In J. Todd Hibbard and Hyun Chul Paul Kim (eds.), *Formation and intertextuality in Isaiah 24–27*. Society of Biblical Literature Ancient Israel and Its Literature 17. Atlanta, GA: SBL, pp. 117–142.
Chow, Simon, 1995. *The Sign of Jonah Reconsidered: A Study of its Meaning in the Gospel Tradition*. Coniectanea Biblica New Testament Series 27. Stockholm: Almqvist & Wiksell International.
Ciuba, Gary, 2000. 'The Worm against the Word: The Hermeneutical Challenge in Hurston's *Jonah's Gourd Vine*'. *African American Review* 34, pp. 119–133.
Darnell, D. R., 1983. 'Hellenistic Synagogal Prayer'. In J. H. Charlesworth (ed.), *The Old Testament Pseudepigrapha*, 2 vols. Garden City, NY: Doubleday, pp. 2:677–697.
Davis, Adam Brooke, 1991. 'What the Poet of Patience Really Did to the Book of Jonah'. *Viator* 22, pp. 267–278.
Davis, Edward B., 1991. 'A Whale of a Tale: Fundamentalist Fish Stories'. *Perspectives on Science and Christian Faith* 43, pp. 224–237. Accessed via http://www.asa3.org/ASA/PSCF/1991/PSCF12-91Davis.html.
Davis, Stephen J., 2000. 'Jonah in Early Christian Art: Allegorical Exegesis and the Roman Funerary Context'. *Australian Religion Studies Review* 13.1, pp. 72–83.
Day, John, 1990. 'Problems in the Interpretation of the Book of Jonah'. In A. S. van der Woude (ed.), *In Quest of the Past: Studies on Israelite Religion, Literature and Prophetism. Papers Read at the Joint British-Dutch Old Testament Conference, Held at Elspeet, 1988*. Oudtestamentische Studien 26. Leiden: Brill, pp. 32–47.

Dell, Katharine J., 1996. 'Reinventing the Wheel: The Shaping of the Book of Jonah'. In John Barton and David J. Reimer (eds.), *After the Exile: Essays in Honour of Rex Mason*. Macon, GA: Mercer University Press, pp. 85–101

Döhling, Jan-Dirk, 2013. 'Jona und des Meeres Wellen: Zum problemgeschichtlichen Horizont und zum traditionsgeschichtlichen Hintergrund'. *Biblische Notizen* 158, pp. 17–37.

Doms, Misia Sophia, 2011. '"Schon gut, Herr, ich verstehen schon": Vom problematischen Umgang mit dem Nicht-Vertrauten in Peters Hacks' Drama Jona'. In Johann Anselm Steiger und Wilhelm Kühlmann, in Verbindung mit Ulrich Heinen (eds.), *Der problematische Prophet: die biblische Jona-Figur in Exegese, Theologie, Literatur und bildender Kunst*. Arbeiten zur Kirchengeschichte 118. Berlin: de Gruyter, pp. 365–389.

Dotson, Esther Gordon, 1979a. 'An Augustinian Interpretation of Michelangelo's Sistine Ceiling, Part I'. *The Art Bulletin* 61.2, pp. 223–256.

Dotson, Esther Gordon, 1979b. 'An Augustinian Interpretation of Michelangelo's Sistine Ceiling, Part II'. *The Art Bulletin* 61.3, pp. 405–429.

Dowling Long, Siobhán, and John F. A. Sawyer, 2015. *The Bible in Music: A Dictionary of Songs, Works, and More*. Lanham, MD: Rowman & Littlefield.

Downs, David J., 2009. 'Specter of Exile'. *Horizons in Biblical Theology* 31, pp. 27–44.

Dox, Thurston, 1991. 'Samuel Felsted of Jamaica'. *American Music Research Center Journal* 1, pp. 37–46. Accessed via http://www.colorado.edu/amrc/sites/default/files/attached-files/0506-1991-001-00-000003.pdf.

Dozeman, Thomas B., 1989. 'Inner-Biblical Interpretation of Yahweh's Gracious and Compassionate Character'. *Journal of Biblical Literature* 108, pp. 207–223.

Dücker, Burckhard, 2011. '"Solitaire" und "solidaire": Albert Camus' Erzählung Jonas oder der Künstler bei der Arbeit'. In Johann Anselm Steiger und Wilhelm Kühlmann, in Verbindung mit Ulrich Heinen (eds.), *Der problematische Prophet: Die biblische Jona-Figur in Exegese, Theologie, Literatur und bildender Kunst*. Arbeiten zur Kirchengeschichte 118. Berlin: de Gruyter, pp. 347–364.

Eagleton, Terry, 1990. 'J. L. Austin and the Book of Jonah'. In Regina Schwartz (ed.), *The Book and the Text: The Bible and Literary Theory*. Oxford: Blackwell, pp. 231–236.

Edwards, Richard Alan, 1971. *The Sign of Jonah in the Theology of the Evangelists and Q*. London: S.C.M. Press.

Elbaum, Jacob. 'Yalkut Shimoni'. In *Encyclopaedia Judaica*. Accessed via http://www.jewishvirtuallibrary.org/jsource/judaica/ejud_0002_0021_0_21181.html.

Eliade, Mircea, 1960. *Myths, Dreams and Mysteries: The Encounter Between Contemporary Faiths and Archaic Realities*. New York, NY: Harper and Row.

Fagan, Deidre J., 2007. *Critical Companion to Robert Frost: A Literary Reference to His Life and Work*. Critical Companion Series. New York, NY: Facts on File.

Feldman, Louis H., 1992. 'Josephus' Interpretation of Jonah'. *ATS Review* 17, pp. 1–29.

Fishman, George, 2008. 'Commentary on Paper by Aviva Gottlieb Zornberg'. *Psychoanalytic Dialogues* 18, pp. 307–316.

Flusser, David, 1976. 'Paganism in Palestine'. In S. Safrai and M. Stern, in co-operation with D. Flusser and W. C. van Unnik (eds.), *The Jewish People in the First*

Century: Historical, Geography, Political History, Social, Cultural and Religious Life and Institutions, Vol. 2. Assen: Van Gorcum, pp. 1065–1100.

Föcking, Marc, 2011. 'Jonah und Pinocchio: Mythen und Plotstrukturen zwischen Altem Testament und italienischem Kinderbuch'. In Johann Anselm Steiger und Wilhelm Kühlmann, in Verbindung mit Ulrich Heinen (eds.), *Der problematische Prophet: Die biblische Jona-Figur in Exegese, Theologie, Literatur und bildender Kunst*. Arbeiten zur Kirchengeschichte 118. Berlin: de Gruyter, pp. 429–440.

Frahm, Eckart, 2016. 'On Doves, Fish, and Goddesses: Reflections on the Literary, Religious, and Historical Background of the Book of Jonah'. In Joel Baden, Hindy Najman, and Eibert Tigchelaar (eds.), *Sibyls, Scriptures, and Scrolls. John Collins at Seventy*. Supplements to the Journal for the Study of Judaism 175. Leiden: Brill, pp. 432–450.

Friedman, John B., 1981. 'Figural Typology in the Middle English "Patience"'. In Bernard S. Levy and Paul E. Szarmach (eds.), *The Alliterative Tradition in the Fourteenth Century*. Kent, OH: Kent State University Press, pp. 99–129.

Friedman, John B., 1988. 'Bald Jonah and the Exegesis of IV Kings 2.23'. *Traditio: Studies in Ancient and Medieval History, Thought, and Religion* 44, pp. 125–144.

Gaines, Janet Howe, 2003. *Forgiveness in a Wounded World: Jonah's Dilemma*. Studies in Biblical Literature 5. Atlanta, GA: SBL.

Gale, Denelle. 'Pinocchio and Religion'. Assessed via http://pinocchioandreligion. weebly.com/jonah-the-whale-and-pinocchio.html.

Gane, Erwin R., 1981. 'Exegetical Methods of Some Sixteenth Century Puritan Preachers: Hooper, Cartwright, and Perkin. Part II'. *Andrews University Seminary Studies* 19 (Summer, 2), pp. 99–114.

Geiger, Friedrich, 2001. 'Art as a Vocation: Vladimir Vogel's Dramma-Oratorio "Jonah ging doch nach Ninive"'. *Tempo*, New Series 218, Swiss Music Issue, pp. 11–14.

Golka, Friedemann W., 1986. 'Jonaexegese und Antijudaismus'. *Kirche und Israel* 1, pp. 51–61.

Gordon, Robert P., 1982. '*Terra Sancta* and the Territorial Doctrine of the Targum to the Prophets'. In J. A. Emerton and S. C. Reif (eds.), *Interpreting the Hebrew Bible: Essays in Honour of E. I. J. Rosenthal*. Cambridge: Cambridge University Press, pp. 119–131.

Gottheil, Richard, and Gotthard Deutsch, 1906. 'Judenhut'. In *Jewish Encyclopedia*. Accessed via www.jewishencyclopedia.com/articles/9046-judenhut.

Greenstein, Edward L., 2016. 'Noah and Jonah: An Intertextual Interpretation'. In Shama Friedman (ed.), *Shmue'el Beqore'e Shemo*: Samuel Leiter Volume [Hebrew]. Jerusalem: Bialik, pp. 23–32.

Gregg, Robert C., 2015. *Shared Stories, Rival Tellings: Early Encounters of Jews, Christians, and Muslims*. New York, NY: Oxford University Press.

Guillaume, Philippe, 2006. 'The End of Jonah is the Beginning of Wisdom'. *Biblica* 87, pp. 243–250.

Guillaume, Philippe, 2009. 'Rhetorical Reading Redundant: A Response to Ehud Ben Zvi'. *Journal of Hebrew Scripture* 9. Accessed via https://journals.library.ualberta. ca/jhs/index.php/jhs/article/view/6235.

Gye, Hugo, 2013. 'Curses, Musical Scores and Jonah'. *Peregrinations: Journal of Medieval Art & Architecture* 4.1. Accessed via http://www.dailymail.co.uk/news/article-2274401/Archaeologists-fascinating-quest-decipher-medieval-graffiti-scrawled-cathedral-walls.html.

Halpern, Baruch, and Richard Elliott Friedman, 1980. 'Composition and Paronomasia in the Book of Jonah'. *Hebrew Annual Review* 4, pp. 79–92.

Haral, Hesna, 2019. 'Prophet Yunus in Islamic Miniature Painting Representation of Repentance, Grief, Patience and Mercy'. In N. Çiçek Akçıl Harmankaya and Ayşe Denknalbant Çobanoğlu (eds.), *Turkish Art History Studies*. İstanbul: Kitabevi Yayınları, pp. 257–295.

Hau, Andreas, 2010. *The Implosion of Negativity: The Poetry and Early Prose of Paul Auster*. Norderstedt, Germany: Book on Demand.

Hard, Robin, 2004. *The Routledge Handbook of Greek Mythology: Based on H. J. Rose's Handbook of Greek Mythology*. London: Routledge.

Hartleben, Otto Erich, 1999. 'Der Prophet Jona'. In Simone Frieling (ed.), *Der rebellische Prophet: Jona in der modernen Literatur*. Göttingen: Vandenhoeck & Ruprecht, pp. 42–48. Accessed via http://gutenberg.spiegel.de/buch/gedichte-6426/115.

Havea, Jione, 2020. *Jonah: An Ecological and Islander Reading*. Earth Bible Commentary Series. London: T&T Clark/Bloomsbury.

Heider, George C., 1999. 'Tannin תנין'. In Karel van der Toorn, Bob Becking, and Pieter W. van der Horst (eds.), *Dictionary of Deities and Demons in the Bible*. Leiden: Brill, pp. 834–836.

Herbert, Jr, T., 1969. Walter. 'Calvinism and Cosmic Evil in Moby Dick'. *Modern Language Association* 84.6, pp. 1613–1619.

Hesse, Eric W., and Isaac M. Kikawada, 1984. 'Jonah and Genesis 1–11'. *Annual of the Japanese Biblical Institute* 10, pp. 3–19.

Hofmann, Petra, 2008. 'Infernal Imagery in Anglo-Saxon Charters'. Ph.D. thesis; University of St Andrews.

Hollander, Harm W., and Marinus de Jonge, 1985. *The Testament of the Twelve Patriarchs: A Commentary*. Studia in Veteris Testamenti Pseudepigrapha 8. Leiden: E.J. Brill.

Holstein, Jay A., 1985. 'Melville's Inversion of Jonah in Moby Dick'. *Illif Review* 42, pp. 13–20.

Irwin, W. R., 1969. 'The Unity of Frost's Masques'. *American Literature* 32, pp. 302–312.

Jacobs, Naomi S. S., 2018. *Delicious Prose: Reading the Tale of Tobit with Food and Drink*. Supplements to the Journal for the Study of Judaism 188. Leiden: Brill.

Jacobson, David C., 1997. *Does David Still Play before You? Israeli Poetry and the Bible*. Detroit, MI: Wayne State University Press.

Jensen, Robin Margaret, 2000. *Understanding Early Christian Art*. London and New York, NY: Routledge.

Jeremias, Jörg, 1975. *Die Reue Gottes: Aspekte alttestamentlicher Gottesvorstellung*. Biblische Studien 65. Neukirchen-Vluyn: Neukirchener.

Johnson, Sara Raup, 2004. *Historical Fictions and Hellenistic Jewish Identity: Third Maccabees in its Cultural Context*. Berkeley, CA: University of California Press.

Juhnke, Anna K., 1964. 'Religion in Robert Frost's Poetry: The Play for Self-Possession'. *American Literature* 36, pp. 153–164.

Kadari, Tamar, 2016. 'Aggadic Motifs in the Story of Jonah: A Study of Interaction between Religions'. In Alberdina Houtman, Tamar Kadari, Marcel Poorthuis, and Vered Tohar (eds.), *Religious Stories in Transformation: Conflict, Revision and Reception*. Jewish and Christian Perspectives Series 31. Leiden and Boston, MA: Brill, pp. 107–125.

Kamp, Albert, 2003. *Inner Worlds: A Cognitive-linguistic Approach to the Book of Jonah*. Transl. David Orton. Biblical Interpretation Series 68. Leiden: Brill.

Keiter, Sheila Tuller, 2012. 'Noah and the Dove: The Integral Connection between Noah and Jonah.' *Jewish Biblical Quarterly* 40.4, pp. 261–265.

Kelly, Joseph Ryan, 2013. 'Joel, Jonah and the Yhwh Creed: Determining the Trajectory of the Literary Influence'. *Journal of Biblical Literature* 132, pp. 805–826.

Kitchen, Robert A., 2011. 'Jonah's Oar: Christian Typology in Jacob of Serug's *mêmrā* 122 on Jonah'. *Hugoye: Journal of Syriac Studies* 11.1, pp. 29–62.

Kitto, John (ed.), 1881. *The Cyclopedia of Biblical Literature*, 2 vols. Edinburgh: Adam and Charles Black. For the full-text, https://archive.org/stream/cyclopediaof bibl02kitt/cyclopediaofbibl02kitt_djvu.txt.

Koertge, Ronald Boyd, 1964. 'A Translation of the Middle English Poem Patience'. MA Thesis; University of Arizona.

Kühlmann, Wilhelm, 2011. 'Modell Jona: Zur biblischen Typologie in der deutschen Essayistik und Erzählprosa des 20. Jahrhunderts' (Andres, Jendryschik, Johnson, Lattmann, Rinser u.a.)'. In Johann Anselm Steiger, Wilhelm Kühlmann, in Verbindung mit Ulrich Heinen (eds.), *Der problematische Prophet: Die biblische Jona-Figur in Exegese, Theologie, Literatur und bildender Kunst*. Arbeiten zur Kirchengeschichte 118. Berlin and Boston, MA: de Gruyter, pp. 317–333.

LaCocque, André, and Pierre Emmanuel LaCocque, 1990. *Jonah: A Psycho-Religious Approach to the Prophet*. Columbia, SC: University of South Carolina Press.

Landes, George M., 1967. 'Kerygma of the Book of Jonah: The Contextual Interpretation of the Jonah Psalm'. *Interpretation* 21, pp. 3–31.

Layzer, Varese, 2001. *Signs of Weakness: Juxtaposing Irish Tales and the Bible*. Journal for the Study of the Old Testament Supplement 321. Sheffield: Sheffield Academic Press.

Lee, Brian S., 1982. 'Jonah in Patience and Prudentius'. *Florilegium* 4, pp. 194–209.

Leiter, Louis H. 1960. 'Echo Structures: Conrad's The Secret Sharer'. *Twentieth Century Literature* 5.4, pp. 159–175.

Levine, Amy-Jill, 1992. 'Tobit: Teaching Jews How to Live in the Diaspora'. *Biblical Review* 8, pp. 42–51, 64.

Limburg, James, 1993. *Jonah*. Old Testament Library. London: SCM Press.

Lindsay, Rebecca, 2016. 'Overthrowing Nineveh: Revisiting the City with Postcolonial Imagination'. *The Bible and Critical Theory* 12.1. Accessed via https://www.bible andcriticaltheory.com.

Lipiński, Edward, 2004. *Itineraria Phoenicia*. Orientalia Lovaniensia analecta 127/ Studia Phoenicia 18. Leuven: Peeters.

Liptzin, Solomon, 1985a. *Biblical Themes in World Literature*. Hoboken, NJ: KTAV.
Liptzin, Sol, 1985b. 'The Literary Impact of Jonah'. In *Biblical Themes in World Literature*. Hoboken, NJ: KTAV, pp. 236–249.
Loreto, Paola, 1999. 'A Man in Front of His God, A Man in Front of Himself: The (Post) Modernity of Frost's *A Masque of Reason*'. *Robert Frost Review* 9, pp. 27–39.
McAuliffe, Jane Dammen, 1988. 'Quranic Hermeneutics: The Views of al-Ṭabarī and Ibn Kathīr'. In A. Rippin (ed.), *Approaches to the History of the Interpretation of the Qur'an*. Oxford: Clarendon Press, pp. 46–62.
McDermott, Ryan, 2013. 'The Ordinary Gloss on Jonah'. *Modern Language Association of America* 128.2, pp. 424–438.
McGregor, Rob Roy, 1995. 'Camus's "Jonas ou L'Artise au travail": A Statement of the Absurd Human Condition'. *South Atlantic Review* 60, pp. 53–68.
McKenzie, Steven L., 2005. *How to Read the Bible: History, Prophecy, Literature—Why Modern Readers Need to Know the Difference, and What It Means for Faith Today*. New York, NY: Oxford University Press.
McLaughlin, Ryan Patrick, 2013. 'Jonah and the Religious Other: An Exploration of Biblical Inclusivism'. *Journal of Ecumenical Studies* 48, pp. 71–84.
Marks, Arthur S., 1997. 'Benjamin West's Jonah: A Previously Overlooked Illustration for the Frist Oratorio Composed in the New World'. *American Art Journal* 28, pp. 122–137.
Masback, Frederic J., 1961. 'Conrad's Jonah'. *College English* 22.5, pp. 328–333.
Meckier, Jerome, 2012. *Aldous Huxley: From Poet to Mystic*. Human Potentialities. Münster, Germany: Lit Verlag.
Melin, Pia (ed.), 2009. *Albertus Pictor: Målare av sin tid. Vol. 1: Bilder i urval samt studier och analyser*. Stockholm: Kungl. Vitterhets historie och antikvitets akademien.
Miller, Christanne, 2000. 'Marianne Moore and the Women Modernizing New York'. *Modern Philology* 98, pp. 339–362.
Modesto, Christine, 1992. *Cena Cypriani und zu deren Rezeption*. Classica Monacensia 3. Tübingen: Gunter Narr.
Moore, Carey A., 1996. *Tobit: A New Translation with Introduction and Commentary*. Anchor Bible 40A. London and New York, NY: Doubleday.
Muldoon, Catherine L., 2010. *In Defense of Divine Justice: An Intertextual Approach to the Book of Jonah*. CBQMS 47. Washington, DC: Catholic Biblical Association of America.
Muradyan, Aram, and Gohar Topchyan, 2013. 'Pseudo-Philo, On Samson and On Jonah'. In Feldman, Louis H., James L. Kugel, and Lawrence H. Schiffman (eds.), *Outside the Bible: Ancient Jewish Writings Related to Scripture*. 3 Vols. Philadelphia, PA: Jewish Publication Society / Lincoln, NE: University of Nebraska Press, pp. 750–803.
Neusner, Jacob, 2007. *Habakkuk, Jonah, Nahum and Obadiah in Talmud and Midrash: A Source Book*. Studies in Judaism. Indiana University: University Press of America.
New, Elisa, 1998. 'Bible Leaves! Bible Leaves! Hellenism and Hebraism in Melville's Moby Dick'. *Poetics Today* 19 (No. 2, Hellenism and Hebraism Reconsidered: The Poetics of Cultural Influence and Exchange II), pp. 281–303.

Newby, Gordon Darnell, 1989. *The Making of the Last Prophet: A Reconstruction of the Earliest Biography of Muhammad*. Columbia, SC: University of South Carolina.

Nichols, Geraldine Cleary, 1986. 'Exile, Gender, and Mercè Rodoreda'. *Modern Language Notes* 101.2 Hispanic Issue, pp. 405–417.

Noegel, Scott B., 2015. 'Jonah and Leviathan: Inner-Biblical Allusions and the Problem with Dragons'. *Hen* 37, pp. 236–260.

Nowell, Irene, 1983. 'The Book of Tobit: Narrative Technique and Theology'. Ph.D. diss.; Washington, DC: The Catholic University of America.

Oren, Michael B., and Mark Gerson, 2007 (21 Sep). 'Jonah's Dilemma'. *Wall Street Journal*, Eastern edition; New York, NY: A.14.

Pardes, Ilana, 2005. 'Remapping Jonah's Voyage: Melville's Moby-Dick and Kitto's *Cyclopedia of Biblical Literature*'. *Comparative Literature* 57.2, pp. 135–157.

Pardes, Ilana, 2008. *Melville's Bibles*. Berkeley, CA: University of California Press.

Parunak, H. van Dyke, 1975. 'A Semantic Survey of NHM'. *Biblica* 56, pp. 512–532.

Person, Jr, Raymond F., 2008. 'The Role of Nonhuman Characters in Jonah'. In Norman C. Habel and Peter L. Trudinger (eds.), *Exploring Ecological Hermeneutics*. Society of Biblical Literature Symposium Series 46. Atlanta, GA: SBL, pp. 85–90.

Plant, Stephen, 2009. '"Jonah": Guilt and Promise'. In Bernd Wannenwetsch (ed.), *Who Am I: Bonhoeffer's Theology through His Poetry*. London: T&T Clark, pp. 197–212.

Plant, Stephen J., 2013. *Taking Stock of Bonhoeffer: Studies in Biblical Interpretation and Ethics*. Farnham: Ashgate, pp. 59–70.

Profitlich, Ulrich, and Frank Stucke, 1995. '"Only Limited Utopias are Realizable": On a Motif in the Plays of Peter Hacks'. *Contemporary Theatre Review* 4.2, Special Issue: David W. Robinson (ed.), No Man's Land: East German Drama After the Wall, pp. 51–61.

Quint, David, 2015. 'The Modern Copy: Dante, Aristo, and Michelangelo's Sistine Ceiling'. *I Tatti Studies in the Italian Renaissance* 18.2, pp. 397–427. Accessed via http://www.journals.uchicago.edu/doi/full/10.1086/683175.

Rathbun, John W., 1991. 'Moby Dick: Ishmael's Fiction of Ahab's Romantic Insurgency'. *Modern Language Studies* 21.3, pp. 3–9.

Reinhard, Miriam, 2011. 'Uwe Johnsons *Jonas zum Beispiel*: Ein Beispiel für das Verhältnis von Beispiel, Lektüre und Sinn'. In Johann Anselm Steiger und Wilhelm Kühlmann, in Verbindung mit Ulrich Heinen (eds.), *Der problematische Prophet: die biblische Jona-Figur in Exegese, Theologie, Literatur und bildender Kunst*. Arbeiten zur Kirchengeschichte 118. Berlin: de Gruyter, pp. 335–345.

Reynolds, Gabriel Said, 2010. *The Qur'ān and Its Biblical Subtext*. Routledge Studies in the Qur'an. Abingdon: Routledge.

Robinson, B. W., 1980. 'Rashīd al-Dīn's World History: The Significance of the Miniatures'. *The Journal of the Royal Asiatic Society of Great Britain and Ireland* 2, pp. 212–222.

Rogerson, John, 1994. 'Jonah'. In Grace Emerson (ed.), *Poets and Prophets: A Companion to the Prophetic Books of the Old Testament*. Oxford: Bible Reading Fellowship, pp. 239–244.

Rosen, Norma, 1992. 'Justice for Jonah, or, a Bible Bartleby'. In *Accidents of Influence: Writing as a Woman and a Jew in America*. Albany, NY: SUNY Press, pp. 87–96.

Russell, John, 1983. 'Limbo States: The Short Stories of Henry Green'. *Twentieth Century Literature* 29, pp. 447–454.

Rubin, Uri, 1984. 'Al-Ṣamad and the High God: An Interpretation of Sūra CXII'. *Der Islam: Journal of the History and Culture of the Middle East* 61.2, pp. 197–217.

Ruether, Rosemary Radford, and Herman J. Reuther, 1993. *The Wrath of Jonah: The Crisis of Religious Nationalism in the Israeli-Palestinian Conflict*. San Francisco, CA: HarperCollins.

Ryu, Chesung Justin, 2009. 'Silence as Resistance: A Postcolonial Reading of the Silence of Jonah in Jonah 4.1–11'. *Journal for the Study of the Old Testament* 34, pp. 195–218.

Saeedimehr, Mohammad, 2018. 'Divine Knowledge and the Doctrine of Badā'. *TheoLogica: An International Journal for Philosophy of Religion and Philosophical Theology* 2(1), pp. 23–36.

Sager, Jenny, 2013. 'The Leviathan in Thomas Lodge and Robert Greene's *A Looking Glass for London and England*'. In *The Aesthetics of Spectacle in Early Modern Drama and Modern Cinema: Robert Greene's Theatre of Attraction*. New York, NY: Palgrave Macmillan, pp. 53–69.

Salberg, Jill, 2008. 'Jonah's Crisis'. *Psychoanalytic Dialogues* 18, pp. 317–328.

Salzmann, Bertram, 2006. 'Jonas, Johnson und Jehova: Uwe Johnsons produktive Bibelrezeption in *Jonas zum Beispiel*'. In Michale Hofmann (ed.), *Johnson-Jahrbuch*. 13. Jg., pp. 139–150. Accessed via http://www.theologie-und-literatur.de/filead min/user_upload/Theologie_und_Literatur/Salzmann_JohnsonJonas.pdf.

Sasson, Jack M., 1990. *Jonah: A New Translation with Introduction, Commentary, and Interpretation*. Anchor Bible 24B. New York, NY and London: Doubleday.

Schellenberg, Annette, 2015. 'An Anti-Prophet among the Prophets? On the Relationship of Jonah to Prophecy'. *Journal for the Study of the Old Testament* 39, pp. 353–371.

Scherman, Rabbi Nosson, 1978. 'Overview: Jonah, Repentance, and Yom Kippur'. In Rabbi Meir Zlotowitz (ed.), *Jonah*. The Artscroll Tanach Series. New York, NY: Mesorah Publications, pp. xix–lxxv.

Schmidt, Gary D., 1995. *The Iconography of the Mouth of Hell: Eighth-century Britain to the Fifteenth Century*. Selinsgrove, PA: Susquehanna University Press/London: Associated University Presses.

Schmidt, Ludwig, 1976. *'De Deo': Studien zur Literaturkritik und Theologie des Buches Jonah, des Gespräches zwischen Abraham und Jahwe in Genesis 18:22ff. und von Hi 1*. Beihefte zur Zeitschrift für die alttestamentliche Wissenschaft 143. Berlin: de Gruyter.

Schwemer, Maria, 2020. 'The Lives of the Prophets and the Book of the Twelve'. In Lena-Sofia Tiemeyer and Jakob Wöhrle (eds.), *The Book of the Twelve: Composition, Reception, and Interpretation*. Formation and Interpretation of Old Testament Literature/Supplements to Vetus Testamentum 184. Leiden: Brill, pp. 415–440.

Scoralick, Ruth, 2002. *Gottes Güte und Gottes Zorn: Die Gottesprädikationen in Ex. 34,6f und ihre intertextuellen Beziehungen zum Zwölfprophetenbuch*. Herders biblische Studien. Freiburg: Herder.

Scoralick, Ruth, 2020. 'Judgment and Grace in the Book of the Twelve'. In Lena-Sofia Tiemeyer and Jakob Wöhrle (eds.), *The Book of the Twelve: Composition, Reception, and Interpretation*. Formation and Interpretation of Old Testament Literature/ Supplements to Vetus Testamentum 184. Leiden: Brill, pp. 469–488.

Seidler, Ayelet, 2019. '"Fasting," "Sackcloth," and "Ashes"—From Nineveh to Shushan'. *Vetus Testamentum* 69, pp. 117–134.

Sherwood, Yvonne, 1997. 'Rocking the Boat: Jonah and the New Historicism'. *Biblical Interpretation* 5, pp. 364–402.

Sherwood, Yvonne, 1998. 'Cross-Currents in the Book of Jonah: Some Jewish and Cultural Midrashim on a Traditional Text'. *Biblical Interpretation* 6, pp. 49–79.

Sherwood, Yvonne, 2000. *A Biblical Text and its Afterlives: The Survival of Jonah in Western Culture*. Cambridge: Cambridge University Press.

Showalter, Jr, English, 1982. 'Camus and Dadelsen's *Jonas*'. *Modern Language Studies* 12, pp. 41–47.

Shulman, Rabbi Dennis G., 2008. 'Jonah: His Story, Our Story; His Struggle, Our Struggle'. *Psychoanalytic Dialogues* 18, pp. 329–364.

Siegert, Folker, 1980. *Drei Hellenistisch-jüdische Predigten: Ps.-Philon, 'Über Jona', 'Über Jona', 'Über Simson' und 'Über Die Gottesbezeichnung 'wohltätig Verzehrendes Feuer'. Aus d. Armen. u. sprachl. Erl. V. Folder Siegert. Vol. I.* Wissenschaftliche Untersuchungen zum Neuen Testament 20. Tübingen: JC.B. Mohr.

Siegert, Folker, 1992. *Drei hellenistisch-jüdische Predigten: Ps.-Philon, 'Über Jona', 'Über Jona' (Fragment) und 'Über Simson'. Vol. II.* Wissenschaftliche Untersuchungen zum Neuen Testament 61. Tübingen: JC.B. Mohr.

Siegert, Folker, 1994. 'Die Heiden in der pseudo-philonischen Predigt *De Jona*'. In Reinhard Feldmeier and Ulrich Heckel (eds.), *Die Heiden: Juden, Christen und das Problem des Fremden*. Wissenschaftliche Untersuchungen zum Neuen Testament 70. Tübingen: Mohr Siebeck, pp. 52–58.

Siegert, Folker, 1996. 'Early Jewish Interpretations in a Hellenistic Style'. In Magne Saebø (ed.), *Hebrew Bible, Old Testament: The History of Its Interpretation*, Vol I/1. Göttingen: Vandenhoeck & Ruprecht, pp. 217–235.

Simon, Uriel, 1994. *Jona: Ein jüdischer Kommentar*. Stuttgarter Bibelstudien 157. Stuttgart: Katholisches Bibelwerk.

Simpson, William, 1899. *The Jonah Legend: A Suggestion of Interpretation*. London: Grant Richards.

Smart, James D., 1956. 'The Book of Jonah'. In *The Interpreter's Bible*, Vol. VI. Nashville, TN: Abingdon Press, pp. 869–894.

Smith, George Adam, 1898. *The Book of the Twelve Prophets*, Vol. 2. The Expositor's Bible. London: Hodder and Stoughton.

Smith-Christopher, Daniel L., 2002. *A Biblical Theology of Exile*. Overtures to Biblical Theology. Minneapolis, MN: Fortress.

Smolar, Leivy, and Moses Aberbach, 1983. *Studies in Targum Jonathan to the Prophets*. New York, NY: Ktav Publishing House/Baltimore, MD: Hebrew College.

Sprang, Felix C. H., 2011. 'Herman Melvilles *Moby Dick* als Jonah-Geschichte'. In Johann Anselm Steiger, Wilhelm Kühlmann in Verbindung mit Ulrich Heinen (eds.), *Der problematische Prophet: Die biblische Jona-Figur in Exegese,* Theologie, *Literatur und bildender Kunst*. Arbeiten zur Kirchengeschichte 118. Berlin and Boston, MA: de Gruyter, pp. 453–457.

Staffell, Simon, 2008. 'The Mappe and the Bible: Nation, Empire and the Collective Memory of Jonah, Biblical Interpretation'. *Biblical Interpretation* 16, pp. 476–500.

Steffen, Uwe, 1963. *Das Mysterium von Tod und Auferstehung: Formen und Wandlungen des Jona-Motivs*. Göttingen: Vandenhoeck & Ruprecht.

Steffen, Uwe, 1994. *Die Jona-Geschichte: Ihre Auslegung und Darstellung im Judentum, Christentum und Islam*. Neukirchen-Vluyn: Neukirchener.

Stökl Ben Ezra, Daniel, 2003. *The Impact of Yom Kippur on Early Christianity: The Day of Atonement from Second Temple Judaism to the Fifth Century*. Wissenschaftliche Untersuchungen zum Neuen Testament 163. Tübingen: Mohr Siebeck.

Strawn, Brent A., 2012. 'On Vomiting: Leviticus, Jonah, Ea(a)rth'. *Catholic Biblical Quarterly* 74, pp. 445–464.

Streete, Adrian, 2009. 'Francis Quarles' Early Poetry and the Discourses of Jacobean Spenserianism'. *Journal of the Northern Renaissance* 1. Accessed via http://www.northernrenaissance.org/frances-quarles-early-poetry-and-the-discourses-of-jacobean-spenserianism

Sutskover, Talia, 2014. 'Directionality and Space in Jonah'. In Athalya Brenner-Idan (ed.), *Discourse, Dialogue & Debate in the Bible: Essays in Honour of Frank H. Polak*. Hebrew Bible Monographs 63/Amsterdam Studies in the Bible and Religion 7. Sheffield: Sheffield Phoenix Press, pp. 203–217.

Thorpe, Benjamin, 1842. *Codex Exoniensis: A Collection of Anglo-Saxon Poetry, from a Manuscript in the Library of the Dean and Chapter of Exeter, with an English Translation, Notes, and Indexes*. London: Society of Antiquaries of London. Accessed via https://ia802607.us.archive.org/16/items/codexexoniensis01londgoog/codexexoniensis01londgoog.pdf.

Tiemeyer, Lena-Sofia, 2005. 'Prophecy as a Way of Cancelling Prophecy: The Strategic Uses of Foreknowledge'. *Zeitschrift für die alttestamentliche Wissenschaft* 117, pp. 329–350.

Tiemeyer, Lena-Sofia, 2016. 'A New Look at the Biological Sex/Grammatical Gender of Jonah's Fish'. *Vetus Testamentum* 66, pp. 1–17.

Tiemeyer, Lena-Sofia, 2017a. 'Jonah and the Foreigners: Interreligious Relations in the Reception History of the Book of Jonah'. In Hallvard Hagelia and Markus Zehnder (eds.), *Interreligious Relations: Biblical Perspectives*. London: T&T Clark, pp. 259–279.

Tiemeyer, Lena-Sofia, 2017b. '"Peace for our Time": Reading Jonah in Dialogue with Abravanel in the Book of the Twelve'. *Journal of Hebrew Scripture* 17, Article 6. Doi: 10.5508/jhs.2017.v17.a6.

Tiemeyer, Lena-Sofia, 2017c. 'Jonah and His Fish: The Monstrification of God's Servant in Early Jewish and Christian Reception History'. In Zohar Hadromi-Allouche (ed.), *Fallen Animals: Art, Religion, Literature*. Lanham, MD: Lexington Books, pp. 47–70.

Tiemeyer, Lena-Sofia, 2018. 'When God Changes His Mind: A Theological Exploration of Jonah 3:9–10 and 4:2'. In Birger Olsson and James Starr (eds.), *Ordet är dig mycket nära: Tolkningar av Gamla testamentet idag*. Skellefteå, Sweden: Artos, pp. 125–146.

Tiemeyer, Lena-Sofia, 2019a. 'Jonah, the Eternal Fugitive: Exploring the Intertextuality of Jonah's Flight in the Bible and Its Later Reception'. In Jesper Høgenhaven, Frederik Poulsen, and Cian Power (eds.), *Images of Exile in the Prophetic Literature*. Forschungen zum Alten Testament II/103. Tübingen: Mohr Siebeck, pp. 255–268.

Tiemeyer, Lena-Sofia, 2019b. 'The Book of Jonah in Jewish-Christian Debate'. *Taiwan Baptist Christian Seminary Journal* 17, pp. 3–53.

Timmer, Daniel C., 2008 'Jonah And Mission: Missiological Dichotomy, Biblical Theology, and the "Via Tertia"'. *Westminster Theological Journal* 70, pp. 159–175.

Timmer, Daniel C., 2013. 'Jonah's Theology of the Nations: The Interface of Religious and Ethnic Identity'. *Revue Biblique* 120, pp. 13–23.

Timmerman, John H., 2002. *Robert Frost: The Ethics of Ambiguity*. Lewisburg, PA: Buckness University Press.

Trible, Phyllis, 1990. 'A Tempest in a Text: Ecological Soundings in the Book of Jonah'. In Stephen L. Cook and Sara C. Winter (eds.), *On the Way to Nineveh: Studies in Honor of George M. Landes*. Atlanta, GA: Scholars Press, pp. 187–200.

Trible, Phyllis, 1994. *Rhetorical Criticism: Context, Method, and the Book of Jonah*. Old Testament Series. Minneapolis, MN: Fortress.

Trible, Phyllis, 1996. 'The Book of Jonah'. *New Interpreter's Bible* 7, pp. 461–529.

Ueberschaer, Frank, 2020. 'The Book of the Twelve in Early Jewish Literature'. In Lena-Sofia Tiemeyer and Jakob Wöhrle (eds.), *The Book of the Twelve: Composition, Reception, and Interpretation*. Formation and Interpretation of Old Testament Literature/Supplements to Vetus Testamentum 184. Leiden: Brill, pp. 352–384.

Urbach, Ephraim, 1949. 'The Repentance of the People of Nineveh and the Jewish-Christian Dispute'. *Tarbiẓ* 29, pp. 118–122 (Hebrew).

Vanoni, Gottfried, 1978. *Das Buch Jonah: Literar- und formkritische Untersuchung*. Arbeiten zu Text und Sprache im Alten Testament 7. St. Ottilien: Eos.

Vawter, Bruce, 1983. *Job and Jonah: Questioning the Hidden God*. New York, NY: Paulist Press.

Vermeulen, Karolien, 2017. 'Save or Sack the City: The Fate of Jonah's Nineveh from a Spatial Perspective'. *Journal for the Study of the Old Testament* 42, pp. 233–246.

Walton, John H., 1992. 'The Object Lesson of Jonah 4:5–7 and the Purpose of the Book of Jonah'. *Bulletin for Biblical Research* 2, pp. 47–57.

Weinfeld, Moshe, 1991. 'Semiramis: Her Name and Her Origin'. In Mordechai Cogan and Israel Ephʻal (eds.), *Ah, Assyria…: Studies in Assyrian History and Ancient Near Eastern Historiography*. Scripta Hierosolymitana 33. Jerusalem: Magnes, pp. 99–103.

Wiegmann, Hermann, 2005. *Die deutsche Literatur des 20. Jahrhunderts*. Würzburg: Koenigshausen & Neumann.

Wiliame, Geraldine V., 2005. 'A Fara Reading of Jonah on Interfaith Dialogue in Fiji'. *Mission Theology in the Anglican Community*. Accessed via www.missiontheologyanglican.org/article-mt/fara-reading-of-jonah-on-interfaith-dialogue-in-fiji.

Wilson, Ambrose John, 1927. 'The Sign of the Prophet Jonah and Its Modern Confirmations'. *Princeton Theological Review* 25, pp. 630–642.

Wineman, Aryeh, 1998. *Mystic Tales from the Zohar*. Princeton, NY: Princeton University Press.
Wolfe, Brendan N., 2014. 'Tolkien's Jonah'. *Journal of Inklings Studies* 9.1, pp. 11–26.
Wright, Charles H. H., 1886. 'The Book of Jonah Considered from an Allegorical Point of View'. In *Biblical Essays: Exegetical Studies on the Books of Job and Jonah, Ezekiel's Prophecy of Gog and Magog, St. Peter's 'Spirits in Prison', and the Key to the Apocalypse*. Edinburgh: T&T Clark, pp. 34–98.
Wright, Nathalia, 1940. 'Biblical Allusion in Melville's Prose'. *American Literature* 12.2, pp. 185–199.
Wright, Nathalia, 1975. 'Melville's Use of the Bible in *Moby-Dick*'. In Roland Bartel with James S. Ackerman and Thayer S. Warshaw (eds.), *Biblical Images in Literature*. Nashville, TN: Abingdon Press, pp. 36–64.
Ziolkowski, Jan M., 1984. 'Folklore and Learned Lore in Letaldus's Whale Poem'. *Viator* 15, pp. 107–118.
Ziolkowski, Jan M., 2007. *Fairy Tales from before Fairy Tales: The Medieval Latin Past of Wonderful Lies*. Ann Arbor, MI: University of Michigan Press.
Zornberg, Aviva Gottlieb, 2008. 'Jonah: A Fantasy of Flight'. *Psychoanalytic Dialogues* 18, pp. 271–299.

Authored Works

Abbot, George, 1600. *An Exposition upon the Prophet Jonah Contained in Certaine Sermons, Preached in S. Maries Church in Oxford*. London: Richard Field. Accessed via https://quod.lib.umich.edu/e/eebo/A16485.0001.001?view=toc.
Adam of St Victor, 12th century. *A short reflection on Jonah*.
Adler, Samuel, 2004. *Der Mann ohne Toleranz* ('The Man Without Tolerance').
Adomnán of Iona, 7th century. *Life of St Columba*.
Agnon, Shmuel Yosef, 1948. *Days of Awe: A Treasury of Jewish Wisdom for Reflection, Repentance, and Renewal on the High Holy Days*. New York, NY: Schocken.
Andres, Stefan, 1963. *Der Mann im Fisch*. Berlin: Union Verlag.
Argento, Dominick, 2010. *Jonah and the Whale* (1973). Accessed via www.bmop.org/audio-recordings/dominick-argento-jonah-and-whale (with a commentary by Michael McGaghie).
Auster, Paul, 1982. *The Invention of Solitude*. London: Faber and Faber.
Babits, Mihály, 1939. 'Jonah's Prayer' (*Jónás imája*). For an English translation, see Peter Zollman. Accessed via http://www.fszek.hu/english/?article_hid=2074.
Barnes, Julian, 1989. 'Three Simple Stories'. In *A History of the World in 10½ Chapters*. London: Jonathan Cape.
Beckwith, John, 1969. *Jonah: Chamber Cantata for Chorus, Four Soloists, and Instruments*. Don Mills, Ontario: BMI Canada.
Bejerano, Maya, 1993. 'Midrash Jonah'. In *Mizmorei 'Iyyou*. Tel Aviv: Hakubbutz Hameuchad.
Beeson, Jack, 1948–1950. *Jonah*. Boosey & Hawkes. Opera in two or three acts to be played, danced and sung. Libretto by the composer, adapted from the play by Paul

Goodman (Boosey & Hawkes). See http://www.boosey.com/pages/opera/moredetails.asp?musicid=1824.

Ben-Chorin, Schalom, 1966. *Die Antwort des Jona: Zum Gestaltwandel Israels, ein geschichts-theologischer Versuch*. Evangelische Zeitstimmen 25/26; Hamburg: Herbert Reich Evangelischer Verlag.

Bonhoeffer, Dietrich, 1944. 'Jonah' ('Jona'). Written in Wehrmachtsuntersuchungsgefängnis Tegel. Original German, see http://www.otthollo.de/JONA/Bonhoeffer.html. English translation, see https://abramkj.com/2014/12/06/jonah-a-poem-by-bonhoeffer. For an alternative English translation, see John Bowden, as cited in Plant, 'Jonah', p. 199.

Bradbury, Thomas, 1721. 'The Repentance of Nineveh: Consider'd and Apply'd, in Two Sermons'. One preach'd on Decemb. 11. 1720; the other on Decemb. 16. 1720. London: Eman. Matthews.

Brentius, John, 1570. *News From Niniue to Englands, Brought by the Prophet Jonas*. Transl. T. Tymme. London: Henrie Denham.

Bridie, James, 1932. *Jonah and the Whale*. London: Constable & Co Ltd.

Burning Sensation, EP 1982. 'Belly of the Whale'. See further https://en.wikipedia.org/wiki/Burning_Sensations.

Camus, Albert, 1958. 'The Artist at Work (*Jonas, ou l'artiste au travail*)'. In *Exile and the Kingdom* (*L'Exil et le royaume*). Transl. Justin O'Brien. Harmondsworth: Penguin Books, pp. 83–115.

Carissimi, Giacomo, 17th century. *Jonas*. Accessed via https://musopen.org/music/32786-jonas.

Collodi, Carlo (pseudonym for Carlo Lorenzini), 1883. *Pinocchio: The Adventures of Pinocchio* (*La storia di un burattino/Le avventure di Pinocchio*). Transl. Ann Lawson Lucas. Oxford World's Classics. Oxford: Oxford University Press, 2009.

Conrad, Joseph, 1897. *The Nigger of the 'Narcissus'*. For on-line access to the book, see www.gutenberg.org/files/17731/17731-h/17731-h.htm.

Conrad, Joseph, 1900. *Lord Jim*. For on-line access to the book, see http://www.gutenberg.org/files/5658/5658-h/5658-h.htm.

Conrad, Joseph, 1902, begun 1899. *Typhoon*. For on-line access to the book, see http://www.gutenberg.org/files/1142/1142-h/1142-h.htm.

Conrad, Joseph, 1910. 'The Secret Sharer'. First published in 1910 in two parts in *Harper's Magazine*. It later appeared in *Twixt Land and Sea* (1912). For on-line access to the book, see http://www.gutenberg.org/files/220/220-h/220-h.htm.

Conrad, Joseph, 1917. *The Shadow Line*. For on-line access to the book, see www.gutenberg.org/files/451/451.txt.

Crane, Hart, 1994. 'After Jonah'. In David Curzon, ed., *Modern Poems on the Bible: An Anthology*. Philadelphia, PA and Jerusalem: JPS, p. 260.

Dadelsen, Jean-Paul de, 1962. *Jonas*. Paris: Gallimard.

Drayton, Michael, 1931. 'The Song of Jonah in the Whales Bellie'. In J. William Hebel (ed.), *The Works of Michael Drayton*, Vol. I. Oxford: Shakespeare Head Press, p. 19

Eich, Günter, 1968. 'Jonas'. In *Maulwürfe*. Accessed in Simone Frieling (ed.), *Der Rebellische Prophet: Jona in der modernen Literatur*. Göttingen: Vandenhoeck & Ruprecht, 1999, pp. 90–91.

Felsted, Samuel. 18th century. *Jonah* (oratorio and accompanying libretto).
Felipe, León, 1942. 'Tal vez me llame Jonás'. Accessed via http://www.prometeodigital.org/SIEMPRE_LEONFELIPE.htm.
Frost, Robert, 1945. 'A Masque of Mercy'. In *Collected Poems, Prose, and Plays*. Library Classics of the United States. New York, NY: The Library of America, 1995.
Grass, Günter, 1959. *The Tin Drum* (*Die Blechtrommel*). Hermann Luchterhand Verlag. Transl. Breon Mitchell. London: Vintage Classics, 2010.
Green, Henry, 1942, 'Mr Jonas'. *Penguin New Writing* 14, pp. 15–20. Accessed in Simone Frieling (ed.), *Der Rebellische Prophet: Jona in der modernen Literatur*. Göttingen: Vandenhoeck & Ruprecht, 1999, pp. 90–91.
Hacks, Peter, 1988. *Jona: Trauerspiel in fünf Akten*. Berlin and Weimar: Aufbau, 1989. First published as 'Jona/Jonah, Beiwerk und Hintersinn'. *Sinn und Form* 40, pp. 1144–1228. See http://www.augsburger-allgemeine.de/kultur/Kuehn-und-glaenzend-Peter-Hacks-Jona-uraufgefuehrt-id6817666.html.
Hartleben, Otto Erich, 1905. 'Der Prophet Jona'. In Simone Frieling (ed.), *Der Rebellische Prophet: Jona in der modernen Literatur*. Göttingen: Vandenhoeck & Ruprecht, 1999, pp. 42–48.
Herbert, Zbigniew, 1965. 'Jonah'. Translated by John and Bogdana Carpenter. In *Postwar Polish Poetry* by Czeslaw Milosz. In David Curzon (ed.), *Modern Poems on the Bible: An Anthology*. Philadelphia, PA, and Jerusalem: JPS, 1994, pp. 257–258. See also Barańczak, Stanislaw. *A Fugitive from Utopia: The Poetry of Zbigniew Herbert*. Cambridge, MA: Harvard University Press, 1987.
Hooper, John, 1831. 'An Oversight and Deliberation upon the Holy Prophet Jonah; Made and Uttered before the King's Majesty, and His Most Honourable Council.' In *Writings of Dr. John Hooper, Bishop of Gloucester and Worcester, Martyr, 1555*. London: The Religious Tract Society.
Housman, Laurence, 1942. *Palestinian Plays: 'The Burden of Nineveh'*. London: Jonathan Cape.
Hurd, Michael John, 1967. *Jonah-Man Jazz*. London: Novello. Accessed via https://www.scribd.com/doc/140375051/Jonah-Man-Jazz-Lyric-Sheet-Michael-Hurd-1966.
Hurston, Zora Neale, 1934. *Jonah's Gourd Vine*. New York, NY: HarperPerennial, 2008.
Huxley, Aldous, 1917. 'Jonah'. Oxford: Holywell Press. For the full-text on-line, see http://johnwsewell.blogspot.co.uk/2007/03/jonah-fish-academy.html.
Jerome, Judson, 1991. 'Jonah'. In *Jonah & Job*. Santa Barbara, CA: John Daniel and Company.
Johnson, Uwe, 1964. 'Jonas zum Beispiel'. Originally published in *Karsch und andere Prosa*, pp. 82–84. More recently reprinted in *Der rebellische Prophet*, pp. 92–95.
Karlfeldt, Erik Axel, 1901. 'Jone havsfärd'. In *Fridolins lustgård och dalmålningar på rim*. Stockholm: Wahlström & Widstrands.
L'Engle, Madeleine, 1967. *The Journey with Jonah*. Sunburst Book. New York, NY: Farrar, Straus and Giroux.
Lihn, Enrique, 1972. 'Jonah' (transl. J. Cohen), in *The Dark Rooms and Other Poems*. In David Curzon, (ed.), *Modern Poems on the Bible: An Anthology*. Philadelphia, PA and Jerusalem: JPS, 1994, p. 267.

Lodge, Thomas, and Robert Greene, 1592. *A Looking Glass for London and England*. Oxford: Printed for the Malone Society at the Oxford University Press, 1932.

Lucian, 2006. 'A True History'. In *Selected Dialogues*. Transl. C. D. N. Costa. Oxford: Oxford University Press, pp. 203–233. https://www.amazon.com/Lucian-Selected-Dialogues-Oxford-Classics/dp/0199555931.

Mathias, William, 1989. *Jonah: A Musical Morality*, with text by Charles Causley. Oxford Choral Music. Oxford: Oxford University Press.

Melville, Herman, 1851. *Moby Dick; or, The Whale*. London: Richard Bentley. For the full text, see https://www.gutenberg.org/files/2701/2701-h/2701-h.htm#link2HCH0083.

Mills, Peter, 1990. *Jonah's Adventure with the Big Fish* (A Bible flap-book – Bible Adventures). Alton, England: Hunt & Thorpe.

Mitchell, Stephen, 1943. 'Jonah', in *Parables and Portraits*. HarperCollins, 1990. In David Curzon, (ed.), *Modern Poems on the Bible: An Anthology*. Philadelphia, PA, and Jerusalem: JPS, 1994, p. 259.

Molodowsky, Kadia, 1965. 'Jonah', in *Light of the Thorn Bush* (*Likht fun dornboym*). In *Paper Bridges: Selected Poems of Kaya Molodowsky*. Transl. Kathryn Hellerstein. Detroit, MI: Wayne State University Press, 1990, p. 491.

Moore, Marianne, 1968. 'Tom Fool at Jamaica', 'Is Your Town Nineveh', 'Sojourn in the Whale'. In *The Complete Poems of Marianne Moore*. London: Faber and Faber.

Nilson, Peter, 1985. *Guldspiken*. Stockholm: Nordstedts.

Orwell, George, 1961. 'Inside the Whale'. In *Collected Essays*. London: Secker & Warburg, pp. 118–159.

Pagis, Dan, 1989. 'Tidings' in *Variable Directions*. Transl. Stephen Mitchell. In David Curzon (ed.), *Modern Poems on the Bible: An Anthology*. Philadelphia, PA and Jerusalem: JPS, 1994, p. 157.

Preil, Gabriel, 1961. 'Jonah'. Transl. Gabriel Preil and David Curzon. In David Curzon (ed.), *Modern Poems on the Bible: An Anthology*. Philadelphia, PA and Jerusalem: JPS, 1994, p. 259.

Prudentius, Aurelius Clemens, 4th century. 'Hymnus Ieiunantium' ('Hymn for those who fast'). Original Latin text and English translation, see https://www.gutenberg.org/files/14959/14959-h/14959-h.htm#p07o.

Quarles, Francis, 1620. 'A Feast for Worms'. In *Divine Poems, Containing the History of Jonah, Esther, Job, Sampson. Together with Sion's Sonnets, Elegies*. Fifth edition. London: Printed for Jeremiah Batley, 1717.

Rodoreda, Mercè, 1984. *My Christina and Other Stories*. Transl. David Rosenthal. Saint Paul, MN: Graywolf Press.

Scliar, Moacyr, 1987. *The Strange Nation of Rafael Mendes*. Transl. Eloah F. Giacomelli. New York, NY: Ballantine Books.

Sewall, Joseph, 1740. 'Nineveh's Repentance and Deliverance'. Congregationalist pastor of South Church in Boston, Massachusetts. Boston, MA and New England: J. Draper.

Shapiro, David, 1988. 'In a Blind Garden'. In *House Blown Apart*. Woodstock, NY: Overlook Press.

Sorescu, Marin, 1990. 'Jonah: A Tragedy in Four Scenes'. In *The Thirst of the Salt Mountain: Trilogy of Plays*. Transl. Andrea Deletant and Brenda Walker. Normanton-on-Cliffe, Grantham, England: Forest Books. First performed in Rumanian in 1968.

Sowden, Lewis, 1974. 'Jonah'. In *The Jaffa Road, and Other Poems From Jerusalem*. Tel Aviv: Eked.

Tandrup, Harald, 1939. *Profeten Jonas Privat*. Translated into English as *Jonah and the Voice* or as *Reluctant Prophet*. Transl. A. G. Chater. New York, NY: Alfred A. Knopf/Translated into German as *Der Prophet Jona—privat*. Transl. H. Georg Kemlein. Leipzig: Paul List Verlag, 1959.

Tavener, John, 1969. *The Whale: A Biblical Fantasy*. London: J&W Chester Ltd.

Tolkien, John Ronald Reuel, 1961. 'The Book of Jonah'. *The Jerusalem Bible*.

Vogel, Wladimir, 1958. 'Jona ging doch nach Ninive'. In Friedrich Geiger, 'Art as a Vocation: Vladimir Vogel's Dramma-Oratorio "Jonah ging doch nach Ninive"'. *Tempo*, New Series 218, Swiss Music Issue. Oct. 2001, pp. 11–14.

Wiesel, Eli, 1981. *Five Biblical Portraits: Saul-Jonah-Jeremiah-Elijah-Joshua*. Notre Dame, IN and London: University of Notre Dame Press.

Index of Biblical Texts

Genesis		3:7	177
1–11	149	3:13	69
1:1–2:4	67	3:17	152
1:2	141	4	9
1:10	49	4:2	149
1:21	92, 98, 103	4:5–6	215
1:26	136	4:10	26
1:26 LXX	92	4:14	50, 215
1:28	136	4:16	215

Jonah Through the Centuries, First Edition. Lena-Sofia Tiemeyer.
© 2022 John Wiley & Sons, Ltd. Published 2022 by John Wiley & Sons, Ltd.

Index of Biblical Texts

6–9	235	28:20	48
6	27, 28	32:10–14	245
6:6	235	32:14	199
6:11	28	32:31–32	33
6:13	28	32:32	35, 213, 245
10:10–11	23	32:33	37
10:10	23	34:6–7	209
10:12	167	34:7	193
10:21	66	34:28	172
11:2	23		
18–19	28	*Leviticus*	
18:20–21	26	16:1	129
18:22–23	234	18	129
19	27, 28	18:5	152
19:17	178	18:28	152
19:21	29	20:22	152
19:23	178		
19:24	173	*Numbers*	
19:25	171, 173	11:15	213
22:4	127	14:18	209
25:23	137	16:30	93, 106
28:12	145	16:33	141
38:14	229	24:17	128
42:18	127		
48:22	128	*Deuteronomy*	
49:15	128	10:12	74
		18:20	30
Exodus		18:22	30
2:20	26	29:22	171
3:1	128	32:1	92
3:11	26	32:39	27
3:13	26		
4:1	26	*Joshua*	
4:10	26	2:16	127
4:13	26	10:12–14	92
7:18	136	19:10–13	16, 17
7:21	136		
14:21–22	123	*Judges*	
14:21	92	1:3	16
14:29	123	1:31–32	16, 17
15:12	93, 106		
15:26	27	*Ruth*	
19:16	127	1:8	149
24:3	198	3:7	96
24:7	198	3:10	149

Index of Biblical Texts

1 Kings
9:26–28	49
14	3
17	3, 13, 238
17:8–10	16
17:9	13, 16, 17
17:13–16	13
17:15	14
17:17–24	141
17:17	13
17:18–21	13
17:22–24	13
17:22	14
17:24	13
19:4–5	223
19:8	172
19:9	50
19:11	54
19:15–18	205
19:19	183
20:35	43
22:11	43
25:25–27	19

2 Kings
1:1	128
2:8	183
2:11	123
2:23	158, 159
4:18	21
6:5	18
8:7–12	205
9:1–4	17, 18
9:1	3, 31
10:30	18
10:31–32	18
14:23–25	3
14:24–25	18, 19, 31, 41
14:25	13, 16, 17, 19, 30, 31, 49, 164, 182
17	205
17:13	36
18–19	199
19:36–37	182
19:36	23
21:1	16

2 Chronicles
2:16	49
7:12	85
9:29	43
30:27	148

Ezra
3:7	49
4:10	182
8:32	127

Nehemiah
9:17	209

Esther
4:1	183
4:3	183
5:1	127

Job
1:19	54
7:1	143
24:12	237
34:12	137
34:22	50
37:12	137
40:25	103
41:1 Eng.	103

Psalms
2:1	98
16:10	141, 147
22:6	226, 227
31:5 Eng.	148
31:6	148
36:6 Eng.	144, 167
36:7	144, 167, 235
39:12 Eng.	66
39:13	66
40:3	141
42:7 Eng.	142, 144
42:8	142, 144
43:8	48
50:13	151
50:14	87

69:2 Eng.	143	45:7			194
69:3	143	50:2			136
69:15	93, 106	50:3			188
72:10	49	53:5			22
75:3 Eng.	147	53:7			158
75:4	147	57:15–58:14			129
77:5 Eng.	148	57:15			129
77:6	148	62:4			16
80:10 Eng.	167				
80:11	167	*Jeremiah*			
86:15	209	2:31			167
88:12	141	7:25			36
97:11	139	18:7–8		193, 194	
102:1	147	18:7			199
103:2–3	27	18:8			196
103:3–4	147	18:11			194
103:8	209	20:16			28
107:10	141	28:1–17			43
113:4	50				
114:4	148	*Lamentations*			
118:5	135	2:11			147
130	132	3:27			58
130:1	135				
139:7	50	*Ezekiel*			
139:13	137	3:17			30
145:8	209	8:2			137
		14:13			55
Proverbs		18:27–28			193
1:12	93, 106	31:3–18			229
15:3	50	31:15			229
		33:1–11			30
Ecclesiastes		33:11			194
1:2	148	33:19			199
8:10	21	47:10			136
Song of Songs		*Daniel*			
8:6	167	2:21			192
		3		96, 124, 153	
Isaiah					
6	140	3:5			128
6:3	50	3:19–30			123
10:5	28	3:27			153
19:21	87	6		96, 153	
23:1	48, 49	6:22			128
31:9	141				
40:6–8	25	*Hosea*			
45:2	92, 147	6:2			127

Index of Biblical Texts

Joel
1:18   184
2:10   188
2:13   209

Amos
3:2   27
3:4   43
3:7–8   44
3:7   43, 171
8:13   229
9:2–4   50

Jonah
1–2   2
1   9, 87, 150, 167, 216
1:1–3   161, 166
1:1–2   24, 33, 199
1:1   13, 19, 23, 26, 28, 31, 35, 41, 50, 141, 144, 149, 157, 164, 231, 238
1:2–3   143
1:2   19, 23–26, 44, 149, 165, 167, 209, 224
1:3   8, 14, 25, 26, 29, 33–35, 44, 48–50, 53, 67, 72, 82, 93, 110, 121, 123, 137, 149, 197, 209, 215
1:4   54, 55, 63
1:5   55, 58, 137, 149, 150
1:6   58–60
1:6 LXX   2
1:7–8   60
1:7   60–62, 64, 68
1:8–9   61
1:8   61, 64, 69
1:9   15, 65, 66
1:9 MT   2
1:10   24, 61, 68, 215
1:11   69, 70, 75
1:12–13   73
1:12   70–72, 82, 90, 107–109
1:13–16   77
1:13   63, 65, 73, 75, 159
1:14   55, 70, 74, 77, 221
1:15–2:1   83
1:15   2, 5, 65, 76, 77, 84, 143, 158, 216, 225
1:16   24, 77, 85, 86, 150
1:17   87, 115, 122
1:17 Eng.   24, 83, 89, 91, 92, 118, 135, 226
1:17 LXX   92
2   59, 89, 99, 122, 128, 129, 131, 141, 142, 149
2 LXX   92
2:1   5, 24, 44, 88, 89, 91–93, 97, 99, 100, 102, 118, 124, 128, 135–137, 140, 153, 155, 226, 238
2:1 Eng.   127, 135
2:1 LXX   92
2:2   42, 59, 89, 102, 123, 127, 134–137, 139
2:2 Eng.   4, 14, 89, 127, 137
2:2–9 Eng.   138
2:3   4, 14, 89, 100, 101, 119, 122, 127, 135, 137, 139–142
2:3 Eng.   59, 122, 137, 142, 143
2:3–10   138
2:4   122, 142, 143
2:4 Eng.   9, 122, 143, 148
2:5   9, 122, 128, 139, 143, 144, 148
2:5 Eng.   144
2:6   102, 139, 144
2:6 Eng.   3, 53, 89, 145, 146
2:7   3, 53, 89, 145, 146
2:7 Eng.   144, 147
2:8   144, 147
2:8 Eng.   148, 149
2:9   139, 148–50
2:9 Eng.   151
2:10   91, 92, 151, 154
2:10 Eng.   83, 89, 130, 135, 147, 151, 152, 221
2:11   6, 21, 70, 75, 88, 89, 113, 130, 135, 147, 151, 152, 154, 162, 166, 221, 223, 225
3–4   207
3   23
3:1–2   167, 193
3:1   20, 164
3:2   3, 24, 164, 165
3:2 Eng.   101

3:2–3	24	7:18	209
3:3	24, 27, 164–68		
3:4	25, 29, 35, 167–171, 173, 193, 237	**Nahum**	
3:5–8	198	1:3	209
3:5	169, 170, 174, 175, 177, 183, 189, 197, 199	3:1	40
3:6–9	177	**Zephaniah**	
3:6–8	177	3:2	36
3:6	174, 177, 181, 182		
3:7	7, 177, 183, 184, 186, 198, 236	**Zechariah**	
3:8	28, 184, 186, 188, 189, 192, 197	3	140
3:9–10	194, 198	4:10	50
3:9	29, 190–192, 195, 239	5:7	56
3:10	29, 129, 180, 191, 193–197, 199–201, 207, 235	6:12	221
4	200, 231	**Tobit**	
4:1–4	122, 207, 217	6:2–4	96
4:1–2	205, 208	6:3–4	97
4:1	204, 205, 207, 214, 215, 217	14	96
4:2–3	206	14:4	96
4:2	9, 17, 29, 30, 32, 169, 194, 195, 205, 207–209, 212	14:8	96
4:3	204, 205, 208, 213, 229	**Judith**	
4:4	82, 110, 149, 213, 215, 217	1:1	24
4:5	33, 207, 217–219, 221, 222	4:9–14	174
4:6	24, 53, 152, 218–20, 222, 224–226		
4:6 MT	3	**2 Maccabees**	
4:6–10	214	7:1	128
4:6–8	225		
4:6–7	6, 83	**Matthew**	
4:7	6, 53, 121, 226, 228, 234	4:2	172
4:8	156, 226, 228, 229	7:18	194
4:9	206, 215, 229, 230	8:10	180
4:10–11	214, 230, 233, 235	8:24	58
4:10	24, 223, 224, 230	10:5–6	164
4:11	24, 149, 168, 209, 230, 232–236, 240, 247	10:29–31	235
		12:38–41	4
4:16–17	217	12:39–41	99, 237
5:10	5	12:39–40	82
6:1–3	161	12:39	4, 5, 87, 118
10:2–3	60	12:40	11, 98, 99, 143
19:10	17	12:41	34, 181
19:13	17	15:24	164
		15:26	206
Micah		16:1–4	4
4:5	55	20:12	208

21:13	202	13:36–38	67
23:37–39	35	14:10–11	144
24:37	4	17:12	151
26:33–35	67	17:21	144
26:38–39	148		
26:39	164	*Acts*	
27:24	76	1:26	61
28:19	164	10:10–23	49
		13:46	206

Mark
1:10	22
7:27	206
14:29–31	67
14:34	148

Romans
3:29	23
4:4–5	208
5:3–5	148
7:24	147
9:1–5	33
11:25	205

Luke
3:22	22
4:25–26	15
11:29–32	4, 99, 237
11:29	4
11:30	5, 99, 118
15:25–32	246
19:41	22
22:33–34	67
22:45	57
23:21	74
23:45	148

1 Corinthians
1:25	39
5:7	151
10:13	143
16:8	40

Colossians
2:17	227

Hebrews
4:15	143

John
1:1	144
1:32–33	22
3:14	4
6:39	151
10:28	151
10:38	144
11:44	123
11:50	75, 247

2 Peter
3:9	26

Revelation
12:9	103
20:2	103

General Index

Early Jewish/Christian Writings	4–5, 26
Hellenistic Synagogal Prayers, 2, 10, 94, 95	6:2, 50
Josephus, *Antiquities of the Jews,* 2, 18,	7:5, 57
38, 48, 71, 85, 86, 106, 107, 200	9:3, 57
Joseph and Aseneth, 2, 10, 94	9:5, 59
Lives of the Prophets, 3, 4, 14, 16, 136,	10:1, 60
159, 161, 237	11, 61
On Jona,	11:3, 61
2:1–3, 27	12, 70

12:3, 70, 75
13:4, 71
14:3, 71, 76
16:1, 134
17:1-4, 136, 138
18:1-3, 128
22:2, 129
25:2-4, 123
26:3-5, 165
27:2, 172
27:3-4, 189
28:4-36:3, 174
28:4, 174
28:7-8, 134
36:1-3, 174
37, 183, 186
38, 187
40, 206
40:3, 223
41, 206
42:2-3, 206
42:7-8, 206
46-53, 233
50:2, 233
Testament of the Twelve Patriarchs, 2, 94
3 Corinthians, 155
3 Maccabees, 2, 95

Rabbinical Texts
Ecclesiastes Rabbah, 21
Genesis Rabbah, 3, 18, 54, 92, 95, 123, 127, 152, 167, 198
Lamentations Rabbah, 35
Leviticus Rabbah, 54
Mekhilta Attributed to Rabbi Ishmael, 15, 34, 50, 71
Mishnah and Tosefta, 43, 129, 130, 197
Midrash Tanhuma, 145, 156
Midrash Tehillim, 21
Midrash Yonah, 100, 182, 223
Pesiqta de-Rab Kahana, 184, 198
Pirqe de-Rabbi Eliezer (PRE), 2, 3, 10, 13, 17, 19, 25, 31, 49, 51, 55, 63, 72, 73, 86, 87, 92, 98, 136, 138, 140, 144, 145, 148, 150, 182, 236, 237

Seder Olam Rabbah, 3, 18, 20
Sifré to Deuteronomy, 43
Targum Jonathan, 48, 50, 51, 55, 66, 86, 135, 182, 218
Yalkut Shimoni, 97, 100, 182
The Zohar, 11, 59, 60, 97, 100, 124

The Babylonian Talmud
Eruvin, 5, 141
Megillah, 129
Nedarim, 52, 136
Rosh Hashanah, 193, 198
Sanhedrin, 17, 43, 171
Shabbat, 219
Sukkah, 72
Ta'anit, 130, 184, 188, 198
Yebamot, 164

The Jerusalem Talmud
Berakhot, 15, 54, 95, 96, 152, 153
Sanhedrin, 35
Sukkah, 17, 49
Ta'anit, 7, 184, 198

Mediaeval and Modern Jewish Commentators
Abarbanel, 3, 4, 14, 20, 28, 36, 37, 48, 50, 57, 68, 72, 73, 141, 175, 193, 205
Chaim Dov Rabinowitz, 73
Ibn Ezra, Abraham, 3, 11, 23, 26, 27, 35, 48, 50, 52, 55, 58, 64-66, 72, 86, 123, 124, 128, 136, 137, 141, 146, 147, 150, 152, 168, 176, 177, 191, 193, 195, 205, 207, 219, 223, 224, 229, 234
Malbim (Meir Leibush ben Yehiel Michel Wisser), 25, 28, 44, 50, 52, 136, 172, 205
Radak (David Kimchi), 3, 17, 25, 27, 28, 35, 51, 52, 55, 63, 64, 86, 92, 128, 135, 136, 140, 143-45, 147, 148, 150, 152, 164, 167, 171, 176, 177, 183, 184, 190, 193, 205, 207, 213, 219, 223, 227, 233, 234

288 General Index

Radal (Rav David Luria), 25, 31, 204
Rashi (Rabbi Shlomo ben Itzchak), 3,
 11, 17, 25, 35, 50, 52, 54, 55, 63, 64,
 87, 136, 141, 143, 145–48, 150, 171,
 188, 199, 204, 223, 234

Writings of the Early Church
Acts of Paul, 155
Constitutions of the Holy Apostles, 121

Writings of the Church Fathers
Adomnán of Iona, 45
Ambrose, 134, 177
Augustine, 4–6, 82, 115, 119, 121, 123,
 124, 172, 182, 194, 219, 227
Basil of Caesarea, 127, 128
Caesarius of Arles, 172
Cassiodorus, 11, 101
Chrysostom, John, 4, 32, 56, 58, 64,
 70, 73, 90, 171, 172, 177, 178,
 184–185, 198
Cyril of Alexandria, 5, 19, 34, 48, 58,
 64, 68, 119, 123, 124, 141, 145,
 146, 148, 164, 166, 167, 169, 179,
 185, 189, 199, 204, 208, 217, 218,
 225, 233, 234
Cyril of Jerusalem, 4, 5, 101,
 119, 124, 145
Diodorus Siculus, 22
Ephraem the Syrian, 179–180
Gregory of Nazianzus, 4, 32,
 127–128, 178
Haimo of Auxerre, 195
Irenaeus of Lyons, 123
Jacob of Serug, 58, 82, 101, 182, 191, 199
Jerome, 4, 5, 15, 21–23, 33, 35, 37, 48,
 49, 57, 65, 66, 71, 74–76, 87, 92,
 99, 118, 119, 123, 124, 140–44,
 147, 148, 150, 151, 154, 164, 166,
 172, 177, 179, 188, 189, 194,
 198, 204, 205, 214, 217, 219–21,
 223, 228, 240
Justin Martyr, 5, 178
Origen, 172
Paulinus of Nola, 51, 54, 90, 134
Rufinus, 220
Salvian the Presbyter, 234

St Methodius, 124
Tertullian, 32, 38, 53, 57, 69, 72, 107,
 153, 173, 194, 200, 225
Theodore of Mopsuestia, 33, 51, 57, 63,
 73, 87, 124, 150, 167, 169, 204, 223,
 233, 234, 236
Theodoret of Cyrus, 48, 119
Zeno of Verona, 102

The Qur'an
6.86, 7
4.163, 7
10.98, 7, 42, 196
21.87–88, 7, 41, 132, 133
21.87, 41, 43, 76, 122
37, 41
37.139–148, 7, 76, 132
37.141, 63, 76
37.146–148, 221
68.48–50, 7, 133

Muslim Authors
Al-Kisai, Muḥammad ibn Allah, 223
Al-Qummī, ʿAlī ibn Ibrāhīm, 8, 42
Al-Ṭabarī, Muhammad ibn Jarir, 42,
 196, 197, 223
Al-Thaʿlabī, Aḥmad ibn Muḥammad,
 17, 42, 136, 159, 161, 223
Al-Zamakhsharī, Abū al-Qāsim
 Maḥmūd ibn Umar, 8, 42,
Ibn Kathīr, Ismail, 8, 42, 43, 63, 76, 132,

Medieval Authored Texts
St Adomnán of Iona, 45
Apollodorus, 93
Cena Cypriani, 158
Letaldus, 117, 159
'Patience',
lines 74–80, 38
lines 134–167, 56
lines 168–174, 63
line 172, 75
lines 225–228, 75, 76
lines 274–275, 102
lines 281–288, 130
line 288, 131
line 306, 102, 135

line 341, 159
lines 392–395, 185
lines 427–428, 204
Prudentius, *Hymnus Ieiunantium*, 82, 102, 169, 173, 181, 185, 200
Pseudo-Cyprian (formerly attributed to Tertullian), *De Jona et Nineveh*, 53, 57, 69, 72, 107, 173, 200
Vercelli Homilies, 103
The Whale, 11, 103

Reform Commentaries
Bugenhagen, J., 4, 22, 140, 180, 191, 192
Calvin, J., 4, 11, 19, 39, 48, 62, 70, 91, 128, 143–45, 148, 151, 154, 166, 168, 186, 187, 195, 198–99, 204, 207, 209, 213–14, 221, 229, 234
Luther, M., 4–6, 11, 15, 19, 22, 23, 28, 33, 39, 44, 48, 49, 52, 56, 58, 60–62, 72, 87, 90, 91, 95, 115, 121, 122, 128, 141–143, 145–147, 151, 154, 167–169, 176–178, 180, 195, 198–99, 206, 208, 221, 227, 234

Other Texts
Codex Palatinus Latinus, 871, fol. 15 r, 84

Exeter Book
Exeter Cathedral Library MS, 3501, folio 96b–97b, 103

Kennicott Bible, folio 305r, 113

KTU, 1.5 I 18, 98

Walters Manuscript, W.34, fol. 131 r, 156

Index of Authors

Abbot, G. 24
Aberbach, M. 86, 145
Abrahams, S. 120
Abusch, T. 235
Ackerman, J. S. 89, 137, 150
Ackroyd, P. 125
Adelman, P. 19, 30, 31, 49, 51, 72, 73, 86, 87, 140, 237
Adler, S. 240, 241

Agnew, S. 242
Agnon, S. Y. 130
Almbladh, K. 137
Amar, I. 22
Andres, S. 37
Andrew, M. 39, 76
Angel, A. R. 94
Argento, D. 39, 131, 161, 188, 242

Jonah Through the Centuries, First Edition. Lena-Sofia Tiemeyer.
© 2022 John Wiley & Sons, Ltd. Published 2022 by John Wiley & Sons, Ltd.

Index of Authors

Arnds, P. O. 126
Auster, P. 45, 46

Babits, M. 108
Band, A. J. 209, 223
Barańczak, S. 243
Barker, W. D. 162
Barnes, J. 110, 230
Barr, L. B. 78, 217
Barrett, B. 143
Bazzana, G. B. 219, 220, 225
Beckwith, J. 133
Beeson, J. 16
Bejerano, M. 47
Ben Zvi, E. 142, 144, 233, 236
Ben-Chorin, S. 66, 68, 69
Berger, Y. 215, 217, 229
Bickerman, E. 30, 90
Boase, E. 242
Bob, S. 58, 135, 205
Bodkin, M. 98
Bolin, T. M. 99, 235
Bonhoeffer, D. 84, 85
Borroff, M. 212
Bradbury, T. 40, 174, 176, 181, 185
Brenner, A. 142
Brentius, T. 23, 24
Bridie, J. 20, 241
Brinner, W. M. 17
Burge, S. R. 15, 16, 42

Calder, N. 87
Camus, A. 108
Carden, M. 48
Carissimi, G. 39, 54, 133, 201
Cary, P. 149
Cathcart, K. J. 86, 182, 218
Cho, P. K.-k. 98
Chow, S. 118
Ciuba, G. 226
Collodi, C. 111
Conrad, J. 79–81
Cook, D. 94
Crane, H. 106

Dadelsen, J.-P. 107
Darnell, D. R. 95
Davis, A. B. 118, 131
Davis, E. B. 39
Davis, S. J. 84, 103, 225
Day, J. 209
Dell, K. J. 142, 223, 236
Deutsch, G. 87
Döhling, J.-D. 98
Doms, M. S. 111, 231, 232
Dotson, E. G. 120, 121
Dowling Long, S. 133, 134
Downs, D. J. 215
Dox, T. 182
Dozeman, T. B. 209
Drayton, M. 142
Dücker, B. 108, 109

Eagleton, T. 30, 209, 210
Edwards, R. A. 99
Eich, G. 109
Eliade, M. 98

Fagan, D. J. 211
Feldman, L. H. 86, 107
Felipe, L. 59
Felsted, S. 182
Fishman, G. 14
Flusser, D. 93
Föcking, M. 113
Frahm, E. 22, 223
Friedman, J. B. 75, 103, 121, 156–159, 221
Friedman, R. E. 24, 53
Frieling, S. 107
Frost, R. 210, 211
Fu, J. 98

Gaines, J. H. 215
Gale, D. 113
Gane, E. R. 77
Geiger, F. 62
Gerson, M. 32
Ginzberg, L. 15, 17, 156, 182

Golka, F. W. 178
Gordon, R. P. 50, 86, 182, 218
Gottheil, R. 87
Grass, G. 126
Green, H. 159
Green, R. 105
Greene, R. 238
Greenstein, E. L. 22, 235
Gregg, R. C. 17
Guillaume, P. 233, 236
Gye, H. 113

Hacks, P. 111, 161, 231
Halpern, B. 24, 53, 221
Haral, H. 159
Hard, R. 94
Hartleben, O. E. 86, 240
Hau, A. 46
Havea, J. 22, 48, 54, 56, 93, 106, 168, 173, 230
Heider, G. C. 162
Herbert, Jr, T. 40, 122
Herbert, Z. 242, 243
Hesse, E. W. 69, 149
Hill, R. C. 123, 169
Hofmann, P. 103
Hollander, H. W. 94
Holstein, J. A. 167
Hooper, J. 77
Housman, L. 126, 227, 228, 239
Hurd, M. J. 91, 189, 201
Hurston, Z. N. 225
Huxley, A. 124, 125

Irwin, W. R. 210

Jacobs, N. S. S. 96, 97
Jacobson, D. C. 47
Jensen, R. M. 84, 225
Jeremias, J. 192
Jerome, J. 189, 190, 240
Johnson, S. R. 95
Johnson, U. 239
Jonge, M. de 94
Juhnke, A. K. 211

Kadari, T. 136, 156, 161, 223
Kamp, A. 67, 209, 235
Karlfeldt, E. A. 64
Keiter, S. T. 22
Kelly, J. R. 209
Kikawada, I. M. 69, 149
Kitchen, R. A. 58, 82, 101, 191, 199
Kitto, J. 115, 116, 234
Kugel, J. L. 156
Kühlmann, W. 110, 126

L'Engle, M. 110, 239
LaCocque, A. 38
LaCocque, P. E. 38
Landes, G. M. 97
Layzer, V. 45
Lee, B. S. 173, 181
Leiter, L. H. 82
Levine, A.-J. 96
Lihn, E. 46, 47
Limburg, J. 95, 235
Lindsay, R. 26, 165, 199
Lipiński, E. 48
Liptzin, S. 37, 66, 85, 90, 218, 241
Lodge, T. 105, 238
Lohrmann, M. J. 22, 140, 181, 192
Loreto, P. 212

Marks, A. S. 183
Masback, F. J. 80, 81
Mathias, W. 20, 25, 77, 110
McAuliffe, J. D. 132
McDermott, R. 238
McGregor, R. R. 108, 109
McKenzie, S. L. 137
McLaughlin, R. P. 28
Meckier, J. 125
Melin, P. 75
Melville, H. 29, 48, 53, 58, 79, 115, 116, 122, 160, 166
Miller, C. 229
Mills, P. 201
Mitchell, S. 126
Modesto, C. 158
Molodowsky, K. 66

Moore, C. A. 96, 97, 212, 213
Moore, M. 228, 229
Muldoon, C. L. 229
Muradyan, A. 27, 174, 193

New, E. 116
Newby, G. D. 17
Nichols, G. C. 216
Nilson, P. 45
Noegel, S. B. 103
Nowell, I. 97

Oren, M. B. 32
Orwell, G. 125

Pagis, D. 161
Pardes, I. 79, 116, 160
Parunak, H. van D. 192
Perlmann, M. 197
Person, Jr, R. F. 235
Plant, S. 84, 85
Priel, G. 46
Profitlich, U. 232
Prudentius 169, 200

Quarles, F. 22, 106, 164, 187, 196
Quint, D. 120

Rathbun, J. W. 29, 40
Reinhard, M. 212
Reuther, H. J. 208
Reynolds, G. S. 42, 43, 132
Rodoreda, M. 215
Rogerson, J. 125
Rosen, N. 78
Rubin, U. 197
Ruether, R. R. 208
Russell, J. 159
Ryu, C. J. 242

Saeedimehr, M. 197
Sager, J. 105, 201, 238
Salberg, J. 47
Salzmann, B. 239
Sasson, J. M. 26, 86, 93, 137, 145

Sawyer, J. F. A. 133, 134
Schellenberg, A. 28, 30, 44, 223
Scherman, R. N. 18, 20, 32
Schmidt, G. D. 102, 103
Schmidt, L. 28
Schwemer, M. 237, 238
Scliar, M. 78, 216, 217
Scoralick, R. 209
Seidler, A. 183
Sewall, J. 170, 181
Shapiro, D. 25, 109, 215
Sharpe, R. 45
Sherwood, Y. 38, 41, 45, 77, 96, 106, 135, 161, 208, 236, 243
Showalter, Jr, E. 107, 108
Shulman, R. D. G. 47
Siegert, F. 61, 71, 76, 90, 129, 192, 193
Simon, U. 235
Simpson, W. 98
Smart, J. D. 125
Smith, G. A. 125
Smith-Christopher, D. L. 125
Smolar, L. 86, 145
Sorescu, M. 109
Sowden, L. 218
Sperber, A. 135
Sprang, F. C. H. 40, 79, 116, 122
Staffell, S. 24, 77
Steffen, U. 197, 221
Stökl Ben Ezra, D. 129
Strawn, B. A. 222
Streete, A. 187, 196
Stucke, F. 232
Sutskover, T. 53, 165, 191

Tandrup, H. 241
Tavenar, J. 77
Thorpe, B. 103
Tiemeyer, L.-S. 30, 37, 67, 78, 87, 137, 162, 171, 202, 215–217, 233, 236, 238
Timmer, D. C. 87, 150, 209, 236
Timmerman, J. H. 210–212
Tolkien, J. R. R. 146
Topchyan, G. 27, 174, 193
Trible, P. 137, 226, 235, 236

Ueberschaer, F. 24, 174
Urbach, E. 178

Vanoni, G. 215
Vawter, B. 223
Vermeulen, K. 236
Verne, J. 139
Vogel, W. 62

Walton, J. H. 198
Weinfeld, M. 22
Whiston, W. 107
Wiegmann, H. 110

Wiesel, E. 78, 110, 224
Wiliame, G. V. 67
Wilson, A. J. 118
Wineman, A. 100
Wolfe, B. N. 146
Wright, C. H. H. 125
Wright, N. 40

Ziolkowski, J. M. 90, 102, 116, 117, 155, 156, 158, 159, 224
Zlotowitz, R. M. 27, 205
Zornberg, A. G. 14, 47

Printed and bound by CPI Group (UK) Ltd, Croydon, CR0 4YY